Maritime Heritage of India

सत्यमेव जयते

With the Compliments of

Embassy of India, Berne

Maritime Heritage of India

Edited by

K.S. Behera

Aryan Books International

New Delhi

MARITIME HERITAGE OF INDIA

ISBN: 978-81-7305-165-4

First Published: 1999

This Edition Published in **2017** by:

Aryan Books International

Pooja Apartments, 4B, Ansari Road, New Delhi-110 002 (India)

Tel.: 23287589, 23255799; Fax: 91-11-23270385

E-mail: aryanbooks@gmail.com

www.aryanbooks.co.in

Designed and Printed in India by

ABI Prints & Publishing Co., New Delhi

Namo vah Sarvasindhūnām ādharebhyaḥ sanātanāḥ
jantūnām prāṇadebhyaś ca samudrebhyo namo namaḥ |

Matsya Purāna ch. 287.11.

"Homage to you, O eternal Seas, the meeting place of all the flowing rivers and life-givers to living beings."

Preface

The volume is a collection of essays in Indian seafaring and maritime activities. The maritime tradition of India is as old as our civilization and as vast as the Indian Ocean. The papers included in part one of the book discuss important and fascinating facets of the theme from different perspectives. The subject matter ranges from archaeological roots to surviving boat-building traditions in Karnataka, Orissa and Andaman & Nicobar islands; from early maritime contacts with Rome to cultural links with Sri Lanka, Southeast Asia and China; and from literary evidence regarding seafaring and ship-building to rivalry in the Bay of Bengal, ports and landmarks in East India. Furthermore, the contributions of the West coast, Tamil Nadu, Orissa and Bengal to the overall Indian pattern have been highlighted on the basis of literary, ethnological, and the most recent archaeological data.

The vivid documentation in Part Two illustrates the chronological development of the seafaring activities in the Indian Ocean and their cultural impact. It is expected to provide a visual feeling of the glorious maritime heritage of India and promote an awareness of the richness of the Ocean.

This volume has grown out of the papers presented at the National level Seminars on *Kalingas in the Indian Ocean* and *Maritime Heritage of India*, held at Utkal University, Bhubaneswar in 1992-93. I am indebted to Shri K.P. Singhdeo, then Minister, Information and Broadcasting, Government of India for inaugurating the Seminar on Maritime Heritage of India. I am grateful to the distinguished scholars for their contributions and participation in both the Seminars. Later on at the request of the editor, Haryati Soebadio, I. Wayan Ardika, Eric Kentley, Hermann Kulke and eminent Indian scholars such as M.K. Dhavalikar, K.V. Raman and N.C. Ghosh sent their valuable papers for this volume. The paper of V. Vitarana was received through the courtesy of the *Universe*, Cuttack. Professor A.R. Kulkarni and Professor Lallanji Gopal kindly allowed their already published papers for inclusion in this volume. The editor is indebted to all the scholars whose contributions have enriched this volume.

The Editor is grateful to Dr. Ashok Jain, Director, National Institute of Science, Technology and Development Studies (NISTADS), New Delhi and Dr. (Mrs.) Lotika Varadarajan for help and keen interest in the subject and to the Council of Scientific and Industrial Research (CSIR) for financial support. The photographs published in this volume are drawn from various sources—published works of others, institutions and individuals who deserve our thanks.

I would like to thank Mr. Vikas Arya, Aryan Books International for undertaking the publication of this important volume.

K.S. Behera

Bhubaneswar

Contents

	Preface	*vii*
	List of Plates	*xi*
1.	Indian Seafaring Traditions: Archaeological Perspectives—*I.K. Sarma*	1
2.	Indian Maritime Activities: Vedic, Epic and Purāṇic Sources—*U.N. Dhal*	11
3.	Indo-Roman Trade—*Kishor K. Basa & K.S. Behera*	15
4.	Early Trade in the Indian Ocean: Perspectives on Indo–South-east Asian Maritime Contacts *(c. 400 BC—AD 500)—Kishor K. Basa*	29
5.	Indian-Indonesian Cultural Relations—*Haryati Soebadio*	72
6.	Ancient Trade Relation Between India and Indonesia—*I. Wayan Ardika*	80
7.	Indian Shipping in Early Mediaeval Period—*Lallanji Gopal*	90
8.	Maritime Tradition of Western India—*M.K. Dhavalikar*	107
9.	Maritime Heritage of the Tamils: Some Recent Findings—*K.V. Raman*	113
10.	Traditional Boats of Karnataka and their Building Practices—*L.N. Swamy*	116
11.	Oceanographic Knowledge among Tribes of Andaman and Nicobar Islands —*R. Sivakumar & G. Victor Rajamanickam*	143
12.	Ancient Ports on the Eastern Coast of India—*A.N. Parida*	155
13.	Maritime Activities of Orissa—*K.S. Behera*	162
14.	Maritime Activities of the Kaliṅgas and the New Light thrown by the Excavations at Khalkatapatna—*B.K. Sinha*	172
15.	Kaliṅga-Śri Lankā Relations—*V. Vitharana*	179
16.	The Sewn Boats of Orissa—*Eric Kentley*	188
17.	History of Shipping in Bengal—*N.C. Ghosh*	196
18.	The Maritime Contacts Between Eastern India and South-east Asia: New Epigraphic Data—*B.N. Mukherjee*	201
19.	Marathas and the Sea—*A.R. Kulkarni*	206
20.	Trade and Politics in Eleventh Century Bay of Bengal —*Hermann Kulke*	214
21.	Orissa in Chinese Historical Records—*Haraprasad Ray*	225
22.	Traditional Navigational Landmarks on the East Coast of India —*B. Arunachalam*	236
	List of Contributors	241

List of Plates
(Photographic Documentation)

A. Deities Associated with the Ocean and Navigation

1. Varuṇa, Bhubaneswar, Orissa State Museum
2. Lakṣhmī, "daughter of the milky ocean", Pitalkhora, c. 2nd century BC, Prince of Wales Museum
3. Avalokiteśvara as a saviour from perils, including of ship wreck, Kanheri
4. Aṣṭamahābhaya Tārā, as a saviour, among others, from ship wreck, from Ratnagiri, Orissa
5. Viṣṇu Anantaśāyīn, Dasavatar temple, Deogarh
6. Viṣṇu Anantaśāyīn, on the bank of the Brchmani river at Sarang, Orissa

B. The Indus Civilization Period

7. Ship on a stone seal, Mohenjo-daro, (after Mackay)
8. Ship on a terracotta amulet, Mohenjo-daro
9. A Dockyard, Lothal
10. Persian gulf seals, Lothal
11. Model of a terracotta boat, Lothal

C. Indo-Roman Period

12. Roman amphora, Roman National Museum, Rome
13. Fragments of Roman amphoras, Arikamedu
14. Fragments of Arretine dishes, Arikamedu
15. Yavan Couple, Pitalkhora, c. 2nd century BC
16. Roman coins found in India
17. Rouletted ware, from Sisupalgarh, Orissa
18. Terracotta bullae, Sisupalgarh, Orissa
19. Small pot with protrusion in the centre from Manikpatna, Orissa
20. Pedestal goblet, from Palur, Orissa
21. Black and red ware sherds, from Palur, Orissa
22. Terracotta pots, Ter, c. 2nd century AD
23. Kaolin figurines, Ter, c. 2nd century AD
24. Roman terracotta lamps, Ter, c. 2nd century AD
25. Roman terracotta lamp, Ter, c. 2nd century AD
26. Bronze mirror, Brahmapuri

27. Repousse emblem depicting the legend of Perseus and Andromeda, c. 2nd century AD, from Brahmapuri
28. Bronze handle of a jug, c. 2nd century AD, from Brahmapuri.
29. Ships engraved on Roman coins
30. Ship with two masts on Sātavāhana coin

D. Cultural Links with Sri Lanka, Indonesia and China

31. Dhyani Buddha, Polonnaruwa, Sri Lanka
32. Coin of Sahasamalla, King of Sri Lanka from Manikpatna, Orissa
33. Borobudur, the perforated stupas, c. 800 AD, Indonesia
34. Representation of a ship, c. 800 AD, Borobudur, (Indonesia)
35. Dhyani Buddha from Borobudur
36. Śiva liṅga, Bali
37. Chinese coins in coastal Orissa (a) from Khelkatapatna (b) from Manikpatna
38. Gaṇeśa, Indonesia

E. Representations of Boats and Ships in Indian Art

39. Representation of a boat, c. 2nd century BC, Bharhut
40. A barge with prow in the form of a griffin, c. 1st century BC, Sanchi
41. A canoe with planks joined together, c. 1st century BC, Sanchi
42. Impression of a seal showing a sea-going vessel, c. 2nd century AD, Chandraketugarh (West Bengal),
43. Seal impression showing a boat c. 2nd century AD, Chandraketugarh
44. Seal with a masted ship flying a banner, c. 3rd century AD, Chandraketugarh (West Bengal)
45. Representation of a ship, Ajanta painting, c. 6th century AD
46. Boats carrying elephants, c. 9th century AD, Bhubaneswar
47. Mahmud of Ghazni's fleet of boats, c. 1026 AD
48. Vīragal showing naval battle with armed soldiers on boats, c. 11th-13th century AD, Eksar
49. Vīragal showing a long canoe-shaped ship, c. 12th century AD, Goa Museum
50. Vīragal showing a naval battle in a shipyard, c. 12th century AD, Goa Museum
51. The clinker style boat, c. 13th century AD, Koṇārak
52. Marttanda Bhairava dancing on a boat, c. 13th century AD, Koṇārak
53. Representation of a clinker style boat on the Bhoga Mandapa, c. 15th century AD, Śrī Jagannātha Temple, Puri
54. Representation of ship in Bustan manuscript, c. 16th century AD
55. Job Charnock founding Calcutta, c. 1690 AD, (after Sir Richard Temple)
56. Representation of boat in a palm leaf manuscript, c. 18th century AD, Orissa

F. Traditional Boats from Eastern India

57. An Orissan *Patia* boat, partly of reversed clinker style. North Coast (Orissa)
58. Details of the boat (of No. 57)
59. Backside of the boat (of No. 57)
60. Bow of an Orissan *Masula* (after Eric Kentley)
61. Taking an Orissan *Masula* to the water (after Eric Kentley)

1

Indian Seafaring Traditions : Archaeological Perspectives

I.K. SARMA

It is admitted by many that the pre-literate developments in Indian archaeology could not have taken place in isolation. India must have received some cultural elements from the other cradles of Asian civilization namely West Asia, China and Far East. Geographically India is sandwiched between the Eastern[1] and Western nuclei. Right from the prehistoric times, India was approachable by sea from west, south,[2] and south-east and the southern peninsula had a bias for seafaring activity.

The Harappans appear in the North-West as early as 3000 BC with a well developed civilised life. Archaeological finds attest to the brisk commercial contacts between Mohenjodaro, Harappa and Lothal on one hand and the Mesopotamian centres on the other hand. The commercial centres mentioned on Mesopotamian tablets of 3rd millennium BC are Dilmun, Magan and Meluhha——Dilmun is the island of Failaka and Bahrain; Magan is Trucial Oman and Baluchistan while Meluhha is identified interestingly with the Harappan city.[3] Indo-Bahrain contacts are exemplified by certain significant finds, like Harappan-type pottery and reserve slipped ware in the Gulf coast sites, Harappan seals from Kajjor and Buni and fire altars like those of Kalibangan and Lothal at Barbar. While a Dilimun-type Gulf seal was found at Lothal (in 1958) by S.R. Rao,[4] K.M. Srivastava[5] reported a steatite Harappan seal from within the burial chamber No. 1757 in Bahrain. This seal has a charging bull, a peacock and four letters of Indus script. Srivastava opines that the buried person was an Indian agent operating from Bahrain.

Certain important finds like mother and child terracotta, mother goddess figures and Mesopotamian cylinder seals from Indus sites (in all seven) and distinctive motifs like ships on Mohenjodaro seals, ship on pottery, clay models of boats from Lothal, Chanhudaro, Mohenjodaro, side rudders indicating seafaring activity, are well known. At Lothal, in particular, a dockyard was found which measured 214 x 36 m lined with walls of kiln-baked bricks. The lock-gate system in the outlet ensured automatic desiltation at high[6] tide. This is a first tidal dock of the world serving the port town of the Harappan Lothal at the head of the Gulf of Cambay. This is also the earliest and probably only one of its kind discovered so far and clearly illustrates the maritime engineering skill and knowledge of hydrography of the Harappans in 3rd millennium BC. The presence of gypsum and the presence of *foraminifera* noted by R. Nigam[7] after a scientific analysis of the core samples from the floor of Lothal dock, confirmed high tidal environment. Coupled with this evidence, seals of Indus origin, were noted in West Asian sites like Tell Asmar, Ur, Kish, Lagash and Susa. Other finds like carnelian beads, bone-inlay, nude male statuary, weights, stamp seals with Harappan characters, point to the overwhelming Harappan contacts. But there is hardly any evidence of such exchange of goods or relics among the coastal Harappan centres either the West Asian, or port towns of Sumeru or even Bahrain, except a lone surface find of a circular Persian Gulf seal of steatite from Lothal reported by S.R. Rao. That shows, the trade was largely one-sided and involving export of Indian goods on a larger frequency, rather than import. Even humped cattle originally from India were introduced to Elam, Anatolia and Syria.

The urban Harappans seem to have kept the sea routes in perfect stance to meet the growing maritime trade. Starting from the Gulf of Cambay, along the coast of Arabian Sea, the ships entered the Persian Gulf, finally reaching the north Euphrates near Ur. The stone seal with ship and a cabin, a terracotta amulet with a ship motif, model boats of terracotta and the extensive Harappan dockyard with perforated anchors from Lothal detailed above clearly point to the modes and means of transport as well.

2. Post-Harappan Evidences

After the wane of the Harappan civilization, for about 600 years there is not enough evidence of the seafaring activity. In recent years, S.R. Rao has brought to the fore a city with inner and outer fortification walls, gateways extending into the Arabian Sea off-Dwaraka.[9] The remains of this submerged city extended over 4 km into the tidal zone of Bet-Dwaraka. In fact, a late Indus type seal of conch and a pottery vessel with post-Harappan script analogous to Semitic script, and a copper metal plate were recovered besides the holed stone anchors. Bet-Dwaraka thus proved to be a coastal town of great significance linked to the Mahābhārata episode.

Certain important relics pertaining to the early maritime contact between the west coast and Nile valley give us an idea of the extent of trade between Neolithic culture of India and Nile. The terracotta headrests found in the Neolithic cultures Andhra-Karnataka (T. Narsipur, Hallur and Piklihal) are reminiscent of similar headrests of ivory, lapislazuli, blue faience, turquoise from the tomb of Tut-Ankh-Amen, Pharaoo of the late 18th century of Egypt found in the Valley of Kings datable to circa 1400 BC. The occurrence of ragi in the Deccan upper Neolithic culture of Karnataka and Deccan Chalcolithic sites is of African origin. Ragi is also found in late Harappan Hulas. Sorghum, bicdor and pearl millet native to East Africa, have been found in late Harappan levels at Rojdi (Gujarat). It would be extremely important to further pursue and pin-point the mechanics of diffusion from East Africa[10] to Western India. There is no doubt that maritime contacts flourished during this proto-historic periods.

3. Some Literary Data

The Ṛgveda, the oldest scripture of India, is familiar with the word *Samudra.* It is difficult to think that it refers directly to sea but more broadly describes the big rivers of the *Sapta Sindhu*[11] region. But the sea as referred in the expression of *Samudrārthāḥ* (ṚV. VII. 49-2) clearly shows that the Ṛgvedic people had knowledge of sea. There is a well known story of Bhujyu, the son of Tugra who was saved by the gods Aśvina when he was caught up in the mid-sea. This Bhujyu was stated to have been rescued in a boat with hundred ores. Sāyaṇāchārya narrates the story how Aśvina went with their army in three ships and brought back Bhujyu. These ships are mentioned as *Nau*, with 100 ores (*Śatāritram nāvam ātasthivāsam).*

In the early historical periods, we have more clear data about the organisation of sea voyages for both cultural and commercial purposes. In the Mauryan period, Chandragupta Maurya had appointed *Nāvādhyaksha,* Commander of the naval fleet and an Officer in charge of trade through waters. The Mauryan impact and spread of early Buddhism from its Magadhan nuclei have been prolific. Several port towns with convenient anchorages encouraged brisk trade. The patrons were religious propagators too. Besides land routes emerging from Afghanistan through Central India to the Gangetic plains provided material evidence which shed new light on the routes of contact between North-West India and South[12] East-Coast. Motifs of boats, sea animals depicted in sculptures, medallions of Bharhut, on the pillars of the western gateway of Sanchi; scenes of Ajanta—the Persian Embassy depicted in cave no. 1 and three-mast ship in mid-sea in the painting of *Purṇāvadāna Jātaka* cave no. 2 (525-630 AD)—apart from the accounts of Chinese travellers Itsing and Huen Tsang amply provide reliable data on overseas trade. The port towns that come to prominence starting from Tamluk (ancient Tamralipti) on the Bengal coast, several important places in descending order were Dosarne (Dhauli, Orissa), Kainapara (Konark), Palura (Gopalapura Dist., Orissa), Kaliṅgapatnam (near Salihundam, Dist. Srikakulam), Veṅgīpura (Peddavegi), Maisolia (Machilipatnam, Dist. Krishna), Utukuru-Krishnapatnam also Dugarajupatnam (Nellore Dist., A.P.), Mālange or Kaḍal Mallai (Mahabalipuram), Mylārpha (Mylarpore, Madras), Poduke or Poduce, Arikamedu (Pondicherry), Soptana (Markanam), Kaberis (Kaveripumpattinam), Nikam (Nagapattinam), Kayalpattinam, Periapattinam, Colchi (Korkai) and Comari (Kanyā Kumārī) on the tip of South India.

4. Ceramics and Sea Trade

The prolific occurrence of NBP ware at the Amarāvatī Dharaṇikōṭa excavations (1974-75) in such early contexts has opened up fresh grounds of study. In recent years, apart from the above evidences from Dhānyakaṭaka *stūpa*, some sites along the coastal Tamil Nadu have yielded precious evidences. The NBP ware from *Korkai,* an ancient port town of the Pāṇḍyas, and more recently Alagankulam (1989) near Ramanathapuram yielded NBP bowls in association with silver punch-marked coins within an early historical cultural assemblage of Mauryan date.[13] It is of great significance to note that NBP ware and punch-marked coins were reported from the earliest levels of some Buddhist sites—especially Gedige and Anurādhapura citadel in Śri Lankā. In the light of these evidences, we may recall with profit the Buddhist legends enshrining certain important events. According to *Mahāvamśa* (XIX, 6 and XIX, 11-12), the Mauryan emperor Aśoka came to despatch the *Bodhivṛiksha* sapling to Simhala in a highly religious manner. He descended into the water up to the neck and set the Bodhi tree on the ship and stood with folded hands on the shore. Again *Mahāvaṁsa* narrates that king Duttagamini of Śri Lankā (101-77 BC) celebrated with pomp the laying of great stūpa inviting many monks and kings from foreign lands (one Mahādeva from Pallava Bhogga and Yona *Mahādharmaraskshita* from Alasandra, i.e. Alexandria. The *Vinaya* texts and *Jātakas* inform us that merchants from Sahajati, Kauśāmbi, Vārāṇasi, Pāṭalīputra and Gompa brought their goods to Tamralipti (Tamluk in West Bengal) for trade with South Asia. The seaport towns of great importance are Tamralipti (Gaṅgāe) and Kanthi on lower Bengal coast, Kainapara (Konark), Dosarene (Dhauli, Orissa), Kaliṅgae (Kaliṅgapatnam) and Maisolia (Machilipatnam) in coastal Āndhra. It is, therefore, becoming clear that the first ceramic viz., the N.B.P. ware with punch-marked silver coins reached South-east Indian port towns and farther beyond Śri Lankā as well, by mid of 3rd century BC along with the Buddhist monks and merchant guild (*Śreshṭhis* and *Nigamas*) who were converts to this popular casteless religious faith.

Vimala Begely's researches[14] have proved that Arikamedu as a port came to prominence in mid-3rd century BC and its contacts with Mediterranean world in late 2nd century BC. A pre-Roman horizon and dating to the amphorae and rouletted ware is clearly indicated in recent excavations under K.V. Raman[15] of Madras University and American team led by Vimala. This evidence amply supports the Śri Lankān evidence not only from the port town of Mantai but also several ports of call in south and south-east Śri Lankā.

Some of the merchant sailors trading with the Mediterranean via the Red Sea seem to be *Draviḍī* people. Tamil-Brāhmi sort inscriptions were found in the Egyptian coastal site of Quseir-al-qadim in the strata of the Roman period.

5. New Evidences from Bengal Coast and South-east Asia

A momentous discovery was recently made by B.N. Mukherjee[16] when recognised, for the first time, numerous Kharoṣhti inscriptions on pots, plaques and seals earlier found from the excavations at Chandraketugarh and nearby places like Bangarh and Hadipur in district 24-Paraganas. The terracotta seals from Bangarh and Chandraketugarh display sea-going vessels containing corn flanked by symbols like conch and taurine. Such vessel types are *Sasyādidhṛtasthāli,* a bowl-shaped vessel filled of corn. The other one of same size has legend in Kharoṣhti-Brāhmī and refers to *Tridēśayātra,* meaning a voyage to three countries or directions. Yet another seal from Chandraketugarh reveals a type of vessel called *Trapyaka* belonging to the wealth-earning *Tasvadaja* family. It may be noted that Trapyaka is a type of ship mentioned also in the *Periplus* and the *Angavijjā*. The above vessel types as well as flanking symbols recall the Sātavāhana ships. It appears that Kharoṣhṭi script using tradesmen settled in the lower Gangetic valley of Bengal in good numbers during first-third centuries AD, mixed up with the Brāhmi using local merchants and developed a *Miṣra*-type Kharoṣhṭi-Brāhmi writing in north-western *Prākritic* expressions. A unique sea-going vessel, single-mast type with an eye-socket symbol engraved thereon indicated an early trade contact with Egypt[17] as well.

Swarṇa Deepa found in Sanskrit and Pāli literature refers to South-east Asia and *Milindapañha* describes this as a land of ports where ships congregated. Recent archaeological excavations in the mainland and peninsulas South-east Asian sites like Chansen, Dontaphet in Central Thailand, Myannar, QC-EO in Mekong Delta, Beikthano and Taungtheman; Semiran on the north-east coast of Bali in Indonesia, revealed certain important objects[18] such as glass and carnelian betched beads, intaglios and seals, etc. Sembiran on the North Coast of Bali excavated between 1987-89 yielded rouletted-ware and most significantly an inscribed sherd with three characters in Kharoṣhṭi script. Besides carnelian, seals in lapis lazuli and garnet inscribed with Brāhmī characters have been found at least in four important coastal sites in South-east Asia datable to early century BC onwards. The use of Kharoṣhṭi and Brāhmī with the typical symbols like *Śrivasta* conch and sun clearly point to the maritime contacts with the Indian subcontinent during this period. In this trade Śri Lankā had also been at the receiving end. Horses from North-Western India were sent by the sea vessels through Bengal coast right from the Mauryan times. Religious involvement provided a cohesion and inspiration to the trading community and through these channels early Buddhism and Brahmanical religious cults found their way to South-east Asia,[19] somewhat later than Śri Lankā.

6. Inscriptions

According to Hathigumpha *Praśasti,* Maharaja Kharavela of Kaliṅga (2nd *c.* BC) captured the market town of Pihunda, as ancient metropolis, a port town on the east coast near Machilipatnam. Seafaring merchants are stated to be travelling by boat from Champa (Kampuchea) to Pihunda even in the days of Mahāvīra. Kudura end Kantakossyala (Ghantasala) are also important centres mentioned by Ptolemy in the country of Maisolia. King Khāraveli of Orissa speaks of even a confederacy of the Tamil countries with whom he had confronted and defeated. This coastal trade had led to extensive religious and cultural expansion not only along the South-east coast but also brought Śri Lankān port towns closer.

In the inscriptions of first-second century AD, we find master mariners residing at Mahānāgaparvata (Guntupalli)[20] and Ghantasala (Ptolemy's Kantakossyla). The Indo-Roman trade of this period is well known and the port towns of Andhra were humming with activity. Mahāyāna Buddhism through its sects spread to coastal towns of South like Mailai (Mylapur), Kāñchī, Kaveripumpattinam and farther Śri Lankā. The Mon race, now known as Tailang in Burma is believed to have come from Telingana or Kaliṅga on the east coast. The script of the oldest inscription found in Mon on a pillar resembles the early Pallava. The earliest Tailang alphabet is identified with the Veṅgī alphabet. According to Burmese tradition the Śālankāyanas of Veṅgī were responsible for the spread of Buddhism to Burma. An inscription of the time of Mahārāja Mūlavarma, the ruler of Malaya refers to a master mariner (Mahānāvika) named Buddhagupta, native of Raktamṛttikā Mahavihara (Rangamati, district Murshidabad, W. Bengal) going to Malaya peninsula in 5th century AD. Again it is exceedingly interesting to note that a 7th century AD inscription in Kavi language and script of Java was found in Mexico which referred to a Mahānāvika Usaluna. It appears that the Mahānāvikas from east coast had undertaken extensive seafaring activity right from 2nd to 7th centuries AD. They were largely followers of Buddhism.

7. Numismatic Evidences

Numismatic sources amply attest to these overseas contacts. As we have pointed out earlier coastal navigation came to prominence under the Mauryas. The occurrence of punch-marked, coins and the Magadhan Buddhist pottery, the N.B.P. ware in Śri Lankān towards of the Mauryan' date (600-450 BC) specially Gedige and Anuradhapura is of great importance. A unique type of punch-marked coins using the ship symbol were obtained from the earliest levels at Chandraketugarh. In northern Śri Lankā we get a single-mast ship in conjunction with a donatory inscription of 1st century BC.

The ship-type coins issued by the Sātavāhana king Vaśisṭhīputra Pụlumāvī, the illustrious son and successor of Gautmiputra Satakarni (the *Trisamudratoya-Pītavāhana, Dakshiṇā Pathapatī),* are classic examples in the domain of ancient coinage. The examples are of lead and circular and depict both double-mast and single-mast ships anchored in mid-sea. Gautamiputra Yajna Sri, his able successor, also continued the type more prominently and are known from many sites on the south-east coast. A unique coin now in the British Museum collection shows the device very clearly and what is more interesting is the portrayal of cargo vessels approaching the anchored ship. The obverse double-mast ship type coins of lead were continued to be issued by the Sālankāyanas (Vijaya Devavarman, AD 280-93) too who succeeded the Sātavāhanas in the Veṅgī country. Śālankāyanas were also powerful kings having trade contacts and furthered the cause of Buddhism as well as Brahmanical religions beyond the shores. Samudragupta, the Guptan king took to the east coast route and subdued all the powers, at least for a brief period, right up to Śri Lankā. Bull and double-mast ship type copper coins were also issued by the Pallavas of pre-Mahendra line.[21]

A galaxy of Buddhist teachers like Buddhaghosha, Buddhadatta, Bodhi Dharma (AD 470-520), Vajrabodhi (Tantrik Buddhism) Dinnaga (Nyaya), Vinitaruchi (AD 570) took Buddhism to the Far-Eastern countries through the sea route. This very zone assumed great importance and as Lokesh Chandra[22] puts it, it was not Bengal, Orissa or Assam but *Oḍḍiyāṇa* meaning girdle, i.e. *Maṇi Mekhalai* i.e. (Kānchī), and *Andhrapatha* were the chief centres transmitting *Tāntrik* Buddhism to Indonesia and China.

Ship symbol occurs on terracotta sealings from central Thailand. Ship type coins of bronze with a cow or bull on the reverse were found from Klong Thom and Khuan Lukpad which were perhaps in circulation amongst the merchants.[23] A stone seal from Nakorn Pathom shows a two-masted ship. Tin used for minting coins, particularly post-Mauryan dynastic issues (Sātavāhana), must have come from Thailand (Phuket province) so also the Malayan gold and tin. Items that were exported from India included ivory, carnelian seals (a pendant of leaping lion from Ban Don Ta Phet), glass beads, knobbed bronze bowls of Orissa-Bengal origin.

The extensive distribution of carnelian beads and seals of Indian origin in South-east Asia shows the impact of organised maritime network between Indian ports, and South-east Asia, Śri Lankā on one hand and Mediterranean world right from early centuries BC on the other hand.[24]

A recently discovered rock inscription (*Pulan Kurichhi*, Ramnathpuram District) refers to a donor as captain of a big naval force during the year 192 of Tamil era founded by Chēndan Kuṟṟan of the Kālabhra family. Kālabhras originally came to the south by sea in 2nd century AD.

8. Evidences from Tamil Nadu

The wharf at Kilaiyur, the reservoir at Vanagiri and the Buddha Vihāra at Malaipur are the unmistakable evidences for the existence of ancient city under the earth of the shores. A shipwreck about 70 ft. depth and 4.5 km away from the seashore was also located. A number of ingots bearing the legend and year 1792, reveal the approximate date of the wreck. A structure somewhat apsidal in shape facing north, was located at Karaiyappar, 4.5

km inwards from seashore, tentatively taken as a part of Poompuhar, the ancient city of Sangam Age.

An account of naval battles[25] and ship wreckage is provided in the Tamil epigraphs. Parāntaka-I is *Maduraiyam Illamum Konda*—conqueror of Śri Lankā, commanding a big naval fleet. Raja Raja I's *Praśasti* gives a vivid account of the naval battle he fought at Kandalur *Kandalur Salai Kalam aruttu aruli*. He bequeathed a strong navy to his son Rājendra-I whose naval power is extolled "*Purvadesamum Gaṅgāiyam Kadaramum Konda*". Kulottunga-I takes pride of his strong navy and sent many naval expeditions.

9. Later Historical Periods: Post-Buddhist and Medieval

In later periods, influences from Far East, Central and South China paved way to the growth of port towns not only in South-east Asian countries such as the Phillippines, Indonesia, Malaysia, Thailand but also in India and Śri Lankā. More particularly, the Chinese ceramics are associated with the forts and palaces but less within temples and mosques during this period. It appears commerce overtook the culture.

There appears to be two distinct waves[26]—the earlier dated to 9th-13th century AD and the second group, 14th to 17th century AD. The former consisted of a few whitish porcelain confined largely to the coastal tracts of Andhra and Tamil Nadu. Noboru Karashima of Tokyo University along with some Indian colleagues (Madras and Calicut Universities) has been doing extensive fieldwork on the Chinese potteries,[27] their distributional patterns, etc. More frequently the Chinese ships touched the South-east Indian ports during the Chōḷa times. From Gangaikondacholapuram and Darasuram, white porcelain was reported. It is well known that great Chōḷa emperors Rāja Rāja-I and Rājendra sent various embassies to China. Even Brahmanical temples were raised and patronised in South China. Chinese porcelain finds attributed to the Jindezhen kilns were found from Periyapattinam, Palayakayal, Devipattinam and Nagapattinam which add substantially to our knowledge on the subject.

Soon after Chōḷas, the Kakatiyas of Warangal rejuvenated the seaborne foreign trade. Marco Polo visited the port of Mottupalli, called *Deśūyakkoṇḍa-Paṭṭana* located in Chirala taluk, district Prakasam of A.P. This great port town is identified with Dabadan mentioned in the Daoyi Zhilue, an important 14th century Chinese work, although Karashima recently put forth the view that *DABADAN* is *Periya Paṭṭiṇam*, Periya (Da) and (badan) = *Paṭṭiṇam,* on linguistic grounds. The famous Motupalli pillar inscription of Gaṇapatideva AD 1244, edited by E. Hultzsch is of far reaching importance as this edict assures safety to traders (*abhaya Śāsana)* arriving from all continents (*Svadēśi* and *Paradēśis*) risking the sea-voyage and its hazards like storm attacks and shipwrecks. The levies (usually 1:30) on the items of import and export have also been listed with great detail and speak of the flourishing international trade from this important seaport which was provided with warehouses. Besides, the mention of several continents, islands, foreign countries and cities, specific mention of *Chīnī* (China) is noteworthy. Confirming this epigraphical evidence is the Telugu work *Harivilāsamu* written by the poet *Śrinātha* (circa 15th century) which details the trading countries in the Āndhra coast and the objects of import, particularly silks and pottery wares from China. In the major excavations at Hampi, the Vijayanagara city, along with Chinese porcelain (white-and-red, white-and-blue and gold hues), Chinese circular copper coins of the times of Ming king Yuang Lo (AD 1403-28) were found. This ruler was a close contemporary to Hari Hara-II and Vijayanagara rulers had kept contacts with China. Several dishes and vessels depict the scenes of Chinese port towns, architecture, ships approaching the coast (particularly from Ginge and Vellore forts of the Nāyaka rulers). Quite recently large quantities of inscribed and painted Chinese porcelain and glazed pottery wares have been encountered in the medieval fortified towns of Daulatabad (Maharashtra), Golkonda (A.P.), Bijapur and Hampi in Karnataka, Champaner in Gujarat, Fatehpur Sikri and Purāṇā Qilā, New Delhi. These bear the marks of long Quan and Fujian kilns of 13-14th century AD. The highly prized table wares from the Jingdezhan kilns, blue-and-white glazed or enamelled ones (Golkonda, Purāṇā Qilā and Red Fort examples) were popular among the Muslim rulers. In the year 1988-89 Noboru Karashimha[28] surveyed some places on the Malabar coast between Kannanur, north of Calicut to Vilinjam, south of Trivandrum. Chinese wares and tiles were noted in the churches and mosques in Cochin, Kollam (Quilon) Kodungallur, etc. datable to 15-17th century AD.

10. The Role of Orissan Ports

Orissa has acted as a gateway for overseas Asian trade. Ptolemy mentions major and prosperous ports like Nanaigam (present Puri) and Konagar (Konarak), both in district Puri, Kosambi (district Balasore), Paloura (Palur), district Ganjam. The entire coast of Orissa[29] from Subarnarekha in the north to river Rishikulya in south is thus dotted with small ports. These ports are on the estuary of rivers, Olandas' on river Burhabalang, Paradeep on the river Mahanadi, Manikapatna on lake Chilka and Khalkatta Pattana on river Kushabhadra.

Clear weather starts from *Kārteeka Pūrṇimā* when the first boat sailed on their Eastward journey, i.e. the festival called *Bāliyātra* which is celebrated in a grand way in Orissa. This *Bāliyātra* appears to be in vogue from very early periods when Buddhism started spreading from Magadha to various port towns of South-east Asia and Śri Lankā.

I am tempted to recall here once again the reference in *Mahāvaṁśa* (XIX. 6; XIX 11-12) as to how emperor Aśōka despatched the *Bodhi Vṛiksha* sapling to *Simhaḷa* in a highly religious manner. He descended into the water up to the neck and set the Bodhi tree on the ship, stood with folded hands on the shore. We get in fact a terracotta sealing which depicts the *Bodhi Vṛiksha* from Chandraketugarh. The excavated evidence recently obtained by B.K. Sinha[30] from Khalkattapatna, 11 km east of Konarka, revealed a brick platform (perhaps a wharf) along with Chinese pottery and a copper coin (circular with square slot) datable to 14th century AD.

NOTES AND REFERENCES

1. I.K. Sarma, "South-east Asia, India and West Asia : A Study on the Beginnings of Food Producing Stages," in S.B. Deo (Ed.), *Archaeological Congress and Seminar Papers,* Nagpur, 1972, pp. 95-112; in S.B. Deo and K. Paddayya (Eds.), *Recent Advances in Indian Archaeology* (Pune, 1985), pp. 49-51; Thai Evidence of Early Beginning of Domestication of Animals and Plants, see, Solheim II G. Wilhelm G. "New Light on a Forgotten Past," *National Geographic* (March, 1971), pp. 330-39; K.C. Chang, "The Beginnings of Agriculture in the Far-East," *Antiquity,* XLIV, No. 175 (Sept. 1970), pp. 175-84. D.D. Anderson, "Excavations of Pliestocene Rockshelter in Krobi and the Prehistory of Southern Thailand." *Prehistoric Studies, The Stone and Metal Ages in Thailand*, Bangkok, 1988.
2. Bridget Allchin, *The Stone Tipped Arrow* (London, 1966), Chapters 4 to 6. Microlithic tools out of rock crystal and quartz found among the assemblages at Teri, Nagarjunakonda, Kuchai (Orissa) provide links to the "Śri Lankān Microlithic Industries."

3. Jagat Pati Joshi, "India and Bahrain—A survey of culture interaction during third and second millennia," in Shaikha Haya Ali Al Khalif and Nichael Rice (Eds.) *Bahrain through the Ages, the Archaeology* (London, 1986), pp. 73-76.
4. S.R. Rao, "Trade and Cultural contacts between Bahrain and India," in *op. cit.* (1986), pp. 376-81.
5. K.M. Srivastava's team worked between Dec. '84 and May 1985. See *The Times Weekend* (May, 1985).
6. S.R. Rao, *Progress and Prospects of Marine Archaeology in India* (Goa, 1987), pp. 1-14.
7. R. Nigam, "Was the large rectangular structure at Lothal (Harappan Settlement), a Dockyard or an Irrigation Tank?," in S.R. Rao (Ed.), *Marine Archaeology of Indian Ocean countries* (Goa, 1988), pp. 20-21.
8. S.R. Rao, *Lothal and Indus civilization* (Bombay, 1972), Pl. XXVI-D.
9. S.R. Rao, "Excavation of the Legendary city of Dvaraka on the Arabian Sea," *Marine Archaeology* (Goa, Jan. 1990), Vol. I, pp. 59-98. Also in *New Trends in Indian Art and Archaeology, S.R. Rao's 70th Birthday Felicitation Volume* (New Delhi, 1992), Vol. II, pp. 479-91.
10. A. Sundara, in S.R. Rao (Ed.), *Journal of Marine Archaeology,* Vol. I (Goa, 1990), pp. 39-40.
11. Ritti Srinivas, "Shipping in Ancient India," in S.R. Rao (Ed.), *Marine Archaeology of Indian Ocean Countries* (Goa 1988), pp. 5-7.
12. I.K. Sarma, "Rare Evidences on Maritime Trade on the Bengal Coast of India," in S.R. Rao (Ed.), *Recent Advances in Marine Archaeology* (Goa, 1991), pp. 38-40.
13. I.K. Sarma, "Ceramics and Maritime Routes of India : New Evidences," *Purātattva,* No. 21 (1990-91), pp. 37-39.
14. Vimala Begley, "Arikamedu Reconsidere, and Rouletted ware at Arikamedu: A New Approach," *American Journal of Archaeology,* 92 (1988), pp. 427-40.
15. K.V. Raman, "Further Evidence of Roman Trade from coastal sites in Tamilnadu," in Vimala Begley and Richard Daniel De Puna (Eds.), *Rome and India: The Ancient Sea Trade,* Wisconsin Press, 1992, pp. 125-33.
16. I.K. Sarma, "Rare Evidences on Maritime Trade on the Bengal coast of India," *ibid* (Goa, 1991), pp. 38-40.
17. P.C. Das Gupta (Ed.), *Bengal's Past,* Department of Archaeology (West Bengal, 1987).
18. "Trade contacts Between India and South-east Asia (200 BC-AD 200), (Mrs.) Janya Manavid, *International Seminar,* UNESCO (Madras, 19-21 Dec. 1990), pp.
19. "Commercial and Cultural Relationship Between India and Thailand during 4th-13th century AD" *International Seminar,* UNESCO (Madras, 19-21 Dec. 199) pp.
20. I.K. Sarma, *Studies in Early Buddhist Monuments and Brāhmi Inscriptions of Āndhradēśa* (Nagpur, 1988), pp. 72-73 and 84-85.
21. I.K. Sarma, *South Indian Coinage : A Review of Recent Discoveries* (Madras, 1992), p.22.
22. Lokesh Chandra, "Oḍḍiyāna—A New Interpretation," *International Journal of Dravidian Linguistics* (Trivandrum 1980), p. 127. Also *Tamil Civilization,* 102.3, No. 4, pp. 9-21 (Tanjore, 1985).
23. C. Higham, *The Archaeology of Mainland South-east Asia* (Cambridge, 1989), p. 207. Himanshu Prabha Ray, "Early Maritime contacts between South and South-east Asia," *Journal of South-east Asian Studies,* Vol. XX, No. 1, pp. 47-48, 51-52.
24. "Trade Contacts Between India and South-east Asia (200 BC-400 AD)," K.V. Raman, "Port Towns of Tamilnadu-Some field data and the prospects of Marine Archaeology," in S.R. Rao (Ed.) (1988), pp. 114-18.
25. P. Venkatesan, "Naval Battles and Ship-wrecks referred to in Tamil Epigraphs," in S.R. Rao (Ed.), *Marine Archaeology of Indian Ocean Countries* (Goa 1988), pp. 26-27.
26. I.K. Sarma, in *Purātattva,* No. 21 (1990-91), pp. 41-42.
27. Noboru Karashima, "Discoveries of Chinese Ceramic Sherds on the coasts of South India," Paper Read at the International Seminar, UNESCO (Madras), 20-21 Dec. 1990.

28. Noboru Karashima, *op. cit* (1990). Also R. Ananda Sivam, "South India and China," in H.M. Nayak and B.R. Gopal (Eds.), *South Indian Studies: Prof. T.V. Mahalingam Commemoration Volume* (Mysore, 1990), pp. 369-88.
29. Sila Tripati, "Ancient Ports of Kaliṅga," in S.R. Rao (Ed), *Recent Advances in Marine Archaeology* (Goa 1991), pp. 192-94.
30. B.K. Sinha, "Khalkattapatna—A small port on the coast of Orissa," in *New Trends in Indian Art and Archaeology* (New Delhi, 1992), pp. 423-28.

2

Indian Maritime Activities : Vedic, Epic and Purāṇic Sources

U.N. DHAL

Our India or Bhāratavarṣa is surrounded by the ocean from the east and the west as well as from the south; the Himalayan ranges stand as a barrier in the north. In this vast country live people of various castes, colours, creed, customs, traditions and culture, speak different languages and move and have their being. Besides moving from place to place on land route and through the river for various purposes inside the country, they also travel through the oceans to distant places for trade and commerce and even for victory over far off countries beyond the sea. The aim of this humble venture is to trace the marine activities of the people as referred to in our Vedas, Epics and the Purāṇas in a broader way. As the Ṛgveda is believed to be the earliest record of the Aryans, we take it up at the beginning for the survey.

The old Vedic god Varuṇa is king of the heaven and the sea. So he is believed to know the movement of the birds in the sky and ships in the ocean——

vedā yo vīnāṁ padam antarikṣeṇa patatām/
veda nāvaḥ samudriyaḥ// (*ṚV.* 1.25.7)

"He (Varuṇa) knows the path of the birds that fly through heaven and as the sovereign of the sea he knows the movement of the ships that are thereon".

In the *Uṣāsūkta* (*ṚV.*1.48), it is said, as like a ship that has anchored during the night moves out to the sea in the morning in search of wealth, the Goddess Uṣas proceeds on her car, attracts her invokers——

uvāsoṣā ucchācca nu devī jīrā rathānām /
ye asya ācaraṇeṣu dadhrire samudre na śravasyava // (*ṚV*.1.48.3)

"Uṣas has dawned and now shall dawn the Goddess, driver forth of cars, which she comes nigh, have fixed their thought on her, like the glory-seekers on the open water (sea)".

Similarly in the *Indrasūkta* (1.56) it is said: Those traders who seek gain move to the ocean on the ship like the followers of Indra who invoke him for pleasure:

taṁ gūrtayo nemanniṣaḥ pariṇasaḥ samudraṁ na
sañ caraṇe saniṣyavaḥ / (*ṚV*.1.56.2)

"To him the guidance-following sons of praise flow full, as those, who seek gain go in company to the ocean (large gathering of water)."

The Maruts are invoked to raise water from the ocean——

udīrayathā marutaḥ samudrato yūyaṁ vṛṣṭiṁ
varṣayathā purīṣiṇaḥ / (*Ṛ V*.5.55.5)

"O Maruts, from the ocean ye uplift the rain, and fraught with vaporous moisture pour the torrents down."

In course of illustrating the heroic deeds of Aśvins, the Ṛgveda (1.116.35) refers to the legend of Tugra's son Bhurju and his recovery from the ocean thus: Rājarṣi Bhurju, the son of Tugra drowned in the ocean. The Aśvins strove for three days and nights to rescue him from the ocean with the help of a ship with hundred oars——

tugro ha bhurjumaśvinodameghe...*(1.116.3)*

xx xx xx

anārambhaṇe tadavīrayethā-manāsthāne agrabhaṇe samudre /
yadaśvinā ūhathur bhujyumastaṁ śatāritrāṁ nāvamātasthi vaṁsam (1.116.5)

"Tugra left Bhujyu in the ocean. Oh Aśvins, you worked such heroic exploits in the ocean for three days and nights without any support and carried Bhujyu to his dwelling in a ship with hundred oars."

In course of invocation to Varuṇa, it is said that Varuṇa accompanied Vaśiṣṭha over the ocean. Because of his acquaintance with him he brought him to prominence as his best eulogizer (*stotā*):

ā yad ruhāva varuṇaśca nāvam pra yat samudramirayava madhyam /
adhi yadapām snubhiścarāva pra preṅkha iṅkhayāvahai śubham kam //3
vaśiṣṭham ha varuṇa nāvyadhād ṛṣam cakāra svāpā mahobhiḥ /4a
(*Ṛ V*.7.88.3-4)

"When Varuna and I embark together and urge our boat unto the midst of ocean; (thereafter) Varuna placed Vaśiṣṭha in the vessel and deftly with his might made him a Ṛṣi."

The Yajurveda refers to the two mantras (VS.21.6-7) in the context of a boat, which are utilized before it is used for the journey. The Pāraskara Gṛhya Sūtra (3.15-10-11) utilizes it for the purpose. The Gṛhya Sūtra enjoins to pray to the boat with the mantra (VS.21.7) from the Yajurveda and states: *nāvamārokṣyannabhi mantrayate* "sunāvamiti" and the complete mantra of (VS.21.7)—*sunāvamāruheya śravantīmanāgasam / śatāritrām svastaye //* "I enter into the boat, which resembles an innocent sacrifice to cross over world like ocean." The other mantra is applied by the Gṛhyasūtra (3.15.11)—*uttariṣyannabhimantrayate sūtramāṇam iti,* for imparting additional strength to the boat and quotes the mantra of Yajurveda (21.6):

sūtrāmānaṁ pṛthivīm dyāmaṇehasaṁ suśarmāṇamaditim suprīṇitam /
daivīṁ nāvam svaritrāmanāgasamasravantīmā ruhemā svastaye //

"(We) mount this divine boat fortified with the beautiful oars in the form of the sacrifice. This great boat without any opening (aperture) is worthy for the welfare of the inmates."

These citations help us to come to the conclusion that the journey by boat or ship was usually conducted for visiting distant countries for trade and commerce.

During the age of the Epics and the Purāṇas (c. 600 BC onwards) such trend is also easily traceable. The *Rāmāyaṇa* informs us of its knowledge of the ocean and the Dvīpas inside it. In this context, Ch. 39 of the *Kiṣkindhākāṇḍa* is remarkable. After the abduction of Vaidehī, Sugriva deputes Hanumāna and his army in search of Sītā. There he comes across the islands like Yāvadvīpa (Java), Suvarṇadvīpa (Sumātrā) and the Rupyakadvīpa inside the ocean:

samudram avagāḍhān śca parvatān pattanāni ca //23b

xx xx xx

ratnavanta yavadvīpaṁ saptarājyopaśobhitam //28b
sumātrā rupyaka caiva suvarṇākara maṇḍitam /29a (*Ram*.4.39.23-29)

Similarly the *Ayodhyākāṇḍa* of the *Rāmāyaṇa* (78.6-7) states—when Bharata proceeds in the forest to meet Rāma, he comes across the kingdom of Guha, the king of the Niṣādas. For fear of Rāma's life from Bharata, as Rama's foe, the king Guha cautions his army to be alert on the occasion:

tiṣṭhantu sarvadāśāś ca gaṅgām anvāśritā nadīm /
balayuktā nadīrakṣā māṅsa-mūla-phalāśanāḥ //6
nāvāṁ śatānāṁ pañcānāṁ kaivartānāṁ śataṁ śatam /
saṁnaddhānāṁ tathā yūnāṁ tiṣṭhantvitya bhyacodayat //7

Like the *Rāmāyaṇa,* the other great Epic, the *Mahābhārata* also refers to the voyage in the ocean: Sahadeva, the son of Mādrī is stated to have conquered the Mlecchas in various islands in the sea:

sāgara-dvīpakāṅś ca nṛpatin mlecchayonijān /
niṣādān purusādāṅś ca karṇa prāvaraṇānapi //44

xx xx xx

dvīpaṁ tāmrāhvayāñ caiva parvatam rāmakam tathā //46 Mbh. 2.28.44-46

The *Karṇaparva* of the *Mahābhārata* (8.60.22) compares the defeat and discomfiture of the Kauravas with the shipwreck of the traders in the sea:

nimajjatastān atha karṇasāgare vipanna-nāvo vaṇijo yathārṇavāt /
uddadhrira naubhirivārṇavād rathaiḥ sukalpitair draupadijāḥ svamātulān //22

In the context of rescuing the Pāṇḍavas by Vidura with the help of a ship the text runs:

tatah pravāsito vidvān vidureṇa naras tadā /
pārthānāṁ darśayāmāsa mano-mārutagāminim //4
sarvavātasahāṁ nāvaṁ yantrayuktāṁ patākinīm /
śive bhāgīrathitīre narair viśrambhibhiḥ kṛtam //
(Mbh. Gita Press edn. 1.148.4-5)

Purāṇa literature is vast and varied. Its date of composition begins along with the Epics or prior to it. This bulk of literature furnishes us with some materials regarding the sea voyage. Of them the *Varāḥa Purāṇa* (Ch. 171. 4-10) states: A trader named Gokarṇa started for a voyage on the sea, during which he accompanied with some examiners of pearls and jewels in his ship:

punas tatraiva gamane vaṇighbhāve matirgatā /
samudrayāne ratnāni mahāmaulyāni sādhbubhiḥ //4
ānayiṣye bahūn yatra sārdham rātnaparīkṣakaiḥ /
evam niścitya manasā mahāsārtha puraḥsaraḥ /
samudrayāyubhiṛ lokaiḥ saṁvidaṁ procya nirgataḥ //5

Thus copious examples direct or indirect even in the form of similes etc., may be traced to have insight into the state of sea voyage during that period.

Books consulted

The Vedic and Puranic texts are referred to from the Nag Publishers' edition. The critical edition of the Rāmāyaṇa, published at Baroda is taken up, but the Mahābhārata (Cr. edn.) published by Bhandarkar Oriental Research Institute, Poona, is taken up along with the Gita Press (edn.) also.

3

Indo-Roman Trade

KISHOR K. BASA & KARUNA SAGAR BEHERA

The possession of Indian products was a sign of wealth at Rome: Tiberius castigated those who squandered their money on Indian gems, while Juvenal tells us of a lady who took no care over her looks for her husband, but saved up her Indian lotions and potions to impress her lover. The East had connotations of luxury that was not quite proper, but the Romans ardently desired the precious stones, the exotic spices and perfumes and rich silks and cottons which the intrepid voyagers brought back from their eastern trips, at great expense.[1]

Much has been written on the theme of Indo-Roman trade.[2] While the earlier works written during the first three decades of the century emphasized primarily the literary sources, the latter works took into account archaeological as well as numismatic evidence. The main reason for opening this issue again is the development during the last decade or so of an Indian Ocean perspective[3] for the early historic maritime trade based primarily on archaeological researches carried out in the Indian Ocean littoral from the area of Red Sea and Persian Gulf to the western and eastern coasts of India, and continuing up to various regions of South-east Asia. Especially the unearthing of archaeological remains showing the Indian maritime trade with South-east Asia during the late centuries BC and early centuries of the Christian era (which was earlier thought to be a 'trickle') demonstrates that the Indo-Roman trade was not an isolated phenomenon confined to the region between the Eastern Mediterranean and the western sector of the Indian Ocean; rather it was integrated to what Glover calls "a world trading system."[4] With this background, an attempt is made here for a comprehensive account of all kinds of evidence—archaeological, numismatic, epigraphic and literary—for the Indo-Roman trade for the period from 2nd century BC to 2nd century AD. Besides brief discussions will also be made as to the favourable conditions for such trade, items of trade, phases of trade and trade routes.

Archaeological Evidence for Indo-Roman Trade

The archaeological evidence for Indo-Roman trade has been discuss by many scholars.[5] Hence we would only provide a summary of various types of evidence which include pottery, bronze, ivory statue, glass, lamp and bullae. The pottery includes both imported ware from the Mediterranean as well as pottery which were Indian imitations of the Graeco-Roman imported pottery and metalcraft tradition. The imported ware includes terra sigillata and amphorae, while Indian imitations of Mediterranean pottery include rouletted ware, mould-made ware. The issue of red polished ware is also discussed since it was, at one time, considered as an Indian imitation.

Terra Sigillata

Terra sigillata[6] is a red-surfaced ware distributed extensively throughout the Rhine and Danube valleys, throughout Britain, south of the Antonine wall in Scotland, throughout France and the Iberian peninsula, Italy, Greece and the Levant and around the southern spheres of the Mediterranean. Such ware is also found at Arikamedu. Previously the term used for such ware in India was the Arretine ware[7] since it was believed that such ware was made par excellence at Arretium (modern Arezzo in Tuscany, Italy) in the late Republican and early Imperial periods, approximately 30 BC to early second century AD. However, this term Arretine ware has been abolished for the term Sigillata, since the provenance for such ware has been determined at different places and not at Arretium as was previously believed. It is now accepted that terra sigillata was made over a longer period in many local varieties. According to Comfort,[8] all varieties of terra sigillata had a red surface called *Glanzton films* and were made by two leading techniques of moulded exterior decoration or of wheel-made plain tableware, and by the very common (though not universal) practice of manufacturers' names stamped on the upper face of the bottom. However, Comfort[9] discussed seven stamped pottery from Arikamedu and concluded that Arikamedu had ITTA from Lyon/La Muette, RVFIO from Pozzuoli, EVHOD from Pisa, plus CAMUR(i) and VIBIE (ni) from Central Italy. Thus not a single signature demonstrably originated at Arrezo and hence he advocated for the abolition of the term Arretine in writing of the period of importation. Rather he suggests the term Sigillata period, which would include Near Eastern wares as well. The stamps were written in two types, in rectangles and in planta pedis (usually a bare foot-sole).[10] However while Comfort places two marbled sherds in the same category as the two sherds from the Roman camp at Mainz,[11] Slane considers them to be South Gaulish.[12] Comfort's identification of two of Wheeler's "Arretine" fragments as Eastern Sigillata B is extremely important for the dating of Arikamedu sequence and the trade on the south-eastern coast.[13] According to Comfort, at least one fragment of sigillata may be dated back to 10 BC, but the majority of stamps are early Tiberian (AD 10-25/30).[14] What Deo referred to as a sherd of Samian ware,[15] Slane identified it as Gaulish sigillata.[16] As to the question of the users of the imported pottery, Comfort suggests that there was a Roman enclave or *conventus Romanorum* comprising Roman citizens or freemen, businessmen, and their families supervising the Indo-Roman commerce.[17] Hence Slane pointed out that "tablewares were not luxurious enough to be traded".[18] However, Begley opines that two previously unpublished sigillata sherds with Indian graffiti, now in the Musee Guimet, Paris, make it necessary to reconsider the question of who the users of sigillata might have been.[19]

Amphora

The distribution of Mediterranean shipping amphoras has been extensive in the Indian subcontinent, from the foothills of the Himalayas in the north to the Coromandel coast in the south.[20] The largest concentration of Mediterranean amphoras in India has so far been found at Arikamedu where amphoras for Greek and Italian wine, Spanish garum and northern Adriatic oil are reported.

At Arikamedu, Will distinguished two types of amphora, the Greek Koan and the pseudo-Koan (primarily Italian), on the basis of dimensions and the fabric of the objects.[21] This is discussed below. At Arikamedu, clay of the Koan pieces is fine, generally pinkish to tannish in colour and contains small inclusions. The surface of the lighter colour is often greenish. Dimensions of rims and handles are regularly smaller than those of the pseudo-Koan varieties. However, no Koan trademark has so far not been found at Arikamedu. These Koan varieties are dated to as early as 2nd century BC.

Like the Greek Koan amphora, Italian pseudo-Koan imitations have two prominent physical characteristics : the double-ribbed handles and the offset between neck and shoulder. But the Italian jars are also taller and narrower than their Greek source, and fragments of some of their components (handles, rims, toes) are usually, except in some early pieces, larger in size. The clay of Italian pseudo-Koan imitations from Arikamedu is uniformly coarse and much darker than the Koan clay, with many inclusions. The surface is regularly a worn, dirty cream colour with no greenish tinge. On the basis of finds at Pompeii, Will dates the pseudo-Koan amphora fragments at Arikamedu between 50 BC and AD 79.[22] Thus it may be inferred that Greek Koan wine which may have been coming to Arikamedu as early as 2nd century BC had been supplemented by the Italian pseudo-Koan wine by about the middle of the 1st century BC.

Will further refers to several Greek Koan amphora fragments covered with pozzolana cement (a distinctive, water resistant cement used by the Romans in the construction of underwater installations) which she argued, were once used in the building of port installations at the site.[23] The fact that Greek Koan amphora fragments are almost the only ones covered with pozzolana cement implies that Italian wine had replaced the Koan wine at Arikamedu by the time of building of permanent port installation.[24]

Besides the Koan and pseudo-Koan imitation amphoras, other Mediterranean amphora varieties at Arikamedu include several fragments of 1st century BC amphora from the Greek island of Knidos, and some from the island of Rhodes.[25] Will further refers to a few fragments of early Spanish jars for garum dated to late 1st century BC and early 1st century AD, two fragments of very early examples of Spanish olive oil amphoras and also a few fragments of jars from the Istrian peninsula in the northern Adriatic for the famous oil from Istria.[26]

Begley emphasizes the importance of Will's work on Arikamedu amphora for the history of trade since they date from the 1st century BC (perhaps even earlier) to the 1st century AD and not the first two centuries AD as was formerly believed.[27] Will found no evidence of amphora dating after the 1st century. According to Slane, amphoras similar to those of Rhodians and Knidians may be identified at more sites in India, but for the moment their presence at Arikamedu coupled with their strong appearance in Egypt suggests that they reached India by the Red Sea route.[28]

Rouletted Ware

Rouletted ware is often regarded as of Mediterranean origin or influence. This ware is invariably wheel-thrown, slipped, and has often lustrous surfaces which are either brown and black or red and grey in colour, with a predominant grey core.[29] The most distinctive feature of rouletted ware is its decoration, i.e. rouletting, which consisted of revolving a toothed wheel on the wet surface of the pot and producing symmetrical picked decoration.[30]

The rouletted decoration was done in the form of minute triangles, diamonds, parallelograms, wedges, or upright crescents, ovals or dots or an eye-shaped device which is only an attenuated diamond.[31] Rouletted ware is widely distributed in India and South-east Asia[32] but it is concentrated in the Coromandel coast with Arikamedu as a major production centre. According to Begley[33] rouletted ware occurs in large quantities in the Cauvery drainage system and eastern coast of South India, but the number gradually decreases when one moves away from these areas. Secondly, this ware seems to occur only at urban or religious centres, not at village sites. Moreover, Begley emphasized that the absolute contemporaneity of the numerous rouletted ware sites cannot be determined.[34] However, Begley's study of contemporary village techniques in India and comparisons with ancient pottery, indicated that the decoration was not rouletted, but chattered.[35] Chattering was produced by the continuous flicking motion of a tool with one or more long twin points which it is held against the surface of the clay vessel rotating on pottery's wheel. Indian archaeologists usually distinguished two types of rouletted ware—(1) a highly glossy black ware with fine grey core, and (2) a dull, coarse black ware.[36] It was widely believed that the former type was an imported ware and the latter an imitation. A new type of rouletted ware has been discovered at the coastal site of Alagankulam with the usual rouletted design on glossy or well-polished red ware which almost resembles Roman red wares.[37] However, Begley[38] opined that while the rouletted ware is a local product, rouletting alone might have been borrowed from the West, with the Syrian made and exported Eastern Sigillata A, a probable source. The technique of rouletting could have been introduced into South India even in pre-Imperial Roman times, in about the 2nd century BC.

Mould-made Ware

A fine red mould-made ware, frequently with relief decoration has been recovered at Nevasa, Ter, Kondapur and Kolhapur in the Western Deccan. The most comprehensive account of such ware is made by Begley,[39] which is summarised below. The vessels are made of fine clay, evenly fired, have red body and core and bright red, sepia, or brownish red surface. A thin slip was frequently applied to vessels of red ware. The vessels are invariably small in size, ranging from 4 to 6.5 cm in height and most were produced from two vertical moulds joined together rather awkwardly. The joints are sometimes off centre and frequently cut through the decorative motif on the body as well as the medallion on the base. The complete vessels reveal four basic shapes—(1) the most common basic shape is a *lota* or cup with outturned rim, flaring wide neck, pronounced shoulder and hemispherical body, (2) a bowl, deep or shallow, straight-sided or hemispherical in form, (3) a deep cup with two very pronounced bulges, one at the juncture of the base and body and the other on the shoulder, and (4) a bottle with bulbous body, flat base and flaring long neck. As to decoration the scheme of decoration on most vessels spreads from the central medallion on the base to the body below the shoulder capped by a final border, each segment separated by one or more ridges. In contrast to the decorated lower body, the neck and rim are plain. The motifs are floral and geometric, never figurative.

As to the origin of the mould ware of the western Deccan, Begley[40] seeks parallels from the West, since there is nothing like it in pre-Hellenistic times in India. Begley referred to the Hellenistic mould-made pottery, commonly known as Megarian bowls, and also numerous metal forerunners (such as Macedonian, Thracian, Egyptian, and late Hellenistic cups and bowls), all believed to have been derived ultimately from Achaemenid prototypes. She further argued that the Deccan shapes, the scheme of decoration, and several individual motifs have analogies in both these ceramic and metallic wares; but the use of the two moulds to produce a single object appears to have been a regional characteristic of the western Deccan. However, Begley mentioned that since mould-made ware from Nevasa can be dated to mid-1st century BC, its foreign prototypes were perhaps imported even earlier.[41]

Red Polished Ware

Red polished ware of Gujarat is made from fine, well-levigated clay, and is evenly fired and has a smooth slipped surface.[42] It appears in strata dated from 1st century BC to the 5th century AD. It was Subbarao[43] who argued that red polished ware, even though an Indian ceramic, derived its major influence in manufacture and finish from the Mediterranean world. Subbarao further argued that, because of its fine quality and lustrous red surfaces, and the fact that it was found in contexts with Roman artifacts, red polished ware closely resembled Roman "Samian" ware and that its manufacturing technique was copied in western India.[44] It was S.R. Rao who on the basis of his study of red polished ware from Amreli, Gujarat, concluded that red polished ware must be an indigenous ceramic, and not an imitation of a Roman ware, especially since the technology for well-fired, finely made pottery existed before the appearance of red polished ware and prior to Roman imports in Gujarat.[45] On the basis of a comprehensive study of red polished ware from many sites in Gujarat, Orton argued against any direct Roman influence on red polished ware.[46] According to her, red polished ware vessel forms are strictly Indian in character. All forms can be found in coarser associated wares of the Early Historical period, except for the "sprinkler" or globuler jars with beaded interior ledges; and hence Orton argued that there is no direct influence on Indian ceramics from the Mediterranean world as a result of contact with Roman traders.[47]

Bronze

The Roman bronzes found at Kolhapur were highlighted by Karl Khandalavala.[48] However these bronzes were restudied by Richard De Puma.[49] De Puma discussed the Kolhapur bronze objects in three categories: figural bronzes (such as the Poseidon statuette, and emblema with Perseus and Andromeda), bronze vessels and handles (for example, the Millingen-type Oinochoe which is a small but fine, trefoil-mouthed jar with solid cast handle; an intriguing pair of almost identical, solid-cast handles; two large basins of Eggers Type 100; fragmentary strainer, a small bronze cup known as Calathiscus) and bronze mirrors. As to the three bronze mirrors, Khandalavala believed that the largest Kolhapur mirror was Roman while the two smaller examples were probably local products copied from or influenced by Alexandrian mirrors.[50] But De Puma rejects this view since, according to him, no Hellenistic mirrors found in Egypt had central protrusions or heavy rims, and no Roman mirrors have tangs—which were the features of Kolhapur mirrors.[51] Thus the Kolhapur mirrors were basically India made, perhaps imported from northern and western India to the Deccan. De Puma[52] considers ten of the Kolhapur bronzes to be Roman, probably from the workshop of Capua in Campania. He dates most of them to the 1st century AD except perhaps the Poseidon statuette and a fragmentary strainer which could be earlier.

Other Archaeological Evidence

References are made to the discovery of Roman pottery lamps in a few sites in India,[53] like Ter,[54] Roman ornaments from the village of Vallalore, near Coimbatore[55] and Roman glass in various Indian sites,[56] especially Taxila in modern Pakistan.[57] Besides, bulla imitations in terracotta or metal, mostly copied from the coins of Tiberius and Augustus, are reported from Ter, Nevasa, Kausan, Kolhapur and Paithan in Maharashtra, a number of sites in Andhra Pradesh (like Kondapur) and Karnataka, at Ujjain and Besnagar in Central India, Rajghat in Uttar Pradesh, Sisupalgarh in Orissa and Tamluk in West Bengal.[58] Another important well known archaeological recovery is an ivory statuette either of Lākshmī or Yakshini from Pompeii.[59]

Numismatic Evidence

Roman coins found in India constitute an important category of evidence for Indo-Roman trade. The earliest find was made 200 years ago, i.e. in 79 (1796) at Nellore.[60] It has been argued that the chronology of the Roman coins recovered from South Indian hoards does not imply contemporaneity of trade with India.[61] However, the most comprehensive and up-to-date account of Roman coins in India is made by Paula Turner.[62] According to her there are two main concentrations, in the Coimbatore district of Tamil Nadu, comprising almost exclusively coins of the Julio-Claudian period, and along the Krishna river in Andhra Pradesh. Judged from the distribution of finds, Turner mentioned that such Roman hoards relate to the Roman seaborne trade. Even the new Laccadive Islands hoard seems to represent the first possible 'shipwreck' hoard, that is, a hoard which accurately reflects the type of silver coin brought from the West. She also summarised certain features of Roman coins in India, such as (a) the scarcity of Republican coin finds, (b) the absence of base metal issues of the early Empire, (c) the absence of comparable finds from Śri Lankā, (d) the predominance of early Imperial *denarii*, especially two common types of Augustus and Tiberius, (e) the difference in composition of the Julio-Claudian gold and silver hoards, and (f) the wider distribution and smaller numbers of second century coins. Moreover, she referred to the incidence of two features which occur only in Indian hoards: the first is the marking of coins in two ways, usually a defacement by slashing but in two cases the emplacement of a small mark or stamp; and the second feature is the presence of imitations in some hoards which are not paralleled within the Empire. However she also admits that the appearance of slashing, punch-marks and imitation of the Roman coin hoards from India is much more restricted than general opinion suggests.

On the basis of Roman coins in India, Turner proposed three phases of Indo-Roman trade. The scarcity of coins of the Republican types in South India and the sudden influx of Early Julio-Claudian silver coins, *denarii,* especially of the two common types of Augustus and Tiberius meant that there was a major thrust of trade in the latter part of Augustus' reign. The two common types were preferred, because they could have been easily recognizable and readily available. Their availability in the region close to the beryl mines of Coimbatore implied that gem stones were important items of trade, although the pepper trade cannot be ignored.

The second phase involved trade of commodities from India in exchange for gold *aurei* of slightly latter Julio-Claudian period. There are more types of these than of *denarii* and their distribution is more widespread implying a diversification of trade. It is believed that sometime in the Julio-Claudian period, local traders might have lost confidence in the *denarius* following its debasement by Nero in AD 64.

From the period of Nero's currency reforms to Trajan's time, there was a distinct shortage of gold. After this, the Roman gold coins, *aurei,* dating throughout the 2nd century AD, occur over a much wider area with minor trade booms during the reign of Antoninus Pius and Septimius Severus, as known from the peaks of coin finds. The new Kerala gold hoard has its most recent coins in uncirculated condition and implies a much greater volume than the earlier hoards suggested; hence is suggestive of the fact that our knowledge of the second century trade is imperfect.

Two further points are important with regard to the Indo-Roman trade.

The first issue is the sporadic occurrence of Roman coins in Western and North-Western India. This paucity in North-Western India may be explained by the fact that goods were only moving through this region, while South India's trade was a terminal one and coins were accumulated there.[63]

Contrasting the Western Deccan and South India, Ray[64] pointed out the local trade in the Western Deccan involved Sātavāhana coinage, and Roman gold and silver coins might have been used as bullion. In contrast, there is hardly any evidence of an established local currency in the South where the Roman gold and silver coins may have been used as high value coins in local transactions.

The second important issue concerns the balance of trade. Pliny's statement that 100 million *sesterces* are drained out of Rome every year for trade with the East causing a monetary crisis has been rightly questioned.[65] However, there is no denying the fact of the unfavourable balance of payment of the Roman trade with India, although its precise amount cannot be determined.[66] The adverse balance of trade for the Romans was not caused by silk alone.[67] Spices played a more important role than either silk or semi-precious stones like beryl or pearls, since both these products were available on or within the frontiers of the Empire.[68]

Epigraphic Evidence

Besides the stamped pottery of the Sigillata variety discovered at Arikamedu and discussed earlier, other epigraphic evidences also indicate the prevalence of Indo-Roman trade. The first is an amphora trademark bearing Latin letters reported from Ambrish Tila at Mathura, excavated by M.C. Joshi and described by Will.[69] The handle is stamped with a two-part trademark. The same type of stamp has been found at Pompeii, Ostia, Carthage, Alexandria, and at Avenches and Vindonissa in Switzerland. The stamp appears to read M. CANSTR (first part) and SVR (second part), or M. CAVSTR (first part) and SVR (second part). According to Will whatever be the correct interpretation of the stamp, its spread from Switzerland to Central India implies that the manufacturer was a person of wealth and influence, and it throws further light on the importance of India as an integral part of the Roman trading network.

Moreover, Slane[70] referred to two rim fragments with stamped amphora handles (at present in Pondicherry Museum). The two pieces appear to have duplicate stamps: the legible stamp is rectangular, reading OEY (retrograde) above a narrow amphora turned on its side; the theta is dotted, the epsilon round, and the upsilon curved. Thus Slane studied two previously unpublished amphora stamps, possibly Knidian, both from Arikamedu, dating from the first century BC

Besides there is an Indian graffiti in the Tamil-Brahmi script of the first or second century AD from Leukos Limen.[71] Incidentally Leukos Limen was the closest to the Nile of all the Roman Red Sea ports in Egypt. One records a male personal name (Catan or Cattan), well attested in the Tamil mercantile community in India.

Textual Sources

Information about sea-trade with Rome is known from the *Periplus of the Erythraean Sea*[72] and the accounts of Greek and Latin writers such as Strabo, Arrian, Pliny, Ptolemy, Cosmas and others. Embassies from kings of India bearing gifts came to Roman emperors such as Augustus seeking friendship and diplomatic alliance. Latin and Greek writers such as Suetonius (1st-2nd century AD), Florus (2nd century AD) Aurelius Victor (4th century AD), Paulus Orosius (5th century AD), Cassius Dio (2nd-3rd century AD) and Flavius Vopiscus (4th century AD), among others, mention such diplomatic missions between the two countries.[73] One obvious objective of such official contact was to ensure furtherance of trade to the mutual benefit. The Indians brought, among their gifts, elephants, pearls, precious stones, ferocious animals, etc.

The Periplus of the Erythraean Sea (1st century AD) or "Sailing Guide of the Erythraean Sea" is a unique text by an anonymous author who was probably a merchant with experience in sea trade.The text provides vital information about the sea routes to India, the principal ports, items of trade, local crafts, etc. According to the *Periplus* the voyage started from Alexandris in Egypt, and going up the Nile, reached the Red sea and Myos Hormos which served as departure point for voyage to India. The knowledge about the pattern of the monsoons (the hippalus or favourable wind) facilitated navigation and sea-trade. The *Periplus* mentions several ports and coastal towns such as Barygaz (Broach), Ozene (Ujjain), Sopara, Kalyana, Naura, Tyndis, Muziris, Nelcynda, Kolkhoi, Masalia, Poduca, Sopatma, etc. The eastern coast upto the Gaṅgas was known to the western sailors and the *Periplus* mentions, among others, Masalia (Masulipattinam) and Dosarene (coastal Oriss) famous for muslins and ivory respectively. According to the *Periplus* India exported several items such as spices, cotton cloth, muslin, pearl, precious stones etc. The balance of trade was in favour of India because of Roman demand for luxury items. Pliny lamented that for the luxury of Roman women "more than fifty million sesterces were spent in India each year." India, received from the Roman world, wine, olive oil, emphoras, terracotta pots typical of Arezzo, lamps, glass vases, engraved cameos, etc.

Strabo (67 BC-20 AD) in the *Geographia* records his geographical knowledge about India "surrounded on two sides by the sea and bounded to the North and West by the Indus and the Gaṅgas"[74] with latter's delta being the farthest point of earth. He touched on the customs and traditions of the inhabitants of India. Arrian in his *Indica*[75] mentions Palimbothra (Pataliputra) as a city of India which was situated near the Gaṅga. He also gives information about the customs and social life of the Indian people. Pliny's *Naturalis Histories* (Natural History) throws light on geography of India and luxury goods involved in sea-trade. According to Pliny, the Indian products that reached Rome included coral and Indian pearls liked by Roman women. Other items exported from India were roots of the costus, ebony, macir, pepper, precious stones like beryls, etc.

The *Geography*[76] of Ptolemy (2nd century AD) despite its limitations, is an important contribution to scientific geography. The work provides valuable information about the ports, towns and commercial activities of India. *The Christian Topography* of Cosmas[77] Indikopleustes (6th century AD) also throws light on India's topography, plants, animals and commerce with the west.

The Tamil texts[78] of the Sangam period, such as *Śilapaddikāram*,[79] *Manimekhalai*,[80] *Nakkirar*, *Mullaipattu*, and others provide date on sea-trade between the west and South India. The Tamil texts indicate the presence of *Yavanas* (westerners) in India. *Yavanas* served as bodyguards of kings. The *Manimekhalai* refers to the *Yavana* carpenters. The *Nakkirar*, mention lambearers of great workmanship made by the *Yavanas*. The terracotta suspension lamp from Ter corroborates the accuracy of the statement in the Tamil literature. The *Nakkirar* also mentions sweet-scented wine carried by the ships of the *Yavanas* to the ports of India. The presence of *yavani* girls in the harems of the rich is known from the Tamil literature. There was a *Yavan* settlement at Pumpuhar or Kaveripattinam at the mouth of the Cauvery river. The *Ahananuru* also mentions *yavanas* who "sail in with gold and sail off with pepper." The early Tamil works, thus provide valuable evidence for the ancient sea-trade between Rome and India.

Favourable Conditions for Trade

Trade between India and Rome was very active during the 2nd-1st century BC as known from the recovery of Republican coins in South India. The political stability ushered in by Augustus Caesar (27 BC–AD 18) and the discovery of the use of the south-west monsoon for trading voyage, said to have been made by Hippalus sometime in the 1st century BC, accelerated this process. In order to face the turbulence of south-west monsoon, the ships of Roman Egypt had supremely strong hulls which were fitted with a conservative rig—meant primarily for safety and not for speed.[81] Moreover such ships were big and sturdy enough to use south-west monsoon over open water. The use of big ships for Indo-Roman trade had tremendous economic implications. Since Indian goods that attracted the Romans were not bulky and cheap commodities, rather compact and costly merchandise, a cargo of such goods would have represented huge investment.[82]

Items of Trade

The items of export from India may be divided into three categories—plant products, animal products and mineral products.[83]

Among the plant products, spices are the most important.[84] Raschke[85] referred to six kinds of spices, malabathrum, pepper, frankincense, myrhh, cassia and cinnamon, that came to the Roman Empire from the East. Out of these, pepper was the most important and it came from India. According to Miller,[86] sesame seed and cardamom[87] were items of export to the West from India for their use as spices. Cotton was also an important export from India to Rome.[88] Cloth and muslins came from Ter.[89] Timber, exported from Broach probably found its way both to the Persian Gulf and the Mediterranean markets; especially teak might have been used for shipbuilding in Arabia.[90]

Animal products, such as ivory, hide, fur, silk, lac, pearl, oysters, conch-shell, tortoise-shell, ghi and musk, were exported from India.[91] Out of these, raw silk, silk yarn and silk cloth were primarily a transit trade coming from China through Bactria to Broach, a port in the western coast of India, from where it was shipped to Arabia. There they were used in making embroidered and silk fabrics for the Roman market.[92] But microscopic analysis of the fibres proved that at least one of the silk textiles found at Dura Europos was of Indian origin,[93] thus implying that Indian silk was also exported along with the Chinese one. But with regard to ivory, there is little evidence that India replaced Africa as the source for the demand of the Mediterranean world.[94] However, a 1st century AD ivory statue of the Indian goddess of prosperity *Lākshmī* was obtained from Pompeii.

With regard to mineral products, semi-precious stones were exported from India to the Mediterranean.[95] The *Periplus* states that carnelian was brought to Broach (section 51),[96] although the Rajpipla mines near Broach are famous for agate and carnelian.[97] According to Pliny,[98] beryl (found in the Coimbatore district of Tamil Nadu) was popular among the Indians and the Indian traders imitated beryls by staining rock-crystals. Roman coins[99] and ornaments[100] were also found in Coimbatore district. Thus, Pliny[101] held that of all the countries that produced gems, India was the most prolific, although India had some rivals in the supply of gems, such as Arabia and Carmania.[102]

The *Periplus* (section 6)[103] states that Indian iron and steel were imported in the West for the inland regions of Ariaka. According to Pliny,[104] iron of the best quality was sent to the West by the Seres of China and Tibet, or the Cheras of South India.[105] But Schoff[106] identified the region around Hyderabad mentioning that the amount of export must have been small.[107] Incidentally, smelting of iron ores is known in India as early as the 7th-6th century BC at Naikund in the Vidarbha region.[108] Moreover, artefacts from the megalithic sites contain a high percentage of iron with little impurity or admixture and iron working continued to be profitable occupation under the Satavahanas.[109]

Trade Routes

There were various trade routes linking the Mediterranean world with the Indian subcontinent during Hellenistic and Roman times. These routes were not direct. For example, the Central Asian silk route to China interconnected with the Bactrian routes to India. There were the Iranian routes through Susa and Persepolis, the coastal routes linking Tigris and the Persian Gulf with Sind and Gujarat and also the sea routes to western and southern India via Arabia or directly from the Red Sea, which link up with Alexandria and other ancient ports on the Mediterranean.[110]

To conclude the Indo-Roman trade has to be understood in the Indian Ocean perspective. Recently, the dominant role of Roman trade in the western Indian Ocean has been rightly questioned.[111] A quantitative analysis of foreign pottery found at Arikamedu and other areas shows that apart from amphorae and terra sigillata, the bulk of pottery from the Early Historical period was locally made. Moreover scholars are now becoming sceptical of the idea that the Roman Empire adopted an economic policy for promoting trade with the East, since maritime trade in antiquity was basically a private venture. There was marked decline of the Roman trade with the East in the 3rd or 4th centuries AD because the great centres of trade were in ruins and the trade routes were impeded by warfare and disturbance.[112] However, in Egypt, it appears that the use of Indian spices in the 3rd and 4th centuries was more widespread than at any previous time.[113] The recovery of a large number of Roman bronze coins of 4th century date and those of Roman copper pieces and local imitations of 4th and 5th century dates near Madras and in Śri Lankā implies a revival of trade during that period.[114] There was an increase in Byzantine international commerce in the 6th and 7th centuries AD following Justinian's stabilization of the Empire, but this was definitely on a lesser scale than Roman commerce with India in the first three centuries AD, and in this latter period the Sasanian Empire dominated trade in the Indian Ocean.[115]

NOTES AND REFERENCES

1. Paula J. Turner, *Roman Coins from India* (London, 1989), preface.
2. H.G. Rawlinson, *Intercourse between India and the Western World* (Cambridge, 1916); E.H. Warmington, *The Commerce between the Roman Empire and India* (Cambridge, 1928); R.E.M. Wheeler, A. Ghosh and Krishna Deva, "Arikamedu: An Indo-Roman trading station on the east coast of India," *Ancient India,* 2 (1946), pp. 17-124; R.E.M. Wheeler, "Roman Contact with India, Pakistan and Afghanistan," in *Aspects of Archaeology: Essays Presented to O.G.S. Crawford,* ed. W.F. Grimes (London, 1951), pp. 345-81; *Rome Beyond the Imperial Frontiers* (Pelican, 1954); M.G. Raschke, "New Studies in Roman Commerce with the East," in *Aufstieg und Niedergang der Romischen welt II. 9* (Berlin, 1978), pp. 605-1361; P.L. Gupta, "Roman Trade in India," in *Dr. S. Mookerji Felicitation Volume* (Varanasi, 1969), pp. 169-80; G.L. Adhya, *Early Indian Economics,* (New Delhi, 1966); H.P. Ray, *Monastery and Guild: Commerce under the Satavahanas* (Delhi, 1986); "A resurvey of Roman contacts with the East," *Topoi* 3 (1993), fasc.2, pp. 479-91; A.K. Singh, *Indo-Roman Trade* (Patna, 1988); V. Begley and R.D. De Puma, *Rome and India: The Ancient Sea Trade* (Delhi, 1992); R. Nagaswamy, "Roman sites in Tamilnadu; Recent discoveries," in *Madhu: Recent Researches in Indian Archaeology and Art History,* ed. M.S. Nagaraja Rao (Delhi, 1981), pp. 337-39; P.J. Turner, *op. cit.* (1989).
3. L. Casson, "Egypt, Africa, Arabia and India: Patterns of sea-borne trade in the first century AD," *Bulletin of the American Society of Papyrologists,* 21(1-4) (1984), pp. 39-47; Sunil Gupta, "Archaeology of Indian maritime traditions: The early historic phase," *Man and Environment,* 19(1-2) (1994), pp. 217-25; L.C. Glover, *Early Trade between India and South-east Asia-A Link in the Development of a World Trading System* (University of Hull, 1989); H.P. Ray, *Winds of Change: Buddhism and the Maritime Links of Early South Asia* (New Delhi, 1994).
4. I.C. Glover, *op. cit.* (1989).
5. See references in No. 2.
6. The most comprehensive account is given by Howard Comfort, "Terra Sigillata at Arikamedu", in Begley and De Puma (eds.), *op. cit.* (1992), pp. 134-50.
7. Wheeler *et al., op. cit.* (1992); A.K. Singh, *op. cit.* (1988), pp. 64-67.
8. Howard Comfort, *op. cit.* (1992), p. 134.
9. *Ibid.*
10. *Ibid*, p. 135.
11. *Ibid.*
12. K.W. Slane, "Observations on Mediterranean amphoras and tablewares found in India," in Begley and De Puma (Eds.), *op. cit.* (1992), pp. 204-15.
13. V. Begley, "Introduction," in Begley and De Puma (Eds.), *op. cit.* (1992), p. 4.
14. Howard Comfort, *op. cit.* (1992), p. 149.
15. K.W. Slane, *op. cit.* (1992), p. 207.
16. H. Comfort, *op. cit.* (1992), p. 145.
17. K.W. Slane, *op. cit.* (1992), p. 205.

18. V. Begley, *op. cit.* (1992a), p. 4
19. L. Will, "The Mediterranean shipping amphoras from Arikamedu," in Begley and De Puma (Eds.), *op. cit.* (1992), p. 151. Recently G. Sengupta claims that one amphorae fragment has been recovered in West Bengal.
20. K.W. Slane, *op. cit.* (1992), pp. 204-5.
21. E.L. Will, *op. cit.* (1992), pp. 151-52.
22. *Ibid.*, pp. 152-53.
23. *Ibid.*, p. 153.
24. *Ibid.*
25. *Ibid.*
26. *Ibid.*, pp. 153-54.
27. V. Begley, *op. cit.* (1992a), p. 4.
28. K.W. Slane, *op. cit.* (1992), p. 205.
29. V. Begley, "Ceramic evidence for pre-*Periplus* trade on the Indian coasts" (1992b) in Begley and De Puma (eds.), *op. cit.*, p. 176.
30. A.K. Singh, *op. cit.* (1988), p. 67.
31. R.E.M. Wheeler *et al.*, *op. cit.* (1946), p. 48.
32. For a distribution, see I.C. Glover, *op. cit.* (1989). Glover has recently reported the evidence of rouletted ware from Central Vietnam.
33. V. Begley, *op. cit.* (1992b), p. 181.
34. *Ibid.*, p. 180.
35. V. Begley, "Rouletting and Chattering : Decoration on ancient and present day pottery in India," *Expedition*, 28(1) (1986), p. 49; *op. cit.* (1992b), p. 176.
36. K.V. Raman, "Further evidence of Roman trade from coastal sites in Tamilnadu," in Begley and De Puma (eds.), *op. cit.* (1992), p. 127.
37. *Ibid.*, p. 128.
38. V. Begley, *op. cit.* (1992a), p. 4; (1992b), p. 176.
39. V. Begley, *op. cit.* (1992b), pp. 157-76.
40. *Ibid.*, p. 166.
41. V. Begley, *op. cit.* (1992a), p. 4.
42. N.P. Orton, "Red polished ware in Gujarat : A Catalogue of twelve sites," in Begley and De Puma (Eds.), *op. cit.* (1992), p. 46.
43. B. Subbarao, *Baroda Through the Ages* (Baroda, 1953), pp. 56-57.
44. B. Subbarao, "The Red polished ware," in H.D. Sankalia, B. Subbarao, and S.B. Deo, *The Excavations at Maheshwar and Navdatoli, 1952-1953* (Poona, 1958), pp. 161-62.
45. S.R. Rao, *Excavations at Amreli: A Kshatrapa—Gupta Town* (Baroda, 1966), pp. 53-59, 80.
46. N.P. Orton, *op. cit.* (1992).
47. *Ibid.*, pp. 46-47; also see K.W. Slane, *op. cit.* (1992), p. 209.
48. K. Khandalavala "Brahmapuri: A consideration of the metal objects found in the Kundangar Hoard," *Lalit Kala* (1960), pp. 29-75.
49. R.D. De Puma, "The Roman Bronzes from Kolhapur," in Begley and De Puma (Eds.), *op. cit.* (1992), pp. 82-112.
50. K. Khandalavala, *op. cit.* (1960), pp. 62-63.
51. R.D. De Puma, *op. cit.* (1992), p. 100.
52. R.D. De Puma, *op. cit.* (1992), pp. 82, 103.
53. A.K. Singh, *op. cit.* (1988), p. 69.
54. *Indian Archaeology—A Review, 1967-68*, p. 35.
55. N. Devasahayam, "Roman jewellery from Vellalore site during the Sangam period," *Lalit Kala* 21(1985), p. 53.
56. E.M. Stern, "Early Roman export glass in India," in Begley and De Puma (Eds.), *op. cit.* (1992), pp. 113-24.
57. M.G. Dikshit, *History of Indian Glass* (Bombay, 1969), pp. 28-31.

58. S.B. Deo, "Roman Trade: Recent archaeological discoveries in Western India," in Begley and De Puma (eds.), *op. cit.* (1992), p. 40.
59. A.K. Singh, *op. cit.* (1988), p. 3.
60. P. Turner, *op. cit.* (1989), p. 1. Some important works on Indo-Roman coins are the following : W. Elliot, "A discovery of Roman coins in the Coimbatore Distirct", *Madras Journal of Literature and Science* 13(30) (1844), pp. 211-15; E. Thurston, *Coins, Catalogue No. 2, Roman, Indo-Portuguese and Ceylon* (Madras, 1894); R. Sewell, "Lists of Roman coins found in India," *Journal of the Royal Asiatic Society* (1904), pp. 591-637; E.H. Warmington, *op. cit.* (1928); R.E.M. Wheeler, *op. cit.* (1951); P.L. Gupta, *Roman Coins from Andhra Pradesh* (Hyderabad, 1965).
61. M.G. Raschke, *op. cit.* (1978), p. 668.
62. P. Turner, *op. cit.* (1989).
63. G.L. Adhya, *op. cit.* (1966), p. 135.
64. H.P. Ray, *op. cit.* (1986), pp. 144-45.
65. M.G. Raschke, *op. cit.* (1978), pp. 636, 670.
66. *Ibid.*, p. 637.
67. *Ibid.*, p. 622.
68. *Ibid.*, p. 671.
69. E.L. Will, *op. cit.* (1992), pp. 153, 156.
70. K.W. Slane, *op. cit.* (1992), p. 205.
71. S.E. Sidebotham, "Ports of the Red Sea and the Arabia-India trade," in Begley and De Puma (Eds.) (1992), pp. 33, 35.
72. W.H. Schoff, *The Periplus of the Erythraean Sea*, New York, 1912.
73. For passages see *India and Italy*, Catalogue by R.M. Cimino and F. Scialpi, Rome, 1974, pp. 8-13.
74. *Ibid.*, p. 6.
75. "India of Arrian," *Indian Antiquary* 1876, p. 86.
76. S.N. Majumdar (Ed.) *Ancient India* as *described by Ptoleny*, Calcutta, 1927.
77. J.W. Mc. Crindle, *Ancient India as described in Classical literature*, Amsterdam, 1871.
78. R. Nagaswamy, *Roman Korur*, Madras, 1995, pp. 96-102.
79. V.R.R. Dikshitar (trans.), *The Silapaddikaram*, Oxford, 1939.
80. N.M.V. Nattar and A.T.Pillai, (Ed.) *Manimekhalai*, Madras, 1951.
81. L. Casson, "Ancient naval technology and the route to India," in Begley and De Puma (Eds.), *op. cit.* (1992), p. 10.
82. *Ibid.*
83. E.H. Warmington, *op. cit.* (1928), pp. 145-260; G.L. Adhya, *op. cit.* (1966), p. 143.
84. J.I. Miller, *The Spice Trade of the Roman Empire, 29 BC to AD 641* (Oxford, 1969).
85. M.G. Raschke, *op. cit.* (1978), p. 652.
86. J.I. Miller, *op. cit.* (1969), p. 87.
87. *Ibid.*, pp. 71-73.
88. E.H. Warmington, *op. cit.* (1928), pp. 210-12.
89. H.P. Ray, *op. cit.* (1986), p. 123.
90. *Ibid.*, pp. 115-16.
91. E.H. Warmington, *op. cit.* (1928), pp. 157-79.
92. H.P. Ray, *op. cit.* (1986), p. 115.
93. M.G. Raschke, *op. cit.* (1978), p. 623.
94. *Ibid.*, p. 650.
95. E.H. Warmington, *op. cit.* (1928), pp. 235-60; G.L. Adhya, *op. cit.* (1966), p. 146.
96. W.H. Schoff, *The Periplus of the Erythraean Sea* (London, 1912), p. 43.
97. H.P. Ray, *op. cit.* (1986), p. 123.
98. D.E. Eichholz, *Pliny Natural History*, Vol. 10 (Cambridge, Mass. 1962), p. 227.
99. P. Turner, *op. cit.* (1989), p. 7.
100. N. Devasahayam, *op. cit.* (1985).

101. D.E. Eichholz, *op. cit.* (1962), p. 329.
102. G.L. Adhya, *op. cit.* (1966), p. 147.
103. W.H. Schoff, *op. cit.* (1912), p. 24.
104. H. Rackham (ed.), *Pliny Natural History,* Vol. IX (London, 1952).
105. G.L. Adhya, *op. cit.* (1966), p. 147.
106. W.H. Schoff, "The eastern iron trade of the Roman Empire," *Journal of the American Oriental Society,* 35 (1915), p. 233.
107. *Ibid.,* p. 235.
108. H.P. Ray, *op. cit.* (1986), p. 124.
109. *Ibid.,* p. 124.
110. V. Begley, *op. cit.* (1992a), p. 3.
111. H.P. Ray, *op. cit.* (1993).
112. M.G. Raschke, *op. cit.* (1978), p. 678.
113. *Ibid.,* p. 669.
114. *Ibid.,* p. 672.
115. *Ibid.,* p. 673.

4

Early Trade in the Indian Ocean : Perspectives on Indo–South-east Asian Maritime Contacts
(c. 400 BC – AD 500)

KISHOR K. BASA

In the first half of this century, the maritime relationships between India and South-east Asia and its all pervasive impact on South-east Asian cultural domain was a common theme of research. In such endeavours, the emphasis was more on the consequences rather than the processes and, in exaggerated versions, South-east Asia was regarded as "an Indian colony" and the best architectural and sculptural specimens were even believed to have been made by Indian artisans. If the issue of early maritime contacts between India and South-east Asia is raised again in this paper at the fag end of 20th century, it is certainly not to reiterate the concepts of 'Greater India' and 'Indian Colony.' The need for discussing the issue emanates from two points. Firstly, archaeological excavations in India and South-east Asia during the last two-three decades have unearthed artefacts which have great implications for the maritime contacts between the two regions. Secondly, with the formation of independent nation states in South-east Asia from the 1950's onwards, the 'Big Brother' attitude of Indian nationalist school was resented, and a distinct 'South-east Asian Personality' has emerged in the writings of ancient history and archaeology. In this framework, South-east Asia is no longer treated as passive recipient of ideas and artefacts, but as an active agent of social process.

With this background, an attempt will be made for a comprehensive review of all kinds of evidence—archaeological, literary, epigraphic and numismatic—for the maritime contacts between India and South-east Asia during *c.* 400 BC – AD 500. It will also be argued that the external trade between India and South-east Asia was an extension of internal trade in the respective zones. Moreover, their mutual interest in such maritime contacts will also be emphasized along with a brief discussion on items of trade, phases of trade and trade routes. In this regard the former date is chosen, because the earliest clear evidence for maritime trade so far between India and South-east Asia comes from Ban Don Ta Phet in west-central Thailand which is dated to 4th century BC.[1] The terminal date is relatively vague. It stands for the beginning of the Early Historic period in South-east Asia with mature states, although in some cases nascent states had already emerged much before.

EVIDENCE OF WESTERLY TRADE OF SOUTH-EAST ASIA (*c.* 400 BC – AD 500)

In this section, evidence of westerly trade of South-east Asia during the period *c.* 400 BC – AD 500 will be discussed under four headings—archaeological, literary, epigraphic and numismatic. However, emphasis will be given to the archaeological sources.

Archaeological Evidence

The archaeological evidence includes glass beads, beads of semi-precious stones—primarily those of agate and carnelian (especially the etched ones), high-tin bronze artefacts, knobbed vessels, rouletted ware and miscellaneous objects such as ivory combs, lamps and coins.[2]

Glass Beads

From a work on survey of early Indian glass,[3] (Fig. 1) it appears that from the middle of the 1st millennium BC at least, India had a number of important manufacturing centres of glass beads with regional specializations. Moreover, glass beads have been found at many sites important in trade. For example, Taxila was a major centre on the silk route; Kausambi, Rajghat, Kumrahar and Chandraketugarh were important stages in the trans-Gangetic trade and Ujjain in central India linked the Ganga valley with Bhrauch on the western coast. In the south, Arikamedu (Podouke of the *Periplus)* and Karaikadu on the Tamil Nadu coast were active in trans-peninsular trade with the Roman Empire and perhaps, given the large number of the *mutisalah* beads in South-east Asia, transmitted Western and Indian goods to the East across the Bay of Bengal. As Glover[4] has argued, there is now evidence to show that the trade routes linking the Mediterranean to India continued on, perhaps at a reduced rate, taking low bulk, high cost items to South-east Asia.

Monochrome beads of different colours, best known collectively as Indo-Pacific glass beads,[5] are the most common bead type in Late Prehistoric South-east Asia. (Fig. 2) Among them, opaque browny red and opaque orange red *mutisalah* beads constitute an important component. They were in great demand in eastern Indonesia till recently.[6] In South Asia, the earliest evidence of red glass beads comes from Rajghat from Period IB (*c.* 600-500 BC)[7] and from the Bhir mound, Taxila (5th century BC).[8] From that time onwards they were plentifully available in various sites in India.[9] However, Arikamedu,[10] which flourished between the 3rd century BC and the early centuries of the Christian era, was one of the most important manufacturing centres of the monochrome beads including the opaque browny red *mutisalah* varieties[11] (Stern 1987a). In Thailand, they have been found in many Late Prehistoric sites such as Ban Chiang, Ban Na Di, Non Muang, Ban Tha Kae, Ban Don Ta Phet, Prasat Muang Sing and Kok Ra Ka.

The earliest evidence for manufacturing glass beads in Thailand comes from Khlong Thom dated from about the 4th century AD onwards.[12] In peninsular Malaysia, the earliest manufacturing evidence comes from Kuala Selinsing which is recently dated to 200 BC-AD 1000.[13] However, the chronology of the glass bead yielding levels is not precisely stated. In Indonesia, Gilimanuk, a coastal site in Bali, of the turn of the Christian era, was a manufacturing centre for glass beads.[14] Oc Eo in Vietnam has yeilded the highest number of glass beads (about 8,000 and mostly from illegal digging) and dated to between the 2nd and 7th century AD on the basis of recent radiocarbon datings.[15] Oc Eo is regarded as a

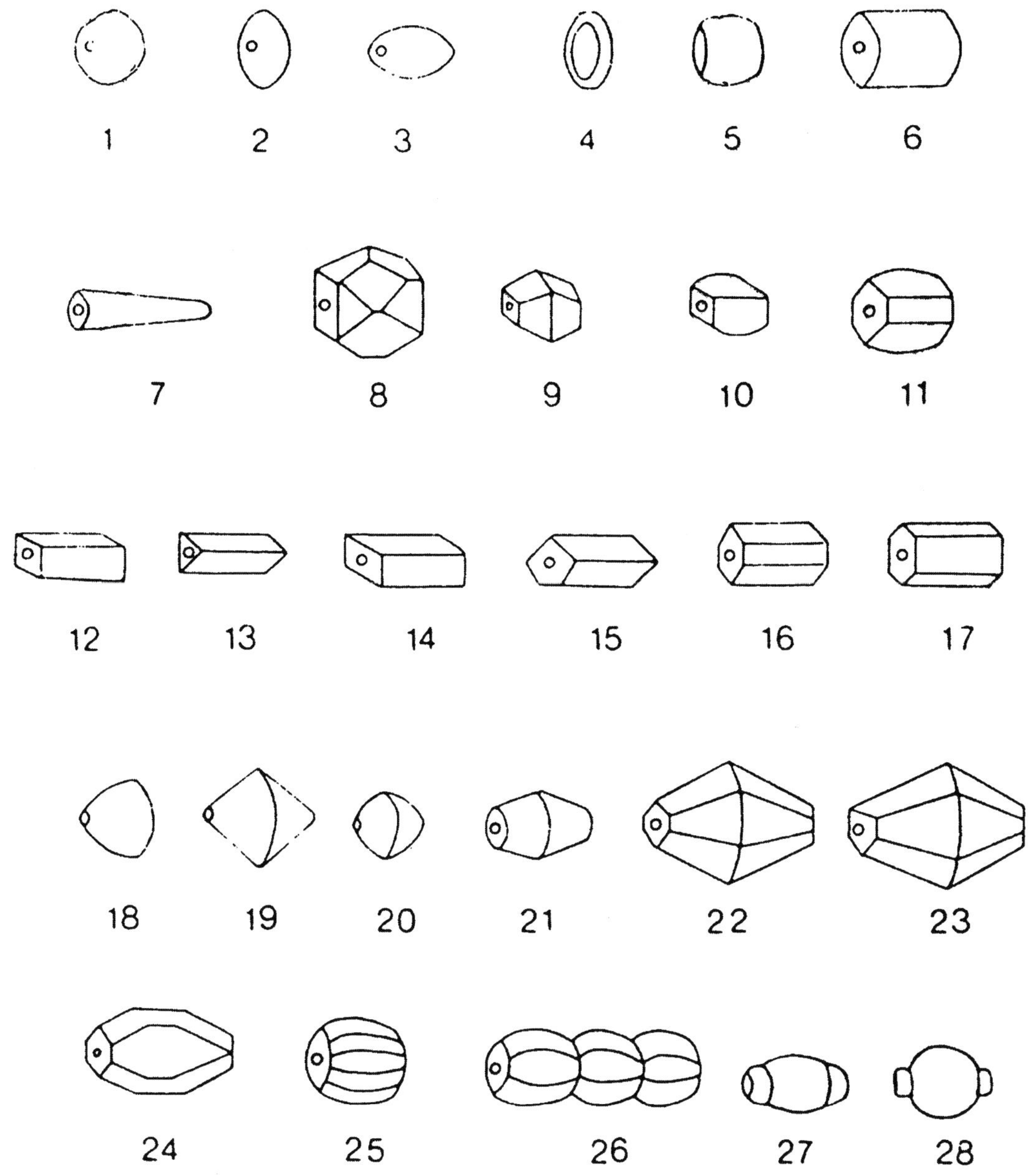

Fig. 1. Typology of glass beads for South and Southeast Asia

1. spherical
2. oblate
3. elliptical
4. annular
5. barrel
6. cylindrical
7. flared cylindrical
8. cornerless cube
9. bipyramidal
10. square barrel
11. square barrel
12. hexagonal barrel
13. triangular prism
14. rectangular prism
15. pentagonal prism
16. hexagonal prism
17. hexagonal tabular prism
18. convex cone
19. bicone
20. convex bicon
21. truncated bicon
22. hexagonal bicon
23. pentagonal bicon
24. diamond shaped tabular
25. melon
26. segmented collared
27. groove collared
28. lug collared

glass bead manufacturing centre, although even there import of glass beads is not entirely ruled out.[16] If we accept this, the problem remains as to the identity of the glass bead makers. One possibility is that some merchants from India could have brought skilled artisans to manufacture glass beads at some sites in South-east Asia partly because there might have been considerable demand in certain areas and partly because of the apprehension of the loss of the cargo of glass beads as a result of wreckage. If the glass bead making was in the hands of the indigenous people, it is difficult to ascertain to what extent they could compete with the glass bead makers of India who had by this time already developed regional specializations and who were manufacturing glass beads on a much larger scale. However, it is unlikely that the local glass could have satisfied the demands for glass beads in the whole of South-east Asia during 400 BC-AD 500 because of the scarcity of evidence of manufacturing centres on the one hand and the abundant recovery of glass beads in many parts of South-east Asia on the other. Thus it is reasonable to infer that most, if not all, of the monochrome glass beads were imported from India. The opaque browny red *mutisalah* beads especially, I think, would have come primarily from South India, and there are some other types, rare in South-east Asia, which are well known from Indian collections.

A type of opaque black round bead with spiral grooves is found at Prasat Muang Sing. It appears that the spiral grooves were originally filled with white strips. A similar bead was found at Ban Chi Nam Lai, Inburi district, Singhburi province from the surface collection (pers. comm. Surapol Natapintu 1988). Rare in South-east Asia, this is a typical North Indian bead, and has been found in the surface collections from Kausambi, and the excavations at Narhan, Chandraketugarh and at Kodumanal. At Kodumanal, it is dated to *c.* 100 BC–200 AD. At Narhan, it is dated to the Gupta period.

Cornerless cube beads of translucent dark blue glass are found at Ban Don Ta Phet. One such blue bead is reported from a cist burial near Tegurwangi in south Sumatra. Similar beads are reported from the Bhir mound, Taxila[17] and also from Sirkap, Taxila, from Phase II, dated about the beginning of the Christian era to AD 50.[18] This shape is said to be very common in the Mediterranean, Egypt, Mesopotamia and Persia.[19]

Ban Chiang and Ban Don Ta Phet have also yielded translucent clear greenish hexagonal prisms, hexagonal barrels, square prisms and square barrels (Fig. 3). For Glover[20], from the point of view of trade with the West, the most interesting glass bead is that of the large hexagonal prism. These are quite similar to the beryl crystals of South India which were very popular in the Buddhist cultures of North India as well as the Roman world and which even caught the attention of Pliny, the Elder. According to Francis,[21] hexagonal prisms closely imitating beryl (which Pliny mentioned) were manufactured at Arikamedu in South India. In my 1988 study of Indian glass beads, I saw only a few similar beads in the surface collections from Ahichchhatra and Kausambi in the Allahabad Museum and a hexagonal barrel type from Narhan. The latter is dated to 290 ± 100 BC, 250 ± 100 BC and 150 ± 100 BC. Two hexagonal barrels of almost colourless glass are also documented from the Bhir mound, Taxila of the 4th-3rd century BC.[22] One hexagonal barrel of green glass is dated to the 3rd century BC and a square barrel to the 4th century BC from the Bhir mound.[23] A hexagonal bead is also obtained from Phase III at Sirkap, dated to between AD 50 and the early 2nd century AD.[24] Even in Western Asia, these beads are not common in collections that I have been able to examine and the Department of Graeco-Roman Antiquities of the British Museum holds only two such beads—one from the surface at Amrit and another

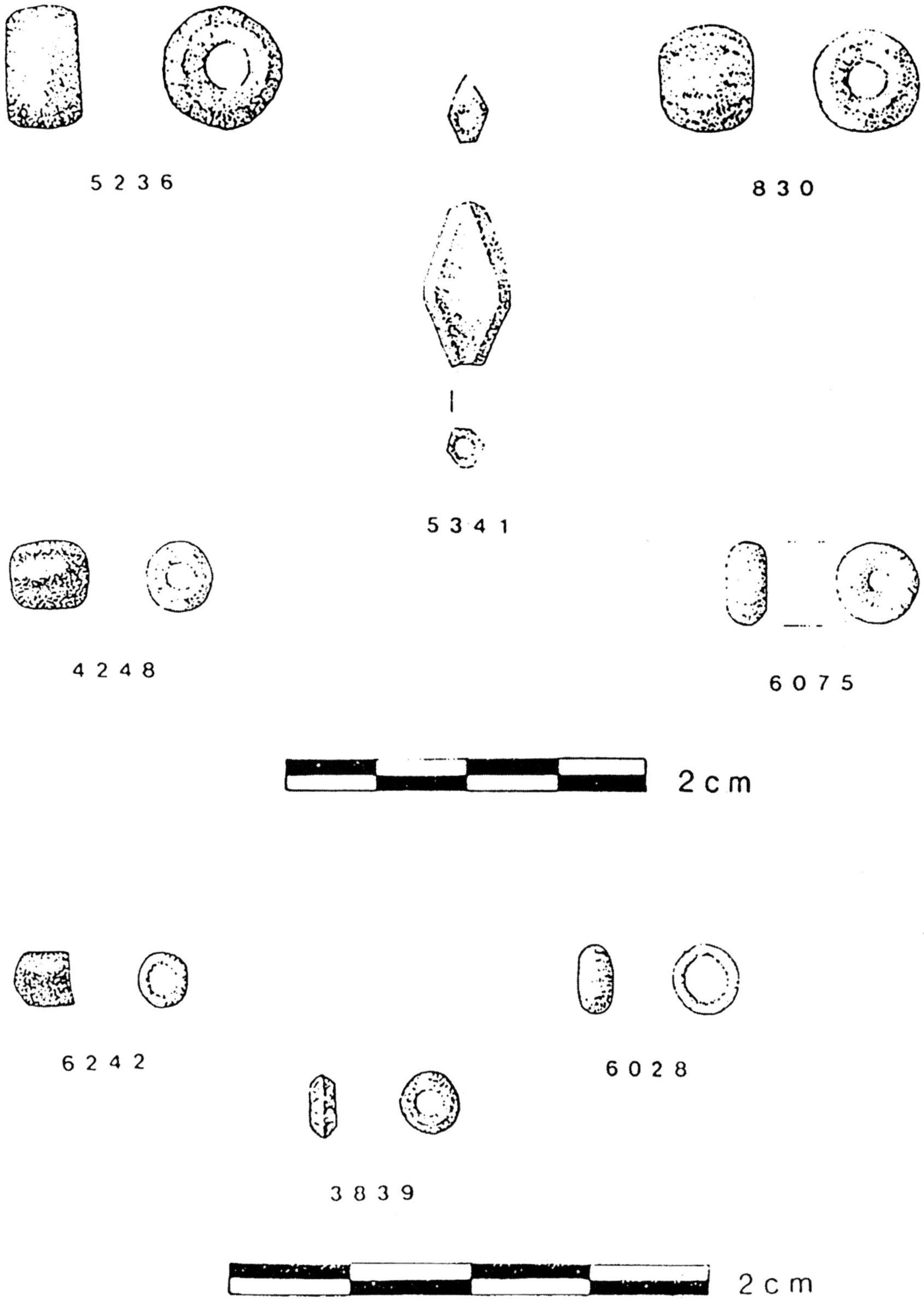

Fig. 2. Glass beads from Ban Don Ta Phet
5236-Barrel, 5341-Diamond-shaped Tabular, 830-Spherical, 4248-Elliptical, 6075-Oblate, 6242-Cylindrical, 3839-Truncated bicone, 6028-Annular, Not numbered Freak Segmented

from Tyre. If it is accepted that the prismatic glass beads imitating beryl were made at Arikamedu, chronological problem remains about their export to Thailand. Arikamedu has been recently dated to the 3rd century BC onwards.[25] But Ban Don Ta Phet is dated to the 4th century BC.[26] However, the chronology of the earliest levels of Arikamedu is still uncertain. Incidentally, three radiocarbon dates on charcoal are available from Kantarodai in Jaffna (Śri Lankā), which displays close connections with Arikamedu in its middle period because of the presence of rouletted ware[27] (Fishman and Lawn 1978: 227). The dates associated with the rouletted ware at Kantarodai are 2020 ± 50 BP (P-2521), 2290 ± 50 BP (P-2518) and 2180 ± 60 BP (P-2520) (ibid.:227-28). When calculated on the basis of the half-life value of 5730 years and corrected by MASCA correction factors, these dates are reported by Fishman and Lawn as 100-10 ± 50 BC (P-2521), 420 ± 50 BC (P-2518) and 390-270 ± 60 BC (P-2520). Hence it might not be impossible that Arikamedu and Ban Don Ta Phet were contemporary.

A hexagonal biconical glass bead of translucent greenish colour—a typical bead of South India—is reported from a stone cist from Tegurwangi. Glass beads of similar shape are also reported from Ulu Sungei, South-east Borneo, but their colour is not mentioned[28] (Heekeren 1958: Plate 13, the 3rd string). Glover[29] also reported a translucent green hexagonal biconical glass bead from the surface at Ban Don Ta Phet, but it is much bigger than the South Indian ones.

Truncated biconical beads of translucent dark blue and turquoise blue glass, from Ban Chiang and Ban Na Di, are typical of north-east Thailand. An illustration of a bicone glass bead of blue colour from Taxila[30] appears to be similar to it. However, its absence from Indian sites, inferred on the basis of my survey, is intriguing.

It is clear that the sources for all kinds of glass beads are not yet fully determined. For example, to my knowledge, there is as yet no parallel to the tubular glass beads with oblique cut ends, obtained from the surface collection of Ban Chiang. Except at Oc Eo,[31] the bipyramidal glass beads from Ban Don Ta Phet do not have any parallel.

Although it is argued that most of the glass beads from Ban Don Ta Phet as with other early glass in South-east Asia were imported in antiquity from India, it is worth pointing out that at least one, a most unusual comma-shaped ear ornament was found during 1975-76 excavations. Although made from a translucent colourless glass such as found in other beads at this site and in India, it is a shape quite uncommon in India, indeed is unique to Thailand, and strongly suggests that some bead manufacture was practised in Thailand, perhaps from imported glass cullet. Some of the bracelets, too, do not resemble ones known from contemporary Indian sites.

With regard to composition, analysis of twenty-four glass beads—eighteen from Ban Don Ta Phet, one from Ban Chiang in Thailand and five from Sembiran (Bali) in Indonesia—shows that the glass can be divided into two main types—mixed-alkali glass and potassium glass.[32] All the six mixed-alkali glass beads analysed had soda as their main alkali along with relatively high alumina (3.5% > and low lime < 5%)—the two most important characteristics of Indian glass, according to Brill.[33] Mixed-alkali glass with soda as the main alkali is reported from Arikamedu and Brahmagiri in South India, from Sar Dheri and Kausambi in North India and from Taxila in Pakistan. Mixed-alkali glass with soda as the main alkali along with high alumina and low calcium oxide is reported from Arikamedu, Brahmagiri and Kausambi. One opaque red bead from Kausambi has a high copper oxide

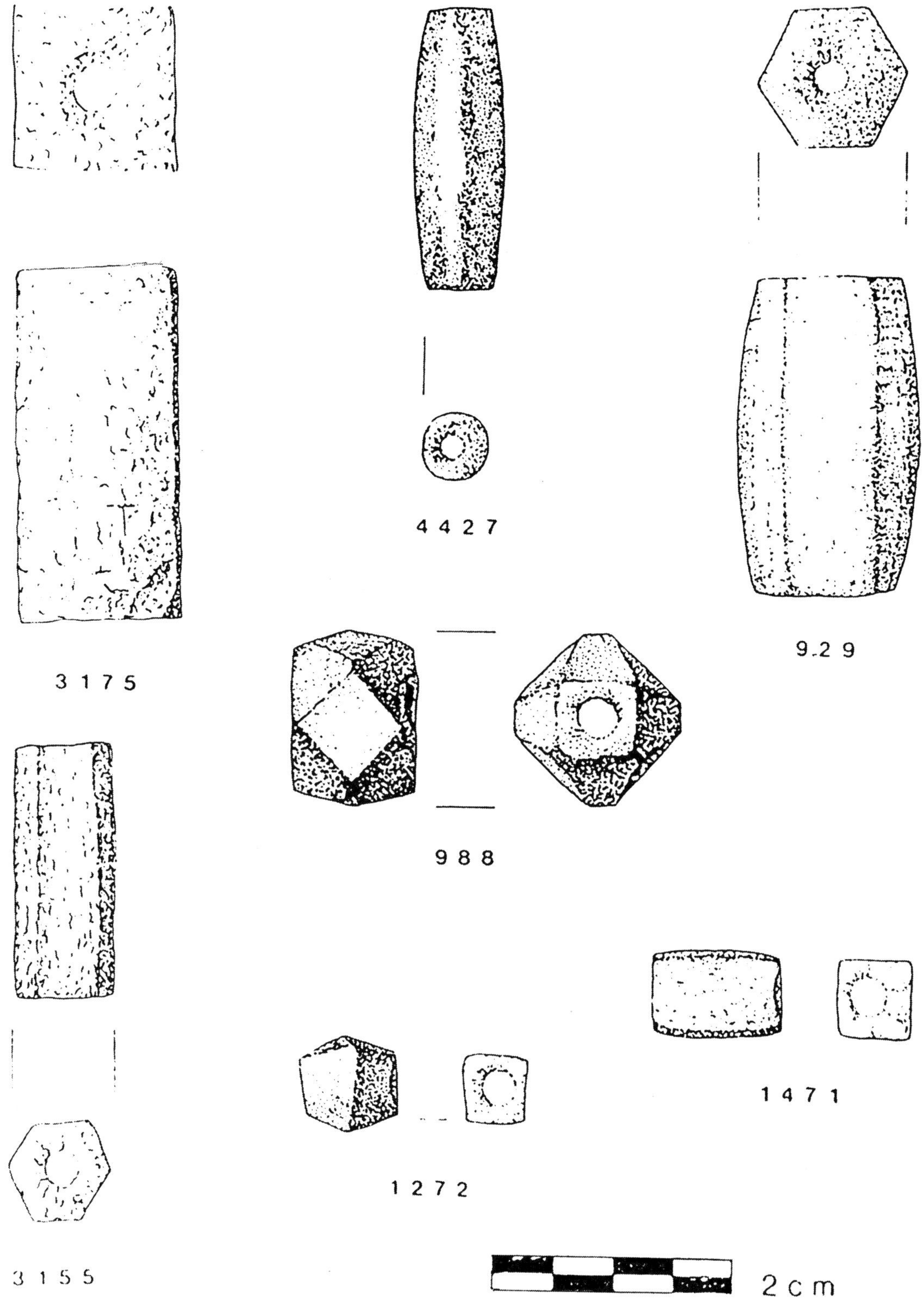

Fig. 3. Glass beads from Ban Don Ta Phet
3175-Square Pris, 4427-Barrel, 929-Hexagonal Barrel, 988-Cornerless Cube,
3155-Hexagonal Prism, 1272-Bipyramidal, 1471-Square Barrel

content (10.9%) like bead S 5 from Sembiran. It is argued that these early mixed-alkali beads with diagnostically high alumina and copper levels are probably also of Indian origin and that mixed-alkali glasses from Ban Don Ta Phet and Sembiran group quite closely with Arikamedu, Kausambi and Sar Dheri glass.

Eighteen glass beads have potassium oxide (K_2O) as their main alkali although in most cases a little soda is also present. Out of these, thirteen are from Ban Don Ta Phet, four from Sembiran and one from Ban Chiang. In contrast to the mixed-alkali glasses, the potassium rich glass has more silica but is low in calcium oxide. However, the view that Bhardwaj[34] expresses, that "potash" glasses (presumbly at least 10% K_2O) from Ter in Western India, Kausambi in northern India and Arikamedu in southern India, are of foreign origin is very unlikely to be true, unless he means soda-lime glasses with potassium oxide at about 1%. Both Han China[35] and India have yielded potassium-rich glass. For example, in addition to the sites mentioned by Bhardwaj discussed earlier, it has been reported from Hulaskhera and Hastinapura in northern India. The import of potassium glass from China to Ban Don Ta Phet in the 4th century BC seems unlikely since the forms of early Thai beads closely resemble those of India and there is no other evidence of Chinese material on the site.

The Sembiran glass beads most probably came from South India, perhaps from Arikamedu, the most important manufacturing centre for the Indo-Pacific glass beads which made both mixed-alkali and potassium glass.[36] The recovery of the Rouletted ware at Sembiran (discussed below) strengthens the link between Arikamedu and Bali. However it does not follow that all the glass beads from the Late Prehistoric Period in South-east Asia were imported only from Arikamedu.

Taking both the typology and the composition of glass beads into consideration, there can be no doubt that India was exporting glass beads to South-east Asia from the late centuries before Christian era. In this trade, more than one centre was involved, although Arikamedu appears, on the basis of present evidence, to be the most important centre. Now, other archaeological evidence will be discussed.

Semi-precious Stone Beads

The site of Ban Don Ta Phet has yielded more than 600 beads of carnelian (both spherical and faceted), agate, rock crystal and jade (possibly nephrite).[37] Two types of faceted carnelian beads are reported from South-east Asia—flattened lozenge shaped with two broad flat sides and the octagonal hexagonal faceted bicones.[38] (Fig. 4).

Faceted carnelian beads are reported in Vietnam from the jar burials at Sa Huynh, Hang Gon and Phu-Hoa and dated to between 700 BC-AD-1 and from Oc Eo of the early centuries AD; in the Philippines from Manunggul Chamber B, Palawan dated 190 ± 100 BC; in Indonesia from Leang Buidane, Salebabu island dated to the 2nd half of the 1st millennium AD and Java in Sarawak from Jaeng dated to AD 900-1100.[39] Carnelian beads are found at Kuala Selinsing in peninsular Malaysia and are believed to have been locally made from imported raw material from India and elsewhere.[40] There are only limited sources for semi-precious stones like carnelian and agate.[41] For example, evidence of recent exploitation of carnelian is known from Khao Mogul, north of Lopburi and unfinished hardstone beads are obtained from Ban Plai Nam near Don Chedi—both in west-central Thailand.[42] Unfinished beads of semi-precious stones are reported from Khlong Thom, Krabi

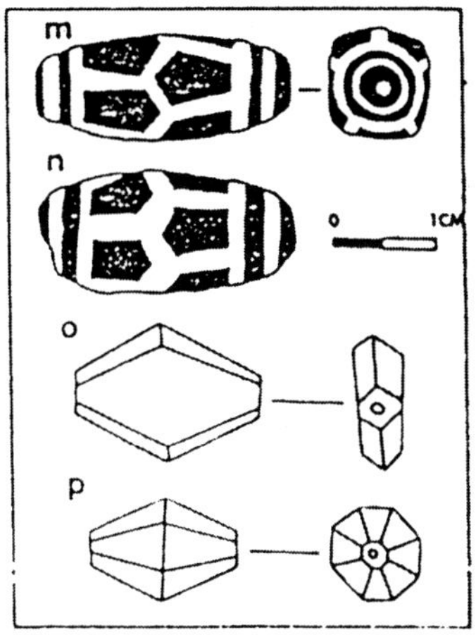

Fig. 4. Two types of faceted carnelian beads from Southeast Asia (see two beads from bottom) (from Bellowood 1976)

province in peninsular Thailand.[43] But their precise period of exploitation is not known. Neither is there much evidence of local exploitation of semi-precious stone beads in Malaysia.[44] Not much can be said about the possibility of exploitation of the local resources of semi-precious stones in South-east Asia in the absence of any precise quantitative and chronological data. Although exploitation of local resources might have been possible, it is not enough to exclude the near certainty of the import of such beads from India to South-east Asia. This is argued for several reasons. Firstly agate and carnelian are abundant in the streams draining the Deccan traps of India and the exploitation of agate and carnelian was carried on from at least the Harappan period (3rd-2nd millennium BC) in the Cambay region of India. Moreover, there was wide distribution of such beads in India during the 2nd half of the 1st millennium BC and the early centuries of the Christian era.[45] Then, on the basis of SEM photographs of the carnelian beads from Ban Don Ta Phet by Williams, it is argued that the concentric circles showed the evidence of diamond-drilling,[46] a technique typical of the Cambay bead-making tradition.[47] In some cases, semi-precious stones like carnelian and agate may have been imported as raw materials from India and beads made locally in South-east Asia.[48]

The best evidence of trade in semi-precious stone beads between South and South-east Asia lies in the etched agate and etched carnelian beads. The technique of etching involves the use of a paste of natural soda and the crushed shoots of the kirar plant (*Capparis aphylla*) which is pasted on before the stone bead is baked on the fire.[49] Following this method in their experiments, Mackay[50], Beck[51] and recently Williams[52] could make white etching; however this could be done without the kirar plant which was a sticky medium. Beck[53] discussed etched beads under three periods—Period I dated before 2000 BC, Period II dated between 300 BC-AD 200 and Period III dated between AD 600-1000. While etched beads were traded to West Asia from South Asia from the Harappan period (Beck's Period I),[54] only Beck's Period II is relevant to trade between South and South-east Asia. More than 50 etched beads were found from Ban Don Ta Phet.[55] Etched beads are also reported, though not from good contexts, from Ban Chiang, U-Thong, Krabi and Khao Sam Kao.[56]

Outside Thailand, etched beads are very scarce. Sporadic recovery has been made from Beikthano in Central Burma,[57] Tanjong Rawa, Kalumpang island and Kuala Selinsing in Malaysia,[58] from Leang Buidane cave, Salebabu island in Indonesia[59] and from the island of Palawan in the Philippines.[60] Interestingly, one cylindrical etched carnelian bead was found in Tomb 13 at Shi Zhai Shan[61] and another in Tomb 24 at Lijiashan,[62] both in Yunnan province, South China—dated to the Western Han Period. The two beads are similar to two of the beads from burial context 73 at Don Ta Phet[63] and to many in Northern India.[64]

Most of these beads belong to Type 1 of Beck,[65] Mackay[66] and Dikshit[67] on which a white design is etched on a polished stone surface of natural red or greyish black colour.

As to Ban Don Ta Phet, Glover[68] pointed out that a closer match to the etched beads from this site comes from the provinces of Uttar Pradesh and Bihar in North India and Taxila in Pakistan. Flat black agate disc beads with radial lines reported by Evans[69] at Kuala Selinsing and seen by Suchitta in peninsular Thailand are rare in South-east Asia, but common in South India.[70] According to Glover,[71] parallels for all the examples of etched beads from South-east Asia (except for one type discussed below) can be found in various collections of India and Pakistan, matching best with Beck's Middle Period (300 BC-AD 200). A large asymmetric banded black, red and white bead—reported from Ban Don Ta Phet, Kok Samrong, Don Makkak and Ban Tung Ketchek—all near U-Thong, does not have a close parallel in India.[72] The closest one can find is one bead reported by Dikshit[73] from Bhita, near Allahabad in North India, dated to between 3rd century BC and 6th century AD what Dikshit refers to as Type III, Variety B, (Fig. 5).

Knobbed Vessels

Glover[74] emphasized the significance of the knobbed-based vessels from Thailand and India and argued that they were associated with Buddhist rituals. About 20-30 bronze bowls from Ban Don Ta Phet have a conical boss sometimes cast integrally with the vessels, but often made separately and riveted through a hole in the base. The conical boss is surrounded by incised circles, often seven. A similar, but unprovenanced piece from Than Hoa province in Vietnam is exhibited in the Musee Guimet, Paris. Parallels for this vessel type are known in a modified form from South Asia in the form of high tin bronze bowls from Nilgiri,[75] a silver dish from Taxila[76] and a splendid granite bowl from Taxila in the British Museum.[77] This is also replicated in a pottery form known as "knobbed ware" in India, reported for the first time, from Sisupalgarh in Orissa[78] and also recovered primarily from northern Andhra Pradesh, Orissa, coastal Bengal and even in Assam. These knobbed wares occur in different fabrics—fine grey ware, Red and Black ware, but mostly it is made in Northern Black Polished ware—which is dated to the late centuries before the Christian era. The precise function of these knobbed base vessels is not known, but Glover[79] argued that these were not meant for any utilitarian purpose. Rather, the knob and the circles perhaps implied a *mandala*, a cosmological symbol with Mount Meru surrounded by oceans.

High-Tin Bronze

Bronze vessels with very high tin content (23-28%), cast with thin walls and manufactured by hot working, quenching and annealing were reported from Ban Don Ta Phet.[80] Despite their brittleness, these high-tin bronze bowls are thought to have been made for their

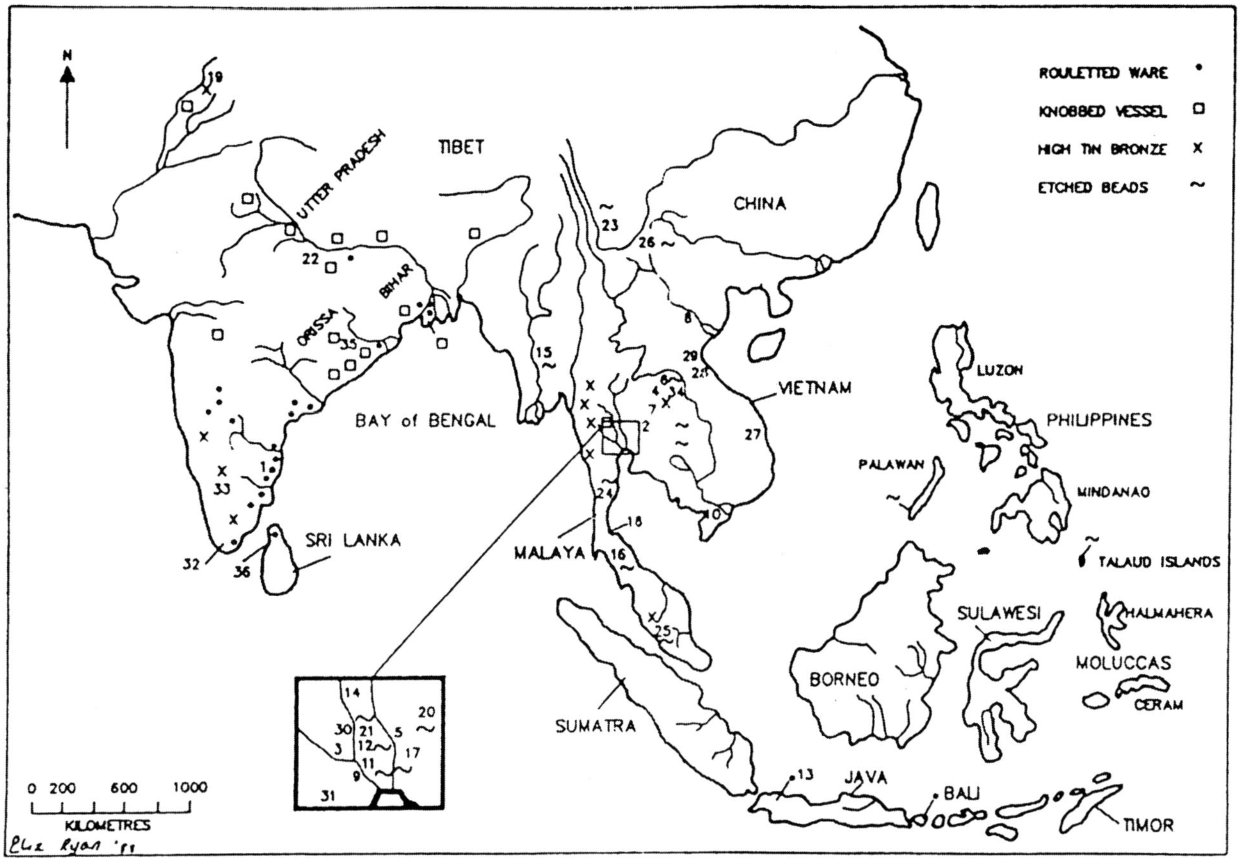

Fig. 5. Distribution of etched beads, knobbed vessels, high-tin bronze and rouletted ware in India and Southeast Asia (from Glover 1989)

Key to the numbered sites: 1 Arikamedu, 2 Kok Charoen, 3 Ban Kao, 4 Ban Na Di, 5 Tha Khae, 6 Ban Chiang, 7 Non Nok Tha, 8 Phung Nguyen, 9 Pong Tuk, 10 Oc-eo, 11 Ban Don Ta Phet, 12 U-Thong, 13 Buni, 14 Chansen, 15 Beikthano, 16 Khlong Thom, 17 Saraburi, 18 Chaiya, 19 Taxila, 20 Khao Mogul, 21 Ban Plai nam, 22 Bhita, 23 Likiang, 24 Khao Sam Kao, 25 kuala Selinsing, 26 Shi Zhai Shan & Lijiashan, 27 Sa Huynh, 28 Xuan An, 29 Dongson, 30 Tham Ongbah, 31 Chombung, 32 Aditanalur, 33 coimbatome, 34 Kok Khon, 35 Sisulpalgarh, 36 Mantai.

yellow, gold-like colour when freshly polished. In Thailand, such high-tin bronze artefacts are also reported from Kok Khon in Sakorn Nakorn province,[81] from the Late Prehistoric Iron Age levels at Ban Chiang and Ban Na Di in Northeast Thailand,[82] from Tham Ongbah on the Kwae Yai river in western Thailand,[83] which is dated to 2180 ± 180 BP (K-300), from Khao Jamook, Suen Peung district, west of Rajburi.[84] Outside Thailand, Batchelor[85] documents a number of high-tin, hemispherical bowls from the tin gravels of western peninsular Malaysia, though not from a good context.[86] Rajpitak and Seeley[87] mention the sporadic recovery of high tin bronze from the Indian subcontinent, from Adichanallur in Tinnevelly district, Tamil Nadu,[88] Coimbatore in the Nilgiri Hills[89] and Taxila, where Marshall[90] found vessels in the Mauryan strata at the Bhir mound. Rajpitak and Seeley[91] also refer to Strabo's *Geography* (15.1.67) which incorporates an earlier observation, made by Nearchus (who had travelled in the Taxila region in the 4th century BC with the Macedonian army) about the local people who used "brass that is cast, not the kind that is forged..." with the result that "when they fall to the ground they break to pieces like pottery". Such a description fits equally well the bowls from Taxila and from Ban Don Ta Phet. Copper-tin artefacts are rare in India—which is deficient in tin and not too brittle brass items were just coming into use. Hence it is argued that the high—tin, cast bronze vessels were imported from South-east Asia.[92]

Rouletted Ware

Rouletted ware is often regarded as important evidence of the Indo-Roman trade. Influenced by the Hellenistic tradition of impressed decoration, rouletting is usually produced by the continuous rolling motion of a toothed-wheel, called a roulette, when it is held against the revolving clay vessel.[93] The rouletted decoration was done in the form of minute triangles, diamonds, parallelograms, wedges, or upright crescents, ovals or dots or an eye-shaped device which is only an attenuated diamond.[94] Before firing, the pot was treated with a slip both inside and outside. Because of inverted firing, its inside usually turned black, while its outside became grey, black, yellow or brown.[95] It was believed that the finer varieties of rouletted ware were imported from the Roman empire, while the coarser varieties were made in India.[96] However, it has been recently argued by Begley[97] that the decoration on some of the rouletted ware at Arikamedu—such as the wedge shapes of the indentations, the occasional change of the indented marks into grooved lines, and the irregularity in spacing, might have been made by the chattering process. Chattering was produced by the continuous flicking motion of a tool with one or more long twin points, when it is held against the surface of the clay vessel rotating on the potter's wheel. According to Begley, the rouletted ware is dated to 2nd-1st century BC and is pre-Augustan in date. The techniques of chattering and rouletting were introduced into India from the West. But rouletted ware was made in India primarily at Arikamedu.

Walker and Santoso[98] referred to the evidence of rouletted ware from the Buni complex in north Java (Fig. 6). It has also been found quite recently at Sembiran on the north coast of Bali, along with monochrome drawn glass beads.[99] This Balinese rouletted ware is almost certainly an import from India, since the mineralogy of the fabric shows it to be close to Indian examples, and quite distinct from local Balinese pottery.[100] Rouletted ware is widely distributed in India,[101] but it is concentrated in the Coromandel coast.

Other Archaeological Evidence

Besides the items mentioned above, some other objects, which are less common, also show the prevalence of westerly trade in South-east Asia. For example, Ban Don Ta Phet in Thailand yielded a large carnelian pendant carved in the form of a leaping lion (and a broken smaller one) which is regarded as a symbol for *Sakyasimha,* a reference to Buddha as a "lion of the Sakya clan".[102] This, along with the knobbed-vessels, can be regarded as the earliest evidence of Buddhist relics, recovered, so far, in any site in South-east Asia, since the site of Ban Don Ta Phet is dated to about 4th century BC. A small lion pendant from Khlong Thom is its strongest parallel. Smaller crouching lions are available in the Buddhist relics of the Gandhara civilization, for example, that of a crystal lion from the Dharmarajika stupa at Taxila[103] and the one illustrated by Wilson.[104]

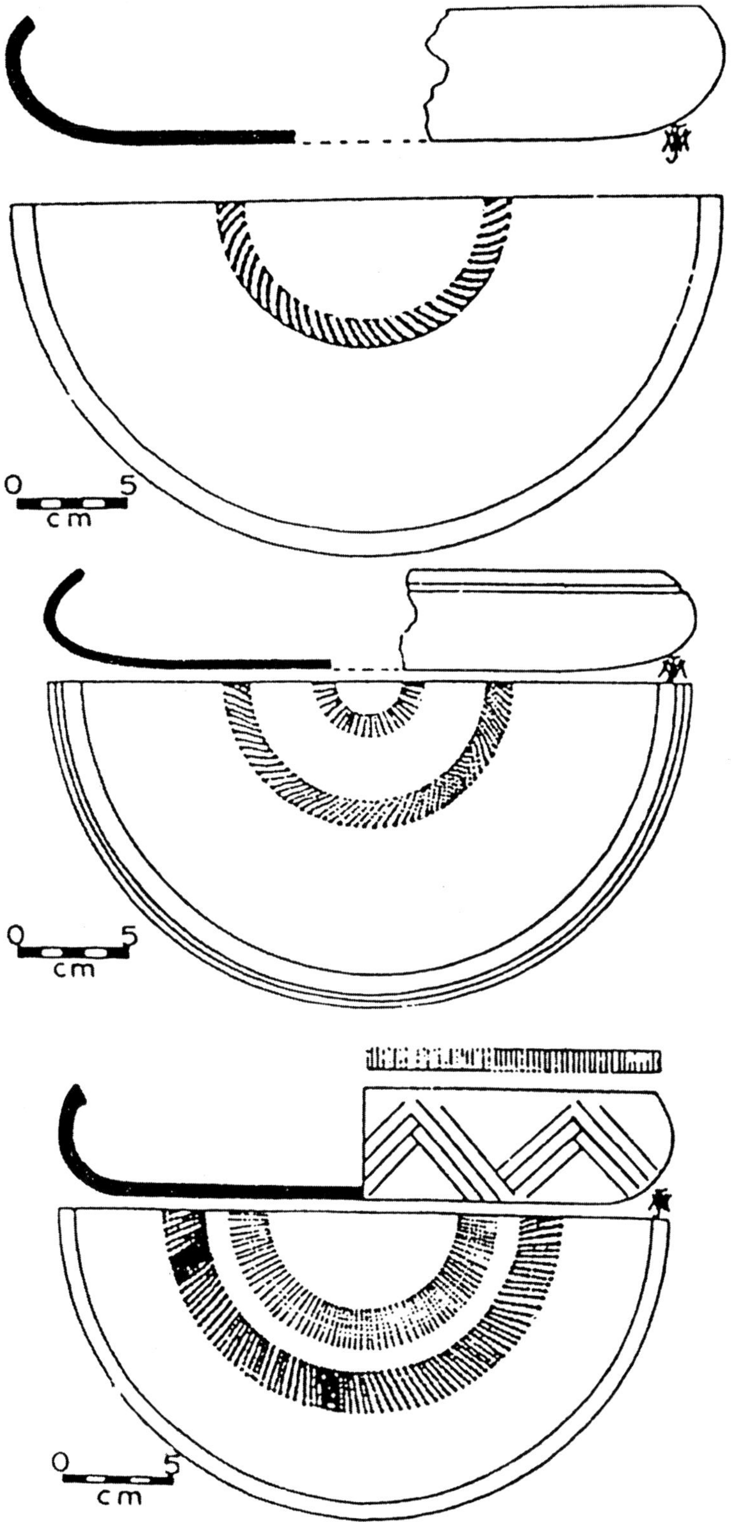

Fig. 6. Rouletted ware from Buni Complex site at Kobak Kendal and Cibutak, Java, Indonesia (from Walker and Santoso 1977)

Glover[105] also refers to scenes of people, houses, cattle and buffalo, incised on some high-tin bronze vessels below the rim, from Ban Don Ta Phet, and from Chombung in Rajburi province, west Thailand, and pointed out the broad similarity to a Kulu vase in the British Museum.

Bronson and Dales[106] illustrate our ivory comb of Indian design from Phase II, dated to the first 250 years of the Christian era, at the moated settlement at Chansen in central Thailand (Fig. 7). The engravings are of horses, an elaborately plumed goose, and a row of Buddhist emblems. All these are broadly related to the Amaravati style which developed in the region of the south-eastern coast of India during the 1st-4th centuries AD. An ivory comb is also reported from Tha Kae.[107] In the Indian subcontinent, ivory combs are reported from many sites from Taxila in the north to Bhokardan and Dhulikotta in the Deccan between the period 300 BC-AD 300.[108]

Moreover, one fine grey ware sprinkler neck with a shiny burnish, from Period III at Chansen (dated to *c.* AD 200-250 to 400-450) has its analogue at Beikthano in Burma and also in India.[109]

Aung Tha[110] mentioned that some of the pottery types of Beikthano also had their parallels in India. For example, spouted vessels with a pouch-like bulge at the base of the spout are also found at Rangmahal, Arikamadu, Yeleswaram and Ahichchhatra in India. Moreover, the sprinkler vessels with the nozzled long bottle neck are also recovered from Brahmagiri and Hastinapura in India.

Hanwong[111] points out some similarities between some ornaments from Tha Kae in central Thailand and from some sites in India. For example, ear plugs, made of clay from Tha Kae are similar to those from Kudavelli[112] and from Khandagiri-Udayagiri in Orissa.[113] Ear-plugs made of clay and lead from Tha Kae are similar to those from Nagajunakonda.[114] An ivory comb from Tha Kae has a similar shape to that of India, although its motif is distinctive.

A thin foliated piece of gold eye-cover is found with a skull at Gilimanuk, Bali.[115] There is a strong similarity between the Gilimanuk find and the 19 diadems recovered from the megalithic graves at Adichanallur on the Tamil coast of India.[116]

A late Roman bronze lamp is reported from a monastic site at Pong Tuk on the Mae Klong river in western Thailand.[117] Ceramic lamps with a similar shape are obtained from Tha Kae[118] and many sites such as U-Thong, Ku Bua and Nakorn Pathom in west-central Thailand. Recently, Brown and Macdonnell[119] argued that the Pong Tuk lamp was similar to a Byzantine type and hence dated to 5th-6th century AD. They also referred to another Roman style lamp (100 BC-AD 100), now in the National Museum, Bangkok, although they were sceptical about its context and period of entry into Thailand.

Recently, Ray[120] has emphasized the intaglios, seals and stampings of Indian origin in mainland South-east Asia. For example, carnelian seals with Brahmi inscriptions have been found at Khuan Lukpad, Kuala Selinsing, Chaiya and Oc Eo. Carnelian intaglios from North-western India were found at Nakorn Pathom, Khuan Lukpad and Oc Eo. Seals and sealings with Kharosthi inscriptions, distributed in the Ganga valley, were found at U-Thong and Oc Eo. Moreover, the ship or boat symbol on coins and sealings was there in both India and South-east Asia.

Fig. 7. Ivory comb of Indian origin from Ban Tha Kae
(from Bronson and Dales 1972)

Literary Evidence

Three types of literary sources—Indian, Chinese and Western classical—are known for external relations, including trade of South-east Asia.

Indian Literature

In Indian literature, three languages—Sanskrit, Pali and Tamil—are important and considerable emphasis has already been placed on these sources by earlier workers.[121]

Three toponyms—*Suvarnabhumi* or *Suvarnadvipa, Java-dvipa* and *Dvipantara,* are frequently mentioned for South-east Asia. Among these, *Suvarnabhumi* (Pali *Suvannabhumi)* and *Suvarnadvipa* (Pali *Suvannadipa*) are referred to most, implying a realm of gold beyond sunrise.

Suvarnadvipa is regarded as the source of a particular class of aloewood (*agaru*) in Kautilya's *Arthasastra.*[122] In the *Ramayana,*[123] this term occurs along with *Javadvipa* where Sugriva, king of monkeys, commands his followers to search for Sita in *Javadvipa* embellished with seven kingdoms and furnished with mines of gold and silver. Gunadhyaya's *Bṛhatkatha,* written in Paisachi Prakrit, probably in the 1st century AD, provided themes for literature of the subsequent period—for example, the *Brihatkatha-slokasamgraha* of Budhaswamin (8th century AD) and the *Kathasarit Sagara* (The Ocean of Story) of Somadeva (11th century AD). The *Brihatkatha-slokasamgraha* narrates the story of Sanudasa—son of a merchant—who undertakes a perilous journey into the interior of *Suvarnabhumi.*[124] The *Kathasarit sagara* contains tales of trade voyages to *Suvarnadvipa* by merchants Samudrasura[125] and Rudra,[126] by Isvaravarma[127] and King Yasaketu.[128] The odyssey of the Brahmana Chandrasvamin[129] throws light on some trade routes. Chandrasvamin sought his lost children at *Narikela-dvipa, Kataha-dvipa, Karpura-dvipa, Suvarna-dvipa* and *Sinhala-dvipa.* The *Kathakoṣa,* a corpus of Jain tales compiled by Jinesvara, relates the story of Nagadatta,[130] who went on a sea voyage with 500 ships in order to acquire wealth. But he had to be rescued by Sundara, the king of *Suvarnadvipa,* from the "hollow of the snake-encircled mountain". The *Mahakarmavibhanga*[131] discussed the calamities of travelling to *Suvarnabhumi.* In the *Jatakamala,* a Sanskrit version of the Jataka tales and composed by Arya Sura probably in the 3rd or 4th century AD, Surparaka, situated on the north-western coast of the Deccan, is mentioned as a port-of-call of merchants trading to *Suvarnabhumi.*[132]

The Buddhist writers, writing in the Pali language, show a more extensive knowledge of South-east Asia. The best known reference to trading voyages to the East comes from the *Millinda-panho* (about 400 AD), which is a Pali translation of a Sanskrit or some North Indian Prakrit text at about the beginning of the Christian era. It states, "...a wealthy ship owner scrupulously discharges his port dues and putting forth on to the high seas, voyages to *Vanga,* to *Takkola, Cina, Sovira, Surattha, Alasanda, Kolapattama, Suvannabhumi* or some other port where shipping congregates."[133]

Other trading areas in the Indian Ocean and South-east Asia (including *Suvannabhumi)* find mention in a gloss on the word *parikissati* (torment) in the *Mahaniddesa,* a part of the Pali Buddhist canons.[134]

The *Divyavadana,* a collection of the Buddhist stories (about 4th century AD), mentions that Supriya, a traveller reached the country (or more likely part of its interior) by scaling a mountain range with the aid of rattan ladders.[135]

The *Jatakatthavannana,* which narrates the stories of the Buddha's former birth, is a store-house of much information regarding the trade network between Indian ports and the *Suvannabhumi.* The core of the narrative had already existed during the late centuries BC. One such story tells of Prince Mahajanaka who joined a group of merchants going to the Land of Gold,[136] and another of the Brahmin Sankha who went on trading adventures to that region.[137] Moreover, two others went there from Bharukaccha.[138]

The *Paramatta-Dipani*, written by Dharmapala probably (about 5th century AD), depicts the regular trade between India and *Suvannabhumi.*[139] This work mentions *Pataliputta* and *Savasti*—both in the Gangetic plain, figuring most prominently as emporia in this trade.

References to *Suvannabhumi* are also found in some ancient Śri Lankān Pali literature. For example, the *Sihalavatthuppakarana* mentions *Suvannabhumi* as a region, where a Buddhist lay devotee and a goldsmith recouped their depleted fortunes.[140] The *Rasavahini* (about 12th century) incorporates stories about the Sinhalese voyage to *Suvannabhumi.*[141]

Suvannabhumi is clearly associated with the spread of Buddhism there from India in the *Mahakarmavibhanga,*[142] the *Sasanavamsa,*[143] in the Sinhalese chronicles, *Dipavamsa*[144] and *Mahavamsa* and in such works as the *Samanta Pasadika, Mahabodhivamsa, Thupavamsa* and *Pujavali.*[145]

It is a pity that despite so many references to *Suvarnabhumi* (or *Suvannabhumi)* and *Suvarnadvipa* (or *Suvannadvipa),* no precise description is available. This has left the task of identifying its location as a field of controversy. For example, the capital of *Suvarnabhumi* was variously interpreted as Thaton in Lower Burma,[146] U-Thong in central Thailand[147] and Chaiya in peninsular Thailand.[148] *Suvarnabhumi* could be also a part or whole of Sumatra.[149]

Javadvipa is another toponym frequently found in Indian literature. An early reference comes from the Ramayana.[150] The term *Yamadvipa* in the *Vayu Purana* is believed to be a variant form of *Javadvipa.*[151]

Moreover, passages mentioning many place names, such as *Kaserudvipa, Kataha* and *Malayadvipa* also occur in the Puranic texts, notably in the *Mārkaṇdeya Purāṇa, Agni Purana, Vāmana Purāṇa* and the *Matsya Purāṇa.*[152] These passages are quite obscure about their geographical connotations.

As to *Dvipantara,* we find more, and relatively less obscure references. This was first brought to notice by Levi[153] in a Sanskrit-Chinese lexicon (7th-8th century AD) which employed *Dvipantara* as a synonym for the Chinese *Kun Lun*—a generalized term for the maritime peoples of South-east Asia. *Dvipantara* also occurs in the *Kathasarit sagara*[154] and the *Mahakarmavibhanga, Agnipurana* and the *Vamana Purana*[155] and also in *Guruparamparai, Arayirappadi.*[156] In the *Raghuvamsa*, written by Kalidasa (4th century AD), mention is made of "the winds wafting the flowers of cloves *(lavanga)* from *Dvipantara.*"[157] According to Wheatley[158] the references as a whole imply a broad regional designation for the archipelago, probably including at least the southern tracts of the Siamo-Malay peninsula.

Wheatley[159] also mentioned that the constituent territories of the broadly designated framework of *Suvarnadvipa* were mentioned more frequently in writings of progressively later dates as conceptions of the geography of the area became more formalised. Perhaps the very names of these kingdoms beyond sunrise were enough to arouse the adventurous spirit of the merchants—*Suvarnadvipa* (the land of gold), *Karpuradvipa* (the land of camphor), *Narikeladvipa* (the land of coconuts), *Takkola* (the land of cardamom). Moreover, Kataha was regarded as "the seat of all felicities" in an account in the *Kathasarit sagara.*[160]

Some passages in early Tamil literature are also relevant. The *Pattinappalai* (about 2nd-3rd centuries AD)—one of the Ten Idylls of the Third *Sangam,* included "goods from Kalagam" as imports into the city of Puhar or Kaveripattinam.[161] According to Nilakanta Sastri,[162] the equation of Kadaram in Kedah with Kalagam is found in the geographical section of the *Divakaram,* the earliest lexicon of the Tamil language available. Nilakanta Sastri also draws attention to a passage from the Silappadikaram (Canto XIV, II, 106-10), one of the five major Tamil epics composed during the early centuries AD. The passage is as follows: "Having entered together with the east wind that came laden with (the aroma) of aloe, silks, sandal, spices and camphor put by the residents of *Tondi* on board a fleet of tall roomy ships."[163] According to Nilakanta Sastri,[164] *Tondi* must have been a Malaysian land across the sea.

Wheatley[165] mentioned that what were originally place names became in the course of time attached to the distinctive commodities exported from them.

Chinese Literature

References to the westerly trade from South-east Asia are also available from Chinese literature,[166] which had a relatively better chronology than their Indian counterparts. However, like the Indian literature, their toponyms are also subject to various interpretations.

The earliest known reference comes from *Jian Han Shu* (Chapter 28).[167] The geographical names mentioned there are variously interpreted. However, according to Wheatley,[168] Rinan was upper Annam, while Xuwen and Hebu were sub-prefectures on the southern coast of Guangdong. The trade by land route referred to is regarded as passing through the Malay peninsula with *Shenli* on the east coast and *Fugandulu* on the west coast. But the term *Huangzhi*—the western terminus of this trade originating from China—is subjected to different interpretations.[169] It has been variously identified as being in Africa, in India and in the Malay peninsula. Irrespective of this, it shows that there was trade between China and the region lying to the west of South-east Asia during that period. Moreover, it implies that there was a trans-peninsular trade route. According to Gungwu,[170] the merchants of the pearl-ports of Xuwen and Hebu in western Guangdong encouraged this mission to obtain better pearls from India for augmenting their business further.

It is mentioned in the same passage of the *Jian Han Shu* (28b, 32b) that Wang Mang sent a mission to *Huangzhi,* with rich gifts, along with a command to its king to send a live rhinoceros.[171] This happened a few years before Wang Mang usurped the throne and established the Xin dynasty. The envoys of this mission came via *Bicong.* Once again, this refers to the voyage between *Huangzhi* and *Jih-nan,* but, unlike the former account, it was entirely a sea-journey. *Bicong* was most probably located on the Malaysian peninsula or a neighbouring island.[172]

It is also mentioned in the *Han Shu*[173] that the Han convoys visited a kingdom south of *Huang-zhi,* known as *Sizhenbu* as *Jijianbu,* which is identified as Ceylon (Śri Lankā) or another port of South India, possibly Kitthipura (Kitur) on the Kaveri river. This visit is regarded as the first Chinese visit to the island of the precious stones.

After the fall of the Former Han Empire in AD 9, the Xin Dynasty ruled for a very brief period (AD 9-23) and was succeeded by the Later Han Dynasty (AD 25-220). During this period, no direct reference to sea trade is available. Brief accounts of tribute missions from kingdoms, such as *Shan, Yediao, Dianzhu* and *Dajin,* imply that China had trade relations with those countries in the south and the west.[174] *Shan* is regarded as Burma, *Dianzhu* was Northern India and *Dajin* was the Eastern Roman Empire. But *Yediao* is variously interpreted as Ceylon (*Sihadvipa*) or Java-Sumatra (*Yavadvipa*).[175] Although China carried out trade, by land routes, with *Shan* (Burma) via Yunnan and with *Dianzhu* (Northern India) and *Dajin* (Eastern Roman Empire) via Central Asia, references to missions from these regions by sea are available from the *Shan* kingdom in AD 132 (*Hou Han Shu* 6, 6a), from *Dianzhu* in AD 159 and 161 and one professedly from *Dajin* in AD 166 (*Hou Han Shu* 118, 10a and 8b-9a) from *Andun,* identified as the Roman Emperor Marcus Aurelius Antoninus. Nothing is mentioned about the merchandise except the tribute brought from *Andun* of *Dajin,* which consisted of elephant tusk, rhinoceros horns and tortoise-shells. Since these were common goods and were without jewels, the authenticity of the missions from *Andun* was suspected (*Hou Han Shu* 14 a-b).[176] Mention is also made about the mission from *Yediao* (*Hou Han Shu* 6, 6a, 116, 6b). *Yediao* is variously identified as Java-Sumatra and Śri Lankā.[177]

It is argued by Gungwu[178] that China's maritime trade with South India was an extension of an earlier Nanhai trade. To begin with, this extension was not prompted primarily by a desire for acquisition of South-east Asian resources,[179] rather for obtaining western luxury items.[180] Hence, for example, the first Chinese references to the Malay peninsula come as a sea route to India rather than as a terminus of trade activity.[181]

With the fall of the Late Han Dynasty (AD 220), China witnessed the emergence of three kingdoms—Wu, Shu and Wei. The Kingdom of Wu was located in South China and hence lost the contact over land with Central Asia. So the Wu government was very cautious in handling the missions. In AD 226, when Jin Lun, a merchant of *Dajin* visited the Wu capital, the emperor Sun Zhuan himself cross-examined him and sent an official with him on his return journey (*Liang Shu* 54, 22a-b).[182] Lu Dai, the Wu Governor of Tong King, sent an envoy to the south soon after AD 226 (*San Guo Zhi Wu*, 15, 9a) and between AD 226-31, tribute was received from Funan and the Chams (*San Guo Zhi Wu,* 15, 9a).[183]

It is interesting to note that the first tributary missions to China came not from the South-east Asians, rather from the North Indians whose first mission by sea was about 70 years earlier than those of Funan and Cham.[184] With the need for a maritime trade, the Chinese sent envoys to Funan for two reasons: (i) to investigate the way in which trickling of the western Asiatic trade was being handled[185] and (ii) to find out whether it was necessary to protect this trade by conquest.[186] Thus Zhu Ying and Gang Dai were sent to Funan most probably between 245-50 AD or possibly 20 years earlier.[187] The data furnished by Kang Dai are preserved in fragments, which mention *Dajin (Dai Bing You Lan* 696, 3105b; 767, 3403b; 816, 3628b; 971, 4306a)[188] and the river system of Northern India (*Shui Jing Zhu*, 1, 16b-17a),[189] but it ignored the relationship between the Indus and the Ganges. With reference to South-east Asia, the description of *Dunsun* in the *Liang Shu* (54, 7a),[190] located at the northern end of the Malay peninsula, is believed to be based on Gang Dai's works.[191]

Dun Sun's importance lies in its strategic location on the trade route from Funan to India, "because at this mart west and east meet together, so that daily there are innumerable people there. Precious goods and rare merchandise—there is nothing which is not there."[192] The *Dai Ping You Lan* (Chapter 28) mentions that in the kingdom of *Dunsun,* a dependency of Funan, "There are five hundred families of *hu* from India, two *fodu* and more than a thousand Indian brahmans."[193] Pelliot[194] believes that the term *hu* refers to a merchant class and *fodu* possibly signified a Buddhist.

Moreover, reference to the despatch of an embassy from Fan Zhan, the King of Funan to India, during the period of the Wu dynasty in China is made in the *Liang Shu* (54, 22b).[195] This mission went through the port of *Zhuli,* which Wheatley[196] considers as being situated somewhere in the Malay peninsula. In response to this mission, *Mou luan,* the Murunda king (who had received the mission), the ruler of some place in the Gangetic valley, despatched *Zhen Song* with four *Yueji* horses to Funan. This is known from the text written by Wan Zhen in the third century AD, which is lost now, but referred to in fragments in *Liang Shu.*[197] Gang Dai met Zhen Song, the Indian envoy to Funan, in the 3rd century AD and learnt that there was no direct contact and trade with North India, that is via the Ganges (*Liang Shu,* 54, 10a), but there was regular trade with *Dajin* through South India, Ceylon, the Malay peninsula and Fu-nan.[198] Two missions came from Dajin in the 3rd century AD—one in AD 226 and another AD 284 (*Liang Shu* 54, 9b-10a and *Jin Shu,* 3, 13a; 97, 8b). According to Gungwu,[199] these two dates are significant, because the first (226 AD) came four years after the establishment of the Kingdom of Wu and the second also four years after the defeat of Wu and the re-unification of China by the Jin Emperor. The implication of sending the missions was perhaps to ensure the resumption of trade and protection for the Dajin merchants.

Horses from *Yueji* were also coming to *Geying*, as known from *Gang Dai (Dai Bing You Lan* 359, 1650a).[200] *Geying* was probably situated in the eastern coast of Sumatra.[201]

With regard to Śri Lankā, two terms were used—*Sidiao* and *Shizi*. The first mission from Śri Lankā came to China with an ivory statue of Buddha towards the end of the Eastern Chin dynasty (AD 317-420) during the period AD 405-19 (*Liang Shu* 54, 11a).[202] Petech[203] pointed out that the Chinese texts do not give much information about Śri Lankā of the 3rd-4th century AD. According to Wolters,[204] the list of products associated with Śri Lankā, as mentioned in the *Dai Bing You Lan* (982, 4347b) included some items from the Middle East, for example, *xunlu,* and storax (items known as the products of *Dajin*). These items might have been imported by Śri Lankā for onward transmission to China.

Fa Xian's account of his return journey from India to China by the maritime route during AD 411-13 is a good example of the sea voyage between the two regions.[205] He boarded a vessel from Tamralipti on the Bengal coast and came to Śri Lankā. He then proceeded to *Yehbodi* for his onward journey to Canton in China. This account has some important implications. Firstly, it highlights the importance of the maritime trade route between India and China. Secondly, a non-stopping voyage between *Yehbodi* and Canton in 50 days is also important.[206] However, there is no mention of any Chinese merchant in India, nor in Śri Lankā. So Gungwu[207] inferred that in the last years of the Chin dynasty, no Chinese personally went to trade in India and Śri Lankā, as the Chinese could obtain Indian, Śri Lankān and Western goods from the marts on the Malay peninsula. Moreover, it might be mentioned that Prince Gunavarmana of Kashmir also followed an India-Śri Lankā-Indonesia maritime route to China, where he died in AD 431.[208]

In the first years of the Liu Song dynasty (AD 420-79), four missions came from Śri Lankā and two from India.[209] From the account of the historian of the Liu Song dynasty (AD 487), it is known that the imports to China included the products of mainland South-east Asia (rhinoceros horns and kingfisher feathers) as well as goods of India, Ceylon and further west (*Song Shu* 97, 12b-13a).[210]

According to Wolters,[211] during the 4th-5th century AD, particularly from the early decades of the 5th century AD, demand for western luxury items in South China was a more important factor in the maritime trade between the West and China than the demand for Chinese silk in India, Persia and the West.

Western Classical Literature

Various regions of South-east Asia find mention in some western classical sources.[212]

Although information about India is known as early as 500 BC from the description of the Earth by Hecataeus of Miletus, the first reference to South-east Asia comes from the popular geographical compendium *De Chorographia* which was written by Pomponius Mela in about 43 AD. The two terms *Chryse* (the land of gold) and *Argyre* (the land of silver) which later became very common references to South-east Asia find only vague mention in that account.[213]

Pliny referred to *Chryse* both as a promontory and an island.[214]

The geographical connotation of both these passages is uncertain, but what is interesting is that in these two paragraphs Pliny seems to attempt combining two traditions—one derived from the overland route across Central Asia and one from the sea route, without realising that they overlapped in South-east Asia.[215]

It is the *Periplus of the Erythraean Sea*—compiled in the 1st century AD by an anonymous Graeco-Roman merchant for the use of merchants—which is the earliest text mentioning the details of trade between India and South-east Asia. Since the author's personal experience seems to have extended not beyond Nelkynda on the Malabar coast of India, his geographical descriptions are relatively vague in relation to the eastern coast of India and to South-east Asia, hence the information about the course of trade is more important than his geographical locations.[216] Thus it is said that very large vessels, called *Kolandia* were used for the voyage from South India to *Chryse,*[217] which was "at the very last land toward the east."[218]

The most detailed account of South-east Asia comes from the *Geographike Huphegesis* or *Guide to Geography*. It was believed to be the work of Ptolemy in the 2nd century AD, but Bagrow[219] and following him Wheatley[220] believe that the *Geography* in its present form is the work of an anonymous Byzantine of 10th or 11th century AD, who based his work on the principles of Ptolemy and who might have incorporated some of Ptolemy's work as well.

For our purpose, Book VII is relevant. Under the rubrics "Location of Trans-Gangetic India" and "Location of Sinai", it lists the coordinates of about 140 settlements and the physiographic features along with descriptive comments. For the present South-east Asia, about 30 settlements were referred to, each as a *polis* signifying an urban centre, six trading ports each specified as an *emporion* (which denoted as an authorised seacoast (not inland) mart in the Orient, where non-Roman dues were levied by non-Roman authorities), five *metropoleis* or chief cities of their respective territories and one *basileion* or royal city. It must be borne in mind that these terms might not connote everything that is usually associated with such terms in the Graeco-Roman world.

The most common cited reference in *Geography* to trade of South-east Asia is the term *Golden Khersonese,* which finds its first mention in Book VII, Chapter 1 in a list of coordinates relating to Peninsular India.[221]

Despite Ptolemy's descriptions of sites in terms of latitude and longitude, precise determination of their present location is very difficult.[222]

The *Golden Khersonese* was identified by some scholars in Lower Burma,[223] but Wheatley[224] located it in the Malay peninsula and Meulen[225] in Sumatra.

Like the above mentioned term, differences also arise as to the location of other toponyms, like *Takkola, Sabara,* the river system of *Khrysoanas, Palanda.*[226]

On the *Geography,* Meulen makes two important points. Firstly, the lines on the map represent sailing routes.[227] Secondly, Ptolemy's toponyms imply considerable influence of Sanskrit.[228]

Wheatley[229] does not accept that Ptolemy mistook sailing directions for coastlines. However, he does appreciate the impact of Sanskrit in some Ptolemaic toponyms in which case corresponding translation is available, but he is very sceptical about extending the principle too far.

General references to the island of *Chryse* are also available from some other sources.[230] Thus, in the 2nd century AD, Dionysius, surnamed Periegetes or the Tourist, mentioned "the island of *Chryse,* situated at the very rising of the sun."[231] The impact of Dionysius is felt in the account of the "Golden Island" by Avienus in his Description of the World, in about AD 370 and by the grammarian Priscianus writing in early 6th century AD. Moreover, *Chryse* and *Argyre* as land of gold and silver respectively find vague mention in the *Collectanea Rerum Memorabilium* of Solinus (3rd century AD), and the *Satyricon* or Nuptials of Philology and Mercury of Marcianus Capella (5th century AD). In the 3rd century AD, Palladius quoted Scholastikos of Thebes as saying that he "arrived among the pepper-gathering *Bisades*", who lived "in rock shelters" and who were "adept at climbing steep crags so that they can collect pepper from the tree."[232] According to Wheatley,[233] these *Bisades* are *Bisatae* of the *Periplus* and probably *Saesadai* of the *Geography* and might be a folk described in Chinese literature as inhabitants of the Malay peninsula.

During the early 5th century AD, Martianus of Heraclea composed the *Periplus of the Outer Sea,* where the *Golden Khersonese* finds specific mention: "In Trans-Gangetic India is the *Golden Khersonese,* and beyond is the Great Gulf in the middle of which is the frontier between Trans-Gangetic India and the Sinai. Then come the Sinai and their capital called Thinai. It is the boundary between lands known and unknown."[234] For Wheatley,[235] this remark on the *Golden Khersonese* is the first specific mention of the Malay peninsula in the Western literature. It is worth mentioning here that after the *Geography,* there is no substantial change in the reference to South-east Asia in the western classical literature.

Epigraphic Evidence

Evidence for westerly trade in South-east Asia can also be supplemented by epigraphic sources. The earliest epigraphic evidence in South-east Asia consists of short inscriptions, often on seals and presumed to be brought by traders.

Beikthano in Burma yielded an unbaked lump of clay bearing two impressions of a circular seal reading *Sangha siri* in Brahmi letters of the 2nd century AD.[236]

In Thailand, the earliest inscription, which was carved on an oval stone seal, is reported from Khuan Lukpad (Khlong Thom) in Krabi province of Thailand.[237] It is written in the Brahmi script of Northern India of the type dateable to the 1st-3rd centuries AD. Using Prakrit or archaic Sanskrit, it reads *rujjo* meaning "destroy". Khuan Lukpad also yields some other short inscriptions, written on seals of carnelian, green stone and gold, in Pallava script and in Sanskrit language, dated on palaeographic ground between the 5th and 7th centuries AD. Some of them refer to their owners—for example, *apralasanasya* (belonging to Apralasana), *virabendhutrasya.* These seals imply the presence of Indian merchants in south Thailand.

Small inscriptions written in Sanskrit language and the Brahmi script of the 3rd-4th centuries AD were recovered from Oc Eo. These are engraved on the carnelian seals and rings[238] and on the gold seals.[239] Some of them bore the names of persons in the possessions, for example, *visnumitrasya, nicitasya.*

A Roman medallion with an inscription of Antoninus Augustus Pius, dated to AD 152 was also recovered from Oc Eo.[240]

An important inscription from Malaysia often cited as an evidence for trade with India is the inscription of Buddhagupta, carved with a Buddhist stupa. The inscription—a prayer written in Sanskrit language and in Pallava script and palaeographically dated to the 5th century AD—was meant for the success of voyage about to be undertaken by a sailing master (*mahanavika*) Buddhagupta, who dwelt in *Raktamrttika.*[241] Majumdar identified it with Rangamati near Murshidabad on the Bhagirathi river. It has been also identified as Rajbadidanga on the Bhagirathi river.[242] However, it is not certain whether this inscription was written before Buddhagupta began his voyage at all or before his return journey. But it can be safely inferred that the estuary of Muda was either the resort of merchants or their home port during the 5th century AD.[243]

Besides these, there is not much epigraphic evidence which has direct implications for trade. However, since the early inscriptions found in many different parts of South-east Asia are all in Indian scripts and/or languages, they will be discussed briefly, because they provide evidence of Indian religious and political influences which flowed along the trade routes.

For example, the Vo-canh inscriptions in the Nha-trang district of Vietnam[244] are palaeographically dated to about 3rd century AD and show close similarity to the inscriptions of the Iksvakus of Andhra Pradesh, South India (dateable to the 3rd century AD), although they have got some minor differences.[245]

The Kutai inscriptions of East Borneo and the Taruma inscriptions of Java[246] are believed to be written in the Pallava script and dated to the end of the 4th or the early part of 5th century AD on palaeographic grounds.[247] However, these inscriptions are not mere replicas of the South Indian Pallava inscriptions.[248]

Numismatic Evidence

From the numismatic point of view, there are two kinds of evidence—(i) a few Roman coins found in South-east Asia and (ii) the extent to which native coins of South-east Asia are influenced by India.

(i) A medallion of Antoninus Pius was reported from Oc Eo in Vietnam.[249] A copper coin of Victorinus (AD 268-70), the Western Roman Emperor and minted at Cologne was found at U-Thong in western Thailand.[250]

At one time, a Chinese coin, found at Chitaldurg near Mysore in South India was dated to the 2nd century BC and was believed to be the earliest evidence for contact between China and India.[251] But it is now said to belong to a much later period in the 8th century AD.[252]

(ii) While discussing the issue of Indian influence on South-east Asian coins, it is worth mentioning that there is no unanimity about the chronology of various native coins of South-east Asia. According to Mitchiner,[253] the earliest evidence of native coinage in South-east Asia comes from Oc Eo, made of silver and dated to about AD 200.

He referred to two series of early symbolic coins.[254] Coins of the commoner series of the "rising sun/temple" type of the Kingdom of Funan and circulated across the mainland, while the second series of coins of the "*sankh* shell/temple without ancillary symbols" type is believed to have been minted in the Mon kingdom of Thaton. Relatively scarcer, the second series circulated more along the coast from southern Burma, Thailand and south Vietnam. On the basis of symbolic designs, Mitchiner[255] divided the coins of Funan into three groups— Early Period (First Series) dated to AD 190-300, Early Period (Second Series) between AD 300 and 400 and the Late Series between AD 400 and 550. Assuming that the origin of the Dvaravati kingdom goes back to the 4th century AD, he dated the early series of the Dvaravati silver coins with a heavier weight standard to about AD 300-550.[256] The Early coins of Sriksetra were said to be in vogue during AD 200-400 and the Intermediate coin series during AD 400-750.[257] On the basis of the Sitthaung Pagoda pillar inscription at Mrohaung, dated to about the 8th century AD, he dated the coins of the Candra dynasty ruling over the Arakan kingdom to about AD 400-630.[258] Gold coins from Krabi in the Malay Isthmus with *sankh*/temple motifs found on silver coins from the northerly region between South Burma to Oc Eo are dated to between the 1st-2nd and the 6th century AD. Similar coins are also reported from Oc Eo.[259]

Cribb[260] disagreed with Mitchiner's chronology and pointed out that these coins cannot be dated earlier than 8th century AD. He emphasized that the coins Mitchiner discussed are mostly from surface finds and not from secure contexts. As regards the date of King Anandacandra who had erected the Mrohaung pillar inscription, he referred to a local chronicle which placed the beginning of Anandacandra's reign at AD 1018.

It was Wicks[261] who made a comprehensive study of the various types of native South-east Asian coins. According to him, an uninscribed silver conch/*srivatsa* type of coin found in lower Burma, Arakan and southern Vietnam is the earliest coinage of South-east Asia and is dated to the 5th century AD. In island South-east Asia, the earliest coinage includes a silver coin of sandalwood flower motif which was recovered from central Java and dated to the 8th century AD. However, the silver coin with the conch/*srivatsa* motif is the model for each mainland coinage during the period about AD 450-1000. Most of the South-east Asian coins are anonymous which could be attributed to geographical areas or culture groups, but hardly to historical figures. However, the most secure date for native South-east Asian coins comes, in his opinion, from those of the Candras of Vesali (Arakan) in Burma, on the basis of Mrohaung *prasasti*. Accepting its date to 8th century AD, he pointed out that some of the inscribed coins (Wicks' conch/*srivatsa* Class B and C) can be attributed to Devacandra (AD 454-76). However, it is not certain whether the Mon-Pegu coins (conch/*srivatsa* Class A of Wicks), obtained primarily near Sittaung in Pegu, date from the 5th century AD or belonged to an earlier period. Devacandra is associated with another type of coin—the bull/*trisula* type, which became later on the Candra standard. He also discussed coins of Pyu-Sriksetra (AD 6th-8th century) and Dvaravati (AD 600-1100). The Harikela coins, post-Candra coins of Arakan, those of the Akara kings of northern Arakaran and the unattributed categories, were, according to Wicks, dated to the second half of the 1st millennium AD.

Although there was a typological link among various groups of coins, Wicks pointed out that there was hardly any metrological link. Moreover, despite the fact that *srivatsa* motif was common to almost all coin types, there were subtle iconographical differences among them catering to the symbolic preferences of various groups. The limited distribution of most of the coin types implied that they were not used in international commerce. Most probably they were used as payment of fines, fees, taxes and religious donations.

According to Wicks, the rising sun/*srivatsa* coin type which is distributed in Burma, Thailand, Cambodia and southern Vietnam, appears to have been acceptable on an international basis and can be regarded as a trade coinage. Malleret[262] regarded it as the coin type of Funan. Boisselier[263] argued on the basis of such finds from U-Thong in Thailand that this was evidence for the conquest of Fan Shih-man of Funan against countries west of Cambodia in the 3rd century AD. Aung Thaw[264] accepted such coins as the criterion for the presence of the Pyu culture in Burma. Wicks[265] questioned such unqualified acceptance in favour of Funan and Pyu, because, typologically, these are late issues and have associations with particularly the southern Shan States region of Burma and Thailand and not with Cambodia. Their presence in Cambodia and Vietnam might be as a result of trade. Unfortunately, the chronology as well as the issuing region could not be determined precisely. With regard to Pyu as a possible candidate for the same, Wicks made two points. Firstly, the metrological and fabric differences between the definite Pyu issues (*bhaddapitha/ srivatsa* Classes A and B of Wicks) and the rising sun have to be explained. Secondly, an explanation has to be made as to the absence of such coins from Hmawza, which was one of the major Pyu sites. Thus, problems remain for the most important South-east Asian coin from the viewpoint of trade.

The issue of the Indian impact on South-east Asian coins is best known from Gutman.[266] In her opinion, the introduction of coinage was the result of South-east Asia's trade with India and so also were the motifs. In this, she emphasised the role of the early Pallavas between 4th and 6th centuries AD. She refuted the argument made by Malleret[267] that all South-east Asian coins had a Scythian origin. There was no doubt that some features of the coins of the Scythian kings in India came to South-east Asia via India. But most of them were already present in the early punch-marked coins of India.

The Guptas of North India and the early Pallavas of South India adopted "Scythian" features such as the beaded surround. But the South-east Asian coins have more similarity with the Pallavas than with the Guptas, because "neither use the likeness of the king, or even anthropomorphic depiction of gods; the coins are often not inscribed and there are no indications of mint markings."[268] With regard to the most common motif of *srivatsa*, she points out that the immediate prototype for the South-east Asian form is found on coins from Chandravalli, in Chitaldurg district of Northern Karnataka from a stratum associated with the Satavahana kings of the 2nd century AD.[269] However, on the basis of the study of Wicks (discussed above), it is difficult to agree with Gutman[270] that some of the early uninscribed coins of South-east Asia conformed to the weight standards of the Roman Empire.

Thus, in this section, four kinds of evidence-archaeological, literary, epigraphic and numismatic—is discussed to demonstrate the culture contacts, including that of secular trade, between South-east Asia and India and, to a certain extent, the Eastern Mediterranean region and China also.

Out of these, the archaeological relics provide the most concrete evidence for trade and the most reliable evidence for its chronology. If the chronology of Ban Don Ta Phet is accepted, the earliest maritime trade between India and South-east Asia so far can be traced back at least to the 4th century BC.

Literary sources also demonstrate the prevalence of such trade. In Indian literature—i.e. Sanskrit, Pali and Tamil, there is no dearth of references to South-east Asia as a geographical region. If one agrees with Sarkar,[271] some of the earliest references come from the *Arthasastra,* dated to *c.* late 4th century BC and the *Mahaniddesa*, dated to *c.* 3rd century BC and this is conformable with the new archaeological evidence from Ban Don Ta Phet. However, often the chronology of Indian literature is uncertain. Secondly, the geographical descriptions are very often vague.

In contrast, Chinese literature has got more secure chronology. The earliest reference to Chinese maritime trade with the West through South-east Asia comes from *Jian Han Shu,* dated to the late 3rd century BC onward. However, the geographical descriptions of places in Chinese literature are subjected to various interpretations like those of India.

Western classical literature bore only vague references to South-east Asia, hence had no consensus in relation to their identification. The earliest reference to South-east Asia can be dated to the 1st century AD from the geographical compendium *De Chorographia* written by Pomponius Mela. More references came from the *Periplus,* Pliny and Ptolemy.

Epigraphically, the evidence of trade comes from the objects with small inscriptions dated to the early centuries of the Christian era and believed to have been imported from India. Moreover, the inscription in Malaysia of the sailing master Buddhagupta and dated to the 5th century AD shows good evidence of trade. Otherwise, the inscriptions bear indirectly on trade but clearly demonstrate Indian influence in the region.

As regards the numismatic source, only two coins from the Roman Empire have been found. However, most probably South-east Asia had only indirect links with the Roman Empire via India. If one agrees with Wicks, the earliest native coins in South-east Asia came from the 5th century AD, that is towards the terminal period under study.

However, taken together, a study of all these sources show that the maritime trade between India and South-east Asia can be traced back to the 4th century BC and was on a considerable scale in the early centuries of the Christian era. On the basis of a study of various sources, it can be said that this trade was not a mere trickling, nor was it a mere drift, rather it continued in an integrated and organized manner. With the emergence of the Roman Empire in the West and the Han Empire in the north, its geographical spectrum extended further to the Eastern Mediterranean in the West and China in the north. This will be discussed in the following section.

After this comprehensive discussion on various evidences of Indo-South-east Asian maritime contacts, it is important to discuss the background for such trade in both India and South-east Asia and their mutual interest in this trade.

India's External Trade as an Extension of Internal Trade

From the Indian point of view, the external trade with South-east Asia may be regarded as an extension of the intense internal trade that developed from the 6th century BC onwards.

From the second half of the 1st millennium BC, most regions of India were interconnected by trade routes.[272] The Grand Route passing through North India connected

Tamralipti—a port in Bengal on the eastern coast—to the northwest of the subcontinent and to Central Asia. Bhrauch was the most important port on the western coast. It connected Western India with North India via Ujjain. Moreover, major routes from the South passed through Western Deccan.[273] By the late centuries BC and the early centuries of the Christian era, maritime traffic was well established in ports on both the western and the eastern coasts of India. While land caravans of carts were the main means of transport in the land-route,[274] shipping technology helped in the maritime traffic.

By the middle of the 1st millennium BC, some indication is available about the private ownership of land and the rise of very rich households of landowners—the *gṛhapatis*—in the middle Ganga valley. The trading communities of *vanijas* and *setthis* arose from the ranks of the *gṛhapatis*.[275] From the age of Buddha (6th century BC) onwards there was a second phase of urbanization in India, and a proliferation of arts and crafts organized with the guild system.[276] Evidence of such diversification was also available in the Western Deccan.[277] In South India, from the site of Arikamedu, places for dyeing vats were recovered.[278] The recovery of punch-marked coins from about the 5th century BC[279] onwards from different parts of the country showed that economy was at least partially monetized, which helped in the intensification of trade and commerce.[280]

According to Sharma,[281] there was state control of agriculture, industry and trade during the Mauryan period. This was because of the need to maintain a huge army, to fund public works and to have some surplus for emergencies. Some officials who played an important role in trade included the superintendent of commerce (*panyadhyaksa*), the superintendent of weights and measures (*pautavadhyaksa*), the superintendent of ships (*navadhyaksa*), the superintendent of tolls (*sulkadhyaksa*) and the superintendent of mines (*akaradhyaksa*). According to the *Arthasastra,* apart from trade in private hands, the state itself should engage in trade on a fairly extensive scale and the state goods (*rajapanya*) may be indigenously produced (*svabhumija*) or produced in foreign lands (*parabhumija*).[282]

Recently Thapar[283] has questioned the extent of direct control of the Mauryan Empire and its role in controlling trade. She argues that the Mauryans did not issue any distinct coinage—which is an important parameter of state intervention in urban trade. According to her, the punch-marked coins were issued by guilds or other local bodies.

Following Thapar, Ray[284] maintained that in Early Historic India, the state only derived revenue from trade, but trade itself was in the hands of private merchants and guilds. The state only tried to monopolize price control of items of royal consumption.

Irrespective of the role of the state, there is no denying the fact that trade was well organized. The profit motive was well established if one considers Kautilya's bemoaning of the profiteering by traders who co-operated with each other in order to raise or lower prices (*Arthasastra* VIII.4.35).[285]

Two more aspects were also important—the first is the technology of ships, and the second is the role of Buddhism.[286]

During the early centuries of the Christian Era, innovations in shipbuilding developed in the Persian Gulf and spread rapidly to other regions of the Indian Ocean. Thus the use of the fore and aft rig allowed vessels to sail closer to the wind. The *Periplus* states that big ships like the *Kolandia* were sailing from South India to *Chryse*. Moreover, the account of the export of horses from Central Asia to Indo-China through sea routes, and the travels of Fa Xian, the monk in the 5th century from Śri Lankā to China in the vessels each of which carried 200 people also imply the use of big ships in the eastern sector of the Indian Ocean by this time.

Buddhism took a more liberal view of trade than the Brahmanical *Dharmasastras*.[287] Manu prohibited sea voyages, for which the *Baudhayana Dharmasastra* prescribed a three-year penance. Visits to foreign countries also led to the loss of purity. Although these rules might not have been applied literally, these must have some restraining influence on foreign voyages. As a contrast, Buddhism rejected the Brahmanical ideas of racial purity and the fear of pollution through contact with the *mlechhas*, and encouraged money-lending on interest which used to be condemned by the Brahmanical law books.[288]

South-east Asia as a Land of Gold

India's interest in trade with South-east Asia also came from the latter's characterization as the *Suvarnabhumi* or the *Suvarnadvipa* or Land of Gold.

Despite a plethora of references to these terms in literature, no precise meaning is given. However, three possible meanings may be considered.

The first is that the terms might literally have referred to real gold. Gold was rare in ancient times. The rumours of gold in some parts of South-east Asia might have created a gold-rush.[289] According to Coedes,[290] the political disturbances in Bactria during the last two centuries BC cut off India from its traditional gold sources in Siberia. India also imported gold coins from the Roman Empire, especially in the 1st century AD. But Vespasian (AD 69-79) tried to arrest the huge outflow from the Roman world and hence India had to look for another source. South-east Asia was an alternative source. This is hard to prove archaeologically, but Malaya, Sumatra and parts of Eastern Indonesia contain low grade gold deposits which have long been worked by traditional methods.

Secondly, the "Land of Gold" might also refer to artefacts of high-tin bronze, an alloy which looks like gold because of its yellow colour.[291] Thailand was a source for such an alloy in the late 1st millennium BC, and vessels of this metal might have been regarded as luxury items. If broken they could have been used as a source of tin—a mineral rare in India.

A third possible meaning is in terms of agro-economic wealth. Spices from South-east Asia—especially cloves and nutmegs from the eastern Indonesian islands—were important items of trade which yielded a lot of profit. Thus trade with South-east Asia meant earning a lot of profit which is explained metaphorically by reference to gold, as a rich location for trade.

India as Middleman

By the end of the 1st century BC, with the emergence of peace and stability during the reign of Augustus, the Indo-Roman trade intensified. In this trade, India could not have met all the demands of the Roman Empire, especially for spices. So India acted as a middleman obtaining spices and other materials from South-east Asia and sending them to the Roman Empire.

The political disturbances in Central Asia during the last two centuries BC also forced the Han Chinese rulers to develop maritime trade with the West via South-east Asia. According to Gungwu,[292] China's maritime trade with South India was an extension of an earlier Nanhai trade. This was for obtaining luxury items from the West.[293] After the fall of the Later Han dynasty in AD 220, this was continued by the kingdom of Wu in South China and which lost direct contact with Central Asia.[294] In this network, India was also playing the middleman.

The Material Evidence from Archaeology for Early Trade and Exchange in South-east Asia

In South-east Asia, good evidence is available from the 2nd millennium BC for the emergence of localised exchange networks for raw materials and exotic goods.[295] For example, arm rings from marine shell species such as *Trochus* and *Tridacna* are reported from the central Thailand sites of Kok Charoen, Ban Na Di, Obluang and Tha Kae; exotic stone for arm rings from Ban Na Di in the north-east and import of lead, tin and copper ores and metal to Ban Chiang, Ban Na Di and Non Nok Tha in the northeast. Moreover, stone adzes—made from igneous and sedimentary rocks—were coming to Khok Phanom Di during 2000-1500 BC from the uplands of Bang Pakong river.[296]

From the late centuries BC onwards, evidence of exchange is available not only in terms of intra-region, but also at inter-regional scale. Welch and McNeill[297] mentioned that while the regional trade around Khorat Plateau in Thailand involved essential resources, long distance trade was mainly in prestige goods. Moreover, fragments of high tin bronze vessels, characteristic of Ban Don Ta Phet in the west-central region, were found at Kok Khon in Sakon Nakhon province in the north-east[298] and in peninsular Malaysia.[299] In peninsular Malaysia, during the Metal Age, evidence of contact between coastal, metal using people and the shifting cultivators of the hinterland was reported in the form of stray iron finds along Pahang rivers, socketed iron implements, pottery with flattened rim in Perlis, a green glass bead, a fragment of the rim of a bronze bowl at Kota Tongkat, Pahang.[300] In Indonesia, citing the case of Gilimanuk in Bali, Soejono[301] believed that the double jar burial at Gilimanuk on the coast seems to have been influenced by the sacrophagus burial which developed in inland Bali. He also talked of the exchange of metal objects, pottery and beads between the inland and the coastal people. In the Philippines, jade ornaments found at the Palawan caves are also reported from the contemporary cave sites in the north-east of Tuguegarao,[302] and they all may have been obtained from Vietnam or Taiwan.

Considerable evidence for inter-regional trade was also obtained from the late centuries BC. For example, the Dongson drum[303] of Heger 1 type, characteristic of north Vietnam, has a wide distribution and is found at Tam Ongbah cave in central Thailand,[304] Khao Sam Kao, Thapak Namrop, Taling Phang, Khlong Khutdvan and Ket Kai in south Thailand.[305] In peninsular Malaysia, bronze drums are reported from Batu Pasir Garam, Sungei Tembeling in Pahang, Kampong Sungei Lang in Selangor, Bukit Kuda, Klang in Selangor and at Kuala Terengganu in Terengganu.[306] In Indonesia, the Dongson drums of Heger 1 type are reported from Sumatra and Java in the west to the Kai islands, and New Guinea in the east.[307] Unfortunately, in most cases, the context of discovery of these drums is not very clear. However, at Tam Ongbah cave they have been dated to about the beginning of the 3rd century BC[308] and at Kampong Sungei Lang to between the 5th century BC and 2nd century AD.[309]

Moreover, high tin bronze artefacts which are characteristic of Ban Don Ta Phet in westcentral Thailand, are also reported from the slab graves from south Perak and north Selangor in peninsular Malaysia.[310]

The Sa Huynh-Kalanay pottery tradition, a term coined by Solheim,[311] shows wide inter-regional contacts in South-east Asia. At first, the Kalanay pottery complex was defined by the pottery available at Kalanay cave sites on the west coast of Masbate island in the Philippines. Since similar pottery types were found throughout the central and southern Philippines, southern Luzon, the Tabon caves and other Palawan sites, coastal Vietnam, Borneo, eastern Indonesia and further west,[312] Solheim developed the term the Sa Huynh-Kalanay pottery tradition. Moreover, the similarity of Phung Nguyen pottery with that from sites in Kalimantan, Sulawesi and Philippines has also been emphasized.[313]

Loofs-Wissowa[314] referred to two types of ear-ornaments—*ling-ling O* and the double-headed beast type—associated with the Sa Huynh culture of south Vietnam, as further evidence of prehistoric contact between the Indo-Chinese peninsula and the Philippines. The *ling-ling O,* made of jade, green glass or nephrite and metal and most typical of north and central Vietnam is also found in Batangan province, Luzon and the Tabon caves in the Philippines, in Samrong Sen in Kampuchea and U-Thong in west-central Thailand and also in Taiwan.[315] The double-headed beast ear ornament, made of jade or nephrite, and typical of the Sa Huynh culture of central Vietnam, is found in Duyong cave, Palawan in the Philippines, U-Thong[316] and Ban Don Ta Phet in west-central Thailand.[317]

South-east Asian Interest in the Westerly Trade

This trend of inter-regional exchange was further intensified by the emergence of chiefdoms (and possibly nascent states in peninsular Malaysia) in South-east Asia during the late centuries BC. This meant that there was a need for exotics for their use as status symbols of the chiefs. This created a congenial atmosphere for external trade. According to Wheatley,[318] once contact was established between the Indian merchants and the coastal/ estuary chiefdoms, the latter were also in favour of its expansion, since they profited from this trade. Moreover, ambitions acquired as a result of association with foreign traders could not be accommodated within the indigenous social and ideological framework, hence arises the development of political authority structured around the divine kingship roughly modelled on Indian patterns.[319]

Item of Trade

In the westerly trade of South-east Asia, the evidence for export is less tangible than that for import. High-tin bronze artefacts, characteristic of Iron Age Thai metallurgy, are the most tangible export item from South-east Asia. These were found at Taxila in modern Pakistan and Adichanallur in South India.[320] In India high-tin was also the characteristic of the Magha coins of Kausambi (17-20%), the Pancala coins of Ahichchhatra (20%), the potin coins of the Satavahanas (23%)[321] and of the bronzes found at Maula Ali in Andhra Pradesh, in the Nilgiris and at Adichanallur in Tamil Nadu (about 23%).[322] Moreover, there are clusters of sites in peninsular Malaysia in the metal rich regions—for example in the west coast states of Perak and Selangor which are famous for tin mines—and along the Upper Pahang-Tembeling river valley in the mountainous interior which produced most of the gold of the peninsula.[323]

However, the most important items were possibly the forest products—like aromatics and wood—which seldom survived. It has been argued that it was the spice trade,[324] which was partially responsible for the Indianization of South-east Asia.[325] The trade in cloves and pepper was particularly important. Cloves are the unopened flower buds of the tree *Eugenia aromatica,* kuntze whose home was restricted to the islands of Ternate, Tidore, Motir, Makyan and Bachan in the Moluccas.[326] India transhipped spices from South-east Asia to the Eastern Mediterranean. These were used for medicinal and preservative purposes there. It is also suggested that cinnamon and cassia were obtained from mainland South-east Asia or Southern China[327] and that sandalwood, sent from Bhrauch might have come from the dry regions of Eastern Indonesia.[328]

The items of import to South-east Asia include glass beads, semi-precious stone beads— especially etched agate and etched carnelian—rouletted ware, ivory combs, Roman coins and medallions, Roman lamps and seals with small inscriptions, and possibly textiles, handicrafts and iron.

Phases of Indo–South-east Asian Trade

The Indo–South-east Asian trade during the period *c.* 400 BC – AD 500 may be divided into three phases. During Phase I (*c.* 400–*c.* 50 BC), organized maritime contacts developed between the two regions. However, it was during Phase II (*c.* 50 BC – AD 300) that it was most extensive, because it was during that period that the stability of the Roman Empire increased the demand for oriental exotics and spices. Moreover, the demand for Western goods by the Han dynasty, the Later Han dynasty and the Wu kingdom also contributed to the intensification of this trade. In South-east Asia during this period, apart from the consolidation of chiefdoms, nascent states developed in some regions. In both these cases, exotics probably played a role in legitimating political authority. In the third phase (*c.* AD 300-500), the Roman Empire was in decline and so also was Indo-Roman trade, implying less demand for spices and other exotics. However, trade between India and South-east Asia continued, which is known from the growing number of inscriptions influenced by Indian script and style, even in some remote regions of South-east Asia. In the absence of adequate data, the quantum of trade involved in different phases cannot be determined precisely.

Trade Routes

Coedes talked of two main maritime routes from India to South-east Asia.[329] The first was from South India either through the 10-degree channel between Andaman and Nicobar or, farther south, the channel between Nicobar and the headland of Aceh (Fig. 8). The former would lead to the peninsula near Takuapa in Thailand and the latter to near Kedah in Malaysia. Then one could go from Kedah to Singora on the east coast of Thailand; from Trang to Patalung in the same direction; also to Ligor or Nakhon Si Thammarat or to Bandon, both on the Gulf of Thailand, or from Kra to Chumphon and especially from Takuapa to Chaiya. The second route was for travellers coming from Central India who sailed along the coast to Martaban, Moulmein or Tavoy in Burma, then continued on foot through the mountains and over the Three Pagoda and other passes, descending to the Menam Chao Pya delta by way of Kanchanaburi and Ratchaburi.

Conclusion

The above survey shows that the maritime trade between India and South-east Asia can be

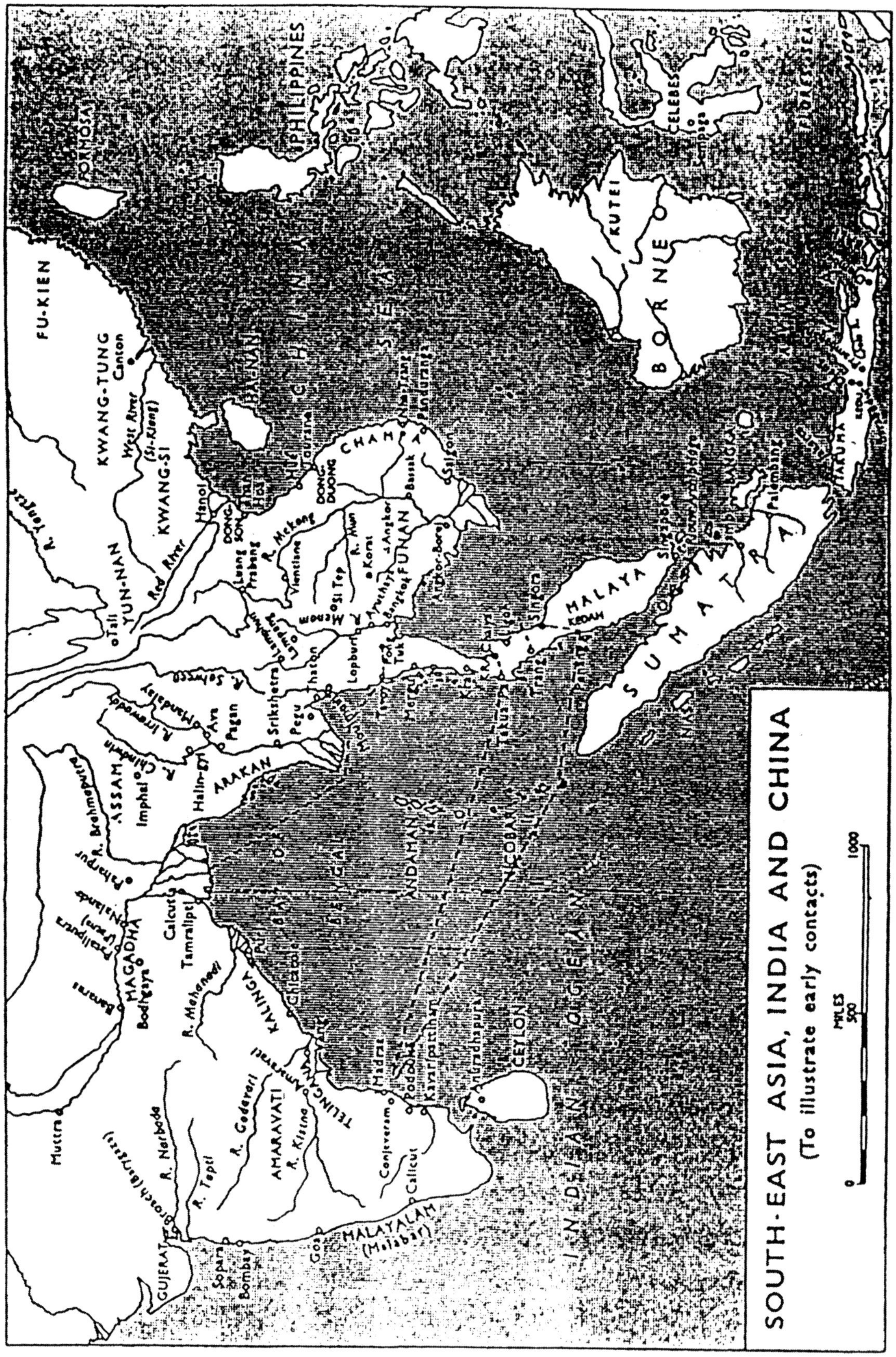

Fig. 8. Trade routes between India and Mainland Southest Asia (after Hall 1964)

traced back to the fourth century BC and was on a considerable scale in the early centuries of the Christian era. On the basis of a study of various sources, it can be said that this trade was not a mere trickling, nor was it as Wheeler thought, a mere drift,[330] rather it continued in an integrated and organised manner. With the emergence of the Roman Empire in the West and the Han Empire in the north, its geographical spectrum extended further to the Eastern Mediterranean in the West and China in the north. From a world system perspective, such trade in South-east Asia operated at three levels—pan-regional, regional and local.[331] At a pan-regional level, between India as the centre (or multiple centres) and South-east Asia as the periphery (or multiple peripheries), the relationship from the world system perspective was primarily economic, partly ideological and cosmological, but hardly political. On the other hand in the case of Han Chinese conquest of North Vietnam, such relationship between the Chinese centre and South-east Asian periphery was more political than economic. Besides, the relationship between the Eastern Mediterranean centre and South-east Asian periphery was primarily economic. Moreover, while the relationship of South-east Asian periphery was direct with the centres of India and China, it was primarily indirect in relation to that of the Eastern Mediterranean. At a regional level in South-east Asia, the relationship between the coast and interior was more economic than political, ideological and cosmological. At a local level in South-east Asia, in the case of the chief and the members of the group, the centre, periphery relation involved primarily a political domination which was ideologically legitimated by Buddhist and Hindu cosmology. Thus the tribal chief derived his *power from* having access to objects of conspicuous display and status symbols (such as exotics from outside). This helped in having *power over* persons and attributes through manipulating the circulation of things.[332] It may be argued that glass beads and semi-precious stone beads were inalienable wealth, which means in the words of Weiner, "keeping while giving."[333] The fact that such beads were imported from outside, and hence exotic, added to their value. So it might not be impossible that the chief used to distribute them among group members as markers of inalienable rank. This enabled the chief to have control over persons, along with the benefit of a return in terms of alienable surplus product from those of low rank. Thus in the centre–periphery relationship between the chief and members of his group, economy, ideology and cosmology were embedded in what was primarily a political domination. It is important to point out here that while the Indian nationalist historians considered South-east Asian cultural splendour as a replica of India, the application of centre–periphery model does not reduce the South-east Asian periphery to a passive ploy in the hands of the Indian centre because of difficulties in communication system (like hazards of journey, such as shipwreck, piracy, weather calamities, dependance on monsoon etc.) between India and South-east Asia as well as the availability of more than one option to the coastal people of South-east Asia enabling them to change partners if the rate of exchange was not advantageous to them. Moreover, in South-east Asia, Indian ideas and artefacts underwent a process, not of Indianisation, but of 'localisation' which Wolters defined as a process by which 'Indian material tended to be fractured and restated and therefore drained of its original significance."[334] It is a process through which foreign materials retreat into local statements.[335] Hence the South-east Asian periphery in antiquity was not a passive recipient, rather an active agent of social process.

NOTES AND REFERENCES

1. I.C. Glover, "Ban Don Ta Phet: The 1984-85 excavation," in I. Glover and E. Glover (eds.), *South-east Asian Archaeology 1986* (Oxford, 1990), pp. 154-55.
2. I.C. Glover, *Early Trade Between India and South-east Asia—A Link in the Development of a World Trading System* (University of Hull, 1989); H.P. Ray, "Early maritime contacts between South and South-east Asia," *Journal of South-east Asian Studies* (henceforward *JSEAS*), 20(1) (1989), pp. 42-54; *Winds of Change: Buddhism and the Maritime Links of Early South Asia* (New Delhi, 1994), Chapter 4; K.K. Basa, *The Westerly Trade of South-east Asia from c. 400 BC to c.AD 500 with Special Reference to Glass Beads* (Ph.D. Thesis, University of London, 1991).
3. M.G. Dikshit, *History of Indian Glass* (University of Bombay, 1969); P. Francis, *The Glass Beads of India* (New York, 1982a); S.N. Sen and M.C. Choudhuri, *Ancient Glass and India* (New Delhi, 1985); R.N. Singh, *Ancient Indian Glass: Archaeology & Technology* (Delhi, 1989); K.K. Basa, "Early Glass Beads in India," *South Asian Studies,* 8(1992), pp. 91-104.
4. I.C. Glover, *op. cit.* (1989).
5. P. Francis, "Glass beads in Asia, Part I, Introduction," *Asian Perspectives,* 28(1) (1990), p.2.
6. A. Lamb, "A note on glass beads from the Malay Peninsula," *Journal of Glass Studies,* 8(1966), p. 94.
7. H.C. Bhardwaj, *Aspects of Ancient Indian Technology* (Delhi, 1979), p. 44.
8. M.G. Dikshit, *op. cit.* (1969), p. 5.
9. For a distribution, see K.K. Basa, *op. cit.* (1992).
10. R.E.M. Wheeler, A. Ghosh and K. Deva, "Arikamedu: An Indo-Roman Trading station on the east coast of India", *Ancient India,* 2(1946), pp. 17-124; V. Begley, "Arikamedu reconsidered", *American Journal of Archaeology,* 87(1983), pp. 461-81.
11. P. Francis, "Bead Report VII: When India was bead maker to World," *Ornament,* 6(2) (1982b), pp. 33-34, 56-57; "Some observations on the glass beads of Arikamedu," *Revue Historique du Pondicherry,* 30(1982c), pp. 156-61; "Bead making at Arikamedu and beyond," *World Archaeology,* 23(1)(1991), pp. 28-43; E.M. Stern, "On the glass industry of Arikamedu (Ancient Podouke)," in *Archaeometry of Glass,* ed. H.C. Bhardwaj (Calcutta, 1987), pp. 26-36.
12. B. Bronson, "Glass and beads at Khuan Lukpad, Southern Thailand," in I. Glover and E. Glover eds., *op. cit.* (1990), pp. 213-29.
13. Nik Hassan Shuhaimi bin Nik Abdul Rahman, "Recent research at Kuala Selinsing, Perak," *Bulletin of the Indo-Pacific Prehistory Association* (henceforward *BIPPA*), 11(1991), p. 148.
14. R. Indraningsih, "Research on prehistoric beads in Indonesia," *BIPPA,* 6(1985), p. 138.
15. Ha Van Tan, "Oc Eo: Endogenous and exogenous elements," *Vietnam Social Sciences,* 1-2(7-8)(1986), p. 93.
16. L. Malleret, *L'Archaeologie du Delta du Mekong, III* (Paris, 1962), p. 155.
17. H.C. Beck, *Beads from Taxila* (New Delhi, 1941), p. 27.
18. A. Ghosh, "Taxila (Sirkap) 1944-45," *Ancient India,* 4(1948), p. 75 and his Plate X; No. 21.
19. H.C. Beck, *op. cit.* (1941), p. 27.
20. I.C. Glover, *op. cit.* (1989), p. 21.
21. P. Francis, *op. cit.* (1991).
22. H.C. Beck, *op. cit.* (1941), p. 27 and his Plate IX: No.3.
23. *Ibid.,* p. 27.
24. A. Ghosh, *op. cit.* (1948), p. 75, his Plate X: No. 19.
25. V. Begley, *op. cit.* (1983).
26. I.C. Glover, *op. cit.* (1990).
27. B. Fishman and B. Lawn, "University of Pennsylvania radiocarbon dates XX," *Radiocarbon,* 20(2)(1978), p. 227.
28. H.R. Van Heekeren, *The Bronze–Iron Age of Indonesia* (S-Gravenhage, 1958), Plate 13, the 3rd string.
29. I.C. Glover, *op. cit.* (1989), Figure 11.

30. H.C. Beck, *op. cit.* (1941), Plate 1, No. 22.
31. L. Malleret, *op. cit.* (1962), p. 250.
32. K.K. Basa, I. Glover and J. Henderson, "The relationship between early South-east Asian and Indian glass', *BIPPA*, 10(1991), pp. 366-85. For a recent comprehensive work on early glass in Asia, see I. Glover and J. Henderson, "Early glass in South and South-east Asia and China," in R. Scott and J. Guy (eds.), *South-east Asia and China: Art, Interaction and Commerce* (London, 1945), pp. 141-70.
33. R.H. Brill, "Chemical analyses of some early Indian glasses," in H.C. Bhardwaj (ed.), *op. cit.* (1987), p. 4.
34. H.C. Bhardwaj, "A review of archaeometric studies of Indian glasses," in H.C. Bhardwaj (Ed.), *op. cit.* (1987), p. 68.
35. Gan Fuxi, ed., *Investigation of Ancient Chinese Glass—Collected papers of the 1984 Beijing International Symposium on Glass* (in Chinese) (Beijing, 1986); Shi Meiguang, He Ouli and Zhou Fuzheng, "Investigation on some Chinese potash glasses excavated in Han dynasty tombs," in H.C. Bhardwaj (ed.), *op. cit.* (1987), pp. 15-20; Zhang Fukeng, "Origin and development of early Chinese glasses," in *ibid.*, pp. 25-28.
36. This is an example as to how correlation can be established between sites or the commodities traded between them, although H.P. Ray (*op. cit.* 1994, p. 95) is sceptical about it.
37. I.C. Glover, *op. cit.* (1989), p. 21.
38. P.S. Bellwood, "Archaeological research in Minahasa and the Talaud islands, Northeastern Indonesia," *Asian Perspectives* (henceforward *AP*), 19(2)(1976), p. 276.
39. *Ibid.*, p. 277.
40. A. Lamb, "Some observations on stone and glass beads in early South-east Asia," *Journal of the Malaysian Branch of the Royal Asiatic Society* (henceforward *JMBRAS*), 38(2)(1965), p. 92.
41. *Ibid.*, p. 92.
42. I.C. Glover, "Archaeological survey in West-central Thailand: A second report on the 1982-1983 field season," *AP*, 25(1)(1982-83), p. 89.
43. Mayuree Veraprasert, "Klong Thom-An ancient bead manufacturing location and an ancient entrepot," in *SPAFA Final Report: Seminar in prehistory in South-east Asia (T-WII)*, Thailand, January, 1987, Appendix 7i, p. 327.
44. A. Lamb, *op. cit.* (1965), p. 92.
45. For a review, see B. Allchin, "The agate and carnelian industry of Western India and Pakistan", in *South Asian Archaeology, 1975*, ed. J.E. Van Lohuizen-de Leeuw (Leiden, 1979), pp. 91-105; P. Francis, *Indian Agate Beads* (New York, 1982d).
46. I.C. Glover, *op. cit.* (1989), p. 21.
47. A.J. Gwinnett and L. Gorelick, "Experimental evidence for the use of a diamond drill in Śri Lankā Ca. A.D. 700-1000", *Archeomaterials*, 1(2)(1987), pp. 149-52; G. Possehl, "Cambay bead making: An ancient craft in modern India", *Expedition*, 23(4)(1981), pp. 39-46.
48. A. Lamb, *op. cit.* (1965), p. 122.
49. E. Mackay, "Decorated Carnelian beads", *Man* (September, 1933), pp. 143-46.
50. *Ibid.*
51. H.C. Beck, "Etched carnelian beads", *Antiquaries Journal*, 13 (1933), pp. 384-98.
52. L. Williams, A New Approach to the Study of Bead-making Workshop Practices, with Special Reference to Carnelian and Agate Beads from Ban Don Ta Phet, Thailand, B.A. Report (Unpublished), Univ. of London.
53. H.C. Beck, *op. cit.* (1933), p. 395.
54. J. Reade, *Early Etched Beads and the Indus-Mesopotamian Trade* (British Museum Occasional Paper No.2, 1979).
55. I.C. Glover, *op. cit.* (1989), p. 24.
56. *Ibid.*, pp. 25-27.
57. U. Aung Thaw, *Report on the Excavations at Beikthano* (Rangoon, 1968), Fig.76.

58. I.H.N. Evans, "On ancient remains from Kuala Selinsing, Perak", *Journal of the Federated Malay State Museums,* 12(5)(1928a), p. 123; "Further notes on remains from Kuala Selinsing, Perak", *ibid.,* 12(5)(1928b), p. 139.
59. P.S. Bellwood, *op. cit.* (1976), p. 277.
60. R.B. Fox, *The Tabon Caves* (Manila, 1970), Colour Plate Ia.
61. Zuo Ming, "Etched carnelian beads found in China", *Kaogu* (6)(1974), pp. 382-85.
62. Zhang Zhenqui, "An analysis of the bronze culture in the area of Dian Chi Lake, Yunnan Province", *Southern Ethnology and Archaeology* 1(1987), p. 110.
63. I.C. Glover, Pisit Charoenwongsa, B.A.R. Alvey and Kamnounket Nawarat, "The cemetery of Ban Don Ta Phet, Thailand: Results from the 1980-81 excavation season", in B. Allchin (ed.), *South Asian Archaeology 1981* (Cambridge, 1984), Fig.46.
64. See S.J. Hassan, "The distribution and types of beads in the Gangetic Valley", *Puratattva,* 11(1979-80), p. 133.
65. H.C. Beck, *op. cit.* (1933).
66. E. Mackay, *op. cit.* (1933).
67. M.G. Dikshit, *Etched Beads in India* (Poona, 1949).
68. I.C. Glover, *op. cit.* (1989), pp. 27-28.
69. I.H.N. Evans, *op. cit.* (1928a, 1928b).
70. I.C. Glover, *op. cit.* (1989), p. 27.
71. *Ibid.*
72. *Ibid.,* p. 25.
73. M.G. Dikshit, *op. cit.* (1949), p. 14 and see his Plate IV.
74. I.C. Glover, *op. cit.* (1989), pp. 42-47.
75. J.W. Breeks, *An Account of the Primitive Tribes and Monuments of the Nilgiris* (London, 1873).
76. Sir J. Marshall, *A Guide to Taxila* (Karachi, 1960), Plate VII.
77. I.C. Glover, *op. cit.* (1989), p. 45 and his figure 31.
78. B.B. Lal, "Sisupalagarh 1948: An early historical fort in eastern India", *Ancient India,* 5(1949), p. 89.
79. I.C. Glover, *op. cit.* (1989), p. 47.
80. *Ibid.,* p. 31; Warangkana Rajpitak, *The Development of Copper Alloy Metallurgy in Thailand in the Pre-Buddhist Period with Special Reference to High-Tin Bronze* (Ph.D. Thesis, University of London, 1983); W. Rajpitak and M.J. Seeley, "The bronze bowls from Ban Don Ta Phet: An enigma of prehistoric metallurgy", *World Archaeology,* 11(1)(1979), pp. 26-31.
81. W. Rajpitak, *op. cit.* (1983), pp. 131-39.
82. N.J. Seeley and W. Rajpitak, "The Bronze technology", in *Prehistoric Investigations in Northeast Thailand,* C.F. Higham and Amphan Kijngam (Oxford, 1984), p. 107.
83. P. Sorenson, "Prehistoric iron implements from Thailand", *AP* 16(1973), Figure 22.
84. Krit Luamai, *2000 years old bronze bowls from Ratburi Khan Chong* (in Thai) (Bangkok, 1986).
85. B.C. Batchelor, "Post 'Hoabinhian' coastal settlement indicated by finds in stanniferous Langat river alluvium near Dengkil, Selangor, Peninsular Malaya", *Federation Museums Journal* (n.s.), 2(1978), pp. 1-55.
86. Also see I.H.N. Evans, "On slab built graves in Perak", *Journal of the Federated Malay State Museums,* 12(5)(1928c), p. 119.
87. W. Rajpitak and N.J. Selley, *op. cit.* (1979), p. 29.
88. Also see A. Rea, *Catalogue of Prehistoric Antiquites from Adichanallur and Perumbair* (Madras, 1915).
89. Also see J.W. Breeks, *op. cit.* (1873).
90. Sir J. Marshall, *Taxila* (Cambridge, 1951), p. 107.
91. W. Rajpitak and N.J. Seeley, *op. cit.* (1979), p. 28.
92. Also see I.C. Glover, *op. cit.* (1989), pp. 31 and 42.
93. V. Begley, "Rouletting and Chattering: Decoration on ancient and present day pottery in India", *Expedition,* 28(1)(1986), p. 47.
94. R.E.M. Wheeler *et al, op. cit.* (1946), p. 48.

95. *Ibid.*, p. 46.
96. V. Begley, *op. cit.* (1986), p. 49.
97. *Ibid.*
98. M. Walker and S. Santoso, "Romano-Indian rouletted pottery in Indonesia," *AP* 20 (2) (1977), pp. 228-35.
99. I.W. Ardika and P. Bellwood, "Sembiran—The beginnings of Indian Contact with Bali," *Antiquity*, 65(247) (1991), pp. 221-32.
100. I.W. Ardika, P. Bellwood, R.A. Eggleton and D.J. Ellis, "A single source for South Asian export quality rouletted ware," *Man and Environment*, 18(1)(1993), pp. 101-9.
101. A.K.Singh, "Pottery and trade—A study of Roman pottery from Indian sites," *Journal of the Bihar Research Society*, 53-54 (1977-78), pp. 140-74.
102. I.C. Glover, *op. cit.* (1989), p. 28.
103. Sir J. Marshall, *op. cit.* (1951), Vol. III and his Plate 49b.
104. H.H. Wilson, *Ariana Antiqua: A Descriptive Account of the Antiquities and Coins of Afghanistan, with a Memoir of the Buildings called Topes by C. Masson* (London, 1841), Plates 1 and 6.
105. I.C. Glover, *op. cit.* (1989), p. 31.
106. B. Bronson and G.F. Dales, "Excavation at Chansen, Thailand, 1968 and 1969: A preliminary report", *AP*, 15(1972), pp. 28-30 and their Figure 7.
107. Thanongsak Honwong, *Artefact Analysis from the Excavation at Ban Tha Kae, Amphor Muang, Changwat, Lopburi* (in Thai), M.A. Dissertation, Silpakorn University (1985).
108. H.P. Ray, *op. cit.* (1989), p. 52.
109. B. Bronson, "The late prehistory and early history of Central Thailand with special reference to Chansen," in R.B. Smith and W. Watson (eds.), *Early South-east Asia* (Oxford, 1979), p. 324.
110. U. Aung Thaw, *op. cit.* (1968), p. 61.
111. T. Hanwong, *op. cit.* (1985).
112. *Indian Archaeology—A Review*, 1978-79, p. 39.
113. R.P. Mohapatra, *Undayagiri and Khandagiri Caves* (New Delhi, 1981), p. 148.
114. K. Krishna Murthy, *Nagarjunakonda: A Cultural Study* (Delhi, 1977), p. 63.
115. R.P. Soejono, "The Significance of excavations at Gilimanuk (Bali)," in Smith & Watson (eds.), *op. cit.* (1979), p. 193.
116. S.J. O.'Connor and T. Harrisson, "Gold-foil burial amulets in Bali, Philippines and Borneo," *JMBRAS*, 44 (Part 1) (1971), p. 76.
117. G. Coedes, "The excavations at Pong Tuk and their importance for the early history of Siam," *The Journal of the Siam Society*, 21(1928), pp. 195-209.
118. T. Hanowong, *op. cit.* (1985).
119. R.L. Brown and A.M. Macdonnel, "The Pong Tuk lamp: A reconsideration", *The Journal of the Siam Society*, 77(2) (1989), pp. 9-20.
120. H.P. Ray, "In search of Suvarnabhumi: Early sailing networks in the Bay of Bengal," *BIPPA*, 10(1991), pp. 357-65.
121. G. Coedes, *op. cit.* (1968), Chapter 1; R.C. Mazumdar, *Ancient Indian Colonies in the Far East*, Vol II. *Suvarnadvipa Part I-Political History* (Dacca, 1937); *Part II-Cultural History* (Calcutta, 1938); *Ancient Indian Colonisation in the South-east Asia* (Baroda, 1955); K.S. Sandhu, *Early Malaysia* (Singapore, 1973), pp. 1-11; H.B. Sarkar, "A geographical introduction to South-east Asia: The Indian perspective," *Bijdragen Tot de Taal—Land-En Volkenkunde*, (henceforward *BTTLEV*) deel 137(1981), pp. 293-323; *Cultural Relations Between India and South-east Asian Countries* (New Delhi, 1985), Chapter 1; *Trade and Commercial Activities of Southern India in the Malayo-Indonesian World (up to AD 1511), Vol I* (Calcutta, 1986), Chapter I; P. Wheatley, *The Golden Khersonese* (Kuala Lumpur, 1961), Chapter 11; *Impressions of the Malay Peninsula in Ancient Times* (Singapore, 1964), Chapter 3; *Nagara and Commandary* (Chicago, 1983), pp. 261-73.
122. R.P. Kangle, *The Kautilya Arthasastra*, Vol II (Bombay, 1963), p. 117.
123. H.P. Shastri, *The Ramayana of Valmiki*, Vol II (London, 1957), pp. 272-74.
124. A.M. Tabard, *Essays on Gunadhyaya and the Brihatkatha* (Bangalore, 1923), p. 131.

125. C.H. Tawney, *The Ocean of Story,* Vol. IV (London, 1925), p. 191.
126. *Ibid.,* p. 190.
127. *Ibid.,* Vol. V (London, 1926a), p. 6.
128. *Ibid.,* Vol. VI (London, 1926b), pp. 15-16.
129. *Ibid.,* Vol. IV (1925), pp. 220-51.
130. C.H. Tawney, *Kothakoca or The Treasury of Stories* (London, 1895), pp. 28-30.
131. S. Levi in P. Wheatley, *op. cit.* (1983), p. 266.
132. J.S. Speyer, *The Gatakamala* (London, 1895), p. 125.
133. Rhys Davids, *The Question of King Milinda* (Oxford, 1894), p. 269.
134. P. Wheatley, *op. cit.* (1961), p. 181.
135. E.B. Cowell and R.A. Neil, *The Divyavadana* (Cambridge, 1886), p. 107.
136. E.B. Cowell (ed.), *The Jataka or Stories of the Buddha's Former Births,* Vol. 6 (Cambridge, 1907), pp. 19-37.
137. *Ibid.,* Vol. 4, (1901), pp. 9-13.
138. *Ibid.,* Vol. 3 (1897), pp. 124-25; *ibid.,* Vol. 4 (1901), pp. 86-90.
139. G.P. Malalasekera, *Dictionary of Pali Proper Names* (London, 1938), pp. 1262-63.
140. Aggamahapandita Buddhadatta Thera (ed.), *Sihalavatthuppakarana* (Colombo, 1958), pp. 91, 107; also see S. Paranavitana, *Ceylon and Malaysia* (Colombo, 1966) pp. 3-5.
141. S. Paranavitana, *ibid.* (1966), pp. 5-6.
142. P. Wheatley, *op. cit.* (1983), p. 266.
143. M. Bode, (ed.), *Sasanavamsa* (London, 1897), pp. 2-8.
144. H. Oldenberg (ed.), *Dipavamsa* (London, 1879), pp. 53-54, 174-75.
145. W. Geiger, *The Dipavamsa and Mahavamsa and Their Historical Development in Ceylon* (Colombo, 1908), p. 115.
146. Maung Htin Aung, *A History of Burma* (New York, 1967), p. 5.
147. J. Boisselier, *Nouvelles connaissances archaeologiques de la ville d'U-Thong* (Bangkok, 1968), p. 26.
148. M.C. Chand Chirayu Rajani, "Background to the Srivijaya story-Part II," *The Journal of the Siam Society,* 62(Part II) (1974), p. 304.
149. P. Wheatley, *op. cit.* (1983), p. 267.
150. H.P. Shastri, *op. cit.* (1957), pp. 272-74.
151. P. Wheatley, *op. cit.* (1983), p. 335, Note 45.
152. O.C. Gangoly, "Relation between Indian and Indonesian culture," *The Journal of the Greater India Society* (henceforward *JGIS*), 7(1940), pp. 57-60.
153. Sylvian Levi, "Kouen Louen et Dvipantara," *BTTLEV,* 88(1931), pp. 621-27.
154. C.H. Tawney, *The Ocean of Story,* Vol. IX (London, 1927), p. 35.
155. O.C. Gangoly, *op. cit.* (1940), pp. 58-60.
156. K.A. Nilakanta Sastri, "Dvipantara," *JGIS*, 9(1)(1942), pp. 3-4.
157. S. Rangachariar and V.S. Aiyar (eds.), *Raghuvamsa* (Tanjore, 1891), pp. 39, 56-57; K.A. Nilakanta Sastri, *op. cit.* (1942), p. 3.
158. P. Wheatley, *op. cit.* (1983), p. 267.
159. *Ibid.,* p. 268.
160. *Ibid.,* p. 268.
161. K.A. Nilakanta Sastri, *The Colas* (Madras, 1955), p. 83; H.B. Sarkar, *op. cit.* (1985), pp. 249-50.
162. K.A. Nilakanta Sastri, "The Tamil land and the eastern colonies", *JGIS,* 11(1944), p. 26.
163. *Ibid.,* p. 26.
164. *Ibid.*
165. P. Wheatley, *op. cit.* (1961), pp. 182-83.
166. For a review, see Wang Gungwu, "The Nanhai trade: A study of the early history of Chinese trade in the South China Sea," *JMBRAS,* 31 (Part II)(1958); H.B. Sarkar, *op. cit.* (1985), pp. 13-21; P. Wheatley, *op. cit.* (1961), Chapters 1 & 2; O.W. Wolters, *Early Indonesian Commerce* (London, 1967).
167. P. Wheatley, *op. cit.* (1961), p. 8.

168. *Ibid.*, p. 10.
169. For a summary of different views, see P. Wheatley, "Possible references to the Malay Peninsula in the annals of the Former Han," *JMBRAS,* 30 (Part I)(1957), pp. 116-17.
170. Wang Gungwu, *op. cit.* (1958), p. 21.
171. P. Wheatley, *op. cit.* (1961), p. 11.
172. *Ibid.*, pp. 11-12.
173. See Wang Gungwu, *op. cit.* (1958), p. 24.
174. *ibid.*, pp. 27-28.
175. *Ibid.*, p. 28.
176. Also see *ibid.*, pp. 28-29; O.W. Wolters, *op. cit.* (1967), p. 42.
177. Wang Gungwu, *op. cit.* (1958), p. 29.
178. *Ibid.*, p. 23.
179. O.W. Wolters, *op. cit.* (1967), p. 39.
180. *Ibid.*, p. 42.
181. P. Wheatley, *op. cit.* (1961), p. 8.
182. O.W. Wolters, *op. cit.* (1967), p. 42.
183. Also see *ibid.*, pp. 42-43.
184. *Ibid.*
185. *Ibid.*, p. 43.
186. Wang Gungwu, *op. cit.* (1958), p. 33.
187. O.W. Wolters, *op. cit.* (1967), p. 43.
188. *Ibid.*
189. *Ibid.*
190. *Ibid.*, p. 44; P. Wheatley, *op. cit.* (1961), p. 16.
191. H.B. Sarkar, *op. cit.* (1985), p. 250; O.W. Wolters, *op. cit.* (1967), p. 45.
192. Quoted in Wolters, *ibid.*, p. 44.
193. Also see H.B. Sarkar, *op. cit.* (1985), p. 250.
194. In Wang Gungwu, *op. cit.* (1958), p. 40.
195. Also see O.W. Wolters, *op. cit.* (1967), p. 47.
196. P. Wheatley, *op. cit.* p. 24.
197. H.B. Sarkar, *op. cit.* (1985), pp. 250-51.
198. Wang Gungwu, *op. cit.* (1958), p. 40.
199. *Ibid.*
200. O.W. Wolters, *op. cit.* (1967), p. 59.
201. *Ibid.*, p. 57.
202. *Ibid.*, p. 81; Wang Gungwu, *op. cit.* (1958), p. 37.
203. L. Petech, "Some Chinese texts concerning Ceylon," *the Ceylon Historical Journal,* 3&4 (1954), pp. 217-27.
204. O.W. Wolters, *op. cit.* (1967), p. 80.
205. For his account, see H. Giles, *The Travels of Fa-hsien* (Cambridge, 1923), pp. 65-83.
206. O.W. Wolters, *op. cit.* (1967), p. 35.
207. Wang Gungwu, *op. cit.* (1958), p. 43.
208. O.W. Wolters, *op. cit.* (1967), pp. 35-36.
209. Wang Gungwu, *op. cit.* (1958), p. 50.
210. Also see *ibid.*, p. 58.
211. O.W. Wolters, *op. cit.* (1967), pp. 82-83.
212. For a general discussion on these sources, see D.G.E. Hall, *A History of South-east Asia* (London, 1964), pp. 14-15; R.C. Majumdar, *op. cit.* (1937), pp. 4-7; P. Wheatley, *op. cit.* (1961), Chapters IX and X; *op. cit.* (1983), Appendix.
213. See the quotation in P. Wheatley, *op. cit.* (1961), p. 129.
214. Quoted in *ibid.*
215. *Ibid.*

216. *Ibid.*, p. 130.
217. W.H. Schoff, *The Periplus of the Erythraean Sea* (London, 1912), p. 46.
218. *Ibid.*, p. 47.
219. L. Bagrow, "The origin of Ptolemy's Geographia," *Geografiska Annaler Arg.27,* Haft 3-4(1945), pp. 318-87.
220. P. Wheatley, *op. cit.* (1961), p. 138; *op. cit.* (1983), pp. 441-42.
221. Quoted in P. Wheatley, *op. cit.* (1961), p. 40.
222. For details see P. Wheatley, *ibid.*, pp. 141-44; *op. cit.* (1983), pp. 439-40.
223. P. Wheatley, *op. cit.* (1961), p. 14.
224. *Ibid.*, pp. 145-46.
225. W.J. Van der Meulen, "Suvarnadvipa and Chryse Chersonesos," *Indonesia,* 18(1974), p. 13.
226. For a detailed discussion of these toponyms, see Col. G.E. Gerini, *Researches on Ptolemy's Geography of Eastern Asia* (London, 1909); W.J. Van der Meulen, *op. cit.* (1974); "Ptolemy's Geography of Mainland South-east Asia and Borneo," *Indonesia* 19(1975), pp. 1-32; P. Wheatley, *op. cit.* (1961), pp. 147-59; *op. cit.* (1983), Appendix.
227. W.J. Van der Meulen, *op. cit.* (1974), p. 5.
228. *Ibid.*, pp. 16-22.
229. P. Wheatley, *op. cit.* (1983), pp. 451-53.
230. P. Wheatley, *op. cit.* (1961), pp. 131-36.
231. *Ibid.*, p. 132.
232. Quoted in *ibid.*, p. 134.
233. *Ibid.*
234. Quoted in *ibid.*, p. 135.
235. *Ibid.*, p. 135.
236. U. Aung Thaw, *op. cit.* (1968), pp. 28, 50.
237. Kongkaew Veeraprajak, "Inscriptions from South Thailand," *SPAFA Digest,* 7(1)(1986), pp. 7-8.
238. L. Malleret, *op. cit.* (1962), pp. 290-92.
239. *Ibid.*, pp. 109-10.
240. *Ibid.*, p. 115.
241. R.C. Majumdar, *op. cit.* (1937), pp. 82-83, 89-90.
242. S.R. Das, *Rajbadidanga: 1962* (Calcutta, 1968).
243. P. Wheatley, *op. cit.* (1961), p. 274.
244. For details, see J. Filliozat, "L'Inscriptions dite de Vo-Canh," *Bulltein de l'Ecole Francaise d'Extreme-Orient,* Tome 15(1969), pp. 107-16.
245. J.C. De Casparis, "Palaeography as an auxiliary discipline in research on Early South-east Asia," in Smith and Watson (eds.), *op. cit.* (1979), p. 382.
246. R.C. Majumdar, *op. cit.* (1937), pp. 105-10.
247. J.G. De Casparis, *op. cit.* (1979), p. 383.
248. *Ibid.*, pp. 383-87.
249. L. Malleret, *op. cit.* (1962), p. 115.
250. C. Landes, "Piece d'epoque romaine trouvee a U-Thong, Thailande," *Journal of Silpakorn*, 26(1)(1982), pp. 113-15.
251. K.A. Nilakanta Sastri, "The beginning of the intercourse between India and China," *Indian Historical Quarterly,* 15(1938), pp. 380-87.
252. G.L. Adhya, *Early Indian Economics* (London, 1966), p. 386.
253. M. Mitchiner, *Oriental Coins and Their Values,* Vol. III (London, 1979), p. 316.
254. M. Mitchiner, "The date of early Arakanese, Pyu and Mon Coinages," *Seaby Coin and Medal Bulletin* (1981), pp. 128-29.
255. M. Mitchiner, *Oriental Coins and their Values,* Vol. II (London, 1978), pp. 656-57.
256. M. Mitchiner, *op. cit.* (1979), p. 318.
257. *Ibid.*, pp. 322-23.

258. *Ibid.*, pp. 323-25; *op. cit.* (1978), pp. 649, 651.
259. M. Mitchiner, "Three hoards of 'symbolic' coins from South-east Asia," *Coin Hoards*, 7 (1985), pp. 322-27.
260. J. Cribb, "The date of the symbolic coins from Burma and Thailand: A re-examination of the evidence," *Seaby Coin and Medal Bulletin*, 75(1981), pp. 224-26.
261. R.S. Wicks, *A Survey of Native South-east Asian Coinage Circa 450-1850* (Ph.D. Thesis, University of Cornell) (1983); also see R.S. Wicks, *Money, Markets and Trade in Early South-east Asia: The Development of Indigenous Monetary System to AD 1400* (Ithaca, New York, 1992).
262. L. Malleret, *op. cit.* (1962), p. 131.
263. J. Boisselier, *op. cit.* (1965), p. 144.
264. U. Aung Thaw, *op. cit.* (1968), p. 54.
265. R.S. Wicks, *op. cit.* (1983), pp. 60-66.
266. P. Gutman, "The ancient coinage of South-east Asia," *The Journal of the Siam Society*, 66(1)(1978), pp. 8-21.
267. L. Malleret, *op. cit.* (1962), p. 376.
268. P. Gutman, *op. cit.* (1978), p. 12.
269. *Ibid.*, pp. 13-14.
270. *Ibid.*, p. 11.
271. H.B. Sarkar, *op. cit.* (1981).
272. For details for trade routes, see Moti Chandra, *Trade and Trade Routes in Ancient India* (New Delhi, 1977), Chapter 1; N. Lahiri, *The Archaeology of Indian Trade Routes* (Delhi, 1992).
273. H.P. Ray, *Monastery and Guild* (Delhi, 1986), p. 92.
274. R.S. Sharma, *Perspectives in Social and Economic History of Early India* (New Delhi, 1983a), p. 126.
275. R. Thapar, "The evolution of state in the Ganges Valley in the mid-first millennium BC," *Studies in History*, 5(2)(1982).
276. R.S. Sharma, *op. cit.* (1983a), p. 118.
277. H.P. Ray, *op. cit.* (1986), p. 112.
278. R.E.M. Wheeler *et al*, *op. cit.* (1946), p. 27.
279. H.P. Ray, *op. cit.* (1989), p. 44.
280. R.S. Sharma, *op. cit.* (1983a), p. 118.
281. *Ibid.*, pp. 128-36.
282. R.P. Kangle, *The Kautilya Arthasastra, Part III* (Bombay, 1965), p. 177.
283. R. Thaper, *The Mauryas Revisited* (Calcutta, 1987).
284. H.P. Ray, *op. cit.* (1991).
285. Also see H.P. Ray, *op. cit.* (1986), p. 107.
286. G. Coedes, *op. cit.* (1968), pp. 20-21.
287. Also see R.S. Sharma, *Material Culture and Social Formations in Ancient India* (New Delhi, 1983b), pp. 117-34; H.P. Ray, *op. cit.* (1994).
288. R.S. Sharma, *ibid.*, pp. 124-25.
289. H.B. Sarkar, *Some Contributions of India to the Ancient Civilisations of Indonesia and Malaysia* (Calcutta, 1970), p. 6.
290. G. Coedes, *op. cit.* (1968), p. 20.
291. W. Rajpitak and N.J. Seeley, *op. cit.* (1979).
292. Wang Gungwu, *op. cit.* (1958), p. 23.
293. O.W. Wolters, *op. cit.* (1967), p. 39.
294. *Ibid.*, pp. 42-43.
295. I.C. Glover, *op. cit.* (1989), pp. 2-3.
296. C. Higham, "Exchange at Khok Phanom Di and social organisation", *BIPPA*, 10(1991), p. 322.
297. J.R. McNeill and David J. Welch, "Regional and interregional interaction on the Khorat plateau," *BIPPA*, 10(1991), pp. 327-40; also see D.J. Welch, "Late prehistoric and early historic exchange patterns in the Phimai region, Thailandm," *Journal of South-east Asian Studies*, 20(1989), pp. 11-26.
298. W. Rajpitak, *op. cit.* (1983), pp. 131-39.

299. I.H.N. Evans, *op. cit.* (1928c), p. 119; B.C. Batchelor, *op. cit.* (1978).
300. B.A.V. Peacock, "The later prehistory of the Malay Peninsula," in Smith and Watson (eds.), *op. cit.* (1979), pp. 211-12.
301. R.P. Soejono, "The significance of the excavations at Gilimanuk," (Bali) in *ibid.* (1979), p. 197.
302. W.G. Solheim II, "Philippine prehistory," in F.G. Casal *et al* (eds.), *The People and Art of Philippines* (Los Angeles, 1981), p. 47.
303. For a recent review of Dongson culture, see I. Glover and B. Syme, "The bronze age in South-east Asia," *Man and Environment,* 18(2) (1993), pp. 52-53 and for a distribution of Dongson Drums, see *ibid.,* p. 60.
304. P. Sorenson, "The Ongbah cave and its fifth drum," in *op. cit.,* eds. Smith and Watson (1979), p. 84.
305. Tarapong Srisuchat, "The early historic sites and the remains in Southern Thailand," in *SPAFA Consultative Workshop on Archaeological and Environmental Studies on Srivijaya (I-W2A), Indonesia,* (1982), Appendix 4b.
306. B.A.V. Peacock, *op. cit.* (1979), pp. 206-9.
307. P. Bellwood, *Prehistory of the Indo-Malaysian Archipelago* (Sydney, 1985), pp. 280-81.
308. Per Sorenson, *op. cit.* (1979), p. 92.
309. B.A.V. Peacock, *op. cit.* (1979), pp. 212-13.
310. J. Loewenstein, "The origin of the Malayan Metal age," *JMBRAS,* 29(2)(1956), p. 48.
311. W.G. Solheim II, *op. cit.* (1981), pp. 48-49.
312. W.G. Solheim II, "Sa Huynh related pottery in South-east Asia," *Asian Perspectives,* 3(2)(1959), pp. 177-88.
313. J.H.C.S. Davidson, "Archaeology in Southern Vietnam since 1954," in Smith and Watson (eds.), *op. cit.* (1979), p. 218.
314. H.H.E. Loofs-Wissowa, "Prehistoric and protohistoric links between the Indo-Chinese peninsula and the Philippines," *Journal of the Hongkong Archaeological Research Society,* 9(1980-81), pp. 57-76.
315. *Ibid.,* p. 62.
316. *Ibid.,* pp. 69-70.
317. I.C. Glover, *op. cit.* (1989), p. 28.
318. P. Wheatley, "Satyanrta in Suvarnadvipa: From reciprocity to redistribution in ancient South-east Asia," in J.A. Sabloff and C.C. Lamberg-Karlovsky (eds.), *Ancient Civilization and Trade* (Albuquerque, 1975), pp. 238-39.
319. *Ibid.*
320. W. Rajpitak and N. Seeley, *op. cit.* (1979).
321. Also see N.J. Seeley and P. Turner, "Metallurgical investigations of three early Indian coinages," *South Asian Archaeology 1981,* ed. B. Allchin (Cambridge, 1981), pp. 331-33.
322. H.P. Ray, *op. cit.* (1989), p. 47.
323. J. Wisseman Christie, "Port settlement to trading empire: Genesis and growth of coastal states in maritime South-east Asia," (not dated).
324. J.I. Miller, *The Spice Trade of the Roman Empire* (Oxford, 1969).
325. R.F. Ellen, "The trade in spices," *Journal of the Indonesia Circle,* 12(1977), p. 25.
326. I.H. Burkill, *A Dictionary of the Economic Products of the Malay Peninsula* (London, 1935), pp. 976-80.
327. L. Casson, *Ancient Trade and Society* (Detroit, 1984), p. 237.
328. J.I. Miller, *op. cit.* (1969), pp. 86-87.
329. G. Coedes, *op. cit.* (1968), pp. 27-28.
330. R.E.M. Wheeler, *Rome Beyond the Imperial Frontiers* (Penguin, 1954), pp. 206-7.
331. K.K. Basa, "Early Westerly trade of South-east Asia: A world system perspective," *Bulletin of the Deccan College, Post Graduate & Research Institute* 54-55 (1994-95), pp. 357-75.
332. M.J. Rowlands, "Centre and Periphery: A review of a concept," in M.J. Rowlands *et al.* (eds.) *Centre and Periphery in the Ancient World* (Cambridge, 1987), p. 7.

333. A. Weiner, "Inalienable Wealth," *American Ethnologist,* 12(2)(1985), pp. 210-27.
334. O.W. Wolters, *History, Culture and Religion in South-east Asian Perspectives* (Singapore, 1982), p. 52.
335. *Ibid.*, p. 63.

5

Indian–Indonesian Cultural Relations

HARYATI SOEBADIO

Indian influence came into Indonesia most probably as part of the general spread of Indian culture throughout the countries to the East and South-east of the Indian subcontinent, which started around the first centuries AD.[1] However, it remains uncertain when exactly this cultural migration reached Indonesia. Neither do we know what kind of people were involved in bringing it about. Various theories have been put forward, starting from ideas of large aggressive colonial migrations[2] to studies on the influence of merchants.[3] The Dutch professor Bosch[4] has discussed Indian influence and its impact in Indonesia, quoting the welknown expression of the English archaeologist Quaritch Wales, "local genius," which indicates the specific indigenous ability to absorb foreign influence in its own way. This implies that the choice was not imposed on, but was actively made by, the receiver, in affinity with his own culture. This naturally excludes any possibility of large-scale colonisation efforts based on power. Still the problem may still pose controversial features. Nonetheless, concrete evidence of the Indian cultural influence on Indonesia is indisputable, as is the process of "Indonesiation" in the course of time. In the first place we have the many historical remains that are scattered about, mainly on the islands of Java and Sumatra. But less physically obvious features existing to this day are in language, literature, dance and music and also in certain types of religious ritual and philosophical thinking. In this paper we can only touch upon some examples.

A. Evidence of the Historical Remains

The earliest archaeological data are found in two areas in Indonesia and on the basis of the script are dated from approximately the same period, fifth century BC. In Kutei, in the Province of East Kalimantan, inscriptions were found on stone sacrificial poles (yupa-s). The script is based on the Indian Pallava script[5] and the language is Sanskrit.

The prosody used is likewise Indian. We are given the names of three successive kings, one of whom, Mulavarman, held a sacrifice costing "much gold" (bahu-suvarṇaka). Brahmanas, evidently Hindu priests of the highest caste, performed the ceremony for the king. And in commemoration of this they received the royal gifts due to them, as is the custom in a Hindu sacrifice. We are thus undeniably in the atmosphere of Hinduism as it is practised in India. The style and contents of the inscriptions are in fact unmistakably Indian. Still it remains questionable, whether the brahmana-s and other types of priests mentioned and finally the king himself, were also of Indian origin. Certain features of this record pose a problem and deserve a closer view. In the first place it was found that stone sacrificial poles of this Kutei type were seldom used in India. The Dutch Professor Vogel[6] mentions only three places in India where stone sacrificial poles were found, of which two had inscriptions. Secondly, the king of the sacrifice and his father bear indeed Sanskrit names, Mulavarman and Aśvavarman respectively. But the king's grandfather is called Kundunga, which is certainly not Sanskrit and may be original Indonesian[7]. As to their sacrifice, the question we may pose is, whether it could already be seen as a type of Indonesianized Hinduism as we see at a later date in Java. But, the sources are scant and do not justify a definite answer.

The other place where remains of the fifth century are unearthed, is West Java. Two inscriptions of King Purnavarman of the Kingdom of Tarumanagara[8] are angraved below the representation of the king's feet that are likened to the god Viṣṇu's. Another inscription shows the imprint of the king's elephant. The fourth is the most interesting. It dates from the twenty-second year of the king's accession and commemorates the construction of a watercourse, also mentioning the gifts bestowed on the Brahman priested at the ceremony. As in India, the gifts consist mainly of cows, whereas Indian chronology is likewise used in dating the inscription.

But again it seems more likely to consider the king, who was able to rule twenty-two years and had the power to cause an important watercourse to be dug, as a Hinduized West Javaneses.[9] Both the Kutei and West Java inscriptions testify that the kingdoms concerned were Hindu, or, with the older term, Brahmanic of religion, not Buddhists. This is supported by records of the same period, a report by the Chinese pilgrim Fa Hsein,[10] who in *circa* 414 AD on his way home from Ceylon was forced to stay five months in Indonesia on account of bad weather. Fa Hsein mentions that Yeh-p'o-t'i[11] was a country where "the heresy of Brahmanianism" reigned supreme, adding that "whatever one perceives of Buddhism is not noteworthy."

Nevertheless, statues of Buddha, dating from the same or may be even earlier period were recovered in Sulawesi, East Java and Sumatra, corresponding to the so-called Amaravati or Gupta style.[12]

Thus it seems, that Buddhism spread throughout Indonesia approximately at the same time as Hinduism. Towards the end of seventh century we find another eyewitness account from the Chinese Buddhist I Ching[13] who wrote two works on the life of Buddhist saints and his experiences, when he was in Sumatra between 689 and 692 AD. The report of Ching is important, not the least because it testifies the Kingdom of Srivijayn capital are outside the scope of this paper.

Hinduism and Buddhist archaeological remains are, however, nowhere to be found in such a quantity as in Java. From the eighth century onwards we find both historical buildings as well as inscriptions.

One feature attracting attention is, that the inscriptions are no longer written in Sanskrit, but in Old Javanese. At the same time the script has developed closer to the Javanese form we know today. It may therefore be expected that this "Javanizing" process occurred also in the field of religion and culture in general. But in Central Java this process had not yet reached the proportions we encounter in East Javanese times.

For this Central Javanese period one Buddhist sanctuary is famous in the world as being unique. The Borobudur, which was extensively restored[14] between 1972 and 1982, and inaugurated in February 1983 by the President of Indonesia, has no equivalent in any Buddhist country, past or present. So, rightly this is a monument of national pride for Indonesians.

But we have other historical remains, both Buddhist and Hindu. Some are already restored and others may never be able to be rebuilt in their original form. The main religions are Mahayana Buddhism and Sivait Hinduism. An interesting feature has to be pointed out, and that is that Hindu and Buddhist sanctuaries are sometimes found at one and the same place[15] and were apparently also built in the same period. The problem whether there were two dynasties involved at the same time, one Buddhist and one Hindu, or that both religions were represented by one dynasty only, cannot be taken up in this paper. I have elsewhere[16] discussed it more extensively.

Archaeological data testify to the deterioration and afterwards complete abandonment of Central Java in the tenth century.

At the same time foundations and other historical remnants were unearthed in East Java, dating from around AD 930. We may assume therefore, that the central power of administration moved to East Java. No inscription or text provides us with the reason of this sudden change. But the recent discovery of a temple complex at Sambisari, near the city of Yogyakarta, that shows partly finished buildings covered by lava, indicates that the most probable reason was a serious volcanic eruption.

The archaeological remains in East Java show the same religious background as in Central Java, Buddhism and Hinduism. However, the temples show in their reliefs a different style, as it were more Javanized, whereas on some we find clear indications of the local beliefs.[17]

With respect to this "Javanizing" effect, the texts that survive give further information.

B. Evidence of Texts

From Central Javanese period only one text has survived. This is the Old Javanese poem, *Ramayana Kakawin,* considered to date from ninth century.[18]

The poem is obviously a literary text and may not be used as historical evidence. It is however interesting for its implications of how Indian influence developed in Indonesia. Right from the start of research on the text, it was realized that it does not contain a literal or free translation of the Valmiki Rāmāyaṇa. In fact, scholars have shown its affinity to the *Rāvaṇavadha* or *Bhattikavya,*[19] while others have noted parts of the *Bhāgavadgīta.*[20] More exhaustive research, involving literal sentence by sentence, or even word to word, comparison, is, however, needed to evaluate the actual extent of the use of the Indian texts and how many were in fact available to the poet. Various versions of the story of Rāma as one of Viṣṇu's incarnations existed in India for centuries. It is conceivable that some of these variations were known in Indonesia. The story of Rāma as depicted on the reliefs of the Prambanan, for instance, does not conform to the text of the Ramayana Kakawin, although the basic story is evident.[21]

We may expect that, as in India, this story would have had religious implications in the Java of the time. Unfortunately we do not know the exact extent of its role in Javanese Hinduism. At present, the Rāmāyaṇa has even in Bali, no more than literary value and is popularized through Wayang, the Indonesian ballet *sendratari* and also comics.

All the other texts that have survived, literary or religious, originate from the East Javanese period. As with the temple buildings we discern a gradual development of "Javanizing" from the older to the younger texts. The older texts have both Sanskrit and Old Javanese sections, the Old Javanese being prose translations or free renderings from the Sanskrit parts, that were mostly written in verse. As time went on, the texts became completely written in Javanese, which also developed from Old to Middle and Younger Javanese.

The most interesting thing is the doctrine that emerges from the older religious texts. This is rigorously monistic. In the end everything becomes one. The abstract conception of the highest power as well as the personal god, and finally also the doctrine itself, the ascetic striving at the goal, which is Complete Annihilation and in fact this goal itself, are identified as One and the Same.[22] So far no exact Indian equivalent could be traced, but this does not mean that future research may not reveal parallels as yet undiscovered.

Next to the religious manuscripts, a number of literary texts have survived. As the Ramayana Kakawin, these texts are called *kakawin-s*. The name testifies relation to the Indian kāvya literature. The heroes in the older kakawins are also Indian heroes from the epics, both the Mahābhārata and the Rāmāyaṇa. The pantheon appearing in these older texts are likewise Indian. Judging from the place these stories have in temple reliefs since the Central Javanese period, there should be no doubt as to their close relationship with religion. Nonetheless the exact role of these kakawins themselves, whether they were prepared for reading at religious ceremonies[23] or were meant as literary products only, is not known. Some scholars, in fact, have connected the kakawins with a cult of kings,[24] as the texts were prepared by court poets. The king was considered as an incarnation of a godhead. This means that writing the history of the king was in fact relating the story of the godhead, which means a religious act. Evidence of this is remarked for the Old Javanese *Bharatayuddha,*[25] written for East Javanese King Jayabhaya, and also the Harivaṁśa.[26]

The stories from the Indian epics, Mahābhārata and Rāmāyaṇa survive popularly to this day, despite influence from more recent date through globalization of Western culture.

C. Sanskrit Influence in Indonesia

Sanskrit has a very deep impact on Indonesian languages, including modern Indonesian. We know from the ancient texts, that Sanskrit influenced Old Javanese in such a way, that at first Old Javanese was considered an Indo-European language.[27] We may remark, that Old Javanese leaned heavily on Sanskrit vocabulary, primarily in its root-form, but retains its specific character as an Austronesian or Malayo-Polynesian language. These Sanskrit words have penetrated into other Indonesian languages as well, including Malay and many other dialects.[28]

But we may add, that the Sanskrit root-forms show their influence and adaptability to modern Indonesian up to this day.[29] We see, that the Sanskrit roots as borrowed by Indonesian, are treated as features of any modern living language, which means able to create new formations based on its fundamental meaning. One example is the modern Indonesian word *swasta* ("private" as in "private enterprise"), that is formed from the Sanskrit roots *sva* (self) and *stha* (to stand). It is obviously not a direct borrowing of the

Sanskrit word *svastha*, meaning "healthy". This root *"swa"* has further proved very productive. Conceivably influenced by the Indian *svadeshi*, it created words with the basic meaning in the vein of "self-supporting", such as "*swadaya*", "self-relying", "*Swasembada*", "self-supporting" and two official such as "*swapraja*" and "*swatantra*", "autonomous or self-governing". Many other examples of new formations are easily pointed out. But borrowed from more ancient times are also surviving, such as the word "*menteri*" for "minister", "*wisma*" from Sanskrit "*vesman*", etc.

It should be remarked that the present-day tendency of choosing some times rather grand sounding slogans and names for official buildings, uses unmistakably Sanskrit elements, although the forms are taken from Old Javanese. But we should remember, that Old Javanese borrowed extensively from Sanskrit.

D. Influence on Religio-Philosophical Thinking

Other interesting Indian elements may be shown at certain types of local beliefs in the Javanese context that are influenced by Indian religious or philosophical thought. These are popular beliefs known as *"kebatinan"* (may be translated as "knowledge of one's self") or *"kejawen"* ("Javanism"), that generally show miscellaneous influence from various sects of Hinduism, including the tradition of certain types of meditation.[30]

As another example of Indian influence we may mention a kind of physical exercise, called *Orhiba* (an acronym for *Olahraga Hidup Baru*, Sport of the New Life),[31] that may be pointed out as influenced by yoga.

In addition we could mention certain features of traditional ceremonies that may be reconstructed as originally of Indian, usually Hindu, character, as some well-known ceremonies at the various Javanese palaces, but research in depth is still needed to show the extent of these Hindu elements.

Bali, that has largely remained Hindu of religion, quite naturally shows many Indian elements both in religious as well as cultural life. Nonetheless the Indonesianizing influence is unmistakable. This is as may be expected. In the first place it is well known that Balinese courts were influenced by those in Java. In addition we may mention that the many sanctuaries we find in Bali are different from those in India, but for that matter already different in which a statue of the principal god is placed. The gods are considered to come down on the stone seats especially erected for them in the area at the back of the temple compound that is considered sacred. Thus the Balinese temples[32] may be seen as a continuation of the pre-Hindu Indonesian sanctuaries where gods (originally divine ancestors) were expected to come down on the megalithic stones erected for them. Balinese Hinduism is also no longer confined to Bali or the Balinese only. All over the Archipelago we find non-Balinese Indonesians who adhere to Hinduism. The religion is therefore no longer called "Agama Hindu Bali", Balinese Hinduism, but in general "Agama Hindu" (Hinduism) or sometimes "Agama Hindu Indonesia", Indonesian Hinduism. The official term used in Bali is "Hindu Dharma".

Many more examples may be cited, as for instance Indian influence in Indonesian dance and music, that have been, or may still be in the process of being, researched upon, by various Indonesian as well as Indian scholars.

In fact, we are justified in saying what was mentioned at the start, that Indian influence is still in evidence up-till these modern times in Indonesia, albeit in the more or less Indonesianized form. Many scholars have in fact commented on the apparent deep impact of Indian influence on Indonesians, despite many other influences of a later date.

NOTES

1. Coedes, 1964, p. 39.
2. R.C. Majumdar, *The History of Hindu Colonization*, 1937.
3. This has been rejected with the consideration that if merchants had been of primary influence, Sanskrit would not have spread so widely in the archipelago.
4. Bosh, *The Problem of Hindu Colonization in Indonesia.*
5. Some scholars use the term *Brahmi*-script, as it is not certain whether the term *allava* denotes the whole area of the Pallavas or only the period of the Pallava Dynasty, 4th to 8th century. See Gonda, 1973, revised edition, pp. 84-86; Sarkar, 1985, p. 173.
6. J. Ph. Vogel, 1918, p. 198 ff.
7. The name Dungga is not uncommon in Indonesia. We seem therefore more justified in considering these kings as Hinduized Indonesians than as Indonesians of Indian descent.
8. The name survives in the name of the West Jananese river *Citarum.*
9. Gonda, 1973, revised edition, p. 178.
10. See Coedes, 1964, p. 107.
11. The Chinese rendering of the Sanskrit *Yavadvipa,* which according to Coedes, 1964, pp. 104-6), could either be Java or Sumatra.
12. We may also point to a Chinese biography of Buddhist saints which mentions that the Kashmiri Prince Gunavarman, as a Buddhist thought throughout the country with the cooperation of the queen Mother. However, this record dates from AD 519 (edited by Paul Pelliot, 1904) and has therefore no eyewitness value.
13. Before setting off to the monastery of Nalanda in Bihar, I. Ching had first to study Sanskrit grammar, which he did in Srivijaya (discussed in Krom, 1931, p. 82 and Zoetmulder, 1965, p. 233).
14. With international aid through UNESCO.
15. The Ratu Baka complex in the Yogyakarta area, for instance, is obvious Hindu sanctuary, but contains also a Buddhist stupa dating from the same time and constructed of the same kind of stone as the other buildings. The Buddhist Candi Sewu, dating from AD 992 is built at the same area as and closely to the Sicait Prambanan temple of in fact an earlier date (9th century).
16. Soebadio, 1978, pp. 67-69.
17. An interesting example is the Candi Sukuh in East Java, that shows very obvious reliefs and statues suggesting the ancient cult of fertility.
18. Poerbatjaraka, 1926, 1932.
19. Sarkar, 1934; Poerbatjaraka, 1952 and Hooykaas in his Ramayana publications between 1955 and 1958.
20. Poerbatjaraka, 1932 and B. van Nooten (as yet unpublished).
21. Consult also, Stutterheim, *Rama-Legends and Rama-Relief in Indonesia*, English translation, 1989 of the German publication of 1925, published in India.
22. Soebadio, 1971.
23. As we find until today in the Balinese tradition of *mabasan.*
24. Berg, 1938, quoted by Zoetmulder, 1965, p. 261.
25. Gunning, J.G.H., 1903 *Bharatayuddha*
26. Teeuw, A., *Hariwansa.*
27. Due to the research on Old Javanese by Van Humbolt in the 19th century, it was cleared that Old Javanese is an Austronesian language. However, until century, at the Dutch University in Amsterdam,

Old Javanese is taught in the Department of Indo-Iranian languages, on par with Sanskrit, as I know from personal experience.

28. Gonda, *Sanskrit in Indonesia.*
29. Compare Haryati Soebadio, "New Sanskrit Loan formations in Bahasa Indonesia," *Cultural Forum 39 Special Issue on India in the Eyes of South-East Asia,* pp. 22-30 (Notes pp. 129-31), publication of the Ministry of Education and Youth Services, Government of India, July 1969.
30. I have conducted a general survey though the paper remained unpublished. It was, however, very obvious that unification of one's "inner self" with the godhead through meditation, possibly influenced by the *brahmanatman* unification in Hinduism, was seen as the final target of these beliefs.
31. Haryati Soebadio, "Orhiba, a modern Indonesian concept of Yoga," a paper read out at the UNESCO sponsored First Sanskrit Conference, New Delhi, 1973, and published in *Studies in Indo-Asian Art and Culture,* Vol. 3, edited by Perala Ratnam, 1974.
32. See Goris, "The Temple System," in *Bali,* Vol. I, 1960, pp. 103 ff, for a succinct description of the Balinese temples.

REFERENCES

Berg, C.C., 1938, "Javaansche Geschiedschrijving" in F.W. Atapel, ed., *Geschiedenis van Nedrlandsch-Indie,* II pp. 5-148.

Bosch, F.D.K., 1946, "Het Vraagstuk van de Hindu-kolonisatie van de Archipel, Leiden. English translation, 1961." *Selected Studies in Indonesian Archaeology,* The Hague.

Chavannes, E., 1894, Memoire composee a I'epoque de la granda dynastie T'ang sur les religieux eminents qui allerent chersher le Loi dans les pays d'Occident, Paris.

Coedes, G., 1986, Les Etats Hindouises d'Indocchine et d'Indonesie, Paris.

Gonda, J., 1973, *Sanskrit in Indonesia,* 2nd edition, New Delhi.

Goris, R., 1960, "The Temple System," in *Bali, Studies in Life, Thought and Ritual* (Selected Studies on Indonesia by Dutch Scholars), The Hague and Bandung.

Gunning, J.G.H., 1903, *Bharatayuddha,* Den Haag.

Hooykas, C., 1955, *The Old-Javanese Ramayana kakawin with special reference to the problem of interpolation in kakawin*, Vol.16, The Hague.

——, 1957, *Love in Lenka*, an episode of the Old-Javanese Ramayana compared with the Sanskrit Bhattikavya, *BKI* 113, pp. 274-89.

——,1958a, The Padadise on Lenka, *BKI* 114, pp. 265-91.

1958b, From Lenka to Ayodhya by Puspaka, being the Old-Javanese Ramayana Sarga XXV mainly, *BKI* 114, pp. 359-83.

——, 1958c, *The Old-Javanese Ramayana, an exemplary Kakawin as to form and content,* Amsterdam.

Krom, N.J., 1931, Hindou-Javaansche Geschiedenis, Den Haaq.

Pelliot, p., 1904, "Deux intineraires de Chine en Inde a la fin du Vllle siecle," *BEFEO* 4, pp. 132-413.

Poerbatjaraka, R. Ng., 1926, "De Dateering van het Oud-Javaanche Ramayana," in Gedenkschrift Koninklijk Instituut, pp. 265-72.

——, 1932, "Het Odu-Javaanche Ramayana," *TBG* 72, pp. 151-214.

——,1934, "Bharatayuddha," translation, in *Djawa* 14, pp. 1-86.

Sarkar, H.B., 1985, *Cultural Relations between India and Southeast Asian Countries,* India.

Soebadio, Haryati, 1969, "New Sanskrit loan formations in Bahasa Indonesia" in *Cultural Forum* 39, pp. 22-30, India.

——, 1971, *Jnanasiddhanta, Secret Lore of Balinese Saivapriest,* The Hague.

——, 1974, "Orhiba, a modern Indonesian concept of Yoga," in Perala Ratnam (ed.), *Studies in Indo-Asian Art and Culture*, pp. 105-27, India.

——, 1978, 'Indian Religions in Indonesia," in Haryati Soebadio and Carine A. du Marchie Sarvaas, *Dynamics of Indonesian History,* pp. 61-96, Amsterdam.

Stutterheim, Willem, 1989, *Rama-Legends and Rama-Relief in Indonesia,* English translation of 1925 German publication, India.

Takakusu, J., 1896, *A Record of the Buddhist Religion as Practised in India and the Malay Archipelago,* Paris.

Teeuw, A., *Hariwansa,* The Hague.

Vogel, J.Ph., 1918, "The Yupa inscriptions of King Mulawarman from Koetei (East-Borneo)," *BKI* 74, pp. 167-232.

Zoetmulder, P.J., 1965, "Die Hochrrligionen Indonesiens," in W. Stohr and P.J. Zoetmulder, *Die Religionen Indonesiens,* second part, Stuttgart.

6

Ancient Trade Relation Between India and Indonesia

I. WAYAN ARDIKA

Introduction

This paper attempts to describe the ancient trade relation between India and Indonesia, particularly with Bali. As Polanyi (1975: 133, 136) has pointed out, institutional trade is a method of acquiring goods that are not available on the spot. The institutional features of trade must involve personnel, goods, transportations, and two-sidedness of people or groups who engage in the movement of goods. Based on this notion, our knowledge about process and mechanism of early trade between India and Indonesia is still obscure. Several questions may rise including what class or level of people were involved in trade, what were their motives (status or profit motives), what kinds of goods that were traded in and out, what kinds of transportations that they have been used.

Many scholars believe that forest products, spices, aromatic woods and tin had attracted the attention of Indian traders to come to Indonesia (Van Leur 1960; Miller 1969; Ellen 1977; Ray 1989). On the other hand, beads, pottery and probably textile were traded into the Indonesian archipelago. Glover (1990) suggests that 'Big Man' prestige goods reciprocal type of economy might have been occurred for earlier societies in South-east Asia as well as for many other parts of the prehistoric world.

As far as early contacts or ancient trade relation between India and Indonesia are concerned, textual and archaeological data provide some information on this activity. The main sources of data will be described in the following sections.

Textual Data

Indian texts dated from the third century BC onwards mention several places in South-east Asia. For instance, the *Arthasastra* of Kautilya (*c.* 300 BC) mentions *Suvarnabhumi* as does the *Sanka Jātaka* (*c.* 300 BC). It is mentioned that the Brahmin Sanka sailed from Varanasi to *Suvarnabhumi* (Sarkar 1981: 303). Sarkar (1981: 296) suggests that *Suvarnabhumi* was located somewhere in Lower Burma, but other authors consider it refers more generally to South-east Asia as a whole.

The *Maha Nidessa* from about the middle of the third century BC refers to 24 places, among which are *Java* and *Suvarnabhumi.* The *Ramayana* of Valmiki, which is usually dated between the fourth century BC and the second century AD, describes the island of Java

(*Javadvipa*) with its seven kingdoms, and the island of Sumatra (*Suvarnarupyakadvipa*). (Coedes 1975; Wolters 1967; Hall 1979; Sarkar 1981). The *Manyunnulakalpa,* dated to *c.* AD 800, is the only text to mention specifically the island of Bali. The text also refers to Java (Sarkar 1981:308).

Historical Indonesian accounts also state that contacts with foreign traders occurred during the late first millennium AD. The inscription of Telaga Batu, dated to AD 686, mentions several specialists such as *sthapaka* (sculptor), *puhawang* (ship's captain), and *vaniyaga* (long-distance or seafaring merchant) (Casparis 1956: 32, 37; Wheatley 1975: 267).

The term *banyaga* which derived from Sanskrit word *vanij* means seafaring merchant also mentioned in several old Javanese inscriptions dated from the ninth to eleventh century AD. These inscriptions include Harinjing A (AD 804), Kaladi (AD 909), Palebuhan (AD 927) and Kamalagyan (AD 1037). The inscription of Kaladi (AD 909) mentions a group of foreigners called the *wagga kilalan* (group of collectors). These foreigners include Kalingas, Aryas, Sinhalese, Dravidians, Pandikiras, Chams, Mons and Khmers (Barrett Jones 1984: 186). Some of these foreigners are identified as merchants by Barrett Jones (1984). In addition, the inscription of Bebetin AI, dated to AD 896 also mentions *banyaga* (seafaring merchant) landing at an unidentifiable location called Banua Bharu in North Bali (Goris 1954: 54-55; Wheatley 1975: 268).

The term *banigrama* (Sanskrit *vanigrama*) means a merchant guild. This is also mentioned in several East Javanese and Balinese inscriptions. The inscriptions of Kaladi (AD 909) and Kambang Śrī (AD 1042) mention *banigrama* as a member of tax collectors (Wheatley 1975: 268).

Old Balinese inscriptions of Sembiran B (AD 951) and Sembiran AII (AD 975) also mention the term *banigrama* (Goris 1954: 73, 78). These inscriptions refer to the village of Julah in North Bali as an ancient port.

Given the notion that Indian traders had already reached Indonesian archipelago by the beginning of the first century AD, the question then arises of what sorts of commodities were traded. On the basis of the archaeological evidence, it is presumed that Indian pottery, beads and perhaps textiles(?) were traded into Indonesian archipelago and other regions in South-east Asia. In terms of exports the *Ramayana* text refers to gharu wood and sandalwood from eastern Indonesia (Wolters 1967: 65-66). The *Raghuvamsa* of Kalidasa, who is believed to have been alive in AD 400, mentions cloves (*lavanga*) from a place called *dvipantara.* Wolters (1967: 66) argues that the term *dvipantara* referred to Indonesian archipelago. Sandalwood is found from East Java to Timor and the clove tree is indigenous to the five small islands of Ternate, Tidore, Moti, Makian and Bacan in the Moluccas (Wheatley 1959; Miller 1969: 60-62). Sandalwood and cloves were also mentioned in the *Periplus* (Schoff 1912:286). Spices, aromatics, woods and tin from South-east Asia, especially Indonesia have attracted Indian traders (Ray 1989: 47-49). These products were also highly required by West during Roman period in the beginning of our century.

Archaeological Data

Recent archaeological discoveries in Sembiran, north-eastern Bali suggest that contacts between India and Indonesia were already occurring at the beginning of the Christian era (Ardika 1991; Ardika and Bellwood 1991). These archaeological data were found between

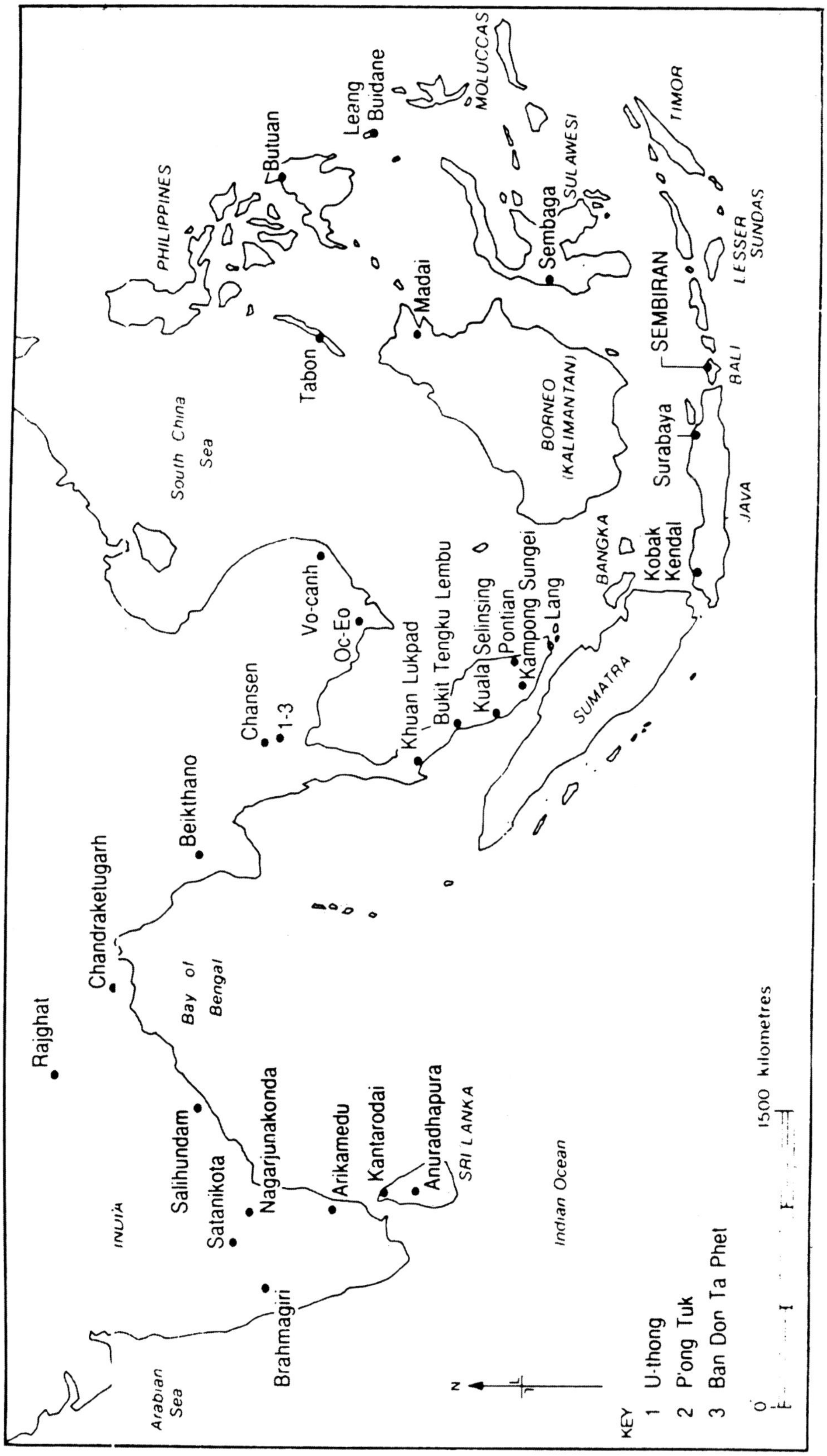

Fig. 1. Sites mentioned in the text

2.4 and 3.6 m below the surface which include Indian rouletted wares, one rim sherd of Wheeler's Arikamedu type 10, a body sherd with Kharoshthi characters and hundreds of glass beads.

Archaeological excavations in Sembiran* produced 79 pieces of Indian rouletted wares. It consists of 8 rims of rouletted wares, 11 rouletted body sherds, and 59 plain body sherds (many probably from rouletted wares). So far, Sembiran produced the largest collection of Indian rouletted wares in terms of form and decoration in South-east Asian sites. Rouletted wares have also been found accidentally in Kobak Kendal and Cibutak in north-west Java (Walker and Santoso 1977: 230, Fig.1.c). The rouletted vessel from Cibutak is different from those found in Sembiran. It is notched on the rim and has incised decoration on its exterior.

Ten of the Bali sherds have very fine rouletting and only one sherd from spit 29 in the trench of Sembiran VII can be described as coarse. Typologically, the rouletted sherds from Bali fall entirely within the range of those from Arikamedu and other sites in India (see Figure 1).

X-ray diffraction (XRD) analysis indicates that samples of rouletted ware from Arikamedu (India), Anuradhapura (Ceylon) and Sembiran (Bali) are very similar. Quartz is dominant in their fabrics (see Figure 2) (Ardika 1991: Appendix A). The analyses were undertaken by Christ Foudoulis and Dr. Tony Eggleton in the Department of Geology at ANU.

Besides XRD, nine sherds of rouletted ware from India, Ceylon and Bali and other samples of sherds from Sembiran (Bali) were also analysed by neutron activation analysis (NAA). The samples were submitted by Dr. Bruce Chappell of the Geology Department of ANU to the Australian Nuclear Science and Technological Organisation (ANSTO) at Lucas Heights in Sydney for the NAA analyses.

The result came back from ANSTO in the form of parts-per-million readings for 22 trace elements. Visual inspection showed that all rouletted ware samples were so closely related that a single source of manufacture seemed to be the only possible conclusion. These results have also been supported by two statistical methods of average link cluster analysis and principal components analysis (see Figures 3 and 4) (Ardika 1991: Appendix B).

In India, rouletted wares have been used widely to date many Early Historical sites. However, there is still debate about the most appropriate date range. Wheeler (Wheeler *et al.* 1946) dated rouletted ware at Arikamedu to between the late first century BC or the beginning of the first century AD, and AD 200. Chakravarti (Wheeler *et al.* 1946: 109) and Subrahmanyam (1964: 8-9), on the basis of palaeography, suggested that the reported examples of inscribed rouletted ware date between the second century BC and the third or fourth centuries AD. Begley (1983: 468-71; 1986) also argues on the basis of stratigraphy and palaeography that the tentative dating of rouletted ware in India should be between the second century BC and AD 200. Recent C14 dates from Gedige, Anuradhapura, indicate that the rouletted ware there dates between 250 BC and AD 1 (Deraniyagala 1986: 46-47).

---

* More Indian potteries were discovered in Sembiran in the last two years. These include: Rouletted sherds, Arikamedu type 10, Arikamedu type 18, Arikamedu type 141. More than 100 Indian sherds have been discovered in Sembiran. So far, Sembiran hs produced the largest collection of Indian potteries in South-east Asia. This indicates that contact between Bali and India must be very intense during the beginning of first century.

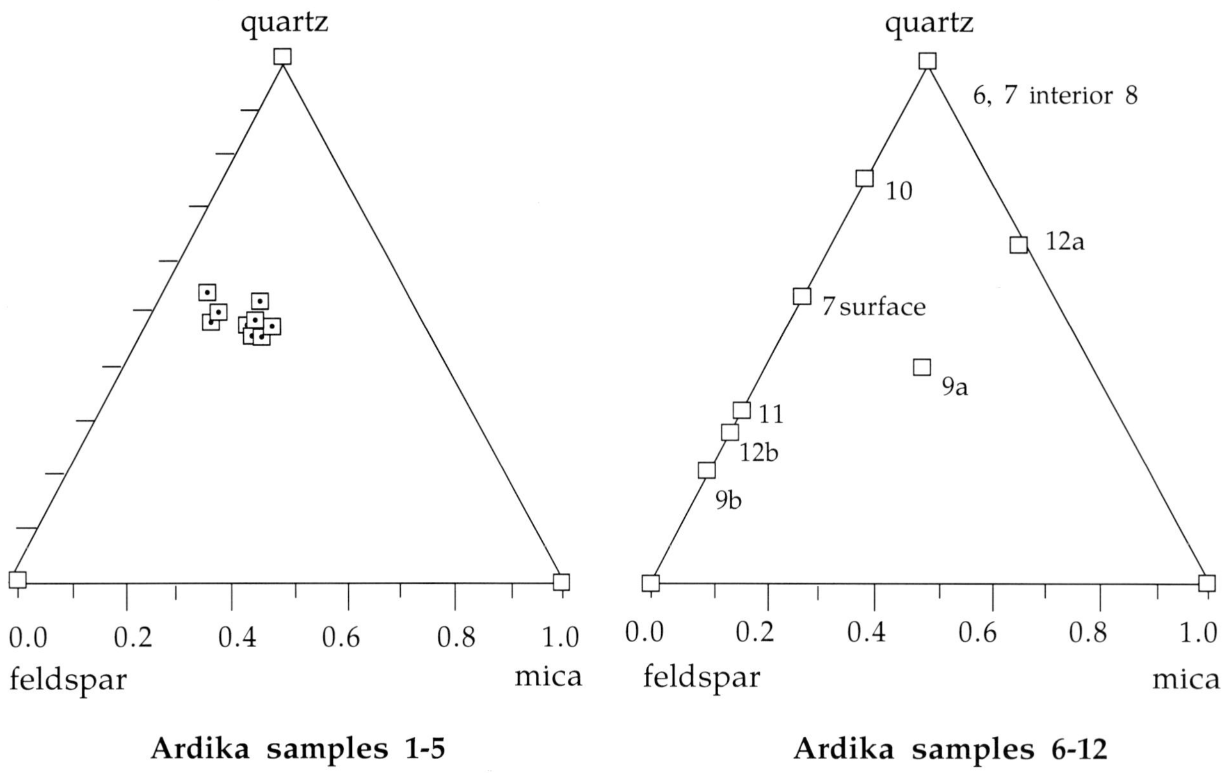

Fig. 2. Triangular coordinate diagrams of XRD results for samples nos. 1-12

In the Sembiran excavations, one C14 date of 1010 ± 110 BP (ANU 7218) was obtained from spit 25 (2.5 m below the surface) in SBN VI. The calibrated age for this is AD 900 (1015) 1160 (ANU 2178) (Ardika and Bellwood 1991). This sample derives from the upper part of layer 6, and rouletted ware first appeared about 0.5 – 1 m below this level.

Another date by AMS radiocarbon on rice husks in a sherd from the 3.5 m level in trench SBN VII is 2660 ± 100 BP (CAMS 732). This gives an age of 910 (818) 790 calibrated BC (Ardika and Bellwood 1991). This AMS date is obviously several centuries earlier than that for rouletted ware according to the Indian evidence, and its interpretation poses a number of unsolved problems.

Given the overall date ranges of rouletted ware in India between 200 BC and AD 200, it seems that the most likely date range for the rouletted ware from Sembiran and Pacung in north-eastern Bali falls in the same time span. However, since Mukherjee (1989a, b; 1990a, b) dates the Kharoshthi inscriptions in West Bengal to between the first and fifth centuries AD, the most likely date span for the rouletted ware in Bali is probably the first and second centuries AD.

Another type of Indian pottery was found in spit 35 of SBN VI. It belongs clearly to a specimen of Arikamedu type 10 (Wheeler *et al.* 1946: 57, 59, fig. 17). This rim is direct, everted, and has an unthickened lip. Both interior and exterior are glossy black-slipped. Impressed decoration occurs on the inside of the rim in the form of a rectangular panel with a bird, probably a peacock, depicted between bands of horizontal incision. This type of pottery has also been discovered in the site of Chandraketugarh in West Bengal and at Alangankulam on the Vaigai river in Tamilnadu (Dr. H.P. Ray pers. comm. 1990). No

```
***Dendrogram ****
** Levels    100.0    90.0    80.0    70.0

           1  ..)
           5  ..)
           2  ..)
           4  ..)
          10  ..)
           6  ..)
           8  ..)
           3  ..)
           7  ..)
           9  ..)
          14  ..) ..
          12  ..    )
          13  ..)   )
          22  ..) ..)...............
          11  ..                    )
          19  ..)                   )
          16  ..)                   )
          20  ..) ..                )
          18  ..)   )               )
          24  ..) ..)               )
          17  ..    )               )
          23  ..) ..)..             )
          15  ..       )            )
          25  ..)      )            )
          21  ..) .....)..          )
          26  ............).... .....).......
```

Fig. 3. Dendrogram of Cluster Average Analysis of NAA results for sherds from Śri Lankā, India and Bali.

Note:

* Samples no. 1 & 2 (Rouletted sherds) from Anuradhapura (Ceylon)
* Samples no. 3 & 4 (Rouletted sherds) from Arikamedu (India)
* Sample no. 5 (Rouletted sherd) from Karaikadu (India)
* Samples no. 6, 7, 9 & 10 (Rouletted sherds) from Sembiran (Bali)
* Sample no. 8 (Rouletted sherd) from Pacuig (Bali)

information is at present available on its occurrence elsewhere, so the Bali find could be of great significance.

An inscribed sherd was found in spit 35 of SBN VII. The sherd is black-slipped inside and outside and the fabric is coarser than that of the rouletted and Arikamedu type 10 sherds. According to Prof. B.N. Mukherjee of Calcutta University, the script is Kharoshthi, and his preliminary reading is *riravi.**

* The surviving letters, according to Prof. Mukherjee may be read as *Tośavi.*

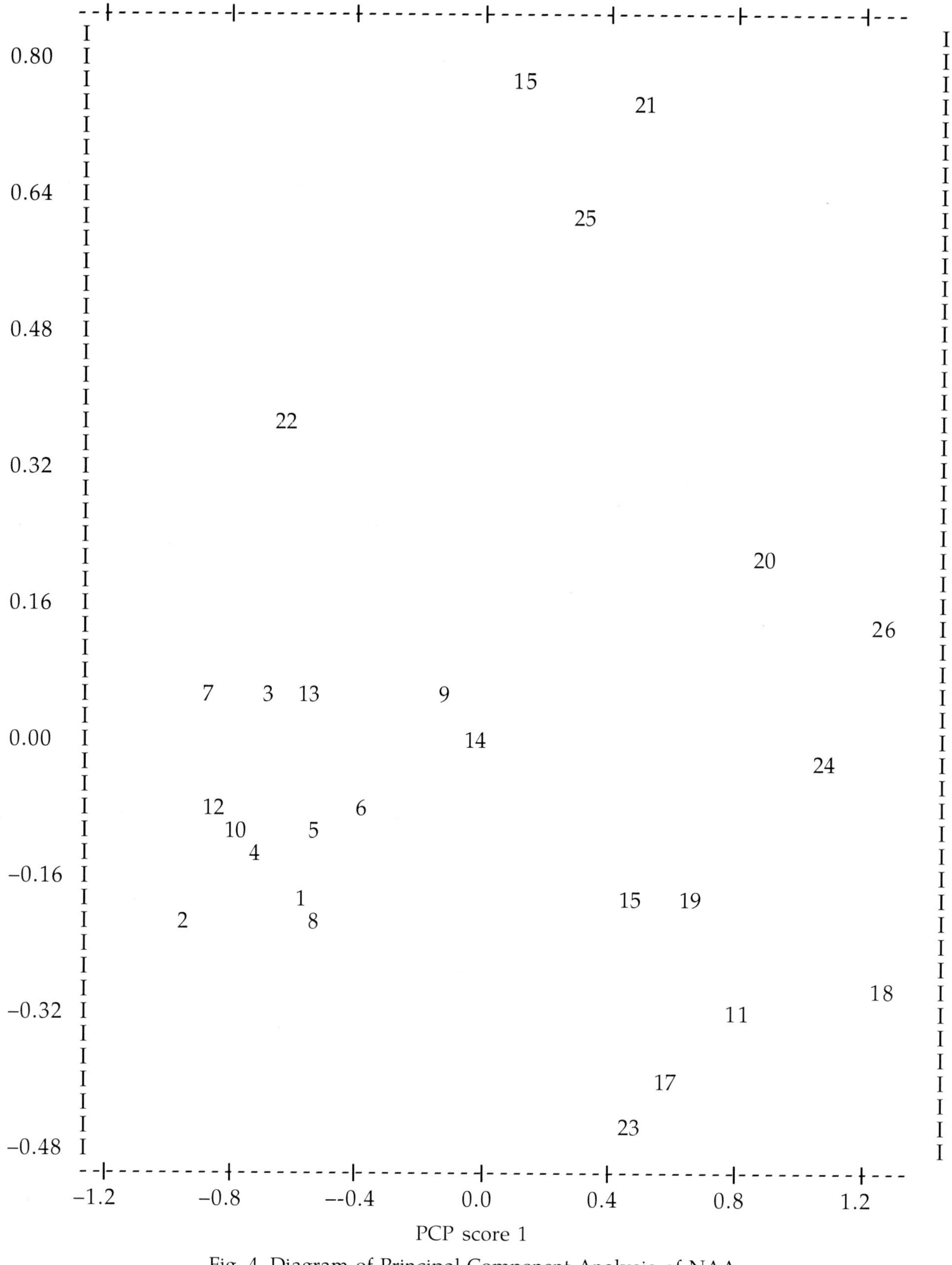

Fig. 4. Diagram of Principal Component Analysis of NAA results for sherds from Ceylon, India and Bali.

The Kharoshthi script was written from right to left. Buhler (1963: 112) believes that the Kharoshthi alphabet is derived from the Aramiaic of the Achaemenian period. It might thus have been introduced to India by the Persians after Darius I conquered the greater portion of Punjab and Sind in 518 BC (Konow 1929: xiii; Gupta 1958:283; Buhler 1963). The script became an official alphabet in North-west India between the third century BC and the fourth or fifth century AD (Konow 1929; Dani 1963: 251-58).

Prof. B.N. Mukherjee (1989a, b; 1990a, b) believes that a group of people who used the Kharoshthi script extended their interests from North-west India to West Bengal, where they became very active as traders from about the last quarter of the 1st century AD to about the beginning of the fifth century AD. They were known as *Yueh Chih* or Khusana. These traders probably conducted maritime commerce with South-east Asia and reputedly had access to a supply of Central Asian horses (Mukherjee 1990a: 2). In mainland South-east Asian sites examples of scripts have been found on seals in Oc-Eo in Vietnam and U Thong in Thailand (Mukherjee 1990a: 2; 1990b). If the script on the sherd from SBN VII is definitely Kharoshthi, it is clearly important evidence for the beginnings of contacts between Bali and India.

Apart from Indian pottery, more than five hundred beads of glass, two of carnelian and one of gold were found in the Early Period layers of several trenches in Sembiran, north-eastern Bali. These beads were found in association with the Indian sherds and they tended to be concentrated close to the burials in the trench of Sembiran VII.

Red glass beads or *mutiralah* were the most common ones at this time in this region of north-eastern Bali. A similar situation also occurs in other sites in South-east Asia such as Oc-Eo (Vietnam), Kuala Selinsing and Pangkalan Bujang (Malaysia) (Lamb 1965: Table VI). Many scholars suggest that red glass *mutiralah* beads are very rare in North India, but are common in South Indian sites, particularly Arikamedu (Lamb 1965; Francis 1990).

Other colours of glass beads, including yellow, green, black, white and brown are rare in Sembiran as other sites of this age in South-east Asia. Overall, the colours of the glass beads from Sembiran are very similar to those from other contemporary sites in Indonesia, including Gilimanuk, Plawangan and Leang Bua (Ratna Indraningsih 1985: 137), although no percentages for different colours from these Indonesian sites have yet been published.

Five glass beads from Sembiran IV have been analysed by Dr. Kishor Basa at the Institute of Archaeology in London. One can be categorized as mixed alkali glass and four are potash glass (Basa 1991; Basa *et al.* 1991). Basa (1991) believes that the Sembiran beads are similar to South Indian samples in terms of raw materials, and were probably manufactured at Arikamedu.

Several authors have suggested that glass beads were manufactured in South-east Asia using raw materials imported from the Mediterranean or India (Harrisson 1964; Lamb 1965; Bronson 1986; Francis 1990). Such manufacturing sites include Kuala Selingsing and Pangkalan Bujang in Malaysia, Khuan Lukpad in southern Thailand, and Oc-Eo in Vietnam. It is not clear whether beads were actually manufactured in Sembiran, since only one possible fragment of scrap glass blue in colour was found (in SBN VI).

Two carnelian beads were discovered in the trench of Sembiran VII. Carnelian beads have also been discovered in Balinese sarcophagus burials at the sites of Nongan, Bona, Selasih, Margatengah, Pujungan and Ambiarsari, as well with the burials at Gilimanuk

(Ardika 1987: Fig.3.2). These carnelian beads are generally believed to have been imported from India, although some may have been made in South-east Asia since carnelian scrap occurs in some sites, including Kuala Selinsing in West Malaysia.

It is worth noting that gold foil eye covers have been found in Gilimanuk and in sarcophagus burial sites at Pangkungliplip in west Bali (Soejono 1977; Miksic 1990: 41-42). Similar gold foil eye covers have also been discovered at Oton on Panay island in the Philippines and at Santubong in Sarawak (O'Connor and Harrisson 1971: 72-73). These gold foil eye covers are similar to the artifacts reported from graves at Adichanallur on the Tamil Nadu coast (O'Connor and Harrisson 1971; Ray 1989: 51).

Conclusion

Based on Indian texts, it is possible that the islands of Sumatra and Java were known to Indian traders as early as the third century BC. Bali might also have been reached by Indian traders at that time.

The increasing demand for spices during the Roman period encouraged Indian traders to search for these products in South-east Asia, particularly in Indonesia. The *Ramayana* and *Periplus* both mention cloves and sandalwood. The clove tree is native to the islands of Ternate, Tidore, Motir, Bacan and Makian in the Moluccas, and the best sandalwood occurs in Sumba and Timor. Sembiran might have been one of the trading centres in northern Bali located on a major spice trade route between western and eastern Indonesia.

The discoveries of Rouletted Ware sherds, a rim sherd of Arikamedu type 10, a sherd with characters in Kharoshthi script, as well as hundreds of glass beads in Sembiran suggest that contact between Bali and India had already begun by about 2000 years ago. It is likely that Indian traders visited Sembiran searching for spices and aromatic wood from the eastern regions of the Indonesian archipelago.

Historical Indonesian accounts also mention foreign traders (*banyaga*) and a merchant guild (*banigrama)* in several port sites in East Java and Bali. These foreigners include Kalingas, Aryas, Singhalese, Dravidians, Pandikiras, Chams, Mons and Khmers.

As Ellen (1977) has pointed out, the spice trade was partially responsible for the Indianization of South-east Asia, and which facilitated the spread of Islam. It was the spice trade which led to the first serious involvement of Europeans in South-east Asia and to the formation of colonies empire there.

REFERENCES

Ardika, I Wayan, *Bronze artifacts and the rise of complex society in Bali.* M.A. thesis. Canberra: Australian National University, 1987.

——, *Archaeological research in northeastern Bali, Indonesia,* Ph.D. thesis. Canberra: Australian National University, 1991.

Ardika I. Wayan and P. Bellwood, "Sembiran: The beginnings of Indian contact with Bali". *Antiquity.* 65, 247:221-32, 1991.

Barrett Jones, A.M., *Early tenth century Java from the Inscriptions,* Leiden: Koninklijk Instituut voor Taal, Land- en Volkenkunde, 1984.

Basa, K.K., *The Westerly Trade of South-east Asia from 400 BC to AD 500 with Special Reference to Glass Beads.* Ph.D. thesis. London: University of London, 1991.

Basa, K.K., Ian Glover, and Julian Henderson, "The relationship between early South-east Asian and Indian Glass". *BIPPA,* forthcoming, 1991.
Begley, V., "Arikamedu reconsidered". *American Journal of Archaeology* 87: 461-81, 1983.
Bronson, B., "Glass beads at the Khuan Lukpad, Southern Thailand". In Glover, I. and E. Glover, (eds), *South-east Asian Archaeology 1986,* 213-29. Oxford: BAR International Series 561, 1990.
Buhler, G., "On the origin of the Indian Brahmin Alphabet". *The Chowkhamba Sanskrit Studies, vol. 33,* 1963.
Coedes, G., *The Indianized states of South-east Asia.* Canberra: Australian National University, 1975.
Dani, A.H., *Indian Palaeography.* London: Oxford University Press, 1963.
De Casparis, J.G., *Selected Inscriptions from the 7th to the 9th century AD.* Bandung: Masa Baru, 1956.
Deraniyagala, S.U., "Excavations in the citadel of Anuradhapura: Gedige 1984". *Ancient Ceylon.* 6: 39-47, 1986.
Ellen, R.F., "The trade in spices". *Indonesia Circle* 12: 21-25, 1977.
Francis, P., "Glass beads in Asia". Part two. "Indo-Pacific Beads". *Asian Perspectives,* 26, 1: 1-23, 1990.
Glover, I.C., *Early trade between India and South-east Asia.* Centre for South-east Asia Studies. London: University of Hull, 1989.
Goris, R., *Prasasti Bali I & II.* Bandung: Masa Baru, 1954.
Harrisson, T., "Monochrome glass beads from Malaysia and elsewhere". *Man,* 50: article 50, 1964.
Konow, S., *Corpus Inscription Indicarum,* vol. II, Part I, 1929.
Lamb, A., "Some observations on stone and glass beads in Early South-east Asia". *JMBRAS* 38(2): 87-124, 1965.
Leur, J.C. Van, *Indonesian trade and society.* Bandung: Sumur Bandung, 1960.
Miksic, J.N., *Old Javanese Gold.* Singapore: Ideation, 1990.
Miller, J.I., *The spice trade of the Roman Empire.* Oxford: Clarendon, 1969.
Mukherjee, B.N., Decipherment of the Kharoshthi-Brahmi script. *Asiatic Society,* XVIII. 8:1-10, 1989a.
——, "Discovery of Kharoshthi inscriptions in West Bengal". *The Quarterly Review of History Studies,* XXIX.2: 6-14, 1989b.
——, "A Kharoshthi-Brahmin seal-matrix from Oc-Eo (S.E. Asia)". *Asiatic Society,* XIX 6: 1-4, 990a.
——, "A sealing in the Lopbhuri Museum (Thailand)". *Asiatic Society,* XIX. 11: 1-2, 190b.
O'Connors, S.J. and T. Harrisson, "Gold-foil burial amulets in Bali, Philippines and Borneo". *JMBRAS,* 44. 1: 71-77, 1971.
Polanyi, K., "Traders and Trade". In J.A. Sabloff and C.C. Lamberg-Karlovsky (eds), *Ancient civilization and trade.* Albuquerque: University of New Mexico, pp.133-54, 1975.
Ratna, Indraningsih, "Research on Prehistoric beads in Indonesia". *BIPPA* 6: 133-41, 1985.
Ray, H.P., "Early maritime contacts between South and South-east Asia". *Journal of South-east Asian Studies,* XX, 1: 42-54, 1989.
——, "Seafaring the Bay of Bengal in the early century AD". *Studies in History.'* 6.1.n.s., 1990.
Sarkar, H.B., "A geographical introduction to South-east Asia: The Indian perspectives". *BKI.* 137: 293-323, 1981.
Schoff, W.H., *The Periplus of the Erythrean Sea.* New York: Longmans, Green, and Co., 1912.
Soejono, R.P., *Sistem-Sistem penguburan pada akhir masa prasejarah di Bali.* Unpublished Ph.D. thesis. Jakarta: Universitas Indonesia, 1977.
Subrahmanyan, S., *Salihundam.* Hyderabad: Government of Andhra Pradesh, 1964.
Walker, M.J.S. and S. Santoso, "Romano-Indian rouletted pottery in Indonesia." *Mankind,* 11: 39-45, 1977a.
Wheatley, P., "Satyanrta in Swarnadvipa: From reciprocity to redistribution in South-east Asia". In Sabloff, A.J. and C.C. Lamberg-Karlovsky (eds), *Ancient Civilization and Trade,* pp. 227-83. Albuquerque: University of New Mexico, 1975.
Wheeler, R.E.M., A. Ghosh and Krishna Deva, "Arikamedu: An Indo-Roman trading station on the east coast of India". *Ancient India,* 2: 17-24, 1946.
Wolters, O.W., *Early Indonesian Commerce.* Ithaca and London: Cornell University Press, 1967.

7

Indian Shipping in Early Mediaeval Period

LALLANJI GOPAL

It will be a platitude to lament the paucity of evidence to reconstruct the history of Indian shipping. There are casual references in scattered texts which do not cover all aspects of shipping activity and make it different to present a systematic and comprehensive account. Moreover, as we do not have full details for shipping in the earlier period, it is not always possible to speak in terms of changes and development in our period. It is with these reservations that we may approach the task of reconstructing the history of Indian shipping in the early mediaeval period.

It does not require evidence to prove that ships were made of wood.[1] Due importance, however, was attached to selecting wood best suited for the construction of ships. Wood was classified into several kinds according to its characteristic properties. The *Yuktikalpataru*[2] ascribed to Bhoja says that a ship built of the Kṣatriya class of wood is to be used as means of communication where the communication is difficult owing to vast water; ships made of other kinds of timbers do not last for a long time, they soon rot in water and are liable to be split at the slightest shock and to sink down. In the account of the naval expedition of Samaraketu described in the *Tilakamañjarī*[3] of Dhanapāla, Tāraka, the chief sailor, reports the construction of ships out of strong timber. From the early Bengali literature we learn that ships were generally made of teak, *gāmbhāri*, *tamāl, piāl* and *kāṭhāl* wood, though the wood of the fabled *manapaban* tree was considered to be best.[4] Al-Mas'ūdī also confirms that ships of the Indian Ocean were made of teak.[5] Indian teak and coconut wood were in demand by the Arabs for constructing ships.[6]

In the earlier period the wooden planks of a ship were stitched together.[7] The stitches are represented on the figures of ships from Bharhut[8] and Sanchi[9] belonging respectively to the second and first century BC. Stiching remained the general method with Indian sailors down to the century and even now survives in the boats of some coastal areas.[10] Sulaimān,[11] Al-Mas'ūdī[12] and Ibn Batūta[13] notice the use of sewn or lashed timbers in Indian ships. A number of European travellers of the period mention that the ships were stitched and point out their weakness. These include Ibn-Jubayr,[14] Jordanus,[15] John of Montecorvino,[16] Marco Polo,[17] Friar Odoric[18] and G. Carreri.[19]

But the use of iron nails seems to have been known in our period, even though it was very much sparse and restricted. One may suspect nails in the upper part of the ship, with horsemen in it,[20] painted in Cave no. XVII of Ajanta, in the scene depicting the conquest of Ceylon by Vijaya. It is clear from a reference in the *Upamitibhavaprapañcākathā*[21] that the use of iron in a ship was negligible. The *Yuktikalpataru* classifies ships into two types, *dīrghā* and *unnatā,* on the basis of their bottom being covered with copper or iron plate.

But from this text itself it is clear that the use of iron was not favoured.[23] It says that nailed timbers should not be used in seagoing vessels because the iron will be attracted by loadstone and the ship will sink; hence Bhoja favours rope joints.[24] Elsewhere also the text speaks of the presence of magnetic rocks in the sea. The legend of magnetic rocks is mentioned by Jinadattasūri in his *Kālasvarūpakulakam.*[26] He says that a ship which is riveted with iron is attracted by loadstone and breaks; it sinks and cannot cross the sea. A ship without iron is seen sailing in deep sea in strong wind; it crosses the sea and brings profit and prosperity to the merchant. In the *Bhavisayattakahā*[27] the ship used by a merchant in a successful sea voyage is described being "without iron" (*ṇilloham*). The legend of magnetic rocks was widespread in the contemporary world. It is mentioned by Procopius and two fourteenth century works, the *Travels of John Mandeville* and an Arabic account of the *Expedition against Alexandria.*[28]

Al-Mas'ūdī attributed the tendency to avoid iron nails to the greater degree of salinity in the Indian Ocean.[29] But, scientifically the explanation is not correct, because the Indian Ocean is not saline to such an appreciable extent. The real reason probably lay elsewhere. Iron seems to have been introduced late in the south.[30] In view of the less advanced processes of mining, smelting and manufacture, stitching with fibres locally available must have been easier and cheaper. The proverbially conservative sailor cannot be expected to have given up his traditional ways for the slight superiority of the nails over stitching.[31] Moreover, iron nails were not without disadvantages, which were probably magnified by popular imagination. Ibn Jubayr, Al-Idrīsī and Ibn Batūta observe that stitched hulls are pliant and resilient; if they strike any reef they are less easily broken than nailed ships.[32] The attribution of magnetic properties to all rocks may then have been "a false interpretation of a very real peril."[33]

Montecorvino[34] denies caulking in the ships on the Arabian Sea. Likewise Procopius[35] denies smearing with pitch. But they are controverted by other sources. According to Al-Idrīsī[36] caulking was done with flour and whale oil. But according to Chau Ju-Kau,[37] the oil was mixed with lime. The fish oil was also used for coating ships.[38]

As the ships were made of wooden planks stitched together, there was a constant danger of their sinking as a result of water entering through leakings.[39] In the texts of the earlier period we find references to sailors whose specific duty was to pour out water[40] or to stop holes.[41] The Jain text *Ācārāṅgasūtra*[42] speaks of the holes in a ship being blocked, in case of emergency, with any part of man's body, metallic dishes, clothes, clay, grass or lotus leaves. From the *Tilakamañjarī* we find a more regular practice of caulking. Before the ships set sail, the crevices were caulked.[43] In another reference we read that the chief sailor examined all the joinings and caulked even small holes with wool and wax.[44]

We do not have much evidence about the nature of decks and cabins on Indian ships. The accounts of foreign travellers mention open ships. Thus, Jordanus notes in connexion with Malabar: Nor are the vessels ever decked over, but open.[45] But, whatever might have been the practice with small ships of early times, the sculptured representations from Borobudur show some form of decking and fencing in ships. On Figure nos. 1 and 3 one may notice a deck and a trapezoid object suggested by Prof. Basham to be a deckhouse.[46] The

Yuktikalpataru[47] mentions that ships can be of two types, with or without cabins, and classifies the former into three sub-types differentiated on the basis of the length and position of their cabins. The *sarvamandirā* vessels had the largest cabins extending over the entire area of the ship and were used for the transport of royal treasure, horses and women. The *madhyamandirā* vessels had their cabins only just in the middle part and were used in the pleasure trips by kings or during rainy seasons. The *agramandirā* vessels had their cabins towards their prows and were used in the dry season or in cases of long voyages or wars. In the *Tilakmañjarī*[48] Samaraketu when proceeding to punish turbulent feudatories of Dvīpāntara is said to have entered the cabin erected in the forepart of the vessel. Here are mentioned the two important characteristics of an *agramandirā* type of vessel, its association with a naval expedition and its cabin towards the prow.

The *Yuktikalpataru* does not have any detailed discussion about masts and sails. At one place, however, it remarks that a vessel is to be painted white, red, yellow or blue respectively as it has four, three, two or one mast.[49] A large number of figures of ships from Borobudur contain two masts,[50] though there are also some which have only one mast.[51] The Borobudur sculptures depict ladders to climb up the masts.[52] The sail most common with Indian sailors was one of the square type. The sculptures from Borobudur show square sails. Of the two square sails in the ships depicted at Borobudur one is large while the other is a small one. Besides these two sails there was also one stay-sail in front of the ship.[53] In view of the clear depiction in sculptures, confirmed by the *Yuktikalpataru,* it seems that John of Montecorvino[54] and Marco Polo mention the general practice to have one mast and one sail only.[55]

From the *Tilakamañjarī* we get some idea of the way the sails and masts were actually regulated. The first thing that Tāraka, the chief sailor, does after hearing of the proposed naval expedition of Samaraketu is to get ropes tied to the sails.[56] In a favourable wind the sails are raised and the ship sets on its course.[57] The ship proceeds on, while the mast is erect and ropes are attached to the sails.[58] The commander says that the navy should take a rest because, among other reasons, the crew is too tired to keep the mast erect. They decide to sew in the mean time the sails, tattered due to violent wind, and to tie ropes to them.[59] In order to halt the ship the sails are loosened and collected.[60] Tāraka, the chief sailor, proves his efficiency by replacing broken ropes by new and by testing even strong sails.[61] The *Samarāiccakahā* of Haribhadra Sūri also contains informative references to sails. In the story of Dharaṇa we read that when the ship was agitated by a violent storm the sails were removed.[62] In other story we find that the sails were spread before the ships set sail and when the ship went out of control the sails were gathered.[63] All these details are confirmed by Borobudur sculptures representing the crew as working hard over the mast and the sail.[64]

The ships from Borobudur are narrow in shape and top heavy, hence to ensure their safety outriggers were attached to them.[65] We can notice outriggers in three of the six illustrations given by R.K. Mookerji.[66] They were probably fastened with rope to the body of the ship. In one case, we find a man clinging to the outrigger, most likely to steady the ship.[67] There were also wash-brakes to check the force of waves.

The Sanskrit word for anchor is *nāṅgara*. In the *Tilakamañjarī* we read that when a ship halted its heavy anchors made of rocks were lowered down.[68] The text further refers to ships being tied to strong wooden poles thrust deep into the earth.[69] At the time of the departure of a ship, the rocks used to restrict its speed were pulled up[70] and the ropes that tied it to the pole were cut.[72] The *Samarāiccakahā*[72] refers to the anchors being loosened to stop the drifting of the ship. The *Milindapañho,*[73] which belongs to an earlier period, mentions two qualities of an anchor: it fastens the ship and keeps it still even in the mighty sea, in the expanse of waters agitated by the crowding of ever varying waves, and lets not the sea take it in one direction or another; and secondly, it floats not, but sinks down, and even in water a hundred cubits deep holds the ship fast, brings it to rest.

We do not find references to indicate the nature of the rudder being used in the period. Probably the rudders were not very convenient. Johan of Montecorvino says: "And they have a frail and flimsy rudder like the top of a table, of a cubit in width in the middle of the stern; and when they have to tack, it is done with a vast deal of trouble; and if it is blowing in any way hard, they cannot tack at all."[74]

The sailors sailing to distant lands found it safe to have a smaller boat attached to their ship for use in case the bigger one was somehow destroyed. In the *Bṛhatkathāślokasaṅgraha* there is the story of Sānudāsa who was rescued by sailors of a ship who spotted his flag in an island and went there in their smaller ship.[75] The *Samarāiccakahā* also speaks of Kumāra and Dharaṇa being likewise approached and helped.[76] On one of the Borobudur sculptures we find an actual representation of a boat tied to a ship.[77]

The *Yuktikalpataru* has an elaborate classification of ships according to their size.[78] Of the two broad divisions, the class of ordinary ships is said to contain ten kinds of vessels with different lengths, breadths and heights. Seagoing vessels are placed as ships of special class with two subdivisions termed as *dīrghā* and *unnatā*. The *dīrghā* subclass of ocean-going ships has ten types, all remarkable for their length. On the other hand the five types of ships included in the *unnatā* subclass are characterised by their considerable heights. Prof. Basham[79] rightly remarks that the measurements are theoretical and that the author of the text had little first hand knowledge of ships. Calculating on the basis of 1 *rājahasta*=16 ordinary *hastas* or 24 feet, he shows that the largest river going vessel will measure 180'×90'×90' and the largest seagoing ships will measure 264'×33'×26'. The ships will be far too long and their beams far too narrow. There are grave doubts if these ships could have been of much practical use on the high sea. R.K. Mookerji justifies the measurements by quoting Nicole Conti who says that some Indian ships were larger than those of Europe.[80] The measurements seem to have little practical validity and have only a theoretical and academic interest. It is, however, interesting to note that a ship of Surat stopped off Aden by Sir Henry Middleton in 1612 was found by Captain John Saris to measure 153'×42'×31.'[81] The ships depicted at Borobudur are also longish.

The ships were dependent upon trade winds to a very great extent and it was only with a favourable wind that a ship set sail. It is significant that in philosophical works the motion due to direct contact with a body exercising continued pressure (*nodana*) is illustrated by the motion of sailing vessels under the impelling force of the wind.[82] In view of the close dependence of the naval activity upon winds, it was but natural that winds were carefully observed and studied. It is interesting to note that the names of twelve winds mentioned by Abū Hanifa Dainūri, an Arab pilot of the twelfth century, in his work on nautical science[83] are included in the list of sixteen types of winds given by the *Āvaśyakacūrṇi*.[84]

The progress of astronomical study may also have facilitated the activities across the sea. The clear tropical sky provided the sailors with a constant guide to point out their direction. The importance of astronomical knowledge for shipping is clear from a reference in the *Tilakamañjarī*.[85] In this passage when the ship is threatened by a storm Tāraka, the chief sailor, addressed his crew thus "Rājilaka, the ship is sailing towards the South, even when I have ordered otherwise. It seems that you have lost all sense of direction. Even being told you do not know the North side. Look at the group of seven stars and turn the ship back."

In the earlier period we find that sailors kept crows to find out the direction in which land was situated.[86] It is significant that in our period we do not have many references to the use of these birds.[87] As the different routes, countries and islands became familiar through repeated voyages, the necessity for using these crows was probably not so pressing as in the beginning.

Though some scholars have suggested that mariner's compass was known to the Hindus,[88] we do not have any definite evidence for its use in the earlier period.[89] The *Milindapañho*[90] says that the pilot of a ship had an instrument (*yanta*=Skt. *yantra*) of which he took great care. He put a seal on it so that no one should touch it. But as the reference is silent about the nature and precise use of the instrument we cannot necessarily infer that it was the mariner's compass. Likewise the circular object depicted as mounted on a pedestal in the stern of Indian ships in the Borobudur sculptures[91] need not be a compass. Prof. Basham[92] points out that the object appears mounted also at the very extremity of the bowsprit which will be a very inconvenient position for the ship's compass. The circular objects at the two ends probably represented fore and oft lights.[93]

The question has to be studied in its proper historical perspective.[94] The magnetic needle was known in China from very early times. But, even there, there is no clear evidence for its nautical use in the early centuries of the Christian era.[95] The earliest available reference is in the account of *P'ing-chou-k'o-tán*[96] which belongs to the second half of the eleventh century. Another early mention is found in Sü-king's narrative of his mission to Korea in 1122.[97] In the beginning the compass does not seem to have played any significant role in navigation.[98] The oldest Arab references belong to the close of the twelfth and beginning of the thirteenth century.[99] The knowledge may have reached Europe through the Arabs in the age of the Crusades. The French poem of Guyot de Provins (c. 1190 AD) is the earliest European reference.[100]

There is some evidence to show that towards the close of the early medieval period the Indians were introduced to the use of the compass. Jacques de Vitry in his *History of the Kingdom of Jerusalem* (c. 1218 AD) refers to the use of compass in India. An Arabic manual of mineralogy (c. 1252 AD) says that Indian seamen steered by an iron fish, floating in a bowl of oil. The Sanskrit origin of *maccha-yantra,* the Marathi word for the compass, supports the suggestion.

It is, however, clear that the compass could at best have been used only sporadically. It must be remembered that in the indigenous literature of the period we do not find any reference to its use by sailors for determining the directions in emergencies. The foreign travellers and writers are silent about its use in India.[102] On the contrary Nicolo Conti definitely says that Indians never used it.[103] Moreover, in the Indian Ocean under a clear sky the luminary bodies are generally visible without much obstruction and the sailors can easily determine the direction with their help. In such conditions the compass could not have played a major part in navigation.

Probably the Indian method of magnetization was not strong.[104] The dry needle on a pivot had not been invented. The magnetic needle was floated on water or oil. Hence it could not be mounted on a windrose and the direction could not be determined accurately from the centre.

It seems that in early medieval period Indian sailors maintained a record of the location of places visited by them or known to them otherwise. They utilised this knowledge in their subsequent voyages. In the *Bṛhatkathāślokasaṅgraha* we read that Manohara, in the course of his voyage, found out the Śṛṅgavān mountain and the city of Śrīkuñjanagara and in a book recorded it clearly together with the sea and the location of direction in which it was situated.[105] It may be suggested that the sailors on the basis of a first hand information probably prepared and maintained works like the *Periplus of the Erythraean Sea.* It is really unfortunate that no single specimen of such a record has survived to illustrate the geographical discoveries made by Indian sailors.

We have elsewhere discussed Indian shipping activity in the early medieval period.[106] The combined testimony of a Chinese account of 749[107] and Al-Mas-ūdī[108] shows that ships from India ascended the Canton river and reached Canton. But in the later period India's maritime contacts with China gradually dwindled. India is not mentioned among the countries which according to the *Sung Annals* were trading at Canton in 971.[109] But Indian states, especially of the south, occasionally tried to assert themselves. It is clear that the Cola kingdom participated in the lucrative maritime trade with China obviously through the intervention of Kiḍāra or the empire of the Śailendra.

The activities of Indian sailors and merchants extended in the East mostly only to Indonesia. The *Liang-shu* states that central T'ién-chu had much sea trade with Fu-nan, Jï-nan and Kiau-chi (Indo-China).[110] There were frequent voyages of Indian merchants to the Indonesian lands. The *Upamitibhavaprapañcākathā*[111] implies that, besides trade, sightseeing was another reason for people coming to these islands.

In the maritime connexions with the Muslim countries, the areas on the western coast of India had a significant role. Abū Zaid[112] suggests that Indian merchants visited Siraf in large numbers and had very friendly relations with the Muslim merchants of that place. Indian merchants like Jagaḍu had Indian agents at Hormuz and maintained regular trade with Persia, transporting goods in their own ships.[113] The western terminus for the Indian ships appears to have changed from time to time. In the seventh century it was Basra, from where it was transferred to Siraf and then successively to Kish and Hormuz.[114]

The Indian sailors and merchants appear to have concentrated on coastal trade. They generally ventured only up to Ceylon.[115] Gradually they left the major part of actual shipping to the foreigners, confining themselves to distribution. The Indonesians had dominance up to Quilon and the ports to its north were frequented by the Muslims.[116] The relative insignificance of Indian shipping explains the absence of any reference to it in the Chinese and Arab accounts.[117]

As we have shown elsewhere,[118] Indian shipping had to face serious rivals. To start with, the Arabs were the foremost maritime power, pushing the sphere of their influence towards the East. From the tenth century they yielded a part of the monopoly, especially to the West of the Indonesian countries, to the ports of Sumatra, Java and Malaya. From the twelfth century they had to face a strong rival in China which eventually established its commercial hegemony up to Malabar port. Ceylon enjoyed the advantages of its central position.

We have seen that the decline of Indian shipping might have been due to the apathy and inability of the Indian states to protect its interests.[119] Whereas in the earlier period the state actively participated in the sea-trade, in the early medieval period it appears that the coastal powers often resorted to piracy.[120]

In this period piracy appears to have increased. Previously piracy was confined to small areas, but now it had become quite widespread.[121] Piracy must have deterred Indian merchants from resorting to frequent voyages to distant areas.[122]

The Indian traders do not appear to have done much by way of providing for the safety of their ships. It is not without significance that whereas references for the Arab[123] and Chinese[124] ships being manned with soldiers are forthcoming, we have not much to suggest this for their Indian counterparts.[125]

Religious considerations also affected shipping activities. As early as the times of the *Baudhāyana Dharmasūtra,*[126] sea voyage (*Samudrasaṃyānam*) was one of the five reprehensible practices followed by the Brāhmaṇas of the north. Manu[127] describes Brāhmaṇas who undertake sea voyage (*Samudrayāyī*) as not fit to carry out their religious functions and hence are not to be invited to religious feasts. According to Nārada,[128] a seagoing merchant (*Sāmudravaṇik*) is not a reliable witness and his statement is not to be accepted as evidence in a court of law.

But from these very sources it follows that in the beginning religious feelings were not very strong against sea voyage. We have evidence to show that Brāhmaṇas undertook voyage. But, in the early medieval period we notice that there was a definite growth of a taboo against sea voyage. The *Mitākṣarā*[129] quotes with approval the earlier views of Baudhāyana and Manu. Al-Bīrūnī[130] says that a Brāhmaṇa must live between the ocean in the east and west. The *Bṛhannāradīya Purāṇa* mentions the undertaking of sea voyage as one of the practices which, being unfavourable for the attainment of heaven and disliked by the people, have been forbidden for the Kali age.[132] Hamādri explaining the rule about seagoing being a *Kalivarjya*, adds that by penance the offender may regain ritual purity but his caste privileges cannot be restored and he is cut off from his family and friends.[133] V.P. Kane interprets the relevant passages as showing that the prohibition against sea voyage affected only Brāhmaṇas and even then they did not become altogether unfit to be associated with. But, if we can use the *Vyavahāramayūkha,*[134] of a slightly later period, to reflect the conditions in the early medieval period, the taboo was against a *dvija* who constantly undertakes sea voyages for trade.

The reason for the religious objection seems to have been that on a ship one cannot perform the religious rites and rituals in their full details, respecting the rules of ritual purity. From the times of Vasiṣṭha[135] and Āpastamba[136] we notice that intercourse with barbarians was advised to be avoided. It was believed that sacrifices and other religious rites could be performed only in a well defined region.[137] For this reason the countries in the bordering areas were enumerated by name as unfit for stay.[138] It may have been felt that with the expansion of Islam, the chances of religious contamination increased. It should be noticed that in this period the impact of the Lokāyatas and Buddhism had weakened.[139] The Lokāyatas advocated a more practical attitude for enjoying worldly happiness and did not subscribe to the orthodox religious scruples.[140] The religious objections were not respected by Buddhists who are known to have undertaken journeys to other countries for missionary work.[141]

We have seen above that foreign travellers belonging to the close of the period of our study point out in clear terms the defects of Indian ships. It seems that "Indian techniques of ship construction and navigation had by this time fallen behind those of the Arabs and Chinese."[142] We have shown elsewhere that Indian ships were smaller than those of China[143] and lagged behind the Chinese and Arab ones in the matter of speed.[144]

There are clear indications of the decline in Indian shipping in one respect at least. For people away from coastal areas it had ceased to be of much concern. This can be easily inferred from the way Medhātithi and Lakṣmīdhara, two Smṛti writers of the period, explain away the emphasis on sea voyages in earlier authorities. There is a provision in Manu[145] that the interest to be paid is to be fixed by persons expert in sea voyages. In his comments Medhātithi[146] remarks that the sea voyage is mentioned only by way of illustrating a journey; the sense is that interest is fixed by traders, who know all about journeying by land and water. Likewise Lakṣmīdhara[147] explains the expression "experts in sea-voyage" to refer by implication to the merchants in general.

It seems that in some areas at least there was a more active participation in sea-trade which may have resulted in a more intimate knowledge of shipping. It is to be noted that the *Vaijayantī* and the *Abhidhānaratnamālā*, two lexicons of the period, collect at one place terms connected with sea and shipping. But, whereas the *Abhidhānaratnamālā*[148] provides more space to terms for sea, waves, shore, tide and aquatic animals, the *Vaijayantī*[149] gives an elaborate list of terms for different types of ships, the principal parts of a ship and the important categories of sailors and passengers. In the *Deśīnāmamālā* we find some Deśī terms for a ship. Of these the testimony of the *Vaijayantī* is very useful. It mentions Sāmudram as the name of the mixed caste born of a Karaṇa and a Vaiśya woman. This class earned its livelihood from commodities obtained from the sea.[151] The necessity for a special term may refer to conditions when there arose a large number of merchants of this type.

As rightly remarked by Prof. A.L. Basham,[152] in ancient Indian literature one does not find a passage praising the seaman's life and the implicit attitude to the sea is one of fear and distaste. But, by way of exception we may refer to the glowing description of the sea and its riches given by Varāhamihira in the Agastyācāra chapter of the *Bṛhatsaṁhitā*.[153] The *Vārāhapurāṇa*[154] also refers with admiration to merchants who sailed fast far into the shoreless, deep and fearful waters of ocean in search of valuable pearls. In the early medieval period Kṣemendra in his *Avadānakalpalatā*[155] exaltingly refers to the unbounded zeal of those brave people who treat oceans like ponds. In Jain story books we find stories of traders going out for trade with foreign countries. We may make special reference to the *Samarāiccakahā*,[156] *Upamitibhavaprapañcākathā*,[157] *Kathākośa*[158] and *Bṛhatkathākośa*.[159] The descriptions of sea voyage in the *Tilakamañjarī*[160] and *Bhavisyattakahā*[161] are so detailed and graphic that they seem to have been based on the direct knowledge of the authors. The Siddha poets employ images referring to ships and sea voyage which suggest that these details connected with shipping formed part of the common knowledge.[162] The *Yuktikalpataru*[163] gives a detailed account of boats and ships in its section on conveyances. It discusses the wood to be used for their construction, the types of the ships and their cabins. As pointed out earlier, the description involves much that is theoretical. But, in any case it may be inferred that ships and shipping could interest a king of a land-locked kingdom like that of Malwa to occupy so much space in the text.

In the early Bengali literature we find a vivid description of the construction of ships.[164] The parts of a vessel mentioned in this source are *dāṛa* (helm) or *pātwāl, mālumkāṣṭha* (mast), *talā* (hold), *māthākāṣṭha* (prow), *chhaighar* (shed), *pāṭātan* (deck), *daṅḍakarwāl* (oar), *baṅśakarwāl* or *dhvaji* (bamboo-pole), *fās* (chord), *naṅgar* (anchor), *pāl* (sail) and *dāṛā* (keel).[165] The *Varṇaratnākara*[166] mentions the important parts of a ship and several varieties of ships known to it.

In the *Samarāiccakahā* we find that the merchant before boarding the ship gives alms to the poor, offers homage to the ocean and bows down to the gods and elderly persons.[167] The performance of auspicious rites seems to have been a necessary part of the preparations made for sailing a ship.[168] The *Bhavisyattakahā* also refers to the special rites to be performed when floating a ship for the first time.[169] From the *Tilakamañjarī* we learn that before proceeding on a voyage God Ratnākara (ocean) was worshipped in course of which groups of ladies in beautiful dress sang songs in praise of his serenity, grandeur, honour and other qualities.[170] Before the ship set sail maid servants applied the auspicious paint of gruel with their five fingers.[171] The *Nāyādhammakahā* gives more details of these rites and formalities. It says that the relatives, grandfather, father, brother, maternal uncle and others, wished those on the ship *bon voyage;* flowers were offered to propitiate the deity presiding over the sea, impression of five fingers was made with the paste of real sandal, *dardara* and other things, incense was burnt, and other *pūjā* rites were performed. The ships started amidst the joyous roar of the cheering crowd, which emulated the roar of the lion, or of the great sea. The soothsayer was loudly uttering benedictions: "Successes to you all, fulfilled be your desires." Greatly pleased were the crew—the captain, the rowers, the officers of the boats, and the merchants.[172]

From earlier texts[173] we learn that sons of chief navigators received education in the nautical science, so that they may also become successful sailors and captains. We do not know the details of the instruction given to these trainees. According to the *Jātakamālā* at Sopārā a pilot could handle ships only after he had learnt the *Niryāmakasūtra.*[174] The reference is probably to some text and not to nautical science. But there is no ancient work of this name. In the library of the old college of Fort St. George (Madras) there were manuscripts of a work on *Nāvāśāstram* (which in one case is called *Kappal Śāstram).*[175] The text has not been edited and studied. It seems to have been a late text. It is chiefly astrological with some directions about the materials and dimensions of vessels.

It seems from the *Tilakamañjarī*[176] that the training given to sailors was essentially practical. We learn that Tāraka was made the chief of the sailors by Candraketu who regarded him as his own son-in-law. Functioning as chief Tāraka very soon learnt the complete art of shipping (*naupracāravidyā*), knew all the duties of a helmsman, journeyed back and forth in deep waters several times, visited the countries of *dvīpāntara* even though they were far removed, saw with his own eyes even small waterways and carefully observed rough and smooth places there. In a subsequent passage[177] he is described as having properly practised the works connected with sailing a ship.

Another reference in the same text would indicate that the sailors could make a practical use of astronomical knowledge.[178] It would seem from the *Bhavisyattakahā*[179] that the sailors studied texts on medicine or rather chemistry, because the reference is to sealing vessels of gold and embossing names on them.

But it seems that as compared with the sailors of other countries the technical skill of Indian sailors was not of a high order. John of Montesorvino speaks of Indian sailors thus: "Moreover their mariners are few and far from good. Hence they run a multitude of risks, insomuch that they are won't to say, when any ship achieves her voyage safely and soundly, that 'tis by God's guidance, and man's skill hath little availed."

In the story books we generally read that before setting sail, the sailors collected an abundance of food material, filled up all the water jars with sweet water and also stored fuel.[180] Such a description may not require an actual experience of sea voyage. But in some cases we find the texts adding details of a specialised nature. Thus the *Tilakamañjarī*[181] says that ghee, oil, blankets, medicine and other things essential for maintaining the body which were given by experts were also taken. From another reference it is clear that the sailors gave attention to preserving ointment necessary for moving in the sea water, kerosene oil and other things and also blocked the holes in the flanks of the reservoir of sweet water.[182] In the *Nāyādhamma Kahā*[183] we read that sailors took with them for viaticum, molasses, rice, oil, ghee, milk products, water in water jars, medicinal drugs, grass, fuel, coverings for the body, wearing apparels, besides many other necessary things required for sailing the boats. In the *Jātakas*[184] we have some indications of the actual use of these things. We find that facing shipwreck people on the ship took as much sugar and ghee as they could digest and covered their bodies and garments with oil to sustain them.

From the story books of the period, we find that the survivals of a shipwreck on reaching an island hoisted a flag on some high place, so that the passing ships may notice it and come to their rescue.[185] The *Samarāiccakahā* uses a technical expression for such a flag[186] *(bhinnapoyaddhao=bhinnapotadhvaja)*. The *Bṛhatkathāśloka-saṅgraha*[187] refers to the custom of sailors of wrecked ships *(bhjnnapatavaṇijavṛtta)* to place a flag on the top of a tree and burn fire so that passing ships may see and come to rescue. The use of the special term shows that sea-voyage and consequent shipwrecks were not uncommon. It was probably a professional courtesy (like that of the highway ethics of modern motor drivers) to go to the rescue of such people.

NOTES AND REFERENCES

1. R. Samkrtyayana (ed.), *Dohākośa of Sarahapā*, Patna, 1958, XIV, 12, 58.
2. Ed. Isvara Candra Sastri, Calcutta, 1917, p. 224, vv. 84-87. The text utilises the Varṇa nomenclature in classifying several other objects also. We find the classification being applied by other writers to other categories of things. Apparently theoretical, it shows the hold of the Varṇa scheme on Indian thought. However, the characteristic qualities of the four Varṇas were probably taken into consideration for such classifications.
3. P. 131 द ढ़काष्ठगुम्फनिष्ठुरा नावः।
4. T.C. Dasgupta, *Aspects of Bengali Society*, Calcutta, 1935, p. 13.

5. G.P. Hourani, *Arab Seafaring in the Indian Ocean in Ancient and Early Medieval Times,* Princeton, 1951, p. 90.
6. *Ibid.,* pp. 89-91. See Ibn-Jubayr, *Travels,* ed. W. Wright, revised by M.J. de Goeje, London, 1907, p. 71.
7. L. Gopal, *University of Allahabad Studies,* Ancient History Section, 1959, pp. 3-4.
8. Barua, *Bharhut,* Vol. I, Pl. LX. 14, no.85.
9. Marshall, *Sanchi,* Vol. II, Pl. LI.
10. Hornell, 'Indian boat designs', in *Mariner's Mirror,* XXVII, pp. 54-68.
11. R. Ferrand, *Voyage du Merchande Arabe Sulayman en Inde et en Chine,* Paris, 1922, p. 93.
12. H. Yule and H. Cordier, *Cathay and the Way Thither,* London, 1915, II, pp. 113-14: "In this country men make use of a kind of vessel which they call Jase, which is fastened only with stitching of twine. On one of the vessels I embarked, and I could find no iron at all therein."
13. Translated by H.A.R. Gibb, London, 1929, p. 243. "The Indian Ocean is full of reefs and if a ship is nailed with iron nails it breaks upon striking the rocks, whereas if it is sewn together it is given a certain resilience and does not fall to pieces."
14. "For they are stitched with cords of coir (*qinbār*), which is the husk of the coconut : this they (the builders) thrash until it becomes stringy, then they twist from it cords with which they stitch the ships." Quoted by Hourani, *op. cit.,* p. 92.
15. *Mirabilia Deseripta.* Translated by H. Yule, London, 1963, p. 53.
16. H. Yule and H. Coodier, *Cathay and the Way Thither,* London, 1915, III, p. 67: "Their ships in these parts are mighty frail and uncouth, with no iron in them, and no caulking: they are sewn like clothes with twine. And so if the twine breaks anywhere there is a breach indeed! Once every year therefore there is a mending of this, more or less, if they propose to go to sea."
17. *The Book of Ser Marco Polo,* translated by H. Yule and edited by H. Cordier, London, 1903, I, p. 111.
18. M. Komrof, *Contemporaries of Marco Polo,* London, 1928, p. 217.
19. Quoted by A.W. Stiffe, former Trading Centres of the Persian Gulf, in *Geographical Journal,* Vol. XII, p. 294.
20. Herringham, *Ajanta,* Plate XLII. 57(A).
21. Ed. P. Peterson, Calcutta, 1899, p. 420—

    भिनक्ति नावं मूढ़ात्मा स महोदधौ। सूत्रार्थ दारयत्युच्चैर्वैङ्र्थ रत्नमुत्तमाम्।।
    प्रदीपयति कालार्थ देवद्रोणी महत्तमाम्। रत्ननस्थाल्यां पचत्यांब्लखलकं मोहदोषतः।।
22. P. 225, v.96—

    लौहताम्रादिपत्रेण कान्तलोहेन वा तथा।
    दीर्घा चैवोन्नता चेति विशेषे द्विविधा भिदा।।
23. P. 227, v.9—

    धात्वा दीनामतो वक्ष्ये निर्णयं तरिसंश्रयम्।,
    कनकं रजतं ताम्रं त्रितयं वा यथाक्रमम्।।
24. P. 224, v.88—

    न सिन्धुगाद्यार्हति लौहबन्धं, तल्लोहवान्तैः हि लौहम्।
    विपद्यते तेन जलेषु नौका, गुणेन बन्धं निजगाद भोजः।।
25. P. 138, vv.14-15—

    यद्दूरादपि लौहानि समाकृष्यति वेगवत्।
    अयस्कान्तमिदं ज्ञेयं तदर्थ द्विविधं बुधैः।।
    प्रायः समुद्रतोयेषु लक्ष्यते प्रस्तरा इति।।
26. L.B. Gandhi (ed.), *Apabhraṁśakāvyatrayī,* Baroda, 1927, p. 79, vv.29-30—

    लोहिण जड़िउ जु पोउ स फुट्टइ, चुंबुकु जहि पहाणु किब बट्टइ?।
    नेय समुद्दह पारु सु पावइ, अंतरालि तसु आवय आवइ।।

लोहिण रहिउ पोउ गुरुसायरु, दीसइ तरतु जाइवि जड़वायरु।
लाहउ करइ सु पारु वि पावइ, वाणियाह धाणरिद्धि वि दावइ।।
See also *Dohākośa,* XLV. 106.

27. Eds. C.D. Dalal and P. D. Gune, Baroda, 1923, p. 22 (III.23.1.ff).
28. Hourani, *op. cit.,* p. 95. See also René Basset, La Montagne d' Aimant. *Revue des Traditions populaires,* July, 1894, pp. 377-80.
29. Quoted by Hourani, *op. cit.,* p. 96—"Now this kind of structure (stitching) is not used except in the Indian Ocean; for the ships of the Mediterranean and those of the Arabs (there) all have nails; whereas in ships on the Indian Ocean iron nails do not last because the sea-water corrodes the iron, and the nails grow soft and weak in the sea; and therefore the people on its shores have taken to threading cords of fibre instead, and these are coated with grease and tar."
30. L. Gopal, "Antiquity of iron in India", *Uttar Bharati,* X, pp. 71-86; N.R. Banerji, *Iron Age in Ancient India.*
31. Hourani, *op. cit.,* pp. 96-97.
32. Hourani, *op. cit.,* p. 96 adds: "Similarly on the Coromandel and Malabar Coasts of India sewn boats can ride ashore on the heavy surf and stand the shock of being landed on a sandy beach from a breaker."
33. A.L. Basham, *Arts and Letters,* Vol. XXIII, p. 65 (Reprinted in *Studies in Indian History and Culture,* Calcutta, 1964).
34. Yule and Cordier, *op. cit.,* II, p. 67. See *supra,* f.n. 16. Ibn-Jubayr mentions "dusur" (cakum) from the wood of the date palm as being used for caulking—Wright's *Glossary to Ibn-Jubayr,* Ist edn., p. 22.
35. *Persian Wars,* Book 1, p. 19: "For neither are they smeared with pitch, nor with any other substance."
36. "The pieces. . . are. . . caulked with flour and whale oil. . . . They catch the smallest, which they cook in cauldrons, so that their flesh melts and changes into thick liquid. This only substance is famous in the Yemen, at Aden, on the coast of Fars, of Omen, and in the seas of India and China. The people of these regions use this substance to block the holes in their ships"—Reinaud, *Relations,* I, pp. 144-46.
37. P. 131—"Every year these are driven on the coast (of Chungli or Somali) a great many dead fish measuring two hundred feet in length and twenty feet through the body. The people do not eat the flesh of these fish, but they cut out their brains, marrow and eyes, from which they get oil often as much as three hundred odd long (from a single fish). They mix this oil with lime to caulk their boats."
38. Kazwani in Reinaud, *Relations,* I, pp. 145-46: "The people harpooned them (whales) and got much oil out of the brain, which they used for their lamps and smearing ships." Ibn-Jubayr regards shark oil as the best—Hourani, *op. cit.,* p. 98.
39. L. Gopal, *University of Allahabad Studies,* Ancient History Section, 1958, p. 3. See also *Dohākośa,* XIV. 87; Rewah Stone Inscription of Karṃa (Kalacuri era 800)—*E.I.,* XXIV, no.13, v.23.
40. *Arthaśāstra,* II.28.13.
41. K.A.N. Sastri, *Gleanings on Social life from the Avadānas,* p. 20.
42. II.3.1.10-20.
43. P. 132 स्थगित निःशेष संधिरन्ध्रया
44. P. 145 सुलिष्टबन्धानपि फलकसन्धीन्निरुन्धातूर्णमूर्णासिकथकेन
45. See Hourani, *op. cit.,* p. 98.
46. R.K. Mookerji, *A History of Indian Shipping and Maritime Activity,* London, 1912, pp. 46-48; A.L. Basham, *op. cit.,* pp. 66-67.
47. P. 228, vv.19-25.
ब्रह्मक्षत्रे द्वितये एकैके वैश्यशूद्रयोनी।
निग हं सग हं वाथ तत्सर्व्वं द्विविधं भवेत्।।

निग हं पूर्व्वमुद्दिष्टं सग हाणि यथा (च) श्रणु।
सग हा त्रिविधां प्रोक्ता (नोक्ता) सर्व्वमध्याग्रमन्दिरा।।
सर्व्वतो मन्दिरं यत्र सा ज्ञेया सर्व्वमन्दिरा।
राज्ञां केशाश्वनारीणां यानमंत्र प्रशस्यते।।
मध्यतो मन्दिरं यत्र सा ज्ञेया मध्यमन्दिरा।
राज्ञां विलासयात्रादि (त्वं) वर्षासु च प्रशस्यते।।
अग्रतो मन्दिरं यत्र सा ज्ञेया त्वग्रमन्दिरा।
चिरप्रवासयात्राणां रणेकाले घनान्यये।
मन्दिर(रा) मानं नौका प्रसरत एवार्द्धभागतो न्यूनतम्।।
भोजस्तु।
दीर्घव त्तवसुषट्–दिवाकरानेक–दिङ् नवमिता यथाक्रमम्।
राजपंचभुजजसम्मितोन्नतिर्मन्दिरे तारिगते महीभुजाम्।।
भास्करादिक–दशाभुवां पुनर्धातु निर्णयनमत्र पूर्व्ववत्।
पताकाकलसादीनां निर्णयो नवदण्डवत्।।

48. P. 131—सपरिग्रहे च पुरोभागवर्तिनं मनवारणकमध्यमध्यास्य तद्धासने
49. P. 227, vv.10-11—
ब्रह्मादिभिः परिन्यस्य नौका चित्रण–कर्म्मणि।
चतुःश्ंगा त्रिश्ंगामा द्विश्ंगा चैकश्ंगिणी।।
सितरक्तापीतनीलवर्णान् दद्याद् यथाक्रमम्।
केशरी महिषी नागो द्विरदो व्याघ्र एव च।।
There is no apparent connexion between the number of masts and the colours suggested. The *Jātakas* refer to three masts of a ship—II, 212; III. 126: IV. 17.21. A painting from Ajanta represents a ship with three masts—Yazdani, *Ajanta,* II, Plate XLII.
50. R.K. Mookerji, *op. cit.,* pp. 46-48, nos. 1, 3, 5. For the ship on Andhra coins see *A.S.I.* (New Imperial Series), XV, p. 29; Elliot, *Coins of South India,* Plate No. 45.
51. R.K. Mookerji, *loc. cit.,* nos. 2, 4, 6.
52. *Ibid.,* nos. 5, 6.
53. *Ibid.,* no. 1, 3, 5. The ship in the Ajanta painting has square sails. The stay sail is depicted here also. Yazdani, *Ajanta,* II, Plate XLII.
54. Yule and Cordier, *op. cit.,* III, p. 67: "They have but one sail and one mast, and the sails are either of matting or of some miserable cloth. The ropes are of husk."
55. Marco Polo also speaks of one mast and one sail.
56. P. 130. आगत्य च मया कृतानि सर्वाण्यपि सुसूत्राणि यानपात्राणि
57. P. 132 प ष्ठतो नुकूलपवनास्फालन तरंगितेन फेनपाण्डुना लसिससंधातेन पुरस्ताच्च सितपटेन प्रवर्त्यमानया व्रजन्त्याप्यतिजवेन दुर्दिभावत्याद्वतेरनुज्भितस्थानयेवोह्यमानया नावोह्यमानः....
58. P. 134 कूपस्तम्भकानुत्तम्भयभिदः सितपटानासूत्रयाभिदः....
59. P. 138 श्रमविकलवाहवो... न शक्रुवन्ति निद्रावशीकृताः कर्तुमवष्टम्भं कूपस्तम्भकेषु कर्णाधाराः, समीरो पि संप्रति प्रतीपगतिः प्रवाति... ।... प्रगुणीकृत्य यदुपवनपातितसितपटानि...
60. P. 140 मुकुलितसितपटेषु
61. P. 145 अनिल संक्षोभेषु नूतनाः संयोजयता रज्जूरजर्जरस्यापि वारं वारमापादयता सितपटस्य वाटवम्...
62. VI, p. 38— ओसहिओ सियवडो
63. Bombay edition, pp. 398 ff.
64. R.K. Mookerji, *op. cit.,* nos. 1-6.
65. *Ibid.,* p. 47.
66. *Ibid.,* pp. 46-48, nos. 1, 3, 5. See also A.L. Basham, *op. cit.,* pp. 66-67.
67. R.K. Mookerji, *loc. cit.,* no.5.

68. P. 140 सर्वतो वलम्बितस्थूल नागरशिलानिगडितपोतेषु
69. *Ibid.* द ढ़निपातनिष्ठुरकाष्ठकीलनियमितनौकेषु
70. *Samarāiccakahā*, VI, p. 37— आगंढियाओ वेगहारिणीओ सिलाओ; (Bombay edition), pp. 264 ff, *Bhavisyattakahā*, VII.3.3 (pp.48-49); *Nāyadhammakahāo,* Agamadaya Samiti edition, pp. 131 ff.
71. *Divyāvadāna*, p. 230.
72. VI, p. 38 तओ समं गमणारम्भेण ओसारिओ सियवडो जीवियासा विय विमुक्का नंगरसिला निज्जामएहि। Bombay edition, pp. 298 ff.
73. II, p. 299.
74. Yule and Cordier, *op. cit.,* III, p. 67.
75. XVIII, 314 ff.
76. VI, p. 39, Bombay edition, pp. 398 ff.
77. R.K. Mookerji, *op. cit.,* p. 48, no.5.
78. Pp. 224 ff, vv. 89 ff.
79. *Op. cit.,* p. 65.
80. *Op. cit.,* p. 46.
81. Purchas, *His Pilgrimes,* Mac Lehose edn., III, pp. 193, 396 : see also Hirth and Rockhill, *Chau Ju-Kua,* Introduction, p. 34, f.n.2.
82. मेघादीत्यादिपदेन यानपोतादिपरिग्रहस्तेषामपि वायुना प्रेर्य्यमाणत्वात्।
    Śrīdhara as quoted by B.K. Sarkar, *Positive Background of Hindu Sociology,* Appendix D, p. 351.
83. *Islamic Culture*, 1941, p. 443.
84. P. 386.
85. P. 146— राजिलक तर्जितो पि नोपरमसि प्रगुणयायिनीमपि नावमागस्ती गतिं ग्राहस्यरित कश्चिन्न ते दिङ्मोहो यद्युदाहृतामप्यहृदय न जानास्युत्तराशावर्तनीं प्रवर्तनीम्। प्रवर्तय द ष्ट्वा द ष्ट्वा सप्तर्षि मण्डलित्यादि।
86. *Ṛgveda,* VI, 62.2; *Jātaka,* III, 267; *Dighanikaya,* XI.85.
87. *Dohākośa,* IX (ख), 23-24. See also Hirth and Rockhill, *Chau Ju-Kua*, Introduction, p. 28.
88. Moti Chandra, *Sārthavāha,* Patna, 1953, pp. 147-209; R.K. Mookerji, *op. cit.,* pp. 47-48; *Bombay Gazetteer,* XIII, Part ii, Appendix A, p. 725.
89. L. Gopal, *University of Allahabad Studies,* Ancient History Section, 1959, pp. 16-17; A.L. Basham, *op. cit.,* pp. 66-67.
90. VII.2.16. T.W. Rhys Davids, *The Questions of King Milinda,* II, p. 301 translates *yanta* as steering apparatus. *Dhruva* mentioned in the *Vasudevahindi* (pp. 145-46; Gujarati translation, pp. 188-89) has been translated as a mariner's compass—*Journal of Oriental Institute*, X, p. 10.
91. R.K. Mookerji, *op. cit.,* pp. 46-48, illustration no. 1. The object can be noticed in some other illustrations—A.L. Basham, p. 67.
92. *Op. cit.*
93. A.L. Basham, *loc. cit.* They could as well have been more ornamental designs—L. Gopal, *University of Allahabad Studies,* Ancient History Section, 1959, p. 16.
94. J. Needham, *Science and Civilization in China,* VI, 1, pp. 245-50.
95. E. Speak, *Hande lsgeschichte des Alterthums,* I, pp. 29, 209 refers it to the first century AD and Beazley, *Dawn of Modern Geography,* I, p. 490 to the third century.
96. "The ship masters know the configuration of the coasts, at night they steer by the stars and in the day-time by the sun. When the sun is obscured they look at the south-pointing needle or use a line a hundred feet long with a hook, with which they take up mud from the sea bottom; by its smell they determine their whereabouts. In mid-ocean it never rains; whenever it rains (they know) they are nearing an island (or headland)"—Hirth and Rockhill (Eds.), *Chau Ju-kua,* Introduction, p. 32.
97. He refers to the "south-pointing floating needle" being used on the ships sailing from Ning-po. It seems from the description that it was a new invention—Edkins, *JCBRAS,* XI, pp. 128-34.

98. The "south-pointing ship" mentioned by the *Sung-shi* for the period of the Tsin dynasty (E.H. Parker, *China Review,* XVIII, p. 197) does not necessarily imply a compass. See also J. Chalmers, *China Review*, XIX, pp. 52-54 (discusses "south-pointing chariots" of early Chinese records); A. Wylie, *Magnetic Compass in China.* Chou Ku-fei also shows that the captains relied on wind and stars—Hirth and Rockhill, *Chau Ju-kua*, Introduction, p. 34.
99. AD. Reinaud, *Geographie d'Aboulfeda,* I, pp. cciii-cciv; S.S. Nadvi, *Arbon Ki Jahāzrāni* (Azamgarh, 1935), pp. 148-52. Nadvi quotes Ali Idrīsī (AD 1154) but admits that he himself did not see the passage. Thus the earliest known reference is by Muhammad 'Aufī in his *Jāmi'ul Hikāyāt* (AD 1232) and Bailak Qibajaqi (death in AD 1282) in his *Kanzul Taijar.*
100. Hourani, *op. cit.,* pp. 108 f.
101. *Bombay Gazetteer,* Vol. XIII, Part II, Appendix A, p. 725.
102. E.g., Marco Polo.
103. Marco Polo and Nicolo Conti. Translated by J. Frampton and edited by N.M. Penzer, London, 1929, p. 140.
104. It was realised that cleaning (*saṃmārjanam)* and right placing of the magnet (*ṛjusthāpanam)* are necessary. But, while commenting on the movement of the needle towards the magnet as an example of unexplained motion in matter Śaṅkara Misra adds that needle meaning iron rod stands for iron in general सूचीनां लोहशलाकानां, अयस्कांताभिमुखगमनम्, सूचीत्युपलक्षणम् अयस्कान्ता कृष्टलोहोहमात्रमाभिप्रेतम्– As quoted by B.K. Sarkar, *Positive Background of Hindu Sociology*, Appendix D, p. 357.
105. Ed. F. Lacote, XIX 107 सहसागरदिग्देशं स्पष्टं संपुटके लिखन्
106. L. Gopal, *The Economic Life of Northern India* (c. AD 700-1200 AD) Varanasi, pp. 119-60.
107. K.A.N. Sastri, *Foreign Notices of South India*, Madras, 1939, p. 19.
108. Quoted in *Age of Imperial Kanauj,* p. 401.
109. *Chau Ju-kua*, p. 19.
110. *Ibid.,* p. 11, 41-42, 113.
111. Pp. 996-98.
112. Ferrand, *Voyage du Marchand Arabe Sulayman,* p. 138.
113. A.K. Majumdar, *Chaulukyas of Gujarat,* Bombay, 1956, p. 267.
114. Yule and Cordier, *op. cit.,* I, pp. 84-85.
115. L. Gopal, *The Economic Life of Northern India,* p. 143.
116. *Ibid.,* pp. 144-45.
117. *Ibid.,* p. 125.
118. *Ibid.,* pp. 119-25.
119. *Ibid.,* pp. 126-27.
120. *Daśakumāracarita,* Tr. Ryder, Chicago, 1927, p. 164; *Prabandhacintāmaṇi,* ed. Jinavijaya Muni, Santiniketan, 1933, p. 14; Motupalli Pillar Inscription, *E.I.* XII, p. 195; Ibn Batūta, tr. H.A.R. Gibb, pp. 233, 254.
121. L. Gopal, *loc. cit.,* p. 129.
122. *Bodhisattvāvadāna Kalpalatā*. Bibliotheca Indica Series, pp. 113-14.
123. Ibn Batūta, H.A.R. Gibb, p. 230.
124. Ibn Batūta, *Voyages,* eds. C. Defremery and B.R. Sangiunetti, III, pp. 88-91.
125. *Upamitibhava Prapañcā-kathā,* pp. 870-72.
126. T.1.22; II.1.51.
127. III.158.
128. IV.179. A.L. Basham, *op. cit.,* p. 68 finds its confirmation in a statement by Dion Chrysostom, *Oratio,* XXXV, 434 (R.C. Majumdar, *The Classical Accounts of India*, Calcutta, 1960, p. 433): "...and some few do come in pursuit of trade. Now these do business with the inhabitants of the seacoast, but this class of Indians is not held in repute, and are reprobated by the rest of their countrymen."
129. On Yājña, III, 292.
130. II, 134 f.

131. XXII, 12-16. समुद्रयात्रास्वीकारः कमण्डलुविधारणम्।
द्विजानामसवर्णासु कन्यासूयमस्तथा।।...
इमान् धर्मान् कलिपुये वज्योनाहुर्मनीषिणः।।
See also *Smṛtyarthasāra,* p. 2; *Udvāhatattva,* p. 112, *Nirṇayasindhu,* p. 367; *Kalivarjyavivaraṇa;* Kṛṣṇabhaṭṭa (on *Nirṇayasindhu,* p. 1288) makes it clear that expiration is to be undergone when the sea-voyage is undertaken from worldly motives and not as part of pilgrimage - एतच्च प्रायश्चित्तं रागप्राप्ते समुद्रयान एव। शंखोद्धारादितीर्थे यात्राविधिनान्तरीयकं समुद्रयानमतो दोषाभावान्न प्रायश्चित्तमित्यन्यत्र बिस्तरः।
132. *Caturvargacintāmaṇi,* Calcutta, 1895, III. Pt. 2, p. 667.
133. *History of Dharmaśāstra,* III, p. 934.
134. Quoted by Kane, *History of Dharmaśāstra, III,* p. 936.
135. VI.41.
136. I.32.
137. Manu II.23— कृष्णमारस्तु चरति म गो यत्र स्वभावतः।
स ज्ञेयो यज्ञियो देशो म्लेच्छदेशस्त्वतः परः।।
Al-Bīrūnī II, pp. 134-35.
138. Devala quoted in *Mitākśarā* on Yājñavalkya, III, 292; *Āditya Purāṇa* quoted in *Smṛticondrikā,* I, p. 9; *Ādi Purāṇa* quoted in *Paribhāṣāprakāśa,* p. 59.
139. L. Gopal, "Economic Pursuits in Indian Ideal of Life", *Gopinath Kaviraj Abhinandan Granth,* Varanasi, 1968, p. 411.
140. *Ibid.,* pp. 409-11.
141. For example traditions about the missions of Sona and Uttara to Suvaṇṇabhūmi (*Mahāvaṃsa,* XII.6, 44, ff: *Dīpavaṃsa,* VIII, 12; *Samantapāsādikā,* I. 64) and Mahindra and Saṅghamittā to Ceylon. See also traditions about Guṇavarman (Pelliot, *B.E.F.E.D.,* IV, pp. 271 ff). Dharmapāla (Kern, *Manual of Buddhism,* p. 130) and Atiśa Dīpaṅkara (S.C. Das, *Indian Pandits in the Land of Snow,* p. 50) sailing to Suvarṇadvīpa.
142. A.L. Basham, *Arts and Letters,* XXIII, p. 69.
143. L. Gopal, *Economic Life of Northern India,* p. 125.
144. *Ibid.,* p. 126.
145. VIII 157— समुद्रयानुकुशला देशकालार्थदर्शिनः।
स्थापयन्ति तु यां व द्धि सा तत्राधिगमं प्रति।।
146. समुद्रयानग्रहणं यात्रोपलक्षणार्थम्। स्थलपथिका वारि पथिकाश्च वणिजो यां व द्धिं स्थापयन्ति सा तत्राधिगमं प्रति निश्चयं प्रति। सैव निश्चेतव्येत्यर्थः।
147. *Kṛtyakalpataru, Vyavahāra,* p. 284— 'समुद्रयानकुशला' इति वाणिङ्मात्रोपलक्षणम्।
148. III, 652-660. In 655 it gives terms for a sea-trader, a ship, the mast of a ship and a helmsman. Later on in the context of rivers it mentions terms for oar, rudder and the head of a boat.
149. P. 155, 11. 29-39.
150. I. 122; II. 20; V. 7; VI. 95, 96.
151. P. 75, 1.83 वैश्या सामुद्रमाजीवेत् पण्यं सामुद्रमेव सः।
152. *Op. cit.,* p. 69.
153. XII, 2-6.
154. Quoted in *Yuktikalpataru,* p. 223, f.n.
समुद्रयाने रत्नानि महामूल्यानि साधुभिः।
रत्नपारीक्षकैः सार्द्धमानयिष्ये बहूनि च।।
शुकेन सह संप्राप्तो महान्तं लवणार्णावम्।
पोतारूढ़ास्ततः सर्व्वे पोतवाहैरूपसिताः।।
अपारे दुस्तरे गाधे यान्ति वेगेन नित्यशः।
155. IV.2— हर्म्यारोहणहैलया यदचलाः स्वभ्रैः सदाभ्रंलिहा, यद्वा गोष्पदलीलया जलभरक्षोमोद्धताः सिन्धवः।
लंघ्यन्ते भवनस्थलीकलनया ये चाटवीनां तटाः, तद्वीर्यस्य महात्मानां विलसतः सत्त्वोर्जितं स्फूर्जितम्।।

156. Pp. 264 ff, 398 ff, 585.
157. Pp. 996-98.
158. P. 29.
159. LIII, 3 ff; LXXVIII, 42; LXXXII, 1 ff.
160. Pp. 123 ff. In this account we find the use of many terms connected with ships and shipping. Thus on p. 124 we notice the word *sāgarāvatāradeśa* for the dock.
161. Pp. 21 ff.
162. *Dohākośa:* Sarahapāda's *Upadeśagīti,* III, 53; IX. 23-24, XIV, 5, 7, 8, 11, 12, 14, 21, 22, 38-40, 59, 65, 70-72, 84, 87, 89, 95, 101, 106, 112, 132; *Vinayaśrī,* No.14.
163. Pp. 223-28.
164. D. Chakravarti (ed.), *Manasāmaṅgal* of Baṅgsīdās, p. 286; *Caṇḍi kāvya* of Kavikaṅkaṇ, Bangabasi ed., pp. 221-22.
165. See T. Dasgupta, *Aspects of Bengali Society,* p. 17.
166. Pp. 62, 68. Also p. 56.
167. VI, p. 37 (p.264). See also p. 398.
168. *Upamitibhavaprapañcākathā,* pp. 900-1 (कृतानि मंगलानि); *Bṛhatkathākośa,* LXXVIII, 42 (कृतमंगल सत्कार्यः)
169. Pp. 21 f (III.22.10) जलजंताकम्मंतरु)
170. P. 123 उदारवेषयोषि द्व न्दगीयमानगाम्भीर्यमहिमयर्यादादिजलनिधिगुणाम्... भगवतो रत्नाकरस्य पूजां प्रतिष्ठम्।
171. P. 132 दासपुरंध्रिदत्तपिष्ट पंचांगलया
172. Angamodaya Samiti edition, pp. 131 ff. This may be one of the rare passages which are exception to the general remark made by Prof. Basham. See *supra,* f.n. 152.
173. *Jātaka* IV, pp. 87-88; *Jātakamālā,* pp. 88-89.
174. *JUPHS,* XXIV-XXV, p. 183.
175. Rev. William Taylor, *A Catalogue Raisonee of Oriental MSS in the library of the Late College of Fort St. George,* Madras, 1857, Vol. III, pp. 6 (no. 2226), 444.
176. Pp. 129-30— तत्र च कुर्वताधिपत्यमचिरेणैव शिक्षितानेन सकलापि नौप्रचारविद्या, विदितम्खिलमपि कर्णधाराणां कर्म कृतानि बहुकृत्वः सलिलराशौ गमनागमनानि, द ष्टा दूरप्रकृष्टा अपि द्वीपान्तरभूमयः प्रत्यक्षीकृताः क्षुद्रा अपि जलपथाः, लक्षितानि तेषु सम्यकसमविषमस्थानानि।

    Later on, the text enumerates the good qualities of Taraka for which he is recommended to be Pointed captain of the ship. But here there is no reference to any technical knowledge. The passage simply mentions his courage, cool-mindedness and observation.
177. P. 144— सम्यगभ्यस्त यान पात्रप्रचार कर्मणा
178. P. 146. See *supra,* f.n. 85.
179. P. 48 (VII.1.84-5). He distinctly remembered what was written in books of medicine.
180. *Tilakamañjarī,* p. 130 पुंजितं तेष्वतिप्राज्यमशनम्, आपूरितानि स्वादुना सलिलेन कृत्स्नान्युदकपात्राणि, समारोपितमप्रमाणमिन्धनम्; p. 138 — पूरयित्वा स्वादुसलिलेन रिक्तजलभाण्डानि ग हीत्वा कियन्मात्रमपि सारमिन्धनदारु।
181. P. 130 अपरो पि देहस्थितिसाधनमधिकृतैर्यः कश्चिदर्पितः सो पि सर्पिस्तैलकम्बलोषधप्रायः प्रायशो विन्यस्तः समस्तो पि द्वीपान्तरदुरायो द्रव्याणां कलापः।
182. P. 134 स्वीकृतसलिलमध्यसंचारणोचिता जनैरग्नितैलादिद्रव्यसंग्रहपरैः।
183. Pp. 131f.
184. No. 442, 539.
185. *Bhavisayattakahā,* p. 45 (VI.18.1-2, 12-13). See also *Dohākośa,* XIV.14.
186. VI, p. 39; Bombay edition, p. 399.
187. XVIII, 314 ff.

8

Maritime Tradition of Western India

M.K. DHAVALIKAR

Of the 1,200 km western coastline, the states of Gujarat and Maharashtra cover almost half of it and they have therefore a strong maritime tradition, the antiquity of which goes back to prehistoric times. There is considerable documentary and archaeological evidence which shows that the western coast, more particularly of Gujarat was humming with maritime activity some five thousand years ago. The tradition continues till today and almost our entire maritime contact with the western world is through ports on the western coast.

On the western coast, it seems that Kutch, which is a part of the present state of Gujarat, has the earliest evidence. According to geologists, Kutch was formerly an island separated from the mainland Gujarat. Even in the historical period, a branch of the river Indus-Nararan in a more easterly course flowed first into the Gulf of Cambay, and then into the Rann of Kutch.[1] Even *The Periplus of the Erythraen Sea,* a first century AD work by an unknown Greek sailor, testifies that there was a sea around Kutch in the north-west and the north-east. The local tradition about the Rann is also worth consideration. The local people still talk of the Rann being an arm of the sea and that ships were sailing through it bringing valuable cargo from distant lands. They relate interesting stories about one Jagadusha, a rich and benevolent merchant whose ships brought gold.[2] There is evidence to show that the Rann was navigable till the mediaeval times and contact with it must have been through sea.

It is now well known that the Indus civilization had spread into Gujarat and to some extent in Maharashtra as well.[3] But evidence is now becoming available which points to sea trade between India and Mesopotamia even in Pre-Harappan times in the early centuries of the third millennium BC. It is supplied by the occurrence of long tubular carnelian beads in Pre-Akkadian times and of chank shell at Shahr-i-sokhta in Iran in levels dated to *c.* 2800 BC. The particular variety of chank shell (*Xancus pyrum*) is abundant along the Saurashtra coast, and a shell cutting centre was established by the Harappans at Nageshwar, near Jamnagar on the Saurashtra coast.[4] Evidence from recent excavations at Dholavira, the Harappan metropolis in Kutch, points to the arrival of merchant traders from Sind in pre-Harrapan times.[5]

The Harappans started coming to Gujarat right from 2600 BC. There is some controversy about the manner in which they came because some scholars think that the Rann was already a desert and hence they came overland[6] whereas others are of the opinion that the Rann was an arm of sea[7] which the Harappans had to cross. But it is highly likely that the climate during the third millennium BC being wet, the sea-level was higher with the Ranns being under 2-4 m water.[8] It seems likely that the Ranns, as of now, may not be under water all over the year; they are under water during the monsoon from June to October, and are dry from November to March and were thus crossable.

Why did the Harappans come to Kutch? Kutch does not have good, cultivable soil, nor enough water resources and is not therefore an area of attraction for human settlement. But the Harappans seem to have come to Kutch for using its seaports as is clear from the location of most of the Harappan settlements which are on or near the coast, and it is through Kutch that they came to Saurashtra for exploitation of its raw materials. Saurashtra has an abundant supply of agates, carnelian and other semi-precious stones, chank shell, ivory and also copper. The Harappans needed these materials for fashioning into beads, and bangles which were in great demand in Mesopotamia. The Harappans also established port settlements in Saurashtra of which Lothal near Ahmedabad has been excavated on a sufficiently large scale.[9] The dockyard discovered at Lothal is perhaps the earliest such structure anywhere in the world. It was 710 ft long and 120 ft wide with about 24 ft. deep and ships were brought into it for repairs. It has been described as a dry dock.[10] The type of ships the Harappans used is depicted in a Harappan seal. It also shows a bird flying above which probably is crow because the *Baveru Jataka* refers to boatmen taking crows with them for finding land.

Lothal also had a warehouse which is unique in the annals of archaeology. It had squarish blocks of mud bricks (3.60 m sq and 90 cm high) with passage, in between of 9.20m wide. There were 12 such blocks. In the warehouse were found 65 sealings which bear impressions of seals which indicate that the goods stored here were imported. It is significant that the spot where the warehouse was located was worshipped by the local people as the shrine of the goddess Vanuvati-mata, the sea goddess.

There were many Harappan seaports in Gujarat, mostly in Kutch and Saurashtra. But by 2000 BC, the Indus civilization was on the decline, possibly because of a drastic shift in climate all over the Old World, and as a consequence the trade dwindled. Some trading contact, however, seems to have continued for a huge structure, which has been identified as a warehouse has been discovered at Prabhas Patan.[11] It is built of stone rubble set in mud mortar and consists of small rooms averaging 2 x 1.50 m whereas some of the rooms are squarish. There was no provision for any wooden posts or uprights for supporting the roof as no post-holes were found. This is indicative of the structure being roofless and open to sky. Moreover, the height of the walls was not more than 60 cm. In fact most of the walls had only one or two courses of stones. Only the central wall running north-south was a little higher (80 cm), and two more walls parallel to it were also equally high. It seems likely that a few upper courses of walls have fallen, but in any case they may not be higher, if the fallen debris is any indication. In some rooms, large flat stones were embedded in black clay in the middle. There was no *chulah* or fireplace, and the structure therefore was not residential. Since the ancient site is located almost on the seacoast, and as it has some resemblance with the Lothal warehouse, it can be identified as a warehosue. Formerly we had dated it to the Prabhas period (C. 1800-1500 BC), but the calibrated dates would place it between *c.* 2000 BC to 1700 BC.[12]

The post-Harappan chalcolithic people had rural cultures which flourished in the second millennium BC. The period from *c.* 2000 BC to about 1000 BC was marked by extremely adverse environment; and later still it became so adverse that all the chalcolithic habitations were abandoned by the farming communities who probably resorted to pastoral nomadism. This phenomenon was not confined to western India only but affected a major part of the Old World.[13] Climate again seems to have improved from 500 BC onwards and great empires flourished from 500 BC to AD 500 in different parts of the world.

This period from 500 BC to AD 500 is marked by the rise of civilization in India. It witnessed the second urbanization and the Golden Age under the Vakatakas and Guptas in AD 300-500. The background for this Golden Age was formed in the early centuries of the Christian era when India enjoyed a flourishing trade with the Roman Empire. From north India, the trade was carried overland whereas from the south and west it was maritime. Much has been written about this trade.[14] The trade was carried through western ports in Gujarat and Maharashtra, prominent among which were Broach (Bhrgukachha, Sk.; Barygaza of Ptolemy) and Sopara, near Bombay (Surparaka Sk.; Suppara of Ptolemy) in Maharashtra. It is generally thought that the trade became brisk after the discovery of the monsoon in AD 44 by a Greek sailor, Hippalus by name. Recent studies show that the trade began much earlier, in the 1st century BC even in the pre-Augustus period.[15] The trade was in the hands of Arab middlemen at Alexandria in Egypt and the Indian merchants rarely reached Rome.

Why did the trade not flourish in the Pre-Roman times? There were two reasons: one, the Red Sea is treacherous because of corals, and two, the Red Sea was infested with pirates. We are told that emperor Augustus established naval stations and controlled the piracy. Moreover, the Arab ships were technologically much inferior as compared to Roman ships which were larger and stronger. Hence trade increased by leaps and bounds under Romans so much that one ship left every day for Egypt from India loaded with luxury goods such as silks, muslin, pearls, ivory, lapis lazuli and above all spices. Pliny the Elder lamented the loss to the Roman Empire from this adverse balance of payments, for the price of Indian articles in Rome was one hundred times that in India. For this Rome paid not less than 55 million sesterces (about 6 lakh British pounds) a year.[17] Pliny (XII, 94) was justified in lamenting that "so dearly do we pay for our luxury and our women."

India's trade passed through Egypt and, although Indian traders did not go to Rome, many Roman merchants, probably residents of Alexandria, had come to India. Their presence in Indian cities has been recorded in early Tamil literature;[18] they seem to have concentrated in western and South India. This is evident from their inscriptions which record their munificent donations to Buddhist establishments in Maharashtra, particularly those at Karla, Nasik and Junnar.[19] Many of these *Yavana* donors claim to have hailed from a place called Dhenukakata which has not yet been identified. It may have been the present town of Junnar near Pune.[20] It may be noted that the house of a Roman merchant was found in the excavations at Kolhapur (Brahmapuri) which yielded a number of bronze objects of surpassing beauty. They are of Alexandrian origin and are dated to first century.[21] They include a most beautiful statue of Poseidon, the Roman sea god, candelabra, wine jugs and mirrors.

The trade began to dwindle in the third century AD possibly because of climatic change and foreign invasions. Consequently the Roman Empire witnessed degeneration. But the memory of this trade still survives in western India where the people in the coastal region worship a goddess called Sakotari Mata,[22] so named after the island of Socotra, at the head of the Red Sea, from where the treacherous journey started.

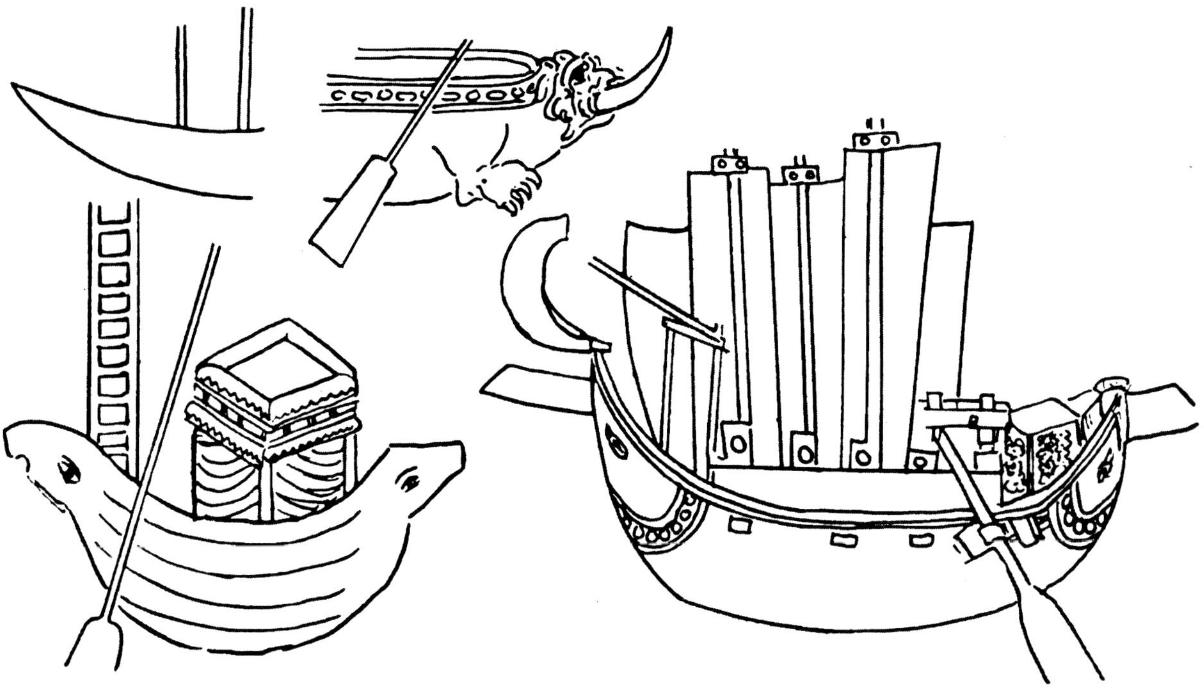

Fig. 1. Refresentations of Ships, Ajanta

In India too, economic condition deteriorates from the 5th century onwards. The Gupta empire is on the decline and the following five centuries are marked by decay. We have ample evidence, literary and archaeological, which gives a fair idea of the decline. This evidence has been very critically analysed by R.S. Sharma.[23] There was no foreign trade worth the name, and frequent famines and droughts caused tremendous hardship to the people. The *Puranas* predict a prolonged famine which was widespread in western India.[24] The *Devi Bhāgavata* (XII, 9, 1-37) refers to a hundred year famine. This was probably the same famine which has been referred to in the *Javanese Chronicles.* They relate that about AD 603, a ruler of Gujarat, forewarned of the coming destruction of his kingdom because of famine, started his son with 5,000 followers, among whom were cultivators, writers, warriors, physicians in six large and a hundred small vessels for Java where they laid the foundation of a great civilization.[25]

The people from western India migrated to South-east Asia in large ships. Such ocean-going vessels have been depicted in the fifth century Vakataka paintings at Ajantā. There are two large panels viz. the Simhala Avadana in Cave 17 and the Purna Avadana in Cave 2[26]. The former depicts the landing of Prince Simhala on the island of Ogresses. There are two ships, one of them carrying three elephants mounted by kings and princes while the other is carrying cavalry. The ship has oars with broad ends, probably attached. It is adorned with *makara-mukha* on the prow; the upper margin of the body contains beaded ornamentation. The early Tamil epic, *Silappadikaram* informs us that there were boats having the shapes of animals.

The finer and the larger ship is to be seen in the panel depicting Purna Avadana in Cave 2 (Fig. 1). It has a high prow and stern with oblong sails attached to as many upright masts. The jib is well filled with wind. A sort of bowsprit, projecting from a kind of gallows on deck, is indicated with the outflying jib, square in form like that borne till recent times by European vessels. The ship appears to be decked and has ports. Steering oars hang in sockets or rowlocks in the quarter, and eyes are painted on the bows. There is also an oar behind and under the awnings are a number of jars while two platforms are fore and aft. This huge ship, with its cabin and masts, is undoubtedly a sea-going vessel. It should clear the doubt of those who are of the opinion that there is no representation of a real sea-going ship in India prior to 10th century AD.[28]

Yet another sea-going vessel is depicted on a stone slab from Eksar near Bombay which is dated to the 10th-11th century AD. It depicts a naval battle of the Silahara period. Unfortunately the whereabouts of this sculpture are unknown, but we have a photograph in Moti Chandra's *Sarthavaha*. Not much is known about the mediaeval period when the Maratha rulers were constantly engaged in warfare with the Muslim rulers of Delhi. Chhatrapati Shivaji, however, evidenced a keen interest in and built up a strong naval force. He built several marine forts in the coastal region of Konkan. He led his first naval expedition in 1664 against Basrur, the chief port of Shivappa Naik of Bidnur in Karnatak.[29] Thana, Kalyan, Bhivandi, Alibag, Vijaydurg, Vasai and Malvan were the chief ship building centres of the Marathas and dockyards were located at Alibag and Vijaydurg. Jadunath Sarkar is justified in his observation that "Nothing proves Shivaji's genius as a born statesman more clearly than his creation of a navy and naval bases."[30] The Peshwas, however, neglected the navy. Thus western India has a glorious maritime tradition.

NOTES AND REFERENCES

1. K.V. Soundararajan, "Kutch-Harappan—A corridor of the Indus Phase," in B.B. Lal and S.P. Gupta (Eds.). *Frontiers of Indus Civilization—Sir Mortimer Wheeler Comm. Vol.* (New Delhi, 1984), p. 217.
2. Y.M. Chitalwala, "Harappan settlements in Kutch-Saurashtra region," in G.l. Possehl (ed.), *Harappan Civilization—A Contemporary Perspective* (New Delhi, 1982), p. 199.
3. M.K. Dhavalikar, *Cultural Imperialism—Indus Civilization in Western India* (New Delhi, 1994).
4. K.T.M. Hegde *et al., Excavations at Nageshwar* (Baroda, 1984).
5. R.S. Bisht, pers. comm.
6. J.P. Joshi, *Excavations at Surkotada* (New Delhi, 1990), pp. 52-53.
7. S.R. Rao, "Shipping and Maritime Trade of the Indus People", *Expedition,* Vol. 7 (1965), pp. 30-37.
8. S.K. Gupta, "Quaternary sea-level changes on the Saurashtra coast", in D.P. Agrawal and B.M. Pande (eds.), *Ecology and Archaeology of Western India* (Delhi, 1977), pp. 181-93.
9. S.R. Rao, *Lothal—A Harappan Port Town (1955-62),* 2 vols (New Delhi, 1979 and 1985).
10. There ranges some controversy about the identification of the structure as dock. See L.S. Leshnik and Junghans in G.L. Possehl (eds.), *Ancient Cities of the Indus* (New Delhi, 1979), pp. 203 ff.
11. M.K. Dhavalikar, "An Early Warehouse on the Western coast," *Puratattva,* No. 9 (1978), pp. 100-03.
12. G.L. Possehl, "The Harappan Civilization in Gujarat—The Sarath and the Sindhi Harappan," in *The Eastern Anthropologist,* Vol. 42 (1992), Appendix A.
13. M.K. Dhavalikar, "Culture-environment Interface—A Historical Perspective." Presidential Address, Indian History Congress, Section V, New Delhi, 1992.
14. E.H. Warmington, *The Commerce between Roman Empire and India* (Cambridge, 1928).

15. Vimla Begley and Richard Daniel de Puma (eds.), *Rome and India——Ancient Sea Trade* (Madison, 1991).
16. Lionel Casson, "Ancient Naval Technology", in Begley and de Puma, *op. cit.*, pp. 8-11.
17. Warmington, *op. cit.*, p. 274.
18. W.W. Tarn, *The Greeks in Bactria and India* (Cambridge, 1951, 2nd ed.), pp. 254-58.
19. S.C. Laeuchli, "Yavana Inscriptions of Western India," *Jr. of the Asiatic Soc. of Bombay,* Vols 56-59 (1981-84), pp. 207-21.
20. *Ibid.*
21. Karl Khandalwala, "Brahmapuri", *Lalit Kala*, No. 7 (1960), pp. 29-75.
22. S.R. Rao, *Lothal,* Vol. I, p. 224.
23. *Urban Decay* (Delhi, 1987).
24. Dhavalikar, *op. cit.*, pp. 984-85.
25. R.K. Mookerji, *Indian Shipping* (Bombay, 1912), p. 51.
26. M.K. Dhavalikar, *Ajanta—A Cultural Study* (Poona 1973), pp. 128 ff.
27. Griffiths' description being most accurate is followed here. See his *Paintings in the Buddhist Cave Temples of Ajanta* (London, 1896-97), Vol. I, p. 17.
28. R.D. Barnett, "Early shipping in the Near East", *Antiquity,* Vol. XXXII (1958), p. 221.
29. A.R. Kulkarni, "Marathas and the Sea", in *Studies in Maritime History* (Pondicherry, 1990), pp. 92 ff.
30. *Shivaji and His Times* (Calcutta, 1952, 5th ed.), p. 245.

9

Maritime Heritage of the Tamils : Some Recent Findings

K.V. RAMAN

Thanks to its peninsula position, South India was destined to play a prominent role in the maritime commercial activities in ancient and medieval times. That there was brisk internal trade both by land and sea within the subcontinent is attested to by literary, epigraphical and archaeological sources. The discovery of Northern Black Pottery as far south as Alagankulam near Rameshvaram, and hundreds of silver punch-marked coins in all parts of South India lend support to the prevalence of the trade network between north and south. Tamil Brahmi inscriptions datable to 1st – 2nd century AD mention the activities of the merchants and merchant guilds (*nigamattōr*) dealing with a variety of materials like gold, gems, semi-precious stones, textiles, salt, grains etc. Similar evidence is available from the Sātavāhana inscriptions about the activities of the *srēnis.* South India's overseas trade both with the West and the East is supported by the accounts of Greco-Roman geographers and writers like Strabo, Ptolemy, Pliny and the author of the *Periplus* besides the ancient Sangam Tamil works. The archaeological discoveries at the sites, both coastal and internal like Arikamedu, Kaveripattinam, Karūr, Kānchipuram, Karaikadu, Vasavasamudram in Tamilnadu, Dharanikota and Nagarjunakonda in A.P., Brahmagiri, Chandravalli, Talakkadu in Karnataka, have provided very interesting and eloquent proof for the commercial relations between South India and the Mediterranean world. Equally eloquent is the discovery of the Roman coins (and more recently of the Phoenician coins at Karur) all over South India. Recent researches have given us valuable data regarding the history of this trade beginning from the Republican period down to the Byzantine period.

This paper focuses attention on the trade relations between Tamil Nadu and South-east Asia. Early references to this trade are found in the Sangam Tamil works like *Pattinappālai* (2nd *c.* AD) and *Manimēkhalai* (5th-6th *c.* AD). The former work gives an interesting list of materials that were pouring in the ancient port-city of the Cholas viz. Kaveripattinam on the east coast. It includes the goods from the Malay peninsula (*Kālagam*) and Ilam (Śri Lankā) and horses from across the ocean. Probably gold, tin, silk were among the chief imports and the cotton fabrics, gems, ceramics were exported.

Recent research studies undertaken by a team of Japanese and Indian scholars led by Prof. Noboru Karashima of Tokyo University have brought to light many new evidences and fresh materials. One of them is an early Chola coin with tiger and elephant emblems discovered in an excavation. This together with small goldsmith's touchstone with Tamil Brahmi inscription datable to 2nd-3rd century AD has been found in Southern Thailand.[1] This would indicate the presence of Tamil merchants and craftsmen in Southern Thailand.

Other important articles exported from South India were lead, semi-precious stones and glass besides some ceramics. The rouletted ware of Indian origin, probably made at Arikamedu, has been found in Bali island of Indonesia as well as Oc Eo in Southern Vietnam.

During the Pallava times, this trade contact seems to have increased and also better organised. This is evidenced by the inscription found at Takuapa, north of Krabi in Malay peninsula identified with Takkola mentioned by Ptolemy. It is a Tamil inscription datable to the 9th century which records the construction of a tank probably for a Viṣṇu temple and the same was put under the protection of the merchant bodies named *Manigrāmattar* and *Sēnamugattār*. The former was a well known merchant guild that flourished in Tamilnadu in the Pallava and Chola times and this inscription provided clear evidence for its activities in South-east Asia. Profs. Noboru Karashima and Y. Subbarayalu suggest that the body *Senamugattār* like the *Vīrakkodiyar* of Tamil inscription might have been the armed guardsmen for the merchants.[2] The name of the tank viz. *Avaninārāṇam,* as suggested by Prof. Nilakanta Sastri and T.N. Subramaniam, was the title of the Pallava king Nandivarman III (AD 846-69), whose date tallies with palaeography of the inscription. Moreover, the beautiful and large-sized stone image of standing Viṣṇu and his consort found along with the inscription are in typical Pallava style. Either it was made by the Pallava sculptors in Tamilnadu or probably made by the Pallava sculptors who accompanied the merchants. This is one of many examples to show the merchant nexus between the trade and religion. This seems to have been a Viṣṇu temple built and maintained by the Tamil merchants of Hindu community living there just as the Sulamani Vihara served the Buddhist colony of merchants at Nagapattinam in Tamilnadu during the time of Rajaraja Chola I (AD 985-1016). A similar case of a merchant body constructing a temple in China can be cited. An inscription dated S 1203 (=AD 1281) was discovered in 1956 in Chuan-Chou (Zayton), a famous medieval port of Southern China. It refers to the installation of a shrine for Śiva (Tirukānisvaram-Udaya-Nāyanar) by one Sambanda-Perumāḷ for the merit of the king.[3]

Tamilnadu's maritime trade with South-east Asia and China further increased and reached a high point during the Chōḷa period especially from the end of the 10th century. This coincided with the rise of the Sung government which followed a more liberal policy towards the development of foreign trade. As pointed out by Prof. Nilakanta Sastri, the Chōḷas took advantage of the new opportunities as is evident from the trade missions sent to China by Rajaraja I and his son Rajendra and also Vīrarajendra in AD 1015, 1033 and 1077 respectively.[4] Some interesting details regarding these missions are available in the Chinese chronicle *Chau Ju-Kua*. It took almost three years for a mission to reach China and it also implied and involved the commerce with the intervening countries of South-east Asia especially the islands of Java and Sumatra. A fragmentary Tamil inscription found at Lobo Toewa near Baros in Sumatra dated S 1010 (= AD 1088) mentions the activities of the Tamil merchant guild *Tisai-Āiyrattainnūtruvar* (the body of one thousand five hundred). This inscription which was first briefly reported by Hultzh in 1891-92 was re-examined recently by the team headed by Prof. N. Karashima and it has added some more interesting information.

It mentions the town as Varosu which had another name Matangari-Vallava-desi Uyyakkonda-paṭṭinam. The term Paṭṭinam indicates it to be a commercial town. It also mentions the levy to be paid by captains of the ships as *marakkala-nāyan* and the boatmen and Vēḷapuram as the place where the merchant body met.[5]

The commercial activity of the well-known merchant guild of South India in Nanadesi in ancient Burma is recorded in a 13th century Tamil inscription found at Pagan.[6] It records the construction of a hall in a Viṣṇu temple and installation of a door and a lamp into the hall by one Śri Kulasekharan Nambi of Magōdayapaṭṭanam in Malaimandalam (Kerala). The Viṣṇu temple was known as Nānādesi-Viṇṇagar (Vishnugraha built by the Nānādesi). The donor hailed from Mahōdayapuram (Mā kōdai puram), the capital of the later Chēras and the town is identified with Cranganore (or Kodungallur), a coastal town of Kerala. Significantly, this Tamil inscription is preceded by a verse from the Sanskrit work *Mukundamāla* composed by the Kerala king-saint Kulasekhara Āḷvār.

Regarding the articles of trade, the *Chau Ju Kua* lists the articles imported by China. These included pearls, elephant tusks, coral transparent glass, betel-nuts, cardamom, cotton stuffs. From the Arab sources, we infer that India exported semi-precious stones, gems, ebony, sandalwood, drugs, perfumes and condiments.

Further interesting information regarding South India's trade with South-east Asia and China in the 13th century is obtained from Marco Polo's accounts of the Malabar coast. The Coromandel coast continued to have its seaborne trade during the Vijayanagar times. Places like Mylapur, Pulicat, Nagapattinam, Trrangambadi, Masulipatnam etc., figure prominently and the merchant guilds played an active part in this long-distance trade. From the 16th century onwards, the Coromandel coast became the scene of intense competition for the European powers, the Portuguese at San Thome, the Dutch at Pulicat, the English at Madras and the French in Pondicherry who acted first as intermediaries between India and the Eastern lands and later on dominated and seized the initiative.

NOTES AND REFERENCES

1. The inscription reads *Perumpatan-kal, i.e.* touchstone of Perunpatan (*Patan* or *pattan* in Tamil means goldsmith and *Perum* literally means 'big' but usually assumed by a leader or royal rank on the analogy of *Perumtachan* royal architect). This inscribed stone is now preserved in the temple museum of What Khlons Thom, Krabi province, Southern Thailand.
2. N. Karashima, *Indian Commercial Activities in Ancient and Medieval South-east India* (1995).
3. T.N. Subramanian, *Keiyyēdu* (1968).
4. K.A. Nilakanta Sastri, *Cholas.*
5. N. Karashima, *op. cit.*
6. *Ep. Indica,* Vol. VII, 1903.

10

Traditional Boats of Karnataka and their Building Practices

L.N. SWAMY

Boat building and navigation are backbone of the economic development of the region. Karnataka is one of the coastal states of India, having a good background of boat building and navigational heritage. The boat building technology was unnoticed till recently. In the recent days scholars have made an attempt to reconstruct this traditional skill and knowledge. For better understanding of the subject, both ethnographical and archaeological studies have been carried out on boat building methods in different parts of the world. This study has attracted scholars in other parts of the world much earlier than the Indian subcontinent.

In India this study has gained momentum in the last decade. A few scholars are studying and conducting researches in different universities and institutions of the subcontinent, on the traditional boats and their building technology. The author has conducted the fieldwork in the Karnataka coast. As a result of that field study, an attempt is made in this paper to record the traditional crafts of the Karnataka coast, its classification, distribution and building technology.

The Karnataka coastline lies on the west coast of India. It is stretched between S. Uchila in the south and Devbag in the north covering about 320 km (see Fig. 1). The Karnataka coast had maintained maritime contacts with foreign countries from very early times. This coast has many ports situated both on the river mouths and river banks. The important ports which helped in the development of Karnataka's maritime trade are Mangalore, Malpe, Barkur, Basarur, Bhatkal, Sirur, Honnavara and Karawara. The history and archaeology of these ports clearly state the existence of foreign trade from very early times (Swamy, 1993). The maritime trading activity of Kannadigas was backed by the local boat building industry. According to the requirements of the overseas trades, the industry had provided good, sturdy and large boats or ships. This boat building technology is not recorded by the craftsmen because they were keeping it as their trade secret. Hence, it is not possible to have the actual method of ancient boat building. But in literature we have some references to names of the boats, types of boats and the method of boat building. By studying the literature we can trace some ancient methods of boat building techniques. With the help of the existing tradition and literature, one can trace some of the ancient methods of boat building traditions.

The Karnataka coastline is dominated by the traditional boats, that too the log boats. But the other types of boats such as extended log boats, plank built boat without and with

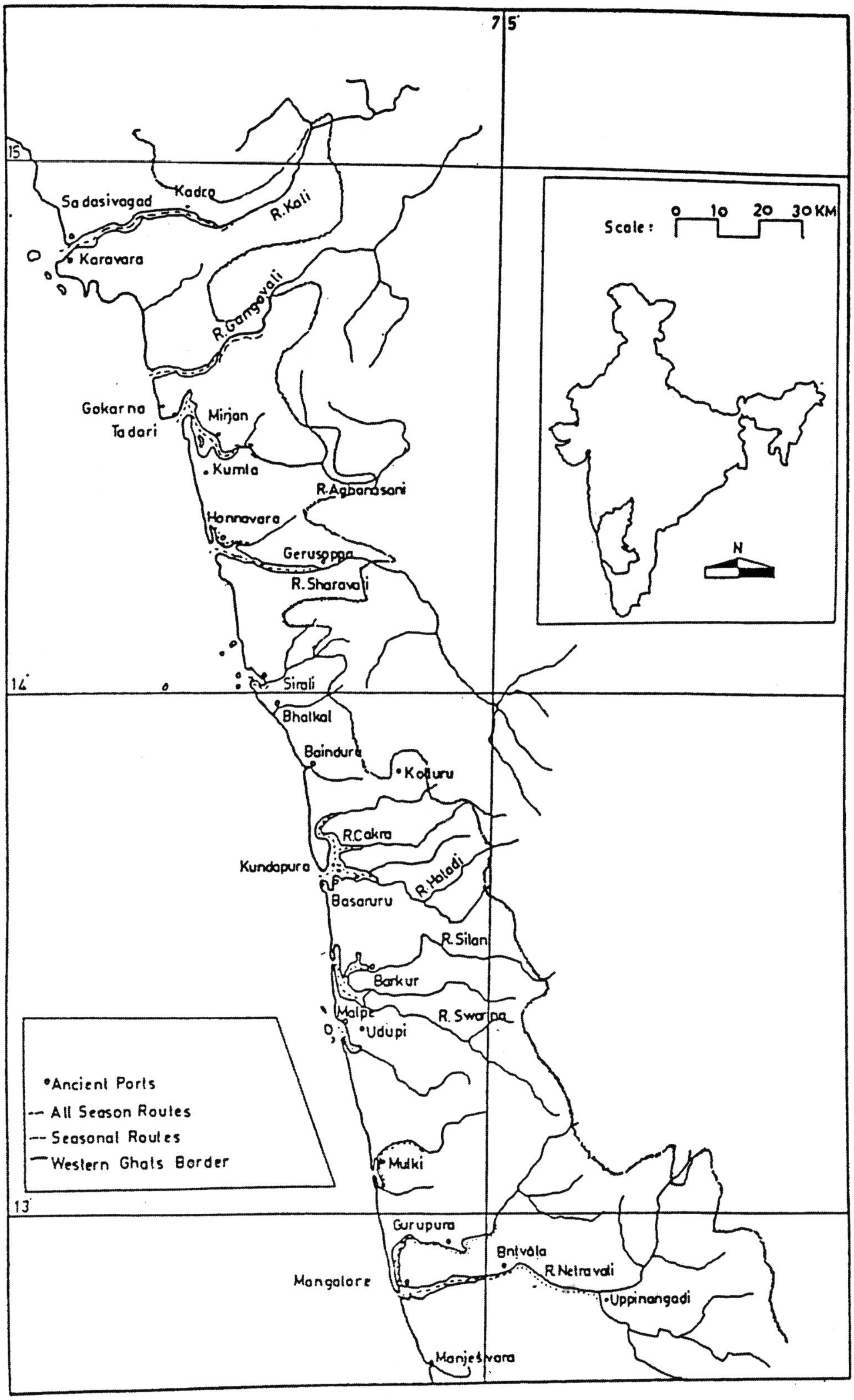

Fig. 1. Map showing coast of Karnataka, ancient ports and navigable rivers of the coast

keel are also seen in some pocket zones. In the log boat category also, there are subdivisions. In the next few pages, a brief sketch of the traditional boats, their classification and distribution is provided, as a background information to the traditional boat building (Swamy, L.N. : 1991). This information is useful in understanding the boat building traditions of ancient Karnataka in a better manner.

I. TRADITIONAL CRAFTS OF THE KARNATAKA COAST

1. Rafts or Floats: *Teppa*

The rafts are called *teppa* in Kannada and they are used only in inland waters like rivers, lakes and ponds. They are used for the purpose of inland transportation and are made of bamboo or dried logs of light and straight wood. One can see the variation in this craft's size, and raw material according to the purpose, for which it is used. Commonly, for temple festival called *tepposthava*, the rafts made of banana tree trunks are used. They use more than three strata (or layers) for that purpose. For cargo, fishing and ferry purposes they are made of wooden logs or bamboo. In this variety also the number of the strakes in the crafts depends on the load they are expected to carry. The rafts are not used by the fisher folk of Karnataka for sea fishing. This type of crafts is propelled by poles and oars.

2. Skin Boats: Coracle: *Harigolu*

Skin boats or coracles are called *harigolu* in Kannada. This boat was the main source of transportation in the downstreams of the rivers, lakes and ponds till recently. The capacity of this boat is estimated to the volume of water it displaces on the water surface. It is propelled by oars and poles. It consists of a wicket work like a woven basket and waterproofing envelope made of skin or any waterproofing material such as synthetic fibre coasted with tar and so on. It is not seaworthy because of its shape and strength. This type of craft is built by skeleton-built method.

3. Log Boats

The log boats (dug-out) are the main type of crafts seen in the Karnataka coastline. The pure log boats are made of a single log and have a good look with pointed bow and aft. The aft end is always shorter than the bow. The log boats are primitive and still exist in this coast.

The width of the log boat is more in the centre and diminishes towards the bow and stern end giving a look of elongated boat. The maximum thickness of the bow and aft point varies from 2.5 to 3.5 inches.

The bow is shaped in such a way as to cut the water easily. The pure log boats are comparatively flat bottomed and used in calm waters, whereas in the surf zones, the same craft is used with outriggers. It is a shell-built craft. The log boats are made in different sizes (see Table 1). The log boats are propelled by sails, oars and poles, according to the place of operation (see Fig. 2). The log boat with outrigger resembles with the pure log boats. The only difference is the use of outrigger (see Fig. 3).

Table 1
Log Boats Measurements

Sl. No.	*Length**	*Width*	*Height/Draft**	*Local Names*
1.	20-22	3.0-4.5	2.0-3.5	Doni, Pati, Pongai, Vada
2.	24	4.0-6.0	2.5-4.5	"
3.	25	3.0-5.0	2.0-2.5	"
4.	30	4.0-4.5	4.5-5.5	"
5.	32	4.0-4.5	2.5-4.5	"
6.	35-36	3.5-4.5	3.0-3.5	"

* Measurements are given in British system (feet).

4. Extended Log Boats

In extended log-boat category, one can see two varieties but they are built in the same way, that is the shell-built method is adopted in the construction. But there are some structural differences in these crafts. The different varieties of this class are given below:

1. Extended log-boat (with one row of plank over the dug-out base): *Pati, Patimarige.*
2. Extended log-boat (with three to six rows of plank on the dug-out base furnished with false stems, ribs, horizontal beam, mast step etc.): *Doni, Hodi, Padava, Pandi.*

4a. Extended Log-Boat: *Pati, Patimarige*

This type of boat is smaller when compared with normal log boat. It is made of a dug-out base and a row of planks on either side of the dug-out base. They fasten the dug-out base and the plank with the help of coir thread. The waterproofing of the joint is made with the help of wax and split bamboo pieces. This variety of craft measures 14.5' to 16.5' in length, 2.3' to 2.6' in width and 1.5' in draft. This craft has operational facilities like yatch. Other features resemble the features of a log boat (see Fig. 4). It is propelled by sails and oars. The sail is used only on rare occasions.

4b. Extended Log-Boat with Outrigger: *Doni, Hodi, Padava, Pandi*

The extended log-boat with outrigger is another variety in the extended log-boat class. This type of craft is classified under extended log-boats because it is built over the dug-out and maintains the shape of log-boat (see Fig. 5). But the bigger vessel of this class namely *padava* or *pandi* has a hanging bow. The building method and technology of the crafts of this class are the same as *doni* and *hodi*. Hence, it is also brought in under the extended log-boats (see Fig. 6). These boats are used only for group fishing in pocket zones, along the Karnataka coast. This type of craft consists of dug-out base and strakes of sewn planks. The number of strakes depends upon the size of the planks and the crafts. The smaller crafts namely *doni* or *hodi* consist of three or four strakes of planks on their side of the dug-out base. The bigger craft namely *padava* or *pandi* consists of seven to nine strakes of planks. These crafts' fore and aft ends that is the sewn edges of planks are covered by false stems. The planks are fastened together by coir thread. Along the first joint that is between the dug-out base and the first strake of planks, the waterproofing is done on outside. In the subsequent joints, the

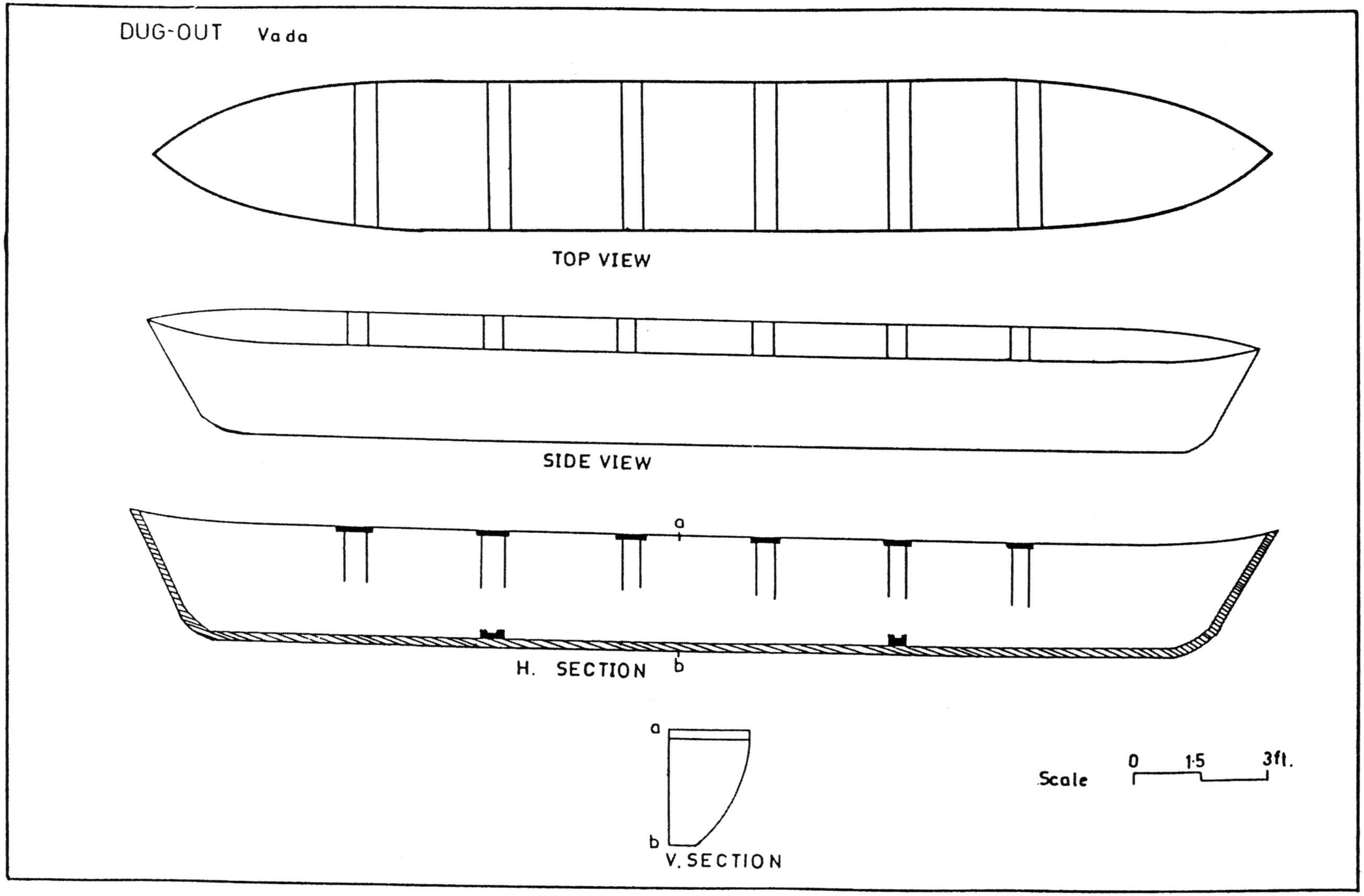

Fig. 2. Line drawing of log-boat

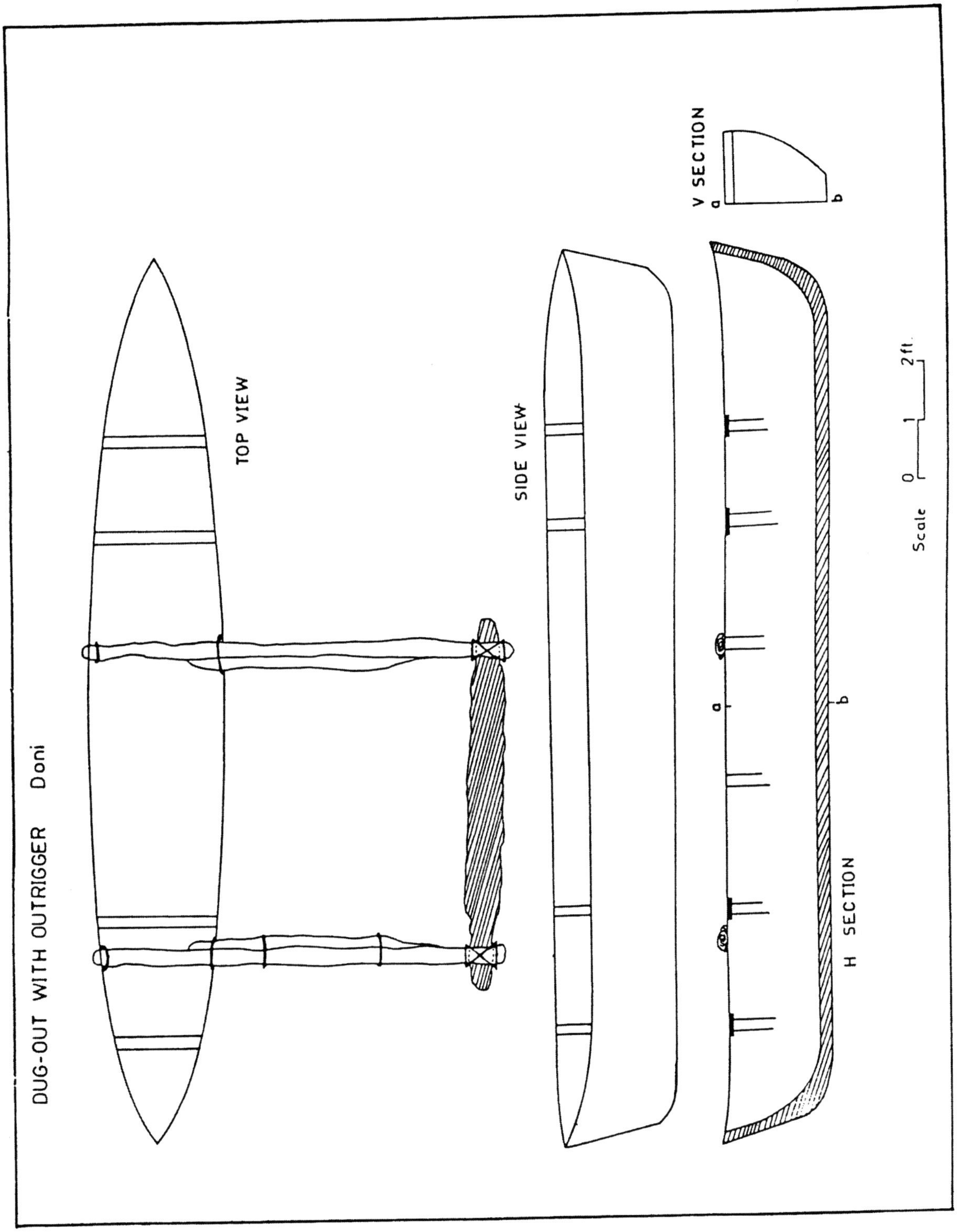

Fig. 3. Line drawing of log-boat with outrigger

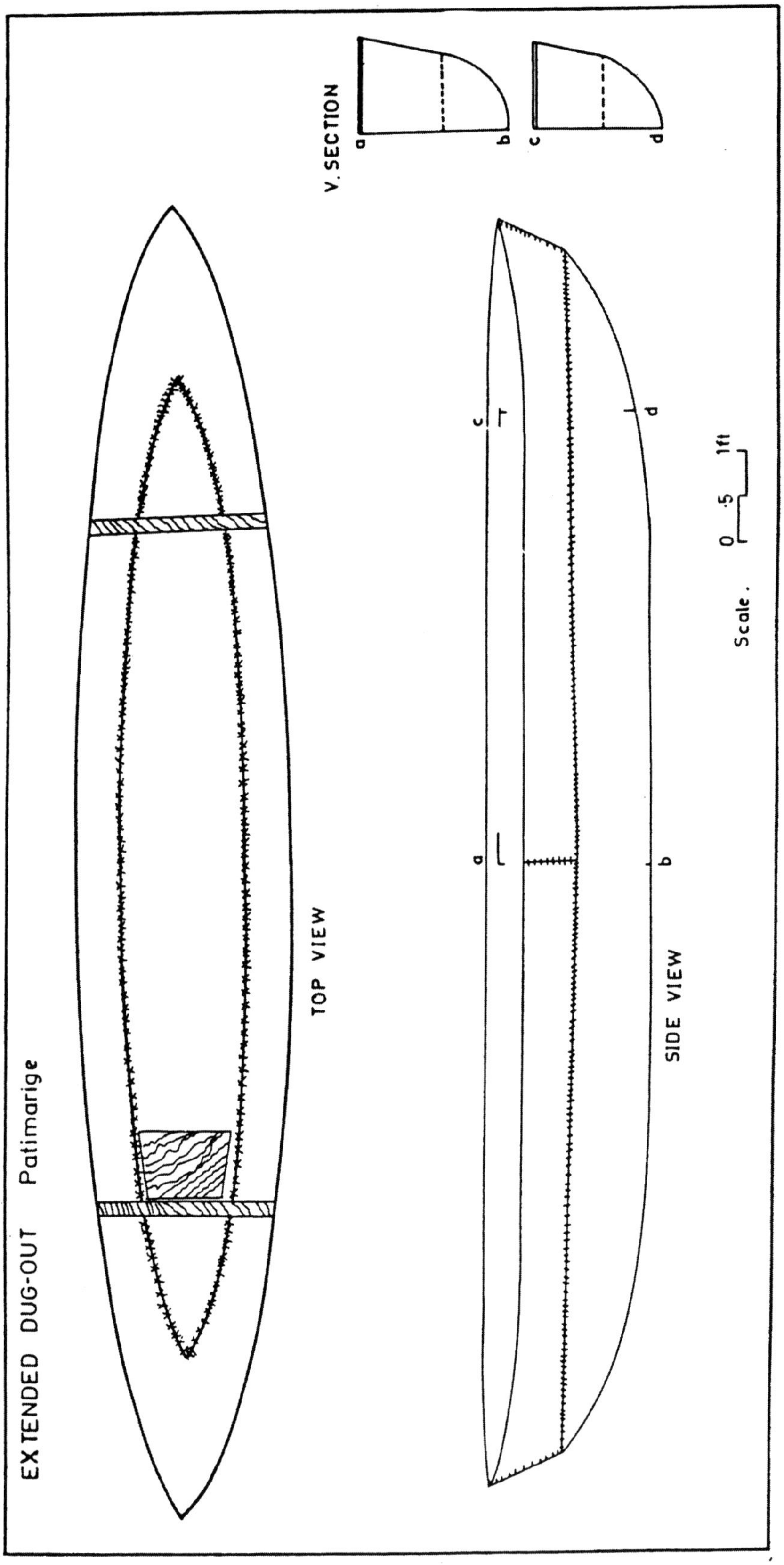

Fig. 4. Line drawing of extended log-boat

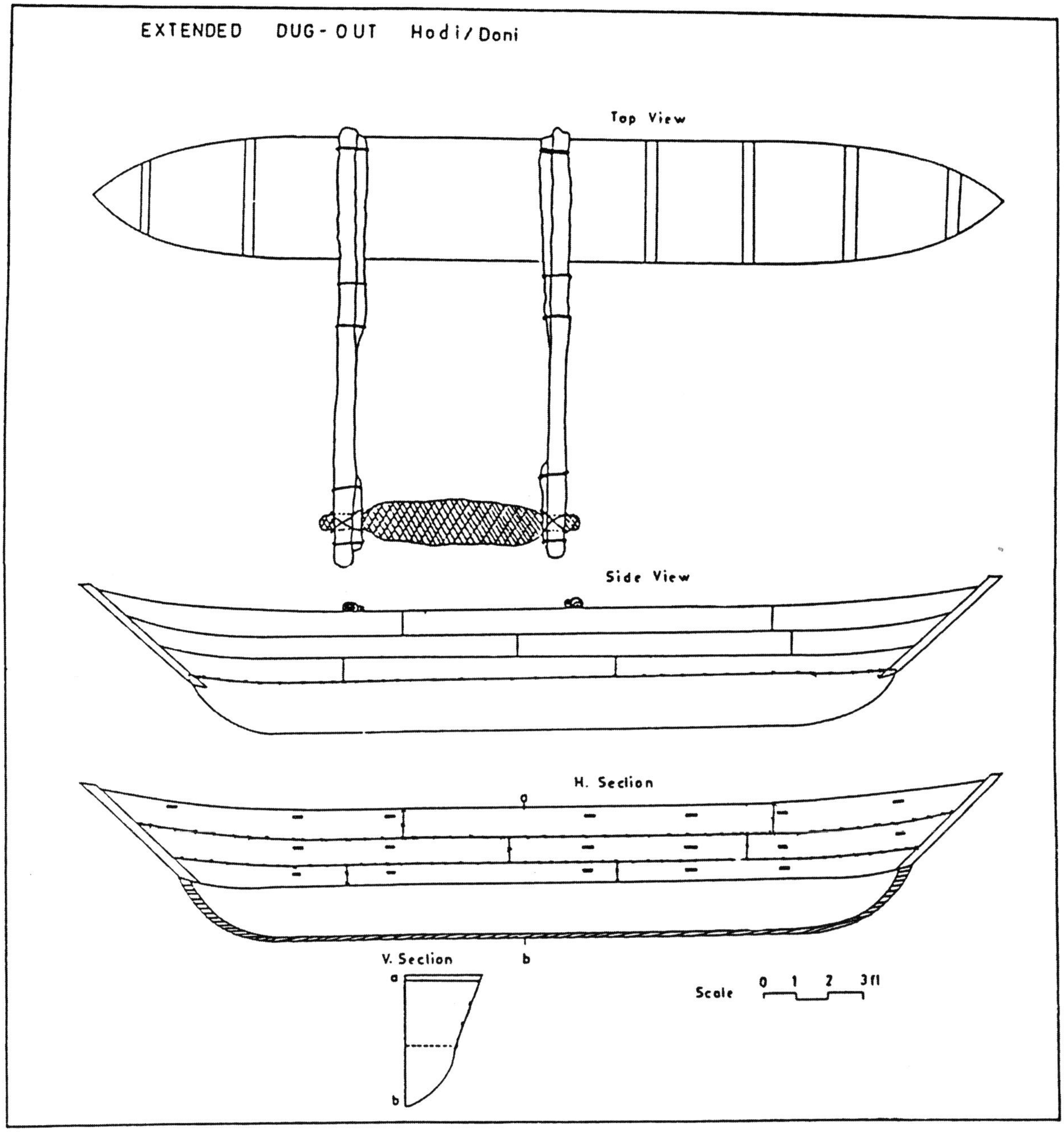

Fig. 5. Line drawing of extended log-boat with outrigger

waterproofing is done in inside only. The ribs (frames) are provided in two different methods:

1. They use the naturally curved tree trunks, according to the curvature of the hull.
2. Rectangular small beams (3x3 inches) are used as ribs or they provide beams in each strake in the form of planks. The horizontal beams are locked properly on both sides of the crafts.

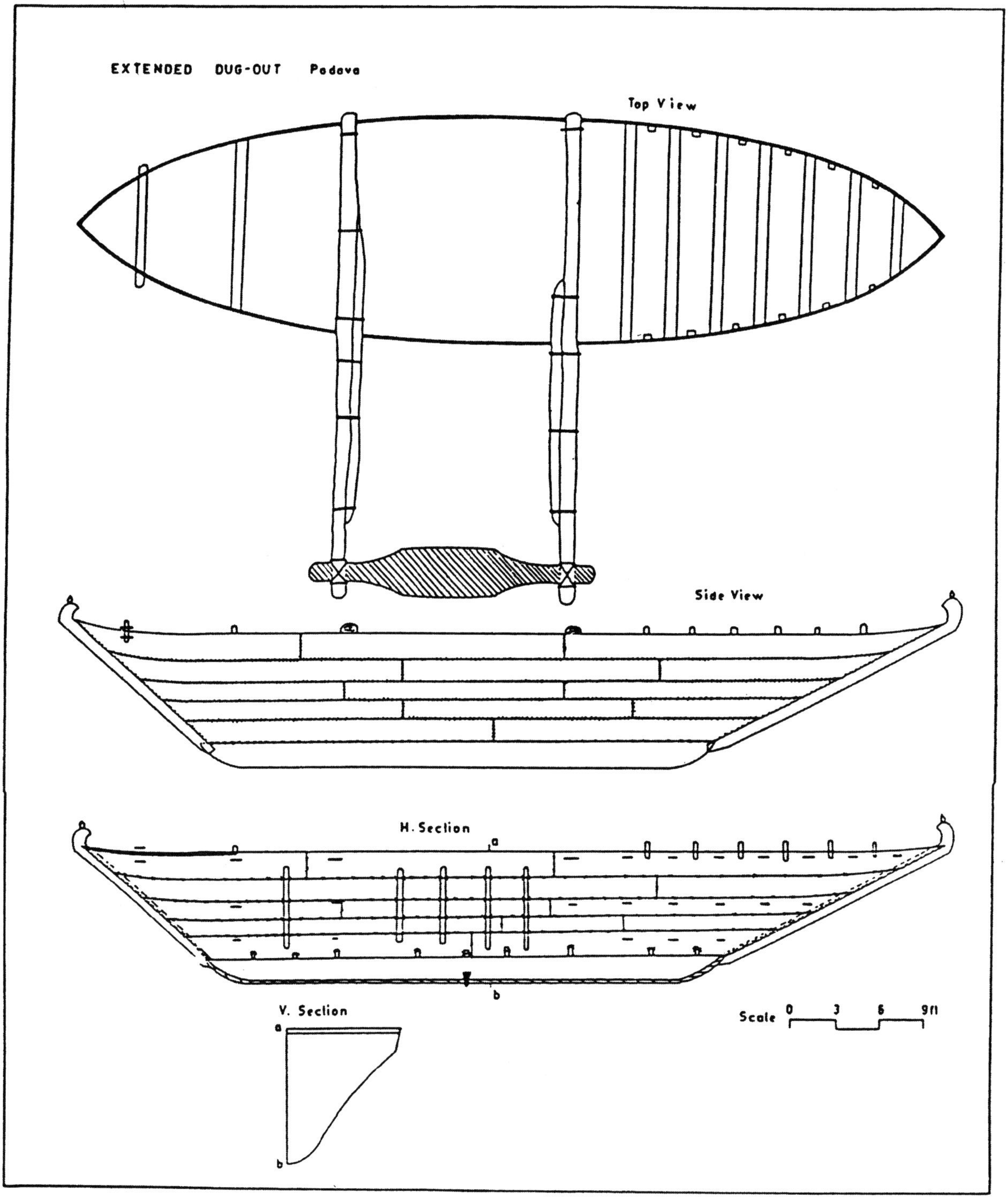

Fig. 6. Line drawing of extended log-boat with outrigger

The bigger vessel namely *padava* or *pandi* is decked in the aft end to facilitate the helmsman. *Hodi* or *Doni* and *Padava* or *Pandi* is propelled by sails, oars and pedal, and oars respectively. The *padava* or *pandi* is used for group fishing only.

5a. Plank built Boat without Keel: *Pati*

The plank built boat without keel (*Pati)* is built by fastening the planks by coir thread. This type of craft is shell built craft (see Fig. 7). It does not have the keel, but in place of keel they use a thick plank. The stem and stern posts are fixed when they start fastening the first side planks. The stem and stern posts are made of either single or multiple piece. The vertical cross section of this boat is shaped like flat bottomed U. The bow end is shaped with an angle of 115-125° without much curvature, which looks like elbow. But the stern is shaped in the same angle with slight curvature in the bottom. In this type of craft, 4 to 6 ribs (frames) are provided with proper curvature on the floor of the boat to retain the shape. The ribs are provided at 1/3 distance from the stem and stern functions as mast steps. The frame consists of a blunt round hole in the centre to house the bottom of mast. Over these frames each, one horizontal beam in the plank form is provided with a circular hole right above the mast step. This beam acts as mast check to uphold the mast in required angle. These crafts are propelled by sails, oars, poles and pedal.

5b. Plank built Boat with Keel: *Machuva, Manji, Phatemara*

In the Konkan and Karnataka coastline, this craft is known by different names. It is known for its sheer speed. It is achieved mainly due to its unique shape and design. The shape of the hull provides more draft which makes it more stable even on the high seas.

The bow of this class is designed specially to cut the water easily. The bow of this class looks like hanging bow. The rudder is fixed in the stern end, resting on the projected keel. It is fixed to the stern post by individual stitches of coir thread or iron clamps. Original design of the stern of this craft was in round shape (James Hornell: 1920). But in the recent past it has been designed like bow without much angle. In this class one can find both sewn and nailed hulls. The smaller crafts are used in major rivers and coastal traffic (see Fig. 8). The bigger vessels are used for long distance and overseas voyages. This type of craft consists of thatched roof in the stern end over the deck. Beneath the deck a cooking galley is provided with an oven. Commonly in the sailing vessels, four masts and five lateen sails are used. While carrying the valuable cargo, the craft is covered by a thatched roof of woven coconut leaves over the bamboo framework.

II. CLASSIFICATION OF KARNATAKA CRAFTS

Scholars who worked on the boats' evolution have tried to classify the boats, based on different criteria. Basil Green Hill (1971: 91-95) classifies the boats/rafts into four major groups based on their origin—they are rafts, skin-boats, log-boats and bark-boats. Sean McGrail (1981:5) classifies the rafts/boats into nine major groups, which is much more a developed one. Kapitan (1987: 135-47) classifies the crafts of Śri Lankā into four major groups such as rafts, log-boats and elevated log-boat, (both with and without outriggers) and enlarged log-boats (flat-bottomed sewn plank boats with elements of dug-outs). Sean McGrail (1989: 4-11) developed his earlier classification in his recent work based on the following parameters:

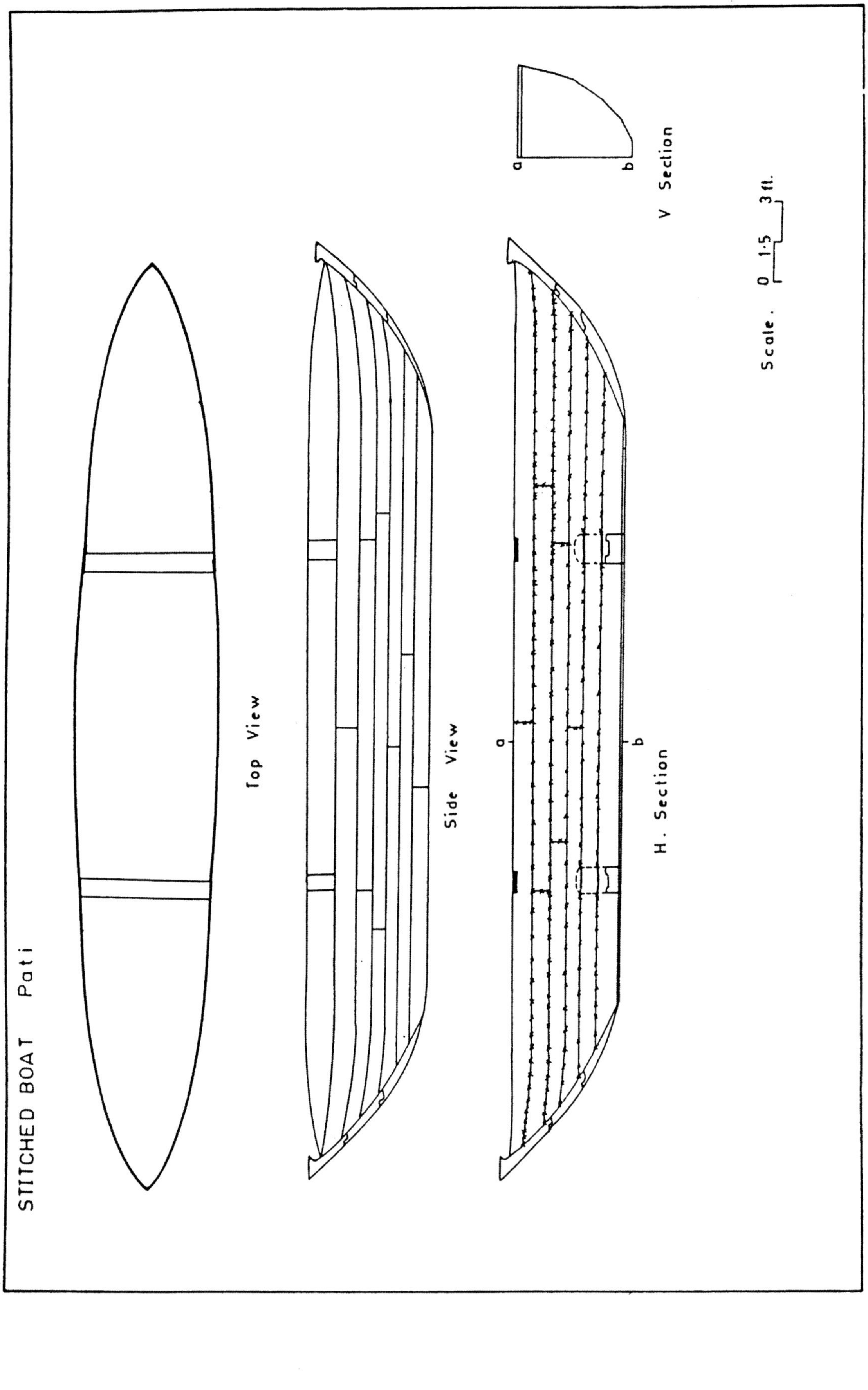

Fig. 7. Line drawing of sewn plank-built boat without keel

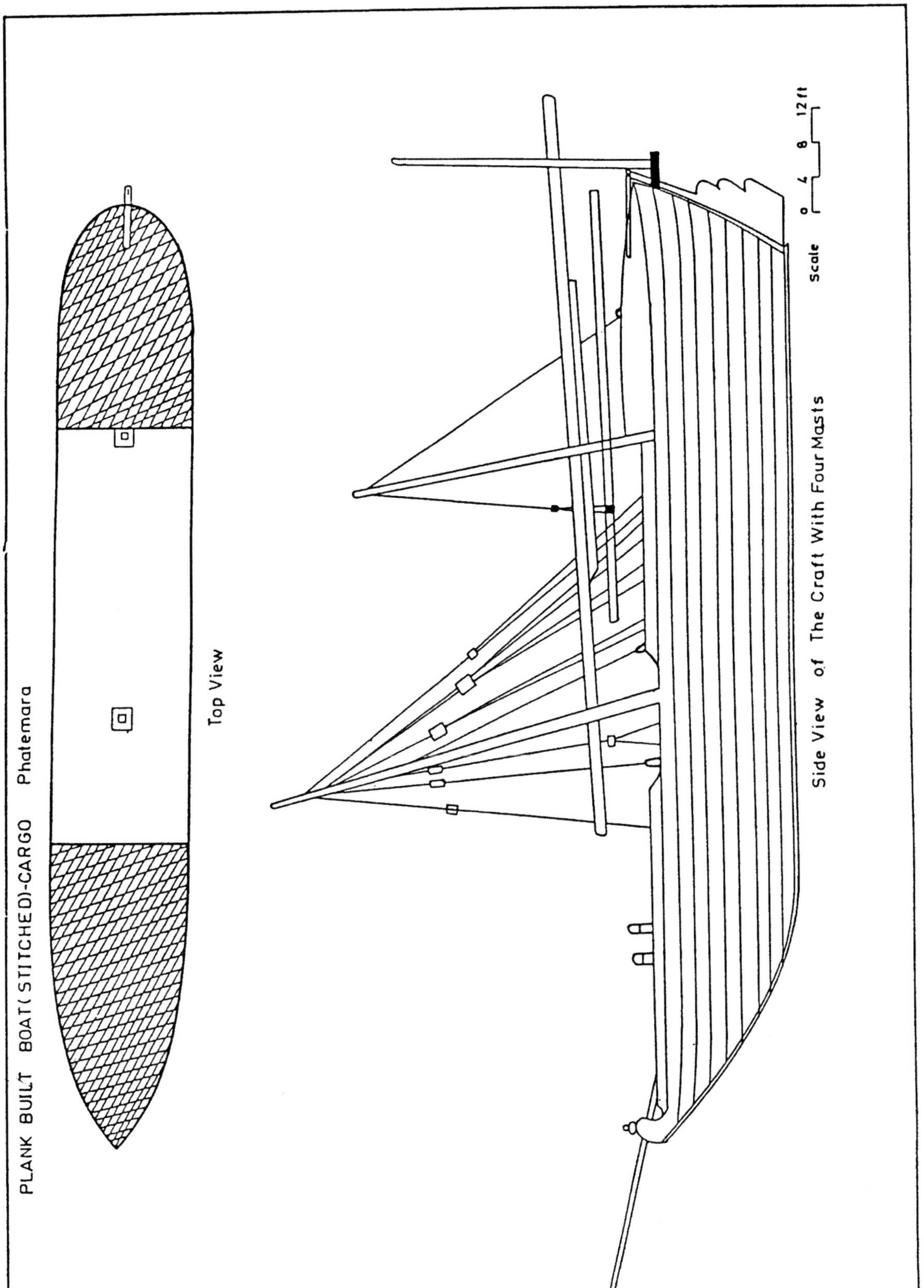

Fig. 8. Line drawing of sewn cargo craft

1. Source and type of buoyancy, e.g. floats, rafts, boats.
2. Principal raw material used, e.g. reed, bark, hide logs, planks, etc.

In the comprehensive classification of the boats he followed the above basic parameters and the construction techniques and methods. In other words by computing the above parameters, the building methods—shell, skeleton built, and building technique—reduction, construction, transformation, he proposed 14-fold classification method. The method of classification employed by Green Hill and Kapitan are not exhaustive one. Sean McGrail's classification of the boats is based on the general buoyancy principles—raw material used, method of construction and construction techniques etc. Hence, this method may be adopted generally.

Before going into details of the classification, distribution of crafts and construction, it is better to discuss the building methods and techniques, followed by the builders. The methods and techniques adopted by the builders help us in classifying the traditional fishing and cargo crafts.

In boat/ship building, two methods namely shell and skeleton-built and three techniques namely reduction, construction and transformation are adopted.

Shell-built: In the shell-built method, the watertight hull is constructed first with keel, stem and stern. After the completion of the hull, they add the internal structures including the ribs, mast step, floor members and so on.

Skeleton-built: In skeleton-built method, builders prepare the skeleton of the boat first which gives the outline of the craft's size, design and curvature. The skeleton of a craft includes keel, stem, stern, ribs along the keel length giving the overall preconceived design of the craft. After the completion of the skeleton, the builder starts providing the waterproofing outer envelope (e.g. planking in plank built boat, covering the skin in skin-boats) and complete the building process (Fig. 9).

Reduction or Substractive Technique

The raw material is reduced in volume into different sizes of planks, keel, beam etc., called reduction. It is not possible to use the logs as such in the boats. Hence, the logs have to be reduced into many shapes like square or rectangular beams for keel, planks, frames and so on. The technology used in building various crafts varies from reduction to transformation. The reduction method is used only in the preparation of log-boats.

Construction or Additive Technique

The plank-built boat, extended log-boats are built by employing this method. In this method the parts of craft obtained from reduction technique are used. In general, a craft using many parts and pieces, built stage by stage, is called construction method.

Transformation or Moulding Technique

Transformation technique means altering the shape of different parts of boat without adding or subtracting, for example, plank bending, rib bending etc.

Some of the crafts are built by adopting any one of the techniques mentioned above or with the combination of all. The log-boats are built by adopting the reduction method but other boats are built by using different techniques described above.

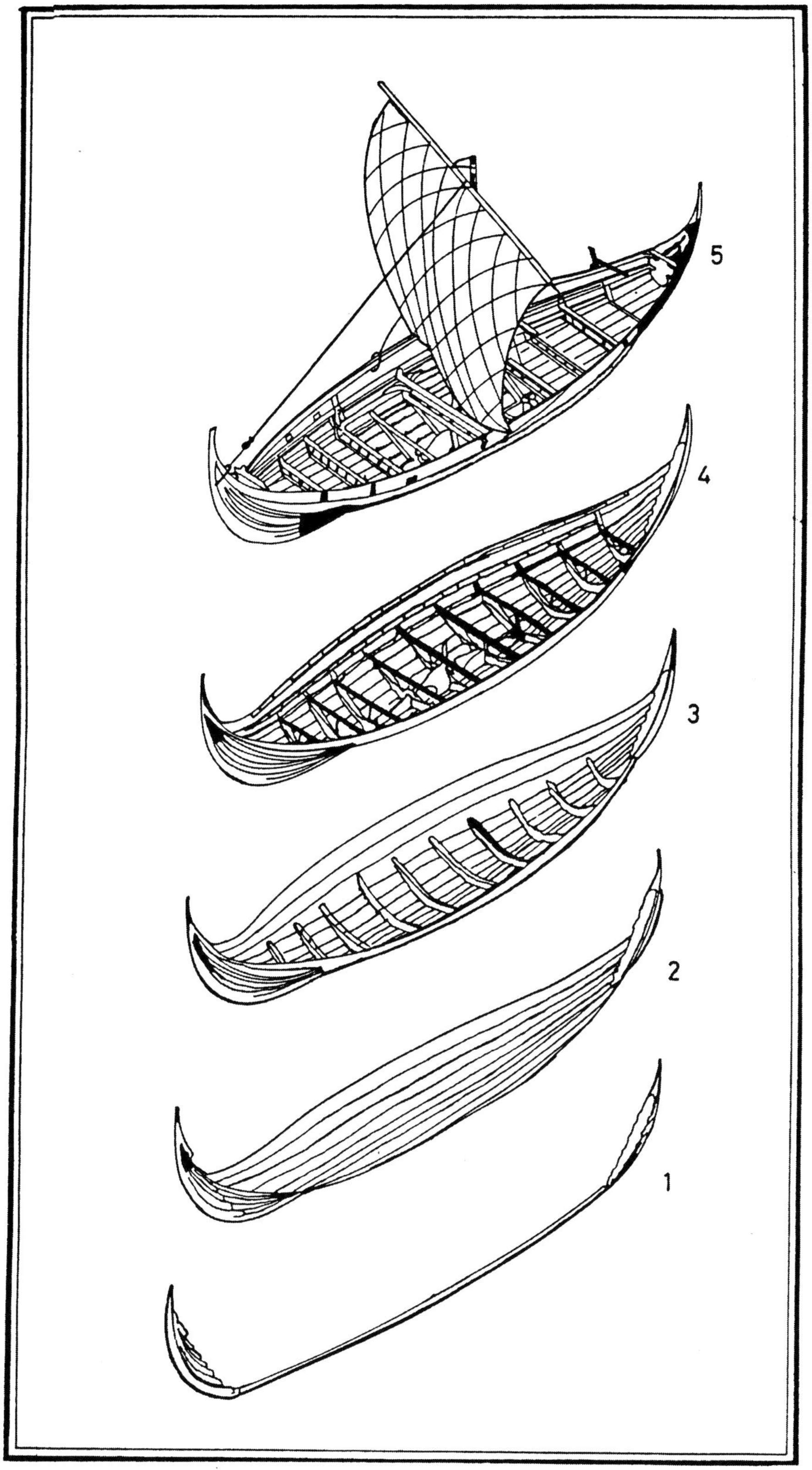

Fig. 9. Five stages of skeleton building method (after Sean McGrail, 1989)

Since the method of classification of boats adopted by Sean McGrail (1989: 4-11) is general in nature, it is acceptable to our coast also, but it is very difficult to accept all the 14 categories. His 14-fold classification is furnished below:

Structural class

1. Shell-built by reduction
2. Shell-built by construction
3. Shell-built by transformation
4. Shell-built by reduction and construction
5. Shell-built by reduction and transformation
6. Shell-built by transformation and construction
7. Shell-built by reduction, transformation and construction
8. Skeleton-built with waterproofing envelope made by reduction, transformation and construction
9. Skeleton-built with waterproofing envelope made by transformation and construction
10. Skeleton-built with waterproofing envelope made by reduction and transformation
11. Skeleton-built with waterproofing envelope made by reduction and construction
12. Skeleton-built with waterproofing envelope made by transformation
13. Skeleton-built with waterproofing envelope made by construction
14. Skeleton-built with waterproofing envelope made by reduction.

It is very difficult to arrange the Karnataka crafts under the above-said classification. But by using the construction and building techniques, an attempt is made here to classify the crafts of Karnataka.

The Karnataka coast is dominated by the log-boats and its varieties. But we can see some other types of boats also. The boats noticed in Karnataka can be grouped under four major headings, namely rafts, skin boats, log-boats and plank built boats (see Table 2).

III. DISTRIBUTION OF THE CRAFTS

Log-boats are the main type of crafts seen in the Karnataka coast. Simple log-boats dominate from south of Mangalore, i.e. Uchila Someshwara to Kundapura in Dakshina Kannada district and Murudeshwara to Gokarna in Uttara Kannada district. Extended log-boats (*pati, patimarige)* are noticed from Baindur to south of Kumta, i.e. Haldipur. Log-boat with outrigger is seen in pocket regions between Gokarna and Karawara. This type of crafts is very rarely seen in Dakshina Kannada district of Karnataka coast.

Extended log-boats with outrigger (*doni, hodi)* are more in number in the area between north of Ankola and south of Sadashivgad. This craft is noticed even in the Goa coast. The bigger craft of this class that is *Padava* or *Pandi* is noticed in the pocket areas along the Karnartaka coast for the purpose of group fishing in a limited number.

The plank built boat without keel (*pati*) stitched is found only in and around Mangalore. The plank built boats meant for cargo purpose namely *Phatemaras* are noticed in almost all the harbours of west coast between Bombay in the north and Kochi in the south. Smaller crafts of this class are found in the big rivers of the Karnataka coast which are navigable, for example, the Kali, the Sharavati, the Gangolli and the Netravati (see Fig. 1).

The rafts and the skin boats are noticed only in the inland waters for transportation of cargo, ferry and fishing. The skin boats are not seaworthy. The rafts are not popular in the Karnataka coast because it has comparatively rocky beach than the Coromandel coast. The Arabian Sea has deep continental shelf. Hence, it is very difficult to sue crafts. The log-boats are more safe in this region because of their shape and design. In the rocky and surf zones of Karnataka coast, that is between Baindur and Haldipur, mariners are using a different type of log-boats which can be used by two men. It is informed that it is more safe than the rafts and this craft has operational facility like yacht in the surf zones. Wherever the pure log-boats are not safe there one can see log-boats with outriggers which increases both the buoyancy and stability of the craft. So, it is more suitable in the surf zones than the other crafts.

Table 2
Classification of Traditional Boats of Karnataka

Sl. No.	*Class*	*Local Name/s*	*Purpose*	*Building method*	*Building technique*
1.	Rafts	teppa	Used for fishing and ferry purpose in inland water (e.g. ponds, lakes, lower valley of river)	-	C
2.	Skin-boats	harigolu	"	Skeleton	RCT
3.	Log-boat	doni, pati, pongai, vada	Used for the purpose of fishing, cargo and ferry in the rivers, coastal waters and high seas	Shell	RC
3a.	Log-boat with outrigger	doni	"	Shell	RCT
4.	Extended log-boat	pati, pati-marige	Used for fishing in near shores of the surf zone	Shell	RCT
4a.	Extended log-boat with outrigger	doni, hodi	Used for the purpose of fishing, cargo, and ferry service in rivers, coastal water and high seas	Shell	RCT
4b.	Extended log-boat with outrigger	padava, pandi	Used only for group fishing in near shore waters	Shell	RCT
5.	Plank-built				
5a.	Plank-built boat without	pati	Used for cargo, ferry and fishing in backwaters, rivers and near shore waters.	Shell	RCT
5b.	Plank-built with keel (sewn and nailed)	machuva, manji, phatemara	Used only for cargo transportation in major rivers, coastal waters and high seas.	Skeleton	RCT

Note : R-Reduction C-Construction T-Transformation

IV. GENERAL BOAT BUILDING STAGES

Karnataka's boat building industry is strongly backed by basic infrastructure such as craftsmanship, skilled labour, technical know-how, availability of wood and other raw materials etc. The knowledge acquired since the inception made Kannadigas as one of the leading boat builders of the west coast. The boat building industry is situated in almost all the major villages along the Karnataka coast. But only a few towns have grown as major boat building centres to meet the demand (see Table 3). Even today the repair work of the traditional crafts is being carried out in almost all the fishing hamlets by the local carpenters.

These centres build the boats, both for local use and for export. The most important craft exported from those centres is *machuva* mainly to the Arab countries. The building activity is not seasonal in the yards, but the traditional builders build their craft generally in summer season.

Technically speaking, the boat building process passes through various stages. Further each craft is built in its own way. The application of methods in building the traditional crafts varies from craft to craft.

So, before going into the details of building technology of each type of crafts it is essential to deal with the general building technique and its various stages. In view of the different techniques employed in different crafts, it is very difficult to draw general method of boat building. An attempt is made here to bring out the common stages of traditional boat building, based on the general methods and techniques adopted by the builders of different types of boats.

The boat building process can be divided into several stages, such as—

1. Selection of wood
2. Cutting and seasoning
3. Bending process
4. Planking and caulking
5. Fastening, and
6. Outside treatment.

Table 3
Boat Building Centres and Type of Craft Built

Taluk	*District*	*Place*	*Craft being built*
Ankola	U.K.	Harwada	doni, hodi
Ankola	U.K.	Keni	doni, hodi
Bhatkal	U.K.	Tenginagundi	pati, patimarige, machuva, padava
Honnavara	U.K.	Honnavara	pati, patimarige (extended log-boat) doni, pati, pongai, vada (log-boat), machuva, padava
Honnavara	U.K.	Kasarakodu	doni, pati, pongai, vada, machuva, padava*
Karwar	U.K.	Karwar	doni, hodi, padava*
Karwar	U.K.	Sadashivagad	doni, hodi, padava*
Kumta	U.K.	Kumta	doni, pati, pongai, vada, machuva, padava*
Kundapura	D.K.	Bindur	pati, patimarige
Kundapura	D.K.	Gangolli	doni, pati, pongai, vada, padava*, machuva
Kundapura	D.K.	Kundapura (Kodi)	doni, pati, pongai, vada
Mangalore	D.K.	Mangalore	pati (stitched), doni, pati, pongai, vada, padava*, machuva*
Mangalore	D.K.	Uchila S.	doni, pati, pongai, vada
Mangalore	D.K.	Ullala	pati (stitched), doni, pati, pongai, vada
Udupi	D.K.	Hangarakatta	doni, pati, pongai, vada, padava*, machuva
Udupi	D.K.	Malpe	doni, pati, pongai, vada, padava*, machuva*

* At present these crafts are not built due to lack of orders.
U.K. Uttara Kannada D.K. Dakshina Kannada

1. Selection of Wood

Selection of wood for the traditional boat building is not an easy job. Sometimes carpenters may have to travel far and wide in search of suitable wood for the craft. Commonly the traditional vessel builder tries to get the required wood without any compromise in quality and size for keel, stem, stern, ribs of plank-built, log-boat and dug-out base of the extended log-boats. On some occasions carpenters purchase side planks of the craft in local timber yard. The timber used for the traditional boat building is supplied by the local forest. Some special types of wood such as sala, Malyan teak, and some other variety of wood are being imported from Malaya, Burma and other South-east Asian countries.

The important varieties of wood used in different traditional boats and its ports are provided in (see Table 4).

Table 4

Different Types of Wood used in Different Traditional Crafts and their Parts

	Name of the wood
Name of the craft	
1. Raft	Bamboo, Indian reed, light and straight timbers
2. Skin boat	Bamboo
3. Log-boat	Mango (*Manigfera indica)*, silk cotton, Dhupa, Banpu
4. Extended log-boat	Mango, teak (Tectona grandise), Honne (Prero-Carpus indicus wild), Banpu, Nandi
5. Stitched plank-built boat without keel	Honne, Nandi
6. Nailed plank-built boat river, and sea cargo	Teak, Honne, Matti (*Ailanthus malabarica*), Banpu, Nandi, Sala, Hebbahalasu (jack fruit tree), Halasu
Name of the part	
1. Keel	Teak, Matti, Hebbahalasu, Sala
2. Stem and stern	Honne, Matti, Nandi, Hebbahalasu
3. Ribs	Honne, Matti, Nandi, Bage, Banpu, Hebbahalasu
4. Planks	Teak, Honne, Hebbahalasu, Halasu, Nandi, Mango, Sala
5. Mast	Teak, Bamboo
6. Mast step	Honne, Matti, Hebbahalasu
7. Pedal	Mango, Honne, Nandi, Casurina
8. Pole	Bamboo
9. Outrigger weight	Any hard and light wood
10. Outrigger poles	Casuarina
11. Pegs used in sewn hulls	Mango, bamboo, silk cotton wood, Honne
12. Rudder Blade	Teak, Honne and Nandi.

2. Cutting and Seasoning

Today wood cutting is done with the help of power saw. But the traditional builders cut the wood with hand saw. This method is adopted to get fine cutting. Traditional boat builders cut the logs in two different ways to obtain planks out of it:

1. By cutting the log vertically
2. By cutting the log vertically in all the faces.

In the first method, the log is roughly shaped into square or rectangular according to its shape. Then they make the planks by following any one face. The planks obtained in this method will have the grains just like straight lines, that too in the planks obtained from the centre part of log. These planks do not withstand more pressure and break easily when pressure is put on them (see Fig. 10).

In the second method, they first shape the log into rough square or rectangular according to its shape. Then they go on making the planks in each face of the log. Ultimately they leave centre portion in square or rectangular shape, which they use for keel or stern and stern posts. If they do not have such requirement they cut that portion also into planks (see Fig. 11). The planks obtained in this method can withstand far more pressure and are also durable than the former. Commonly they prefer to have planks in this method only.

The seasoning of the wood is the most important stage in the process of traditional boat building. The traditional builders employ different seasoning methods for different types of crafts and materials used in different parts of the craft. First they shape the log into required size. Then they keep such logs (except teak wood) in muddy or backwater for about 6 to 8 weeks. After that the logs are removed from the water and dried in shade. After they are properly dried they use them for boat building.

Generally, after selecting the proper sized wood the log-boat builders prepare the rough shape of canoe out of that log and then it will be seasoned in the above-said manner. It is believed that this type of seasoning enhances the resistance power of the wood against wood borers.

The planks and ribs are seasoned by using oil also. In this process, the builders use many kinds of oils such as *honne,* groundnut, cashew, and other oils made out of vegetable seeds. Fish and old engine oil is also used for this purpose. In this process, the traditional builders apply the hot oil on the surface of the plank, or they apply the oil over the plank and then heat it. When they feel it is ready to bend they take it out of the flame and fix it wherever it is required. Once the traditional crafts are prepared, they apply the oil to the craft both in inner and outer surface to make it fully seasoned.

3. Bending Process

The bending process is unique and complicated one in the traditional boat building technique. While constructing the boats, it is very difficult to use straight planks and ribs in all the portions of the boat. Hence, it is very necessary to bend the planks and ribs for the required shape.

In the earlier days the traditional craft builders used to select the natural curved trunks for ribs. If they did not get such bends, they used to carve the straight wooden pieces into ribs according to the required curvature. In this case they found wastage of wood. So, to minimize the wastage of the wood they started employing the bending process of ribs and planks.

The ribs which are to be bent are boiled in water about 12-18 hours. By this process the wood can be bent to a shape of their requirements, without damaging the originality of the wood.

Traditional boat builders of Karnataka use two different methods to bend the plank, such as heating the planks after applying the oil and vice method.

The first method is used wherever the simple bends namely convex and concave bends are required. This type of bends are required in the middle portion of the hull. In this process they apply the oil over the plank surface and heat it with the help of fire. Then, the plank gets flexibility. In this condition, they fix the plank wherever it is required.

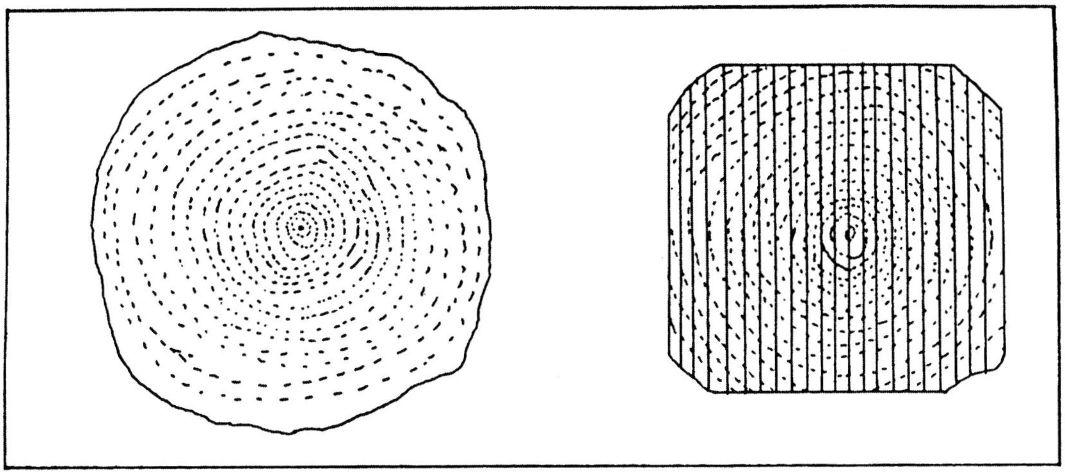

A. Cross-section of a log B. Plank making by following one face

Fig. 10. Method of planking

The second method is employed to obtain the complex bends, specially for the stem and stern portion of the boat. First they fix the plank to the vice made of fixed wooden legs. Three wooden logs are fixed firmly to the ground. Between the centre and side logs a plank thick gap is left out to fix the plank. Once the plank is kept in the provided space, the upper portion of the gap is closed by keeping some plank and the vice is kept intact with the help of bolt and nut. Then the other end of the plank is fixed to the lever. After this, they apply oil where they want the curvature, and put fire on both the sides of the plank at distance. Then the lever is bent to get the required curvature. Once the plank is ready with such curvature they remove it from the vice and use in the required portion of the boat.

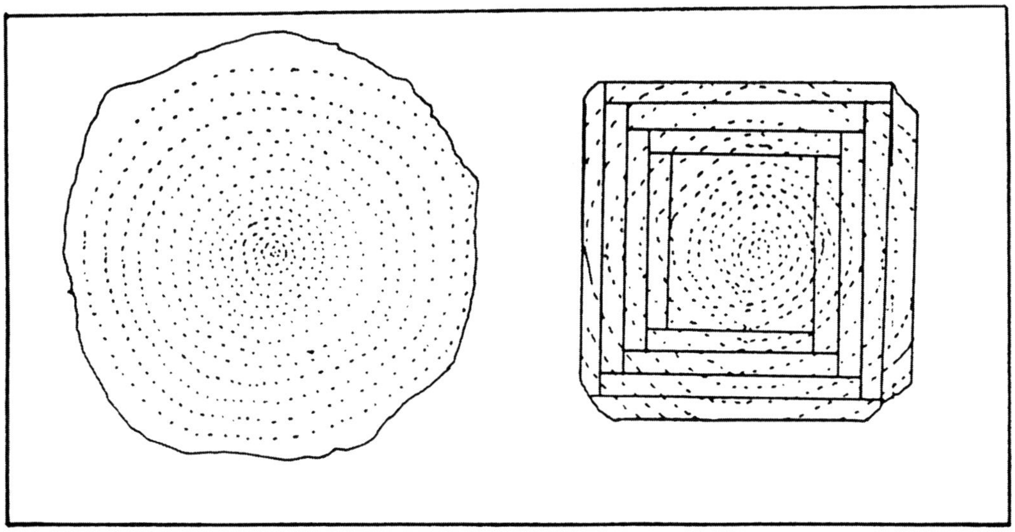

A. Cross-section of a log B. Plank making by following all the faces of the trimmed log.

Fig. 11. Method of planking

4. Planking and Caulking

Almost all the traditional crafts are built with the help of planking. The log-boats are exempted by the large scale planking. In case of log-boats damaged portion, caused while seasoning or scooping, is replaced by same kind of wooden plank.

Patimarige (extended log-boat with one row of plank stitched), the smallest craft of the region consists of one small dug-out base and one row of plank stitched over the dug-out base. Other variety of extended log-boat class such as *doni/hodi*, *padava/pandi* is also constructed with the help of planks and dug-out base. But the number of strakes used varies from craft to craft according to the height and width of the craft.

Commonly, planking is done from bottom to top. The traditional vessels are planked only in outside. The carvel type of planking is noticed in the Karnataka coast. While planking they take proper care to ensure that no leakage occurs in the craft.

The traditional boat builders follow many plank joining methods to make the craft waterproof. They make 'Z' angle cutting in the planks used in the damaged portion of the log-boat. By using the wax and cotton they caulk before nailing the plank to the main body of the craft. In stitched plank built boat without keel (*pati*), in each and every plank joint, they do V groove joints in the lower plank they make male 'V' groove " " and the plank which is to be fixed over that they make female 'V' groove " ". This type of plank joining along with the waterproofing provides 100% waterproof to the crafts. In other boats commonly edge to edge joining is done. In the uppermost strakes, and other sensitive portion they use fish and half-fish joining according to the requirements (see Fig. 12).

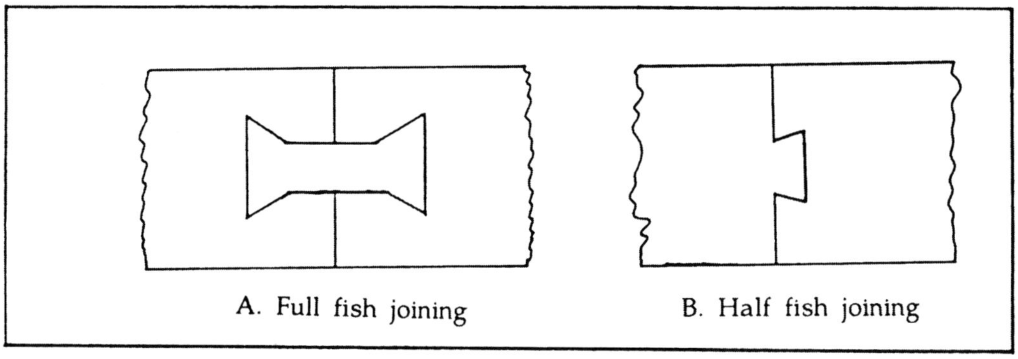

A. Full fish joining B. Half fish joining

Fig. 12. Fish joining method

The traditional boat builders use two different methods of caulking in building the traditional crafts:

1. Caulking while planking
2. Caulking after planking.

Caulking is done even in the log-boats wherever the damaged portion of the log-boat is replaced by the plank. They coat wax (made of tree resin *Dhupa* and vegetable oil) and cotton along the joint and fix the plank. This method is followed in almost all the plank built boats. In the extended log-boat (*Patimarige*) in addition to the cotton and wax a split bamboo is also used as waterproofing material. In all the other crafts such as extended log-boats (*doni/hodi/padava/pandi*) plank built boat without keel (*pati*) sewn sea and river cargo crafts (*Machuva, manji, phatemara*) coir fibre and wax is used for caulking. In the nailed cargo craft they do caulking after the planking is over with the help of cotton and wax. Most of the cargo craft builders use coir fibre and wax for the purpose of caulking. Coir fibre is used for caulking because of its quality, durability and strength. As and when it comes into contact with the water, it gets expanded and closes all the minute gaps which is not possible to caulk with the help of wedge and hammer. Once the caulking is over they coat wax and oil.

5. Fastening

Fastening is done in all the traditional crafts by using different materials. For fastening the planks with the ribs of the traditional craft coir thread/rope, wooden pegs, copper, iron, zinc coated iron nails and bolt and nuts are used. The coir thread/rope and copper nails are the common fastening media of the traditional crafts of Karnataka coast.

In the log-boats, whenever the damaged portion is replaced by wooden plank, they use copper nails. In all other traditional crafts such as *doni/hodi, padava/pandi, pati, machuva* (both river and sea cargo vessel) coir thread is used as fastening material. The stem, the stern and keel are fixed with the help of wooden pegs. Nowadays to provide more strength, bolts and nuts are used in the above-said portions.

In some special cases coir is replaced by nylon thread. The river cargo and sea cargo vessels are fastened by zinc coated iron nails in recent days.

6. Outside Treatment

The traditional crafts are coated with oil. The traditional builders use many varieties of oils such as cahsew, *honne*, groundnut, oils made out of vegetable seeds, fish and shark oils for this purpose. The traditional crafts are coated both on outer as well as inner surface by any one of the above-mentioned oils. The sea-going cargo vessel like *machuva* is coated by specially made wax, which is prepared by mixing animal fat, lime and vegetable oil. This is used up to water level. Free broad portion of the craft is coated by paint or coal tar.

The traditional craft owners coat the craft by oil once in fifteen days, when it is in use. During the off season they coat only twice, first while dry-docking, secondly in the middle of the off season. Nowadays the traditional builders have started using the modern coating materials such as paints and fibreglass.

V. BUILDING TECHNIQUES OF THE TRADITIONAL CRAFTS

With the above background knowledge of the traditional boat building, let us discuss the boat building technology of the different types of crafts (here the earlier classification is followed).

1. Rafts: *Teppa*

The rafts type of boats are made of horizontal logs. The horizontal logs are arranged in two different forms. In the first type, a row of logs are arranged, horizontally, and tied up together by coir or nylon rope with the help of two supporting logs at both the ends.

The second type of rafts contain more than one strata. These strata are pegged in four corners in such a way to peg the remaining logs then and there. These pegs are made of hard wood. Before pegging, craftsmen make a hole in all the corner logs to insert the peg properly. These rafts are made for the purpose of cargo and ferry service in the river.

2. Skin Boat: Coracle: *Harigolu*

The skin boat preparation differs entirely from all the other traditional types. As far as Karnataka is concerned basket boat is considered as skin boat. Here the framework is more complete, made of a wicker like an old-fashioned basket of woven twigs. It is covered by a skin or fabric merely made waterproof with heavy tar or any other waterproof material (Basil Greenhill: 1971).

First they prepare bamboo frame or bowl-shaped basket, or of neatly trimmed bamboo or reed. The prepared wicker is covered by animal skin or any other waterproof fabric in the outside. They stitch the skin to the frame. To prevent the leakage in the joints they apply some wax or coal tar. Nowadays, they have started using synthetic fabric with coal tar instead of skin.

3. Log-boat: *Vada, Pati, Doni-pongai*

Log-boats are prepared by the local carpenters. Traditional boat builders keep the measurements in their memory. By experience and memory they prepare neatly shaped boats with correct measurements. For the preparation of log-boat they prefer mango tree (*mangifera indica*) as a raw material. First they choose required size of a stem or trunk of a mango tree, then they shape into log-boat roughly, then it is seasoned as described earlier.

After seasoning is over they carve the boat to the planned shape. If some portion is damaged during seasoning and carving that will be replaced by the same kind of wood in the form of planks to get required shape. This type of extra planks are fixed with the help of nails. Commonly copper nails are being used for this purpose as iron nails easily get rusted and it may cause havoc during sea operation.

After completion of the building work, they use and apply cashew oil both inside and outside, so as to increase its durability. Once the boat is prepared in the above method it will serve more than 20 years without any problem in the normal working condition, with proper maintenance.

4a. Extended log-boat (one row of planks stitched on the dug-out base): *Patimarige*

This type of boats are smaller when compared to the normal log-boats. During preparation of this type of boat, first they prepare the dug-out base in the same method as described under the log-boat preparation. Once the log-boat is ready they go for planking. On the dug-out base one row of plank will be stitched all around. The coir thread is used by them to fasten the plank and the dug-out base. In between the dug-out base and the plank joint they coat wax which is prepared out of *dhupa* (tree resin white liquid collected from a tree namely *vateria indica*) and vegetable oil. This will help in preventing the leakage. Both the dug-out base and the plank edge are shaped in 'Z' angle to have the compact joint. For making the joint strong enough, and to prevent the leak a split bamboo is fixed along with the wax throughout the joint of the plank and dug-out base. Two supports are given in the sheer line of the boat, in order to give proper shape and strength. Once the boat is prepared in this manner, they apply cashew oil both on the inner and outer surface. This will prevent further cracks. This type of boat is propelled by oars.

4b. Extended log-boat with outrigger: *Doni, hodi, padava, pandi*

When compared to the log-boat, this type of crafts are bigger in width, height and length. It is also made out of dug-out base with more than one row of stitched planks. They are commonly attached with outrigger.

The boat builders prepare the dug-out base in the required size, employing the same technique which is used to make the log-boat. After the dug-out base is ready, they stitch the rows of planks on both the sides of the dug-out to acquire the desired size. They stitch the planks by coir thread. While fixing the first row of plank with dug-out base, waterproofing is provided in the outer surface by using the oakum or other fibre along the joint. In the subsequent joints, waterproofing is done in inside itself. To retain the shape and give strength, they fix the frames in the craft in two different methods. They are:

1. The use of natural U'-shaped ribs, and
2. The use of horizontal beams.

The ribs are shaped by artificial means or by selecting a suitable tree branch which is naturally bent according to their requirements. It is also attached to the hull by sewing only. In the second method, they fix horizontal beams in the form of planks for every row of planking. They make proper holes in the suitable places to keep the planks in the row. It extends on both the sides of the plank row. After the horizontal check is kept in that hole, they fix the check by pegging on both the sides. When the planking is over, false stem and stern posts are fixed to protect the plank joint in the respective parts. These parts are carved on one side to cover the pointed joints of the planks.

Outrigger is commonly used in this class of craft. Outrigger is fixed nearer to the stern end in starboard side. The poles/booms of outrigger are made of hard wood and the weight is always made of light and strong wood. This type of crafts namely *doni/hodi* are propelled by sails and oar. The bigger ones of this class namely *padava* or *pandi* are propelled by oars only.

5a. Plank-built boat without keel: *Pati*

This type of craft is built of planks and noticed in the southern parts of the Karnataka coast. To manufacture this type of boat, builders prefer *Honne* wood. Neatly shaped seasoned planks are used in the construction of the boat. The wooden planks used for the construction is seasoned as described earlier. This craft is built by following the shell built method. In the place of *keel* a thick plank is used. They make holes on each side of the plank giving 3 inches interval between the holes . Once the planks are ready with proper shape and size with holes they stitch the planks with the help of coir thread. Coir fibre is used as waterproofing material along with the wax made of vegetable oil and tree resin (*dhupa*) in all the joints. Then they plug the sewn holes with the help of wooden pegs. Commonly in the stem and stern end more than one piece is used but on some occasions they use single piece. The stem and stern pieces are also fixed by sewing only. To maintain the shape of the vessel they use two to six thick frames at equal distance at the bottom of the craft. Frames fixed at 1/3 distance from bow and stern with blunt round hole function as mast steps. Over these frames each one horizontal check with a round hole is provided on the sheer strake. These checks help in holding the mast upright. After the craft is completely built they coat with cashew oil on both the sides of the vessel. This type of crafts are manoeuvred by sails, oars and poles.

5b. Plank-built boat with *keel* (cargo): *Machuva, Manji, Phatemara*

This variety of crafts are seen in almost all the major harbours of Karnataka, Kerala and southern Maharashtra. These crafts are built rarely in some of the boat building centres of Karnataka such as Gangoli, Bhatkal, Honnavara, Malpe and Mangalore.

These boats are built by following the skeleton built method (with keel, stem and stern). First they lay the keel according to the craft requirement. In ancient days only one piece was used for thc kcel. When they do nol get the required size of keel in length, they use more than one piece. To join the keel they follow the traditional method. They lock the joint by a wooden peg. Nowadays they provide extra strength by steel or brass bolt and nut in the case of two piece keel. In this case, to improve the keel's strength they use keelson over the keel, which is thinner and wider than the keel. If the craft is designed for 100-150 tons they use 1.3 x 1.9-foot thick keel. The length of the keel varies according to the craft's design. Commonly it will be of 80 feet in length in the above, said case. They fix the stem in such a way so as to cut the water very easily. The angle of the stem varies from 130° to 150°. The stern post is fixed with an angle of 105° to 115°. The stem and stern posts are fixed to the keel with proper joints and reinforcement.

The aft and fore posts are generally rectangular in shape. The size of the fore and aft posts varies from the bottom to top. Commonly they are tapered towards the top, but retain the rectangular shape. The aft end is designed in such a way as to accommodate the rudder in between the projected aft and keel.

In order to give strength and to maintain the shape, frames are used along the entire keel length. The size and number of frames differ from craft to craft according to the length of the craft. Before they start planking they use temporary frames for getting the proper shape of the hull. These frames help them in shaping the permanent frames. Both in sewn and nailed cargo crafts, frame joints are not commonly seen. Instead of joint they use another piece along with the earlier one. Generally, the planking will be done from bottom to top. The carvel type of planking is followed in this region. Planks are called *halage palage* and *palai*. The bottom-most plank is called *Malkire* and the second strake is called *Cir;* subsequent strakes are called by general terms such as *Palai, palage* and *halage*. The topmost plank which covers the frame and the planks is called *dande.*

The number of planks in a strake and the number of stakes in the craft depend upon the size of the planks available. In the bottom portion only 6¨width planks are used as it is very difficult to bend the wider planks according to the complexive curvature in the bottom. If they use the above-said sized planks they get the shape very easily.

The bottom-most plank is always fixed to the keel by making a groove in it. The groove is made equal to the thickness of the plank. This type of plank fixing helps in avoiding the leakage. Nowadays copper nails are used for fastening. Generally, one side planking is done. The thickness of the planks used for outside planking varies between 1.5" to 2". In the case of inside planking they use the same size of planks.

In early days, to fix the planks with the ribs, they adopted the sewing method. But, in the recent days, they fasten the planks with frame by using iron rails. After the planking is over they do caulking by using coir rope. Over that they apply some special mixture made of vegetable oil, animal fat, and calcium up to water level. Above the water level that is free board portion is coated with coal tar or any paint. Such crafts are decked in the stern end to provide shelter for the crew. The remaining portion is kept open. While carrying the valuable goods, they cover it by thatched roof of coconut leaves on the bamboo framework.

These crafts are powered by sails, number of sails varing from craft to craft. Maximum four masts and five sails are used. All the five sails are in triangular shape. The height of the mast and sails depends upon the length of the craft. However, the height of the mast and sails should be equal or less than the craft's length.

Conclusion

The Karnataka coast has a unique place in the maritime history of India. The Karnataka coast is mainly dominated by the primitive type of boats namely log-boats and its varieties such as extended log-boats, and extended log-boats with outrigger. Sewn plank built without keel (*pati*) used for the purpose of cargo transportation and ferry service in the rivers and coastal waters are seen in limited numbers. But they are surviving with great difficulty. Sailing cargo vessels (*machuva*) are remodelled as engine boat. Once Karnataka was famous for this type of crafts, especially for their stability and speed. But now hardly a few such boats are surviving in the coastal Karnataka.

The Karnataka coast has a unique affinity with the outriggered boats. These boats are said to have been influenced by the Phoenicians. To establish this theory, further study is needed.

A few boat building techniques such as keel joining, plank joining, seasoning of planks, ribs, logs and other building materials, bending process, planking, caulking, waterproofing methods and the materials which are used by the present day builders are the same as the ancient builders. We can observe a few changes in the field, that is the use of iron nails, paints, cotton and synthetic materials for caulking and coating, an influence of modern development. The existence of these techniques gives us a clear idea about the validity of the ancient knowledge and technical know-how.

The above traditional skills have not been studied properly from time immemorial. This tradition as mentioned in Indian and as well as foreign accounts is an incidental note. So, it is very difficult to get a clear picture of the subject from literary inferences.

The above-mentioned skills are on the verge of extinction. At least now we have to record this heritage properly before it vanishes from our sight, for the sake of future generations.

We have some details about the past in the form of literature and the present in the form of existing tradition. To bridge the past with present, much work is needed in this line especially by the marine archaeologists. In India marine archaeology is confined only to underwater archaeology and that is also in infant stage. This paper is a humble attempt in recording the water transport of Karnataka state. This will impart some information to the learned readers and create some interest in the beginners of the field.

ACKNOWLEDGEMENT

I am grateful to the Head, EMR Division, CSIR, New Delhi, for providing the fellowship in the project entitled *Maritime History of South India* (Indigenous Traditions of Navigation in Indian Ocean). I am also grateful to Dr. G. Victor Rajamanickam, Principal Investigator, CSIR Project, Head, Department of Industries and Earth Sciences, Tamil University, Thanjavur, for introducing me to the field and his able guidance in the research.

REFERENCES

Basil Greenhill, 1976, *Archaeology of the Boat,* A&C Black Limited, London.

Gerhard Kapitan, 1987, "Records of native crafts in Śri Lankā-I single outriggered fishing canoe *oruwa* part I. Sailing *oru",* in *INAUW,* 16:2, 135-47.

James Hornell, 1920, "The origin and Ethnogical significance of Indian boat designs", in *MASOB,* Calcutta, Vol. VII, No.3, pp.139-256.

L.N. Swamy, 1981, Maritime History of South India, Vol. I, Karnatka, (ed) : G. Victor Rajamanickam, (Unpublished report), Dept. of Industries and Earth Sciences, Tamil University, Thanjavur.

——, 1993, Maritime Contacts along the West Coast of India with Special Reference to Karnataka (From the earliest times to 1336 AD), Unpublished thesis, Mysore University, Mysore.

Sean McGrail, 1981, *The Rafts, Boats and Ships,* National Maritime Museum, Greenwitch, U.K.

——, 1989, *Ancient Boats in NE Europe,* Longman, London.

11

Oceanographic Knowledge among Tribes of Andaman and Nicobar Islands

R. SIVAKUMAR & G. VICTOR RAJAMANICKAM

Introduction

The Andaman and Nicobar Islands comprising 306 islets with a geographical area of 8,249 sq.km are situated in the south-eastern part of the Indian subcontinent in the Bay of Bengal between 6° and 14° north latitude and 92° and 94° east longitude over a distance of 700 km north to south. These islands of the marigold sun are separated into two groups viz., Andaman group and Nicobar group by the stretch of the dreaded 10° channel which is about 145 km wide. The Andaman group of islands is delimited as Andaman district, which is occupying 6,408 sq km area. The Nicobar group of islands constitutes the Nicobar district, having an area which is 1,841 sq km. The Andaman group of islands is the homeland of four primitive tribes viz., Great Andamanese, Onges, Jarawas and Sentinelese. All of them are of Negrito stock and are residing in separate pockets. In the Nicobar group of islands, two Mongoloid tribes viz., Nicobarese and Shompens reside. The Shompens are still in primitive food gathering stage, while the Nicobarese who are already in the mainstream of civilization, live in 156 tribal villages (Boden Kloss, 1971; Pandit, 1990; Chakraborty, 1990; Sarkar, 1990; Basu, 1990). In this paper an attempt is made to study the oceanographic knowledge prevailing among the tribes of Andaman and Nicobar Islands.

Methodology

The present study is based on the fieldwork carried out among the tribes of Andaman and Nicobar Islands during November 1991 to March 1992 (Fig. 1). The interviews were conducted with the help of translators and in some cases with local people or a settler who has some knowledge of tribal language. Care has been taken to select those experienced and aged people who are well versed in seafaring activity. A total of 60 interviews have been conducted among these tribes and recorded in the audio cassettes covering the entire islets of Andaman and Nicobar districts. The help of Tribal Welfare officials, settlers and other people who are in close contact with those tribes and are well aware of their maritime activity, has also been utilized. Five to seven days were spent in each island to observe their navigational and related activity.

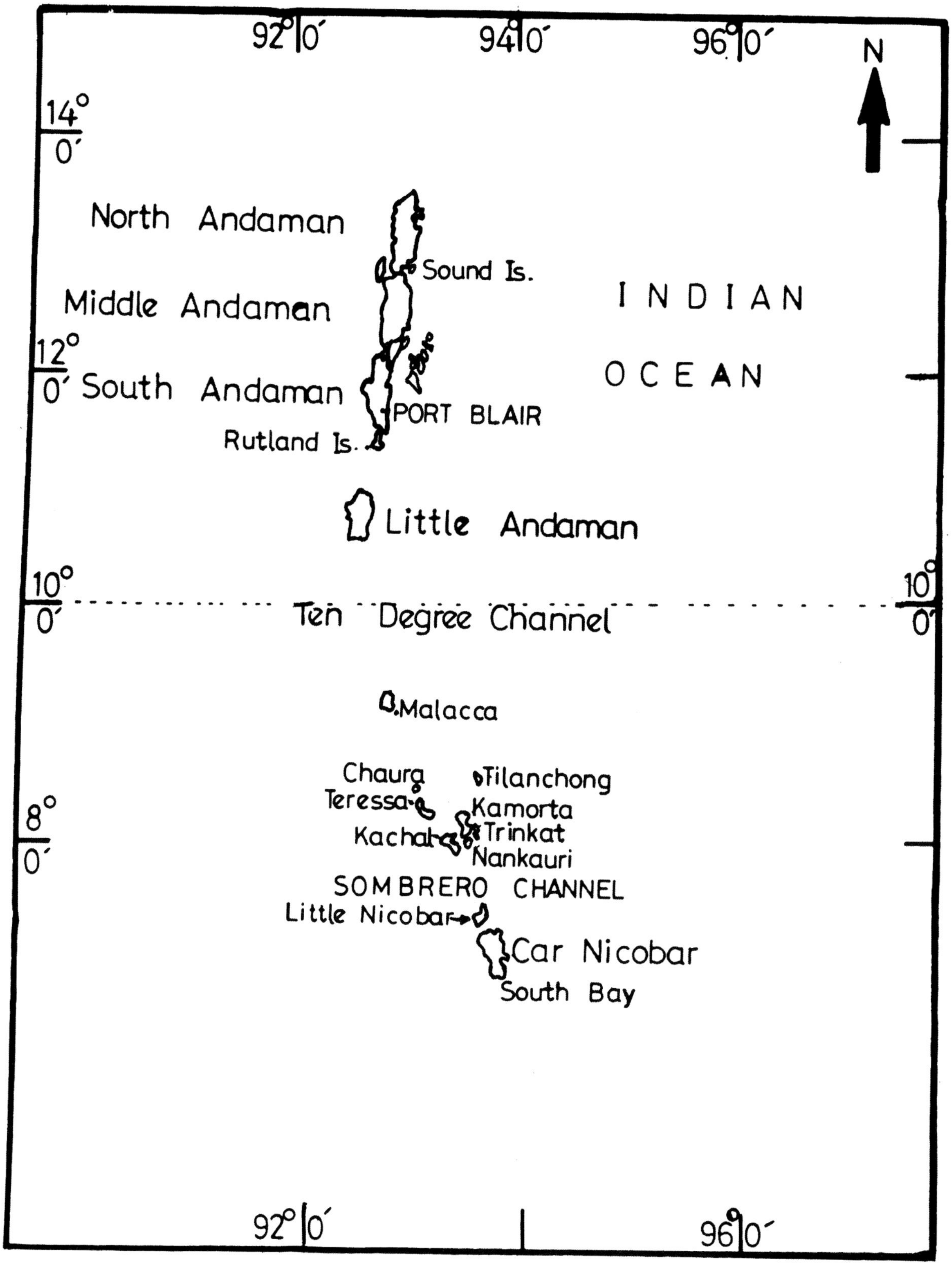

Fig. 1 Location of the Study Area

Navigational Skill of Tribals

Tribals of different islands possess different navigational skills and practices. Generally, the people of Chowra are considered to be the masters in navigation and boat building. The island of Chowra is a revered place for all the Southern Islanders and they visit Chowra every year. The people of Chowra are revered and respected by every one, as they are believed to have some occult power over winds, waves, tides, currents, etc., and manipulate them to their advantage. The people of Car Nicobar, Teressa, Tilangchung, Nancowry, Trinket, Great Nicobar, Camorta, Katchal and Little Nicobar visit Chowra at least once in a year. They learn several navigational techniques from the people of Chowra. Besides this, they practise almost similar navigational techniques with minor variations. For fishing trip, generally a minimum of one to a maximum of three persons go into the sea. More persons are involved for approaching Chowra and other islands.

Waves

The tribals of Andaman and Nicobar Islands do not pay much attention to the waves. They, however, recognise that the waves are more and the sea is turbulent during new moon and full moon days. As a precaution they use to keep away from voyaging at the time when the sea is too rough. As the sea is found to be very rough around these islands on full moon and new moon days even in good weather, their decision to avoid the voyage is highly appreciable. The tribals have acquired much knowledge about different kinds of waves. However, they seem to identify one particular type of wave locally known as "Nayange" which is the principal wave of each set of waves.

Currents

The Nicobarese also like the mainlanders recognise four different types of currents on the basis of direction from which they flow. They are: 1. Heam Kudi—from North, 2. Heam Kulam—from South, 3. Heam Kuli—from East and 4. Heam Kuvath—from West. These four types of currents are prevalent during the four seasons namely Chu, Kaba, Susam and Lohaha, respectively. Among these four currents, the Heam Kuli from East is prevalent during the season of Susam. It is generally considered as favourable, because at that time they get a good fish catching. The presence of any current in a particular place is determined by looking at the surface in which they are able to notice an agitated nature when there is an undercurrent. The nature and direction of the current are known by just putting the Hallis (pedal) over the water for sometime. These currents are sometimes used to move in a particular direction. They are able to state that the currents are very less from 9th day of full moon up to 14th day and after that the currents again gain momentum. During the seasons of heavy currents, they use to carry stone anchor.

Tides

The tribal seafarers and mariners are having a thorough knowledge about tides and their usefulness and they apply this knowledge in their day to day fishing activity. They clearly relate different phases of the moon to the tidal cycle and authentically say that the low and high tides are caused by moon only. However, they calculate the time of occurrence of low and high tides in a clumsy manner. Low tide is generally preferred for fishing. However, for reasons unknown, they avoid fishing both in high and low tides that occur during new moon and full moon days. If a fisherman locates a fishing ground where the catch is plenty, he goes there again in the same phase of the moon, expecting good catch.

Tides are also useful for coastal fishing. Until recently they were in the practice of digging small pits during low tide period in the inter-tidal region. When the tide turns high, it fills the pit. When the tide turns to ebb, water is logged in the pit along with fishes. Women, small boys and girls splash the water with small sticks in order to prevent the fish from returning along with the receding water. The fishes, thus stranded in the shallow pools, are caught with bare hands. Sometimes extract of the seeds of Kanyov tree is sprinkled on the water which has a narcotizing effect on the fishes. If very big fishes are caught and they are not narcotized, they use spears or arrows to poke them. Sometime octopuses of various sizes ranging from 4 inches to 5 feet are stranded in these tidal ponds which are a great delicacy to these people. These octapuses are caught by hand if small or otherwise after spearing and arrowing them down.

Winds

The Nicobarese have recognised 4 different types of winds from 4 seasons. Just as the main-landers and settlers, they recognise these winds and name them on the basis of direction from where they are blowing. Each wind is predominant in a particular season. Though these winds are observed regularly, only on few occasions they are harnessed to propel the vessel. For that their vessels are equipped with a mast and sail. The details about the shape, colour and exact position of the sail are presented in Table 1. These winds are: 1.

Table 1
Triangular Type of Sail

Name(s)	*Exact Position*	*Measurements*	*Shape of the sail*	*Colour*	*Materials used*	*Rigs used*
Thianmang	Quarterway from stem	10x10x8 m	Triangular, rectangular sails are also rarely used	White brown	Cotton & synthetic cloth	Nylon ropes bark fibres coir ropes 3 in number

Materials used in rigs	*No. of persons involved to hoist the sail*	*Method of hoisting*	*Method of partial furling*
Coir ropes Nylon ropes Bark fibres	2 to 3	The upper rig connecting the upper end of the sail is pulled through the mast tope and tied to the stem. The lower two ends are tied to right and left gunwales.	The lower ends connected to right and left gunwales are loosened and sail is furled and tied to the top of the mast.

West wind - Chu - January to March, 2. North wind - Kaba - April to June, 3. East wind - Susam - July to September, 4. South wind - Lohaha - October to December. Among these four winds, the east wind which blows during the season of Tutch is considered to be good for navigation and fishing. These different winds are recognised just by feeling only.

Depth Measuring

As the islands are surrounded by corals in many places they are able to see the bottom and assess the depth of water by mere sight. The Nicobarese practice of depth measuring is quite unique and in contrast to that of mainlanders and settlers. The first method they adopt for measuring the depth is observation of water colour. Their long experience with the sea teaches them that a close relationship exists between colour and depth. If the water is clear blue that place is considered to be deep. Green and pale water indicate shallowness. If it is in-between these two colours, the depth is reckoned accordingly.

The next method of knowing the depth is also indirect. This method involves assessing the depth by hearing the sound produced between the vessel hull and sea surface. By hearing the sound from underneath the vessel due to friction of hull bottom with water, they tentatively determine depth in that spot. They say that the friction sound produced at the interface of water and Odi is different at different depths. By perceiving such different sounds, they approximately determine the depth in that place.

The third method to determine the depth is a direct one. The water of Andaman and Nicobar Islands is crystal clear. So in day time, by simply looking at the water they can see the bottom and determine the depth. Whenever there is a doubt over the depth as much of areas around the islands appeared to be lagoons, they just jump into the water and confirm the depth. After their contact with English and Japanese colonialists, they started to use goggles while they dive. They are known for their ability to remain underwater for a longer time. The depth is tentatively estimated by the aforesaid three methods only. They never use any measuring rope or device for depth finding.

Cyclone Prediction

The tribals of southern islands employ different methods for predicting the arrival of cyclone, bad weather, thunder and heavy rain by observing several natural clues and behaviour of animals around them.

According to many of them, the pigs, which they rear in large number, get agitated and are in a state of unrest, 2 or 3 days prior to the arrival of cyclone. If they have any doubt regarding the cyclone or bad weather, they closely observe the pigs at home. If they are agitated and behave in an erratic way they suspect cyclone. Besides this, they observe the marine snakes rolling together and float like ball. When such balls are washed ashore they indicate them the arrival of cyclone and rough weather. Many of them also said that they observe small bubbles on the surface of the water in offshore areas. Besides all these things, they keep track of clouds. If the dark clouds congregate in large masses with heavy lightning and thunder, it is a sure indication of cyclone. The winds from different directions also become strong, turning into a gale. All these things are collectively considered to predict the arrival of cyclone.

Time, Duration and Place of Navigation

The fishing times of tribes have no standard pattern. They choose the time of their departure for fishing trip according to their food requirements, mood, nature of the tide, availability of odi, phase of the moon, etc. They go for fishing both in day and night hours. Generally, low tide is preferred and sometime, they go for fishing in high tides also. However, while starting a long voyage to adjacent island or during their trip to Chowra, they are particular to start at low tide only. Fishing is undertaken during the days in between full moon and new moon as the sea is calm.

There seems to be a uniformity in the duration of fishing among all Islanders. The fishing time never exceeds 3 to 4 hours and they do not want to remain in sea for a prolonged period of time. The moment they feel that their catch is enough to sustain them for 3 or 4 days, they return. The excess catch is sometimes salt or fire dried and stored for future or distributed among relatives and neighbours. The only occasion the duration of their voyage exceeds several hours or days is during their voyage to far off islands and Chowra. During such voyages, they travel nearly 20 hours per day.

The place of navigation also varies from island to island. While the fishermen of Car Nicobar go up to 10-15 km from the shore, those from Nancowry, Trinket, Teressa and Katchal confine their activity within 5 to 10 km from their shore. Similarly, each villager is expected to fish within the proximity of his island.

Direction Finding and Stellar Knowledge

The fishing range of Nicobarese and other tribals does not impose any necessity to know position and direction as it never exceeds 10 km. However, they know position and direction while undertaking long journeys to visit the adjacent islands which may involve several hours of travel in open sea. They have definite words for 4 directions which are *tangale* (north), *tangange* (south), *tanganae* (east) and *tangaiche* (west).

As in the case of mainland fishermen, Nicobarese also depend on natural objects like sun, moon and stars for direction finding. During day time, the direction is clearly indicated by the sun in its early hours of rising. After this the small islets, hills and other shore features along the way indicate them the correctness of the course. During night hours, the stars are very much relied upon until they reach their target (see Table 2). They generally use the following stars in their navigational activity.

Onchiana (Centaurus): A constellation which appears in South during February to April. They compare this constellation to the chicken cage and hence it is named after a type of chicken cage used by them.

Thyan (Orion): It is a constellation appearing in East. It is visible during summer when East monsoon is in full swing. Among the 3 stars, one is reported to be very bright.

Mahayuvan (Southern cross): It is visible in South like a holy cross. It is most useful to go to islands like Chowra, Terressa and Tilangchung, etc. They sail by keeping the stem of the vessel towards this star. It is visible from December up to April.

Sama (Al de Baron): It is a bright, red coloured star appearing in the East. It is visible from May to September.

Balangkaruvya (Venus): It is a bright star appearing in the eastern horizon between 7 to 8 p.m.

Musaha (Ursa Major): It is a constellation appearing in North and moves South. It is mainly used by them for direction and time finding.

Gna gna hyyam (Pleiades): A constellation appearing in the East. It is regularly watched by them during their long journey. It is visible from September to February along with a bright star nearby.en cage used by them.

Table 2
List of Stars/Planets/Constellations used by Tribals

Sl. No.	*Tribal name of the star*	*International Name*	*Characteristics*
1.	Onchiana	Centaurus	Appears in South from February to April. Used for direction finding. It is a constellation.
2.	Thyan	Orion	A constellation appearing in the East. One star in it is very bright.
3.	Mahayuvan	Southern cross	Visible in South from December to April. Useful for direction finding.
4.	Sama	Al de Baron	Red coloured star. Visible in the East from May to September.
5.	Balangkaruvya	Venus	Single planet in the East.
6.	Musaha	Ursa Major	It is a constellation appearing in North.
7.	Gna gna hyyam	Pleiades	Constellation in the East. Visible from September to February. Most useful for direction finding.

Besides the above stars, they do not look at other stars. The Pole star, despite its brightness and prominence, is never considered. Thus, it seems that the Nicobarese knowledge about heavenly bodies is very limited. Such knowledge is found to be possessed by more intelligent and elderly members of the society who are very few in number. Eliciting this information from them is still more difficult, as these elderly tribes strongly believe that exposure of this knowledge will shorten the life span of the new learner and make them become old very quickly. Hence, they in most of the cases misguide or evade the enquirers. However, this information was collected from some trustworthy people who have some modern outlook. The application of this knowledge about heavenly bodies is solely for direction finding and not for any other purpose like time calculation, etc.

Seafaring in Different Seasons of the Year

Seafaring activity does not take place in all the seasons of the year. There are definite seasons for navigation which is very strictly adhered to fearing sea danger and the curse of Chowra people. The Nicobarese have their own calendar by which the year is divided into 12 months as shown in Table 3. Seafaring is strictly forbidden during the season of 'amu' (April - June) and nobody should go for fishing or into the sea during 'amu'. The arrival of this season is heralded by flowering of some plants. The elders of the village, who keep track of all such natural events announce the arrival of such season. Immediately they plant long poles or branches of a particular tree in knee deep water on the shore to indicate that the season of 'amu' has come and nobody should enter the sea. This season lasts up to the month of 'Sennai' (May - June). The end of 'amu' is perceived by the people of Trinket Island only and when they start fishing and seafaring, it is immediately known to everybody that the month or season of 'amu' has ended. The seasons of 'Mukyop' (December - January), 'Ranecaba' (January - February) and 'Tutch' (February - March) are generally good for navigation and fishing and their catch is also good during this period. From 'Bach' (March- April) the wind force is great and the sea becomes rough. After this comes the 'amu' during which fishing and seafaring are altogether forbidden. Then the wind force becomes normal and fishing and seafaring are resumed again from the month of Tukai (September-October).

Table 3
The Months of a Year in Nicobarese Calendar

English Month	*Nicobarese Month*	*Importance*
October-November	Ramo	East monsoon begins
November-December	Mithus	Uprooting of trees, rough season; no navigation
December-January	Mukhyap	Mild wind; suitable for navigation
January-February	Ranegaba	The wind turns to North for thc first time
February-March	Tutch (silent)	Very calm season. Ideal for navigation
March-April	Bach	Wind in all directions; not suitable for navigation
April-May	Amu	Planting of trees, in the shore; slight disturbances start
May-June	Senni	High disturbance; rough sea; no navigation
June-July	Thanac Bhuva	Wind becomes mild; suitable for navigation
July-August	Lanae	Time of hunger as trees bear no fruit
August-September	Kakathak	East horizon is dark blue; but no rain
September-October	Tukai	The change of wind direction and beginning of East monsoon.

Types of Crafts

The tribals of Andaman and Nicobar Islands invariably use dugouts and outrigger canoes with some difference. The dugouts used by the Great Andamanese are comparatively small in size with an outrigger. Only 2 or 3 persons can be accommodated in this vessel. The Nicobarese fishing dugouts with outriggers present some variations from that of the Great Andamanese in workmanship and structure (Fig. 2). Another peculiar craft unique to Nicobarese is their racing canoes (Fig. 3). These canoes are solely meant for recreation and they are never used for fishing. Onge's dugouts with outriggers mostly resemble that of Great Andamanese with a horizontally extended stem and stern prow (Fig. 4). However, these dugouts are more sturdier than those of Great Andamanese and the mode of attachment of outriggers is also found to vary. The Shompen's dugout with outriggers greatly resembles that of Nicobarese, but the only difference observable is their small size (Fig. 5). The Sentinelese are reportedly using dugouts with outriggers which are small in size than other tribal canoes. The Jarawas neither make nor use dugout canoes or outriggers. However, they are reportedly using a raft made of bamboo or tree trunks.

The Occupation of Fishing

The tribals of all islands pursue fishing for food. Every tribe is expected to possess great skill in the occupation of fishing. Any man exhibiting special talent in this art is respected and accorded special honour. He is often consulted for an efficient fishing trip, who gives

Fig. 2 Nicobarese Fishing Canoe

Fig. 3 Nicobarese Racing Canoe

some tips regarding fishing. The traditional fishing implements of these tribes are arrows, spears, hooks and lines only. The nets were introduced before the arrival of English colonists by Malaysian and Burmese merchants. The youths, if they do not have an odi, go for fishing with a multi-pronged spear by which they poke any big fishes standing at knee deep water. This requires great quickness, a sharp vision and a better agility. They also hunt crabs and shells for food. The line and hook fishing involves standing on a rock in the near shore waters. The hook with a bait is let loose in the water and the fish, generally a big one weighing 2 to 5 kg, are caught at a time.

Some tribes used to go into the sea by their odi during low tide and cast their net. Those who go inside the sea for fishing generally fish for a longer time and catch more than the people who use hook and line and spears. During such trips they generally use different types of pedals and oars for propulsion besides sails. One of their favourite pastime and occupational interest is octopus fishing. The octopuses are used as a bait in the hook as well as food. The people who want to catch octopus go in the night time irrespective of the phase of the tide. They, generally, carry spears, arrows, the seeds of kanyov tree as narcotic, coconuts and lime. They never carry any foodstuff both in night and daytime. They quench their thirst by the coconuts. Large torches with leaves of Pandanus tree loosely rolled around a log are carried which keep burning throughout the trip. By the light of this torch they look into the water and locate the octopus. Many of them believe that the octopus come to the surface when this light is shown to the water. On such occasions, they are easily speared and caught. Though the octopus stings them, it is not fatal. Octopuses are also caught with hook and line. However, the chance of losing the hook and line in octopus fishing is great and they generally do not want to lose their hook and line at any cost. Still they go for octopus fishing since the returns are high. Sometime, they use narcotic agents like seeds of *Baringtonica racemosa*. The extract of these seeds is sprinkled in water which narcotises the octopuses and fishes. In all fishing trips, lime is important as it is being used as repellent to sharks and other animals like sea snakes. When any such dangerous animal approaches their fishing odi, the extract of lime is sprinkled in water which reportedly repels these dangerous animals away from their vessel.

Trip to Chowra and other Islands

The trip to Chowra is considered by the Southern Island tribes a most important event of everyone's life. Boys are not considered grownups until they make their maiden voyage to the Chowra island. This is partly because of the fear instilled by the Chowra islanders who claim to have special powers to alter winds, currents and even directions, if anybody goes against their will. They have also created a dependency so that people of other islands should come to them for cooking pots and building of big racing odis. They strongly believe that it is a sin to cook in vessels not made by Chowra people.

The vessels (odis) that are to sail to Chowra should invariably be Chowra built only. Before starting their voyage, the odis are prepared by adding a strake to the gunwale to prevent water splashes. The common village canoe is sure to be taken in this trip. The canoe is also strengthened by adding palm leaves and additional logs. Some new crossbars are also added. Before the voyage is started, cocks are sacrified whose blood is annointed on the heads of boys who are taking their maiden trip. They also sing song in praise of the canoes.

Fig. 4 Onge's Canoe

Fig. 5 Shompen's Canoe

The journey is started during ebb tide. Each member on board carries food, tender coconut, lime and some materials for presenting to their Chowra friends. Some coconut oil is also carried to rub on the body, in case it rains or it is too hot. At the outset, all the canoes are taken beyond the backwaters and anchored. Then the people and youngsters swim to the canoes and board it, and the voyage is started. The distance of Chowra from any southern island is not less than 30 km. For the people from Car Nicobar it is nearly 60 km. The journey in a favourable wind takes nearly 15 to 20 hours. But occasionally the journey takes as long as 3 days. During the journey, they mostly consume coconuts and yams which they have brought with them. The lime is used to repel shark and other unwanted and dangerous marine forms which cannot bear the pungent taste of lime. Stars like Orion, Venus, Serius and Ursa Major are used to find the direction.

On reaching Chowra, they are accorded a warm welcome by their friends and inmates of Chowra. They are allotted special places for stay and other things. After a stay of around 10 days, they start their return journey.

Conclusion

The navigational practices of tribals of Andaman and Nicobar Islands are quite interesting and vast. The seafaring activity of tribals is different from that of settlers in all aspects. Unlike settlers, who are living in this environment only for 2 or 3 generations, the tribals are living in this environment for hundreds of years and they have a thorough and detailed knowledge about the seas of these islands, as they totally or partially depend on sea for their livelihood. The seafood forms a major part of their diet and almost all tribal settlements are on the seashore. Hence their traditional knowledge about sea is unique and gathered independently without any external influence. However, in the last hundred years, they have adopted several techniques and methods from the settlers and English colonists in their fishing and seafaring activity. At present the only tribe which is actively involved in seafaring and fishing is Nicobarese, especially the people of Car Nicobar. The other tribes like Andamanese, Onges, Shompens have forgotten their traditional sea knowledge. Since every island is separated from each other by sea stretching up to 100 km and they are in dire need to contact tribals of other islands every year they have to undertake long journeys to the other islands. So each tribe is well trained in all aspects of navigation. A thorough study of their navigational practices can bring a lot of unknown facts about their maritime knowledge and activity. There are as many methods and practices as the number of islands. Through the present investigation, it was noticed that people of same races and communities are practicing different techniques and methods by virtue of their living in different islands. The present need is to preserve their traditional oceanography knowledge for future records.

REFERENCES

Badal Kumar, Basu, 1990, *The Onge*. A.S.I. Publication, p. 87.
C. Boden Kloss, 1971, *Andamans and Nicobars*. Vivek Publishing House, p. 373.
Dilip Kumar Chakraborthy, 1990. *The Great Andamanese*. A.S.I. Publication, p. 83.
Jayanta Sarkar, 1990, *The Jarawa*. A.S.I. Publication, p. 77.
T.N. Pandit, 1990, *The Sentinelese*. A.S.I. Publication, p. 53.

12

Ancient Ports on the Eastern Coast of India

A.N. PARIDA

India has a long coastline. In the ancient period several ports flourished on the coast which served the outlets of India's trade with the Roman Empire, Śri Lankā and countries of South-east Asia and Far-East. India's trade through the Bay of Bengal was controlled by the ports on the Bengal-Orissa coast and the Coromandel coast. This paper aims at making a survey of the ancient ports on the eastern coast, highlighting their importance in the context of external trade. The rise and fall of the ports were closely linked with the growth and decline of overseas trade. Therefore the study of the ports constitutes an essential part of the general pattern of trade of a given period.

So far as the ports on the coast of Orissa are concerned, lack of adequate material is a major problem. But, for the ports of Tamil country, the information is forthcoming from literature, particularly Sangam literature, and to a limited extent, from archaeological finds.[1] The principal supporters of Jainism and Buddhism were the merchant community apart from the ruling families. It was because of this, Buddhism and Jainism flourished with the growth of trade and commerce. The coastal towns, especially the port towns, largely represented Buddhist interests.[2] Therefore Buddhist texts abound in references to ports. The Buddhist as well as Jain texts have evidences of ancient Orissa's inland and maritime trade.[3] Buddhist association of Dantapura, a port-town on the Orissa coast, is well-known. Similarly Puhar or Kaveripattinam on the Tamil-Mandala bears evidence of Buddhist association.

Hsuan Tsang's account[4] refers to the port of *Che-li-tā-lo* in *Wu-t'u*, i.e., Oḍra. From his description it is evident that the port was a Buddhist site. It will not be out of place to refer here to another Chinese pilgrim Fa-hsien[5] who returned back to his country in the same sea-route which was followed by the Indian merchants in their trade with Śri Lankā, South-east Asia up to China. The Greek and Latin writings[6] constitute an important source of information. Their writings enumerate the ports on the eastern as well as on the western coasts visited by the ships. The identification of a few of these ports is still not clear. The importance of these texts lies in their references to the flourishing Indo-Roman trade of the early centuries of the Christian era.

Epigraphic reference to the ports is rather scanty. A few inscriptions refer to *Pattanas.* But *Pattana* is not a port in all the cases. The Maranjamura copperplates of the Somavaṁśī king Mahāsivagupta mention *Pattana* Suvarnapura,[7] i.e., Sonepur. It was probably the confluence of two rivers, here the Mahanadi and the Tel. But the references to Kalinga-Pattana,[8] Visakhapattana[9] and Bhimalipattana[10] in the Gaṅga inscriptions were the ports on the coast of northern Andhra Pradesh in the early medieval period. Lastly, the archaeological finds can provide three dimensional evidences about the ancient ports. But in Orissa archaeological excavations of the sites, identified as ancient ports, have not been undertaken on a systematic and regular basis. Whatever a little bit of excavation done, the results are not encouraging. The excavation at Manikapatana in Puri district has been taken up recently, completion of which may provide some new information. But in South India the excavations at Arikamedu near Pondicherry, Kaveripattinam, etc., have yielded substantial results pertaining to Indo-Roman trade.[11] The excavations at Puhar have proved the existence of harbour facilities.[12] Similarly, discovery of Roman objects and Roman factory site at Arikamedu have proved to be quite illuminating.[13]

Sometimes local traditions provide clue to unravel the mysteries of historical facts. In Orissa the *Taapoi* and *Bāliyātrā* traditions speak of the existence of merchant community called *sādhavapuas* and their voyages to oversea countries. It is difficult to say how old these traditions are, but it cannot be denied that they had been built up over the years on the trade relation between ancient Orissa and the countries of South-east Asia. The story of the merchant prince Kovalan and his wife Kannagi found in *Śilappadikąram*,[14] a Tamil work composed in the post-Sangam Age is based on the trade activities, particularly at Puhar, of the Sangam Age. This text gives a very realistic description of Puhar or Kaveripattinam.[15] Besides, *Manimekhalai* and the Sangam literature[16] refer to trade activities in South India in which the ports played an important role.

From the very early times Orissa had trade relations with Śri Lankā, Myanmar, Indonesia and Malay Peninsula. Ports on the Orissan coast handled the trade with the oversea countries. An important port of ancient Kalinga was Tāmralipti (modern Tamluk in the Midnapur district of West Bengal). It was a big port and ships loaded with merchandise sailed to Siṁhala (Śri Lankā), Suvarnadvīpa, Martaban and Myanmar. It seems that there was regular traffic between Tāmralipti and Siṁhala and other overseas countries. In the third century BC emperor Aśoka Maurya sent Mahendra and Sanghamitra to Siṁhala with a branch of the Bodhi tree from this port.[17] The Chinese pilgrim Fa-hsien, on his return journey, boarded a merchant ship in this port and after 15 days' voyage reached Siṁhala[18] and from there he took passage on board of another merchant vessel for Java. From Java he sailed to Canton.[19] The Chinese merchants sailed from Canton to Western Java and Palembeng (Sumatra) where they changed ship for Siṁhala or Śri Lankā which sailed via Nicobar. From Siṁhala they took another ship for Tāmralipti. It took about three months to cover the distance between Canton and Tāmralipti. During the north-east monsoon the Chinese ships sailed to India.[20]

Both the *Periplus* and Ptolemy's *Geography* mention that ships on the eastern coast used to visit the port, among others, Tamalites[21] which can be identified with Tāmralipti. Since this port, situated at the southernmost end of the grand route it became the principal centre of South-east Asian trade of the Gangetic plains, particularly of eastern Uttar Pradesh and Bihar. From Tāmralipti the grand route extended up to Mathura through Pundravardhana in north Bengal, Kajangala (Rajmahal), Rajagriha, Pataliputra, Champa in northern Bihar and Vaisali. From Mathura one of its branches extended up to Broach through Ujjayini and the other passing through the Hindukuśh extended up to Balk in Afghanistan.[22] Goods for South-east Asia channelised through this port.

Brihadkathāślokasaṁgraha of Buddhaswami narrates the story of Sānudāsa. He was the son of a merchant of Champa and came to Tāmralipti. A story[24] in the *Jñātā Dharma*, a Jain literature, refers to sea merchants (*nāva vaniyaga*) of Champa who came to the port of Gambhira with merchandise loaded on bullock carts. At the port the merchandise were unloaded and then reloaded in the ship. It is further mentioned that from this port ships sailed to Suvarnadvipa and Kaliyadvīpa (Zanzibar ?). Moti Chandra identifies this port with Tāmralipti.[25] Fa-hsien also followed the same route. From Pataliputra he went to Champa and then, following the Ganga, he reached Tāmralipti.[26] All these indicate that goods from the eastern part of the Gangetic plain were brought to Tāmralipti for export to Siṁhala and Suvarnadvīpa. Goods from northern part of coastal Orissa were also transported to Tāmralipti which was joined with road. In the 7th century AD the Chinese traveller Hsuan Tsang travelled from Tan-molih-ti to Wu-t'u via Karnasuvarna.[27]

The importance of Tāmralipti continued up to the Gupta period. The decline of the Indo-Roman trade in the Gupta period shifted the emphasis to South-east Asia. Consequently Tāmralipti remained as busy a port as it was before.

Next to Tāmralipti was the port of Che-li-tā-lo. It is evident from Husan Tsang's account that it was a flourishing port in the 7th century AD. According to his account[28] Che-li-tā-lo, situated to the south-western part of Wu-t'u country, was a seat of Mahāyāna Buddhism. The place was well-protected by lofty walls and there stood five great stupas with multi-storeyed towers. It is also evident from his account that it was an emporium of trade. He writes, 'It was a thoroughfare and resting place for sea-going traders and strangers from distant lands.'[29] This place also contained many rare and precious commodities, probably brought to that place either for export and by way of import.

It appears from the above description that the port was of considerable importance. Ships sailed to Śri Lankā from this port. Standing here Hsuan Tsang could visualize the stupa containing Buddha's tooth relic in Śri Lankā. He writes, 'Twenty thousand li in distant in the south, was Seng-ka-lo or Śri Lankā and on calm nights, one could see the brilliant light from the pearl on the top of the tope over Buddha's tooth relic in that country scintillating as a bright torch burning in the air'[30] An ordinary human eye cannot see the light coming from such a great distance. The relation between Che-li-tā-lo and Śri Lankā was so close that it could stimulate the mental vision of the visitor.

The identification of this port is still a subject of controversy. Cunningham identifies Che-li-tā-lo or Charitrapura with present Puri.[31] Waddel[32] restores Che-li-tā-lo as Chitrotpalā. It is the name of the branch of the river Mahanadi. He locates the site at Nendra where Chitrotpala is branched off from the Mahanadi. Rhys Davids[33] reconciles the views of the two and opines that it was Charitrapura and located at Nendra. R.D. Banerji[34] accepts the identification of Cunningham and so also N.K. Sahu.[35] Some scholars, on the authority of Oriya Mahābhārata, have identified it with Chandrabhāgā.[36] Very recently an attempt has been made to identify the place with village Chitreśvarī, about 2-3 km from the excavated Buddhist site of Kuruma near Konark.[37] After subjecting the pilgrim's account to close scrutiny it comes to our mind that the port was not far from the Buddhist complex of Ratnagiri, Lalitagiri, Udayagiri, etc., in undivided Cuttack district. But in spite of the uncertainty in location, it was an important port on the eastern coast and was linked with highways facilitating overland trade.[38]

Another important seaport on the eastern coast was Paloura. It was a famous emporium of trade. Ptolemy (second century AD) writes about this port.[39] He takes it as one of the bases for the preparation of his map.[40] He names a place Allosygne apparently situated somewhere below Paloura, as 'the apheterion (*Samudraprasthāna Pattanam*) from where ships bound for Khryse or the land of gold (*Suvarṇabhūmi*) leaving the shore went to sail in the midsea.'[41] It was one of the ports on the eastern coast visited by the ships. The other ports were Camara, Poduca, Sopatma, Kantakosdyla, Pitundra, Gange and Tamralites.[42] According to Sylvian, Levi Paloura is the Tamil equivalent of Dantapura.[43] But he identifies the city in the neighbourhood of Chicacole and Kaliṅgapatanam.[44] B.C. Sen[45] also equates Paloura with Dantapur, the ancient capital of Kaliṅga.

Pali *Dāthāvaṁśa* of Dhammakitti refers to Dantapura as the famous capital of Kaliṅga.[46] *Mahāgovinda Sutta* of *Digha Nikāya*,[47] *Kurudhamma Jātaka*[48] and *Mahāvastu*[49] refer to Dantapura. There are also epigraphic references to Dantapura.[50] The capital city seems to be a trading centre and thus it was linked with many other kingdoms by good roads.[51] It also finds mention in the Jain *Sūtraktāṅga*.[52]

A good number of scholars have given their own interpretations. According to scholars Paloura of Ptolemy is same as Dantakura of the Mahābhārata[53] and Daṇḍagula of Pliny.[54] According to G. Ramdas it stands on the way from Chicacola to Sidhantam in A.P.,[55] Oldham identifies it with the village named Puluru in Ganjam,[56] Cunningham identifies it with Rajmahendri on the Godavari,[57] and B.V. Krishna Rao identifies it with an old city near Amudalavalsa and Chicacole station which is still known as Dantapuram.[58] But its identification with Palur in Ganjam district seems to be correct.

From this port trade was carried on with Śri Lankā and countries of S-E. Asia. According to an inscription[59] of the 14th year of Māḍhariputta of the later Sātavāhanas Buddhists from Śri Lankā converted people into Buddhism in (P)lura among other places. This Lura was perhaps Palur. If this is accepted then it can be concluded that there was direct contact between Palur and Śri Lankā—the contact being trade contact.

The *Brihad Kalpasūtra Bhāṣya*[60] refers to Kanchanapura, the capital of Kaliṅga. According to its description it was a port and had trade relation with Siṁhala. Very probably it is same as Dantapur, i.e., Ptolemy's Paloura. In that case the antiquity of the port town can be pushed to the third century BC.

Another port on the east coast was Pithuṇḍa. The Hātigumphā inscription of Kharavela refers to Pithuḍaga or Pithuṇḍa.[61] In the eleventh year of his reign Kharavela conquered it. Jaina *Uttarādhyāyana Sūtra*[62] mentions Pihumṇḍa as a seacoast town, i.e., port town. This Pihumṇḍa appears to be the same as Pithuṇḍa of the inscription.[63] Pithuṇḍa is the same as Pityṇḍra metropolis of Maisoloi mentioned by Ptolemy.[64] Both *Periplus of Erythraean Sea* and Ptolemy mention Pitundra as a port on the eastern coast visited by the ships.[65] This port was situated between the mouths of Krishna and the Godavari in present Andhra Pradesh.

The ports on the eastern coast controlled by the Sātavāhanas were Maisolia (Masulipattinam), Kontakosyla (Ghantasala) and Alosygne (Koringa).[66] As stated earlier these ports were mentioned by *Periplus* and Ptolemy.

The lower Coromandel coast or the Tamil coast had several ports. These ports played an active part in the flourishing Indo-Roman trade in the early centuries of the Christian era. Besides, they had a share in the trade with South-east Asia, Far-East and Śri Lankā. *Periplus* states that ports of South India and Śri Lankā were active centres of trade with Far-East employing larger ships in greater number than those coming from Egypt.[67] The Sangam literature throws a good deal of light on the life of the people in the port-towns called *Paṭṭinams*. These *Paṭṭinams* were more commercially active and organized towns located on the coast.[68] These are also called Neidals.[69] The excavations of some of these sites like Kaveriputtinam, Arikamedu, etc., have unearthed material evidences in support of Sangam literature.

The most important port-town in the Tamil coast was Puhar or Kāveripaṭṭinam. It was situated at the mouth of the northern branch of river Kaveri. The Kaveri river is very deep and therefore big ships could enter the port of Puhār without slacking sail.[70] Śilappadikāram gives a very realistic description of this port-town. The caravans brought from land and sea-routes variety of goods which seemed as if 'all the produce of the world had been collected there.' One could see heaps of goods scattered over the city. In this city also lived the Yavanas and 'one could see sailors from all countries who were friendly to each other.'[71] Thus the oversea trade made it a cosmopolitan city.

In Tamil, Puhār means gateway city.[72] It is described that rows of boats, which returned laden with grain in exchange of white salt, were seen in the backwaters of the port of Puhār tied to rows of pegs.[73]

Puhār not only handled the trade of the Tamil country but also collected goods from northern India. It is evidenced from Śilappadikāram, Manimekhalai and other Tamil poems that Tamil merchants went to Varanasi via Ujjayini. Even there is a story that a Brahmin pilgrim from Varanasi visited Cape Comorin with his wife.[74] So there was regular intercourse between Tamil country and northern India. Śilappadikāram further narrates that sealed goods from north India reached the South and the merchants paid duties on them.[75] A portion of these goods channelised to Kaveripaṭṭinam and other ports. Other ports of the Tamil coast were Poduca (Pondicherry), Sopatma (Marakanam situated between Madras and Pondi-cherry),[76] Nirpeyarru (for Kacci or later Kanchi), Korkai of the Pandyan kingdom[77] and Kolapattanam.[78]

The above discussions lead to the conclusion that there were a good number of ports on the eastern coast of India in the ancient period. These were emporia and also handled the trade with Śri Lankā, countries of South-east Asia and Far-East. The ports on the Tamil coast played an active role in the Indo-Roman trade.

NOTES AND REFERENCES

1. R. Champakalaksmi, "Urbanization in South India: The Role of Ideology and Polity," Presidential Address in Section I, 47th Session of I.H.C., p. 6.
2. *Ibid.*, p. 9.
3. D.N. Das, *The Early History of Kalinga,* Calcutta, 1977, p. 249.
4. T. Watters, *On Yuan Chwang's Travels in India,* Delhi, 1961, pp. 193-94.
   S. Beal, *Si-yu-ki,* London, 1906, p. 205.
5. J. Leggi, *Fa-hien's Record of Buddhist Kingdoms,* Oxford, 1886, p. 100.
6. (i) *The Periplus of the Erythraean Sea of an unknown Alexandrian.*
   (ii) Pliny, *Naturalis Historia.*
   (iii) C. Ptolemy, *Geographica Huphagesis.*

7. *JBORS,* II, p. 52.
8. *SII,* VI, Nos. 848-849.
9. *SII,* X., p. 351.
10. *JAHRS,* VII, Part II, p. 129.
11. Reports of the excavations have been published in "For Arikamedu," R.E.M. Wheeler, et al., "Arikamedu—An Indo-Roman Trading Station on the East Coast of India," *Ancient India,* No. 2, 1946. For Kaveripattinam excavations, *IAR,* 1961-62; 1963-64.
12. R. Champakalakshmi, *op. cit.,* p. 46 fn.
13. See the Report of Excavation.
14. Śilappadikāram, trans. by V.R.R. Dikshitar, OUP, 1939.
15. Motichandra, *Trade and Trade Routes in Ancient India,* New Delhi, 1977, p. 154.
16. *Ibid.,* p. 153.
17. T. Thaper, *Asoka and the Decline of the Mauryas,* OUP, Second Edn. (Paperback), 1961, p. 46.
18. J. Leggi, *op. cit.,* p. 104.
19. *Ibid.*
20. Fredrick Hirth & W.W. Rockhill, *Chau-Ju-Kua,* St. Petersberg, 1912, pp. 8-9.
21. K.A.N. Sastri (Ed.), *A Comprehensive History of India,* Vol. II, Calcutta, 1957, p. 438.
22. Motichandra, *op. cit.,* pp. 5-21.
23. *Brihadkathā Śloka Saṁgraha,* Ch.18, p. 71.
24. Motichandra, *op. cit.,* p. 165.
25. *Ibid.*
26. J. Leggi, *op. cit.,* p. 104.
27. T. Watters, *op. cit.,* pp. 194-200.
28. *Ibid.,* pp. 193-94.
    S.Beal, *op. cit.,* p. 205.
29. *Ibid.*
30. *Ibid.*
31. S.N. Majumdar Sastri (Ed.), *Cunningham's Ancient Geography of India,* Calcutta, 1924, pp. 584-85.
32. *Proceedings of the Asiatic Society of Bengal,* 1892.
33. T. Watters, *op. cit.,* p. 195.
34. R.D. Banerji, *History of Orissa,* Calcutta, 1930, p. 138.
35. N.K. Sahu, *Utkal University History of Orissa,* Vol. I, Bhubaneswar, 1964.
36. D.K. Ganguly, *Historical Geography and Dynastic History of Orissa,* Calcutta, 1975, p. 68.
37. U. Subudhi, "A Note on Che-li-tā-lo", *The Journal of Orissan History,* Vol. II, No.2, July 1981, pp. 12-14.
38. D.N. Das, *op. cit.,* p. 251.
39. G.E. Gerini, *Researches on Ptolemy's Geography of Eastern Asia, India and Indo-Malay Peninsula,* p. 743. Ptolemy, VII, 16.
    J.W.McCrindle, *Ancient India as Described by Ptolemy* (Ed. by S.N. Majumdar Sastri), pp. 69-70.
40. D.K. Ganguly, *op. cit.,* p. 25.
41. C. Muller, *Geographic Graeci Minoris,* Vol. I, p. 535, Sections 37-39.
42. K.A.N. Sastri (Ed.), *A Comprehensive History of India,* Vol. II, Calcutta, 1957, p. 438.
43. Motichandra, *op. cit.,* p. 76.
    S. Levi, *Pre-Aryan and Pre-Dravadian in India* (Eng. trans. by P.C. Bagchi), Calcutta, 1929, p. 170.
44. *Ibid.,* p. 175.
45. B.C. Sen, *Some Historical Aspects of the Inscriptions of Bengal,* Calcutta, 1942, p. 44.
46. B.C. Law, *Dāṭhā Vaṁśa* (Punjab Sanskrit Series), *JASB,* XXVIII, pp. 186ff.
47. *Dīgha Nikāya,* XIX, 36.
48. V. Facesbollced, *The Jātakas,* Vol. II, No.276, pp. 251-52.
49. *Mahāvastu,* III, 351.
50. *EI,* XIV, p. 361.

51. *The Jātakas*, Vol. III, No. 301, pp. 3-5.
52. *The Sūtraktāṅga* (1, 6, 22).
53. *Mahābhārata* (Udyogaparvan) XLVII, 1883; (Dronaparvan), LXXVII.
54. *Naturalis Historia,* Book VI, XXIII, p. 72 (see Pliny, *Naturalis Historia,* Loeb Classical Library, pp. 392-93).
55. *EI,* XIV, p. 361.
56. *JBORS,* XXII, pp. 1f.
57. S.N. Majumdar Sastri (Ed.), *op. cit.,* p. 593.
58. *JBORS,* XIV, pp. 110-11.
59. *EI,* XX, p. 6; *EI,* XXXV, Pt.1, pp. 1ff.
60. *Brihadkalpasūtra Bhāṣya,* 3263 ff.
61. LII of Hatigumpha Inscription.
62. *Uttarādhyāyana Sūtra,* XXI, 1-4.
63. *IA,* LV, 1926, pp. 145-47.
64. Ptolemy, VI, I, 15 & 93.
    McCrindle, *op. cit.,* p. 234.
65. K.A.N. Sastri (Ed.), *op. cit.,* p. 438.
66. E.H. Warmington, *The Commerce between the Roman Empire and India,* Cambridge, pp. 115-16.
67. K.A.N. Sastri, *A History of South India,* 4th Edn., OUP, 1966, p. 141.
68. R. Champakalakshmi, *op. cit.,* p. 6.
69. *Ibid.,* p. 4.
70. K.A.N. Sastri, *op. cit.,* p. 139.
71. Motichandra, *op. cit.,* p. 154.
72. R. Champakalakshmi, *op. cit.,* pp. 5-6.
73. *Pattinappalai,* 11, 29-32.
74. Motichandra, *op. cit.,* p. 153.
75. V. Kanakasabhi Pillai, *The Tamils Eighteen-hundred Years Ago,* Madras, 1904, p. 112.
76. Motichandra, *op. cit.,* pp.118-20.
77. R. Champakalakshmi, *op. cit.,* p. 6.
78. S. Levi, *op. cit.,* pp. 35-37.

13

Maritime Activities of Orissa

K.S. BEHERA

Introduction

Maritime contacts and cultural interactions between civilisations, which contribute to the process of mutual enrichment and cross-fertilisation, are fascinating aspects of the history of mankind. This paper attempts to analyse the ancient maritime activities and contacts of Orissa with the outside world in the light of textual data, and archaeological evidence provided by the recent excavations of sites in coastal Orissa.

Orissa's geographical location between North and South India, and her favourable position along the shore of the Bay of Bengal, provided an excellent opportunity for its people for maritime trade and contacts. In the past the region covering a major part of coastal Eastern India had a distinct political identity of its own being known as Kaliṅga, Oḍra, Utkal and Orissa. In ancient times Orissa was famous as Kaliṅga. By the 14th-15th century, however, the name Oḍiśā (Orissa) had already become popular.

Literary and Epigraphic Evidence

In the 3rd century BC Kaliṅga was a major power of Eastern India. Aśoka conquered it eight years after his coronation, around 261 BC, mainly due to political and economic reasons. Aśoka invaded Kaliṅga apparently to gain control of trade centres and its natural resources. Kaliṅga controlled the trade routes to the South which passed through its coastal tracts. The location of Aśoka's Major Rock Edicts at Dhauli and Jaugada suggests the existence of coastal route from Tamralipti in West Bengal to the Andhra coast. Under Kharavela (1st century BC), the greatest ruler of ancient Kaliṅga, the influence of Kaliṅga was felt far and wide. As known from his Hatigumpha inscription, Kharavela defeated the Tamil confederacy and "caused the procurement of pearls, precious stones and jewels from the Pandya king." Kaliṅga's commercial importance and association with the Bay of Bengal are evident from classical texts such as the *Periplus*, Ptolemy's *Geography*, and Pliny's *Natural History*. Pliny places Kaliṅga on the seacoast. He says: "The tribes called Calingae are nearest the sea. The royal city of Calingae is Parthalis. Over their king 60,000 foot soldiers, 1,000 horsemen, 700 elephants keep watch and ward in precinct of war." According to the *Periplus*, Dosarene (identified with coastal Orissa) was famous for its ivory. Ptolemy also mentions several places in the Orissan coast including Paloura, which was a major port of Eastern India for sea voyages to South-east Asia. According to Ptolemy, the point of departure (*apheterion*) for ships bound for Khryse (South-east Asia) was "immediately to the south of a town of the territory on the Gangetic Gulf called Paloura". It was from here that ships bound for Khryse "ceased to follow the littoral and entered the high seas". The Periplous Tes Exo Thalasses, compiled by Marcianus of Heraklea (between 250 and 500 AD) also mentions the *apheterion* from which "all those navigating to Khryse leave." Paloura of Ptolemy is possibly identical with the village of Palur in the neighbourhood of Chilka lake. Digging by local people at Palur has brought to light black and red ware, NBP like ware, dish-on-stand, red ware etc. indicating its archaeological potentiality. With its ideal geographical location near the sea and a hillocle, Palur was a major port of Eastern India for voyages to South-east Asia. Kaliṅga was an important maritime zone of Eastern India and its king, according to Kalidasa, was the "lord of the Mahodadhi." In connection with the seashore of Kaliṅga, the *Raghuvaṁśa* mentions *dvipāntars* (Indonesian archipelago) from which breezes, filled with the scent of cloves, blew:

> *anena sārdham viharaṁburāseh tīresu talivana marmaresu* I
> *dvīpāntaranvita lavaṅga puṣpeiḥ apakṛtasveda lava marudbhiḥ* II
> Raghuvaṁśa 6:57.

The Chinese sources reveal close relations between Orissa and China. The Chinese pilgrim Hsuan Tsang, who visited Orissa in the 7th century, mentions an important port called Che-li-ta-lo: "Near the shore of the ocean, in the south-east, was the city of Che-li-ta-lo, above 20 li in circuit, which was a thoroughfare and resting place for sea-going traders and strangers from distant lands".

In the first half of the 8th century Śubhākar Siṁha, a famous scholar of Orissa, visited the court of Chinese emperor and translated a Buddhist text into Chinese. Another Buddhist monk named Prajñā, "who had settled in the monastery of the king of *Wu Cha* (Orissa)" went to China in AD 795. He carried a Buddhist manuscript autographed by the king of realm of *Wu Cha* (Orissa) for the Chinese emperor Te-Tsong. The name of the Orissan king is mentioned as "the fortunate monarch, who does what is pure, the lion." He is generally identified with the Bhaumakara monarch Śivakara. The visit of Buddhist scholars to China was possible because of merchant vessels which were plying between Orissa and China. The sea route from Eastern India to China passed through Siṁhala and Java. The Chinese pilgrim Fashien returned from India to China in a large merchant vessel which had two hundred other passengers. Orissa's cultural and commercial contact with China seems to have continued to a later period. *The Chu-fan-chi* of Chau-Ju-Kua, written in 1225-26, refers to *Kia-ling* sea-going vessels (i.e. Kaliṅga ships) and their system of trade organisation. Chau-Ju-Kua mentions two types of ships plying between Kaliṅga and Canton:

> On large *Kia-ling* (Kling) sea-going ships every several hundred men, and on small ones a hundred and more men, choose one of the more important traders as headman who, with an assistant headman manages various matters. The Superintendent of merchant shipping (at Canton) gives them a certificate permitting them to use the light bamboo for the punishing their followers. When one (of the company) dies, they (i.e., the headmen) make an inventory of his property.

This reference to *lavanga* from *dvipāntara* would suggest trade in cloves. Orissa evidently derived considerable revenue from sea trade as an inscription of the Bhaumakara period refers to *samudrakara bandha.*

The people of Kaliṅga had an important role in establishing contact with Java. Legends and local traditions of Java mention that "20,000 families were sent to Java by the prince of Kling. These people prospered and multiplied". The term 'Kling" is evidently derived from Kaliṅga and denoted the people of Kaliṅga. In course of time, however, Indian merchants, irrespective of their origin, were called Klingas. Several old Javanese inscriptions, dated between the 9th and the 11th century, refer to foreign merchants and captains of ships. These foreigners include Kaliṅga, Aryas, Simlaese, Dravidians, Pandikiras, Chams, Mors and Khemars. In the inscriptions the Klings or Kaliṅga people were clearly distinguished from people of other parts of India.

The contact of Kaliṅga with Siṁhala is attested by Ceylonese chronicles and inscriptions. *The Dathadhatuvaṁśa* records that the sacred Tooth-relic was taken from Dantapura of Kaliṅga to Śri Lankā. The *Chulavaṁśa* mentions that king Vijayabāhu of Siṁhala (1054-1109) married a Kaliṅga princess named Trilokasundarī. Kaliṅga Parakramabāhu Kīrti Niśankamalla, who ruled the island of Lankā between 1187 and 1198 AD was the son of king Jayagopa of Kaliṅga. He established effective control over Lankā and declared: "Enemies to the doctrines of Buddha might not be installed in the island of Lankā which is appropriate to the Kaliṅga dynasty".

About four years after the death of Virabāhu, son of Kīrti Niśanka Malla, Sāhasamalla was invited from Kaliṅga and installed on the throne in AD 1200. He ruled for two years. The sailors of Kaliṅga were quite familiar with the sea route to Śri Lankā and the maritime contact between Orissa and Śri Lankā continued through the ancient and medieval periods.

Not much is known about the volume of trade and the products involved in such transactions. From the account of Wang-Ta-Yuan (14th century) we know that the natural products of Wu-Tieh (Oḍiyas) were rice, king fisher's feathers, bees wax and fine cotton stuffs. Wang Ta-Yuan further mentioned that "because of the cheapness of living in Orissa nine out of ten persons going here for trade did not like to return home. Rice which was evidently the staple food of the people, was sold at the unbelievably low price of 45 baskets for one cowrie."

The textual data for the early historical period are not adequate to give a clear picture about the role of Orissa in the navigation of the Indian Ocean. Moreover there is complete lack of indigenous Oriya literary sources prior to the 15th century. The identification of places mentioned in the classical texts and Chinese sources, as for example, Paloura, Che-li-ta-lo etc., are problematic and not above controversy. On the whole, the literary and epigraphical data, brought to light so far, are limited and do not provide conclusive evidence. In such a situation, the archaeological evidence is of paramount importance.

Archaeological Evidence

Orissa is rich in archaeological remains which are scattered throughout the state but, unfortunately, archaeological investigations have barely begun. Hence the evidence from excavations is summarised below.

Since V. Ball picked up prehistoric tools in Orissa in the last century, several prehistorical sites have been reported to give us an idea about the progress of society from hunter-food gatherer stage to settled life and food production. The excavations of Neolithic sites of Kuchai and Baidyapur in Mayurbhanj district gave positive evidence of the use of polished shouldered tools, rice and cord-impressed pottery in the Neolithic age. In view of the technological affinites of shouldered adzes with those of South-east Asia, some scholars accept the possibility of Orissa's maritime connections with South-east Asia from the Neolithic period. But the possibility of introduction of shouldered adzes into India through land route via north-eastern India cannot be ruled out. Thus the beginning of Orissa's maritime contact with South-east Asia is unclear.

Excavations conducted B.K. Sinha at Golbai (lat. 20° 01' N and long. 83° 05' E in Khurda district) have provided evidence of "Copper Age" and a sequence of cultures from Neolithic to the Iron Age. The site located on the left bank of Malaguni river, a tributary of the Daya which falls into the Chilka lake, is divided into two parts by road to provide access to a Śiva temple of about 11th century. The site, otherwise, has an undisturbed deposit of 8 m consisting of Neolithic, Chalcolithic cultures and in its last phase giving evidence of iron.

In the centuries before the Christian era, the region underwent transformation in the economic field with the use of iron, development of agriculture, growth of trade and urban centres, etc. Significant changes also occurred in the political field with the Mauryan expansion and the growth of regional empire under Khāravela in the first century BC. The evidence about urban settlements in coastal Orissa comes from the excavations at Dhauli and Jaugada which were also the political nerve centers of Kaliṅga under Aśoka. The excavations at Sisupalgarh provide further evidence of a well-planned early historical city which remained under occupation between 3rd-4th centuries BC, and 4th century AD. Among the objects found are rouletted ware, clay bullae with heads imitated from those of Roman coins, a unique gold medallion showing "Kuṣāṇa design of a standing king and a Brahmi legend in character of third century AD on the obverse and Roman head with a Roman legend on the reverse." A terracotta bullae embossed with the head resembling that of Silenus has also been collected from Sisupalgarh. The discovery of Roman coins was reported in the Bamanghati area of Mayurbhanj district and in Koraput district of Orissa at Gumuda and Kotpad.

A study of the art of the Khandagiri-Udayagiri caves reveals the use of West Asian decorative elements such as honeysuckle, acanthus, stepped merlons, winged animals, etc. Some of the pilasters facing the doorways of the cave of Anantagumpha have *ghata-bases* ornamented in the Hellenistic fashion, very similar in treatment to vessels found from excavations in Western India. A *yavana* guard is shown on the left pilaster of the cave in the upper storey of the Ranigumpha. The kilted foreigner is in boots and wears a fillet on the forehead, while a sheathed sword hangs from the left side. The huge Bell Capital from Bhubaneswar, imitated from Aśokan columns, also shows West Asian motifs in its ornamentation.

The combined testimony of historical sources, material remains, and art evidence suggests that coastal Orissa was somewhat indirectly connected with the early trade between India and the western world. Goods from Orissa could have reached the Southern and Western India through coastal voyages taking advantage of the changing cycle of monsoons and ultimately despatched to the Roman world with which Kaliṅga had no direct maritime connection. Trade and commerce at regional and inter-regional level were facilitated with the circulation of punch-marked coins, Kuṣāṇa copper coins and imitation Kuṣāṇ coins. Kuṣāṇa gold coins, discovered in Orissa, were not the currency of Orissa but mostly used as ornaments. Kuṣāṇa copper coins, coming to Orissa by way of trade, remained there in circulation. Later on these were imitated for use in commercial transactions. While the silver punch-marked coins were in circulation up to *c.* AD 300 the imitation Kuṣāṇa coins (also called Puri Kuṣāṇa coins) continued from about 2nd to 4th-5th century AD. This is suggested by the evidence of stratigraphy at Sisupalgarh and legend *tanka,* which is datable to 4-5th century AD on ground of palaeography.

Between 2nd and 4th centuries Orissa had direct maritime contact with South-east Asia. The importance given to sea-trade with South-east Asia was partly the result of the extension of the inland and inter-regional trade and commerce and predominantly the outcome of the rising demand in the West for spices. It is likely that the Orissan "middleman" merchants took advantage of this situation and involved themselves in the spices trade, especially the trade in cloves. The existence of an Apheterion, point of departure to South-east Asia must have facilitated voyages to South-east Asia.

Recent archaeological discoveries in Śri Lankā, Indonesia, Thailand, Vietnam, Burma, etc., have thrown new light on India's maritime connections with those countries. Archaeological excavations in Anuradhapura prove the introduction of Indian cultural elements including Buddhism into Śri Lankā even before the days of Aśoka. Excavations in Sembiran in north-eastern Bali yielded Indian rouletted ware, one rim sherd of Wheeler's Arikamedu type 10, a body sherd with Kharoshti characters and hundreds of glass beads. These suggest that Bali seems to have been reached by Indians about the beginning of the Christian era. Scientific analysis of the samples of rouletted ware from Arikamedu (India), Anuradhapura (Śri Lankā) and Sembiran (Bali) are very similar. Rouletted wares have also been reported in Kopak Kendal and Cibutak in north-west Java.

The material evidence brought to light from Don Ta Phet in Thailand includes semi-precious stone and glass beads, knobbed base, bronze vessels, etc. The knobbed ware pottery was first identified at Sisupalgarh and this occurs at several sites in Eastern India and the Ganga valley. These prove contact with Eastern India and possibly also with Orissa in view of the knowledge of knobbed ware technique and rich deposits of semi-precious stones in western Orissa in Kalahandi, Bolangir, Baud and Sambalpur areas. In ancient time Kaliṅga was known for its elephants and its tusk could have been an important item of commerce. It is interesting that an Indian ivory comb (dated between 1st-3rd century AD) has been recovered from Chansen in central Thailand. The Śrīvatsa motif on it is analogous to the motif found in the art of Khandagiri, Udayagiri caves and the Hatigumpha inscription of Kharavela (1st century BC). Later on Śrīvatsa motif became fairly common in coins from OCEO in Vietnam at Arakan. Kharoshti inscriptions discovered in Orissa coast (from Manikapatna), Thailand, Bali and possible depiction of a horse on bronze bowl from Don Ta Phet, which is taken to be the earliest evidence about horse in South Asia indicate maritime contacts of Orissa with Kharoshti using horse merchants of lower Bengal and South-east Asia. Prof. B.N. Mukharjee believes that activities of the Yueh-chih horse dealers in South-east Asia are preserved in an engraving on a drum from an Indonesian island, representing two persons clad in Yueh chi dress along with a horse.

Orissa's sea trade seems to have declined in the post-Gupta period, although cultural contacts with other countries such as Śri Lankā, China, Indonesia, etc., continued. Again the active role of Orissa in the maritime trade is witnessed from the 11th to 14th century AD.

The excavation of Khalkatapatna (long. 86° 02' 4" E, lat. 19° 51' 13" N) on the left bank of the Kushabhadra river in Puri district, indicated its importance as a port of coastal Orissa between 12th and 14th centuries AD. The excavation conducted by J.S. Nigam, Superintending Archaeologist of the A.S.I., yielded Chinese celadon ware and Chinese porcelain with blue floral design on white background. The Chinese copper coins (one complete and one fragmentary), with square perforation in the middle and inscription in the Chinese character, provide further evidence for overseas trade links between Orissa and China. Egg-white glazed pottery obtained from the site is supposed to be from the Arab countries and this suggests sea-trade with countries in the West.

The material evidence from the excavations of Manikapatna (long. 94' 5", lat. 33' 5') adds considerably to our understanding of the overseas contacts of Orissa in the medieval period. Manikapatna, located on the left bank of the water channel which connects the Chilka lake with the Bay of Bengal, was identified as a possible port site by the Orissan Institute of Maritime and South-east Asian Studies, Bhubaneswar and was subjected to limited excavations between 1989 and 1993. Puri Kuṣāṇa coins had been picked up from the neighbourhood of Manikapatna in 1993. A Śiva temple, locally called Bhavakundaleswara temple, which stands here was built in the 13th century. In the 16th century Abul Fazal mentions Manikapatna as a "large port where salt dues were collected". The place is mentioned in maps of the 16th-17th centuries and Gujarati sea manuals of the 18th century. Manikapatna is also on the land route from the South and it virtually served as the entrance to Orissa from that direction. The British troops moved to Cuttack in 1803 following the Ganjam-Manikapatna-Puri route.

The deposits of the early historical period (Period I) yielded two Neolithic celts, two sherds of Indian rouletted ware, fragments of what seems to be imitation of an amphora, Puri Kuṣāṇa coins, and a sherd with Kharoshti inscription.

The deposit of Period II, separated from the Period I by a deposit of sand, can be dated between 12th century to the early part of the 19th century. The complete sequence of culture, however, is not clear as digging did not reach the natural soil due to difficulty of drifting sand and extensive flooding of the site. The excavations yielded two types of evidence for maritime connections with China: celadon ware and Chinese copper coins. Celadon ware occurs in abundance. The material awaits proper study and classification but a preliminary study revealed considerable variations in quality and raw material. The very well-made jade green celadon are generally of Chinese origin. A few blue Chinaware fragments have also been found. A good number of sherds showed poor workmanship, both in the use of raw material and finish. A base fragment was without glaze on either side. This suggests that all the celadon ware from the site may not be of Chinese origin. There is a probability that an attempt was made to manufacture celadon ware in Orissa or somewhere in India. They may have been imported from abroad, possibly from Thailand or Burma but not necessarily from China proper. This requires further investigation. Apart from the celadon ware, a fragmentary copper coin with characteristic square perforation in the centre, is of Chinese origin. This evidently came by way of sea trade with China. Wang Tu-Yuan (1330-49) of China gives an idea about relative value of Orissan and Chinese currency. It is said that each of Orissa's silver coin is equivalent in value to ten taecls of Chung-t'ung Ch'ao. It exchanges for 11,520 odd cowries, and each coin can purchase 45 baskets of rice. The use of cowries in Orissa suggests maritime contact with the Maldive islands.

Trade links with Burma are proved by the presence of a brown glazed ware, known as Maratuan ware, after the name of the place located in Burma. This Burmese ware is available both in thick and thin variety.

The two other imported wares from the Arabian countries include a thin egg-white glazed pottery and thick chocolate glazed ware. The former has mainly bowls and the latter are the fragments of storage jars. These were first noticed in the excavations at Khalkatapatna. The presence of giraffe, an African animal in the temple art of Konarak (13th century) suggests contact with Arab merchants who might have been commissioned to bring this animal from Africa to the eastern coast. In the early 15th century the Chinese Admiral Cheng Ho is known to have taken a giraffe to China. Maritime connections with Tamil Nadu coast and Śri Lankā are proved by the recovery of a Chola coin and a copper coin of Sāhasamalla of Śri Lankā. The discovery of Sāhasamalla's coins from Manikapatna in Orissa, Polonnaruwa in Śri Lankā and Kotchina in Indonesia, prove a maritime network linking coastal Orissa, Śri Lankā and Sumatra. It is clear that Manikapatna was an important port and trading centre for indigenous people and foreign sailors and merchants

The expansion of sea trade is closely connected with the development of boat building technology and techniques of navigation. The *Datha dhātu vaṁśa*, while mentioning the transfer of the Tooth Relic from Dantapura of Kaliṅga to Śri Lankā refers to a ship that was "firmly constructed with planks sewed together with ropes, having a well rigged, lofty mast, with a spacious sail and manned by a skilful navigator." Representations of boats in the temple art of Orissa, as at Bhubaneswar, Puri and Konarak, indicate the importance attached to water transport. A detached sculpture preserved in the Orissa State Museum shows elephants on the boat. The boat motif is also associated with the iconography of Aṣtamahābhaya Tārā, Mārtaṇḍa Bhairava (at Konarak) and Mahiṣāsuramardini Durgā. The boats are also shown on illustrated palm leaf manuscripts. Further, several palm leaf manuscripts of the modern period give some details about the construction of flat bottom boats of Chilka lake with illustrations. A study of the boats, depicted in sculpture and manuscripts, indicates the existence of both carvel and clinker construction. The specimens from the Bhogamandapa of the Puri temple and the detached sculpture representing a royal barge from the Indian Museum, Calcutta, reveal the practice of reversed clinker technique. Its continuance till date is proved by a drawing of *Patua* made by B. Solvyns in the early part of the 19th century* and *Patia* boat types, which are found in the northern coast from Dharma to the Suvarnarekha (Fig. 1). The survival of clinker construction, both ordinary and reversed type, is significant as clinker construction of boats is not available in southern and western coast of India. Of course such types are known in the eastern coast from West Bengal and Bangladesh (Fig. 2).

Apart from the documentation of the present boat forms of Orissa, equally rewarding would be the excavation of sites with remains of sunken boats. A trial excavation at Olandazsahi, in the town of Balasore, shows the remains of a boat whose features can be ascertained only after completion of the excavation.

Buddhism played a significant role in the relations between Orissa and South-east Asia. Scholars, so far, have discussed Indian influence in terms of North Indian art styles of Gupta

---

* I am grateful to Jean Deloche for drawing my attention to this and a copy of it.

Fig. 1. *Patua*, engraving by Solvyns B., *Les Hindous*, Paris, 1811, t. III, s.v. *pettoua*

and Pāla periods and South Indian influence in terms of the Pallava art. Comparative studies of Buddhist art of Orissa with that in South-east Asia show several common elements and striking affinities. Excavations conducted in Orissa at Ratnagiri, Udayagiri and Lali-tagiri have brought to light masterpieces of Buddhist art. The Buddha heads from these centres and those from central Java share common traits of massive form, sensitive modelling and spiritual expressions. The Javanese Bodhisattvas from Chandi Mendut have their attributes placed on long lotuses in the style distinctive of the Lalitagiri figures of Orissa.

Conclusion

The available evidence, though inadequate, indicates that Orissa was an important zone of commerce from about the third century BC to the early centuries of the Christian era and

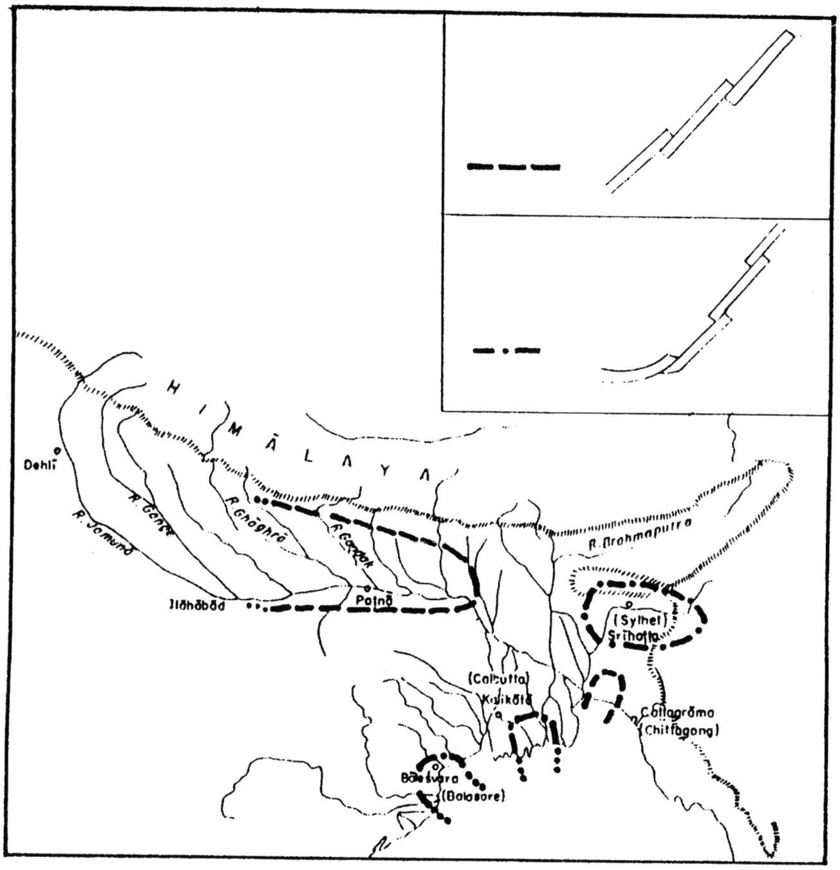

Fig. 2. Distribution of ordinary clinker style and reverse clinker

was connected with the national communication network. It had a share of Indo-Roman commerce though as yet there is no concrete and conclusive evi-dence to show direct maritime links with the Roman world in the beginning of the Christian era. The presence of Indo-Roman rouletted ware, gold medallion combining Kuṣāṇa coin type and a bust from a Roman coin, terracotta bullae with bust imitated from Roman coins, the presence of West Asiatic motifs in the art of Khandagiri-Udayagiri caves, etc., indicate the impact of early sea trade between India and Mediterranean world. By 2nd century AD Kaliṅga seems to have established direct contact with South-east Asia. The overseas contact with Śri Lankā, South-east Asia and China was very much evident between 10th and 14th centuries. The presence of celadon ware and Chinese coins in coastal Orissa provides the evidence for exchange between China and Orissa. The excavations at Manikapatna provide evidence to prove its importance in the East-West maritime trade.

Further fieldwork, identification and excavation of port sites, study of boat building technology, comparative study of art evidence from Orissa and South-east Asia are expected to shed new light on the maritime connections of Orissa with the outside world.

REFERENCES

Ardika, I. Wayan and P. Bellwood, 1991, "Sembiran: The beginning of Indian Contact with Bali". *Antiquity* 65.

Arunachalam, B., 1993, "The route of the Baliyatra—A Scientific Appraisal".

Begley, V. and De Puma, R.D. 1992. *Rome and India: The Ancient Sea Trade,* New Delhi.

Behera, K.S., 1993, "Ancient Orissa/Kaliṅga and Indonesia: The Maritime Contacts", *Utkal Historical Research Journal,* Vol. IV, pp. 122-32.

Bernet Kempers, A.J. 1933, *The Bronzes of Nalanda and Hindu Javanese Art.*

Coedes, G., 1968, *The Indianised States of South-east-Asia.* Kuala Lampur, University of Malaya Press.

Das, D.N., 1977, *The Early History of Kaliṅga,* Calcutta.

Dikshit, M.G., 1949, *Etched Beads in India,* Poona.

——, 1969, *History of Indian Glass,* University of Bombay.

Glover, I.C., 1989, *Early Trade Between India and South-east Asia: A Link in the Development of a World Trading System,* Center for South-east Asian Studies.

Lal, B.N., 1949, "An Early Historical Fort in Eastern India", *Ancient India,* No. 5.

Mukharjee, B.N., 1989. *Post-Gupta Coinages of Bengal,* Calcutta.

——, 1989-90. ,Discovery of Kharoshti Inscriptions in West Bengal", *The Quarterly Review of Historical Studies,* Vol. XXIX, No. 2, p. 61.

——, Coastal and Overseas Trade in Pre-Gupta, Vanga and Kaliṅga: Some New Data (unpublished).

Nigam, J.S., 1993, A Brief Note on the Excavation at Manikpatna (1993) (unpublished).

Ray, H.P., 1989, "Early Trade in the Bay of Bengal", *The Indian Historical Review,* Vol. XIV, Nos. 1-2, pp. 79-89.

——, 1989. "Early Maritime Contacts Between South and South-east Asia", *Journal of South-East Asian Studies,* Vol. XX, No. 1, pp. 42-54.

Sarkar, H.B., 1983, *Cultural Relations Between India and South-east Asian Countries,* Indian Council of Cultural Relations, New Delhi.

——, 1977, The People of Kaliṅga in the History and Economic Life of the Malayo-Indonesian World (up to 16th century)." Paper presented at the Indian History Congress, Bhubaneswar.

Sastri, K.A.N., 1949. *South Indian Influences in the Far East.*

Satish Chandra (Ed.), 1987, *The Indian Ocean: Explorations in History, Commerce and Politics,* New Delhi.

Sinha, B.K., 1993, "Excavations at Golbai Sasan, Dist. Puri, Orissa" (published in the *Puratattva*).

Tripathi, S., 1986, *Early and Medieval Coins and Currency System in Orissa,* Calcutta.

Wheatley, Paul, 1980, *The Golden Khersonese,* Kuala Lampur.

Williams, J., 1989, "The Bird of Hariti: Some questions about the Buddhist Iconography of Orissa and Java," *The Journal of the Orissa History Congress.*

Wolters, O.W., 1967, *Early Indonesian Commerce: A Study of the Origins of Śrī Vijaya.* Cornell University Press.

14

Maritime Activities of the Kaliṅgas and the New Light thrown by the Excavations at Khalkatapatna

B.K. SINHA

नावा न क्षोदः प्रदिशः प थिव्याः
मधुमन्मे परायणं मधुमत्पुनरानम्

Ṛgveda X 24.6

This hymn from Ṛgveda is the earliest literary reference about the maritime activities of Indians. Rigveda also mentions interesting stories about sea voyages as well as hazards during sea voyages. The story of the adventures of Bhujyu, son of Tugra, in the middle of the sea and his rescue by Aśvina is one of such descriptions. (ṚV.I 116.3.5)

There are several stories in Jatakas and works like *Hitopadeśa* and *Kathā Sarit-sāgar* recording adventures of several people on high seas and oceans.

Kautilya's *Arthaśāstra* gives a vivid account of officers led by a *Nāvādhyakṣha* controlling naval or maritime activities. During Mauryan period important ports were developed both on eastern and western coasts, and through these ports Aśoka's messages reached far off places like Egypt, Syria, Macedonia, Cyrene, Epirus and Ceylon. Some historians believe that Aśoka waged a bloody war on Kaliṅga with the sole aim of acquiring control of Orissan ports, so that trade to eastern countries may be controlled.

Ptolemy, in his *Geography*, gives indication of well developed ports on both the coasts of India, including Barygaza (modern Broach) and Tamralipti, as well as a flourishing trade with both western and eastern countries. *Periplus of Erythraean Sea*, a work attributed to AD 50, also mentions about the ports, on both the eastern and western coasts of India along with items imported into India and exported from India.

Literary sources also inform us of the maritime activities of Sātvāhanas, Pallavas and later the Cholas. Sopara, Kalyāna, Hannavar and Gokarna have been referred to as the ports of the Sātavāhanas, whose coins also bear the figures of ships. The Aihole Praśasti refers to the naval expedition by the Chalukian king Pulkesi II to the Puri island. The copperplate grants of his grandson Vinayditta and his successors ascribe Vinayditta the conquest of Parasika, Simhala, Kamera or Kavera (Khymer), present Cambodia.

Pāṇini (5th cent. BC) talks of four types of timber used in the making of ships. *Vṛksayurveda,* a work assignable to circa 1st cent. AD classifies wood used in making ships into four categories, namely (1) Brahman Jati, (2) Ksatra Jati, (3) Vaishya Jati and (4) Sudra

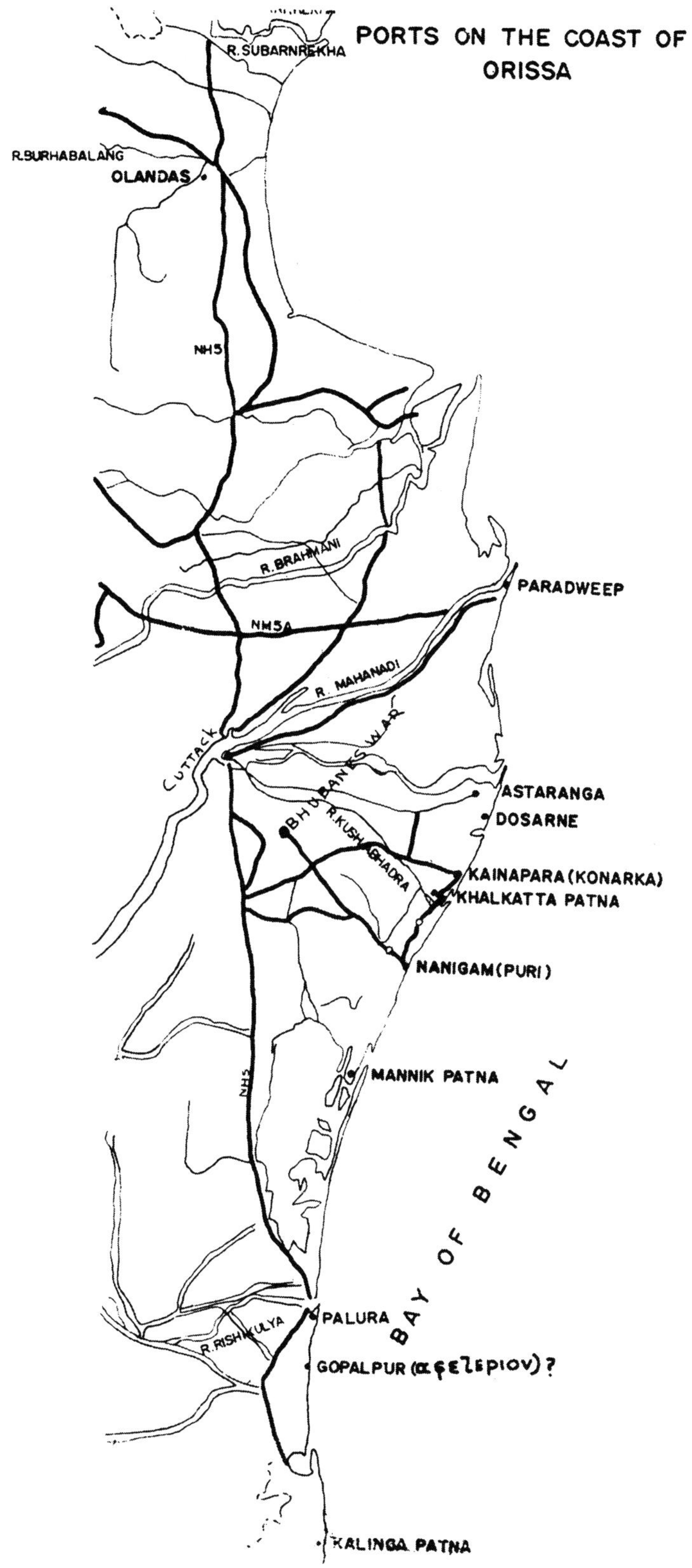
PORTS ON THE COAST OF ORISSA
R. SUBARNREKHA
R.BURHABALANG
OLANDAS
NH5
R. BRAHMANI
PARADWEEP
NH5A
R. MAHANADI
CUTTACK
BHUBANESWAR
ASTARANGA
DOSARNE
R.KUSHABHADRA
KAINAPARA (KONARKA)
KHALKATTA PATNA
NANIGAM (PURI)
MANNIK PATNA
NH5
BAY OF BENGAL
PALURA
R. RISHIKULYA
GOPALPUR
KALINGA PATNA

Fig. 1

Jati. Out of these Ksatra Jati, being strong and sturdy, was used for outer casing and the others for inside works.

Bhoj's *Yuktikalpataru* (11th century AD) gives details of ships and shipbuilding. According to this work, ships have been classified into two categories, 1. Sāmānya, 2. Viśeṣa Sāmānya were ordinary type of ships and were undecorated, while Viśeṣa were specially decorated with foils of iron, copper and gold. Sāmānya was further subdivided into 10 categories based on the size and measurements, e.g., the smallest Ksudra having a length of 16, breadth of 4 and height of 4 cubits while the largest of this category Manthara was 120 x 60 x 60 cubits. The Viśeṣa had two sub-categories: (a) of which length was the main feature and (b) of which height was the main feature. Of the ten types in category (a), the smallest Dirghika measured 32 x 4 x 3 cubits while the longest Vengini measured 172 x 22 x 17 cubits. Of the 5 types under category (b), the smallest Urdhva measured 32 x 16 x 16 cubits while the largest Manthara measured 96 x 48 x 48 cubits.

Archaeological discoveries in India and neighbouring countries have reinforced the descriptions in literature. Mesopotamian clay tablets, datable to 3rd millennium BC, refer to contacts with Dilmun, Magan and Meluhha and the discovery of Mesopotamian seals in the Harappan levels in India and of Harappan seals in Mesopotamia, (Kassite levels) Egypt and Bahrain support this evidence. Dilmun, Magan and Meluhha, always referred in that order in the clay tablets have been identified with the island of Failakand, Bahrain, Oman and Baluchistan and Harappan culture.

Clay boat models and potsherds showing pictures of boats, have been recovered from Mohanjodaro, Chanudaro and Lothal. The discovery of a dockyard at Lothal, associated with Harappan culture, leaves nobody in doubt about Harappans being seafarers. A painted potsherd showing a multi-tiered galley and an inscribed amulet depicting a boat with a motiff of cabin and two sea birds with the inscription reading Pak-Tras-Ap-Par meaning "O guardian of turbulent waters protect" (Rao 1973) found at Lothal further strengthen the evidence of the maritime activities of the Harappans.

India's maritime contacts with South-East Asia and China, in which Orissa played an important role, are traceable to circa 3rd-4th century AD on the basis of some inscriptions in Pallava Grantha script. The Chinese traveller, Fa-Hian, who visited India during the Gupta period, i.e., 5th century AD, took a sea route from the port Tamralipti, on his journey back home passing through Śri Lankā and Java.

Another Chinese traveller Itsing, who visited India in the later part of 7th century AD came by sea and returned by sea, but took a different sea route than Fa-Hian, touching Sumatra, Champa and Canton. The routes taken by these two Chinese travellers indicate that there were at least two sea routes from the east coast of India to China.

Trade contacts with South-East Asian countries also led to religious and cultural contacts. The rise of Buddhism in India added a new dimension to the existing commercial relations. Starting with the exchange of scholars, when need arose to build monasteries and images of Buddha and of Buddhist pantheon, a big demand for architects, sculptors and artisans became apparent in South-eastern countries including China. As a result of this demand there started migration as well as interaction of these classes.

Around AD 800, a king of Orissa is believed to have sent a Buddhist manuscript to the imperial court of China. During the period between AD 800 and AD 1200 Buddhist and

Hindu art were at its peak in Orissa. Monasteries among them Ratnagiri, Lalitgiri and Udaygiri and temples like Lingraja temple at Bhubaneswar and Jagannath temple at Puri had been built. A great number of artisans went to South-East Asian countries from Orissa and the influence of Orissa's Buddhist and Hindu art can be seen in the Buddhist art of Java under the Shailendra dynasty, the art of Bali islands, and the art and architecture of Cambodia during the 11th century AD.

Orissan tradition and folklore are also full of stories which bespeak of voyages by sea, boats, as well as Orissa's contacts with Bali islands, in Indonesia. There are also references to the worship of sea god and goddesses which reflect the concern of the families left behind by the voyagers. *Boita vandana* and the worship of *Mangala gor* are two such ceremonies which are performed till today. *Boita vandana* is celebrated on Kartika Purnima and paper boats are put in the village tanks and worshipped. In remembrance of contacts with the Bali islands, Bali yātrā is celebrated all over Orissa. In older days all the journeys to far off lands started on Kartika Purṇima day, i.e., at a time when after rains the weather was clear and strong easterly winds started. The main Bali yātrā festival is celebrated in Cuttack at the Gadgadia ghāt on river Mahanadi. Here in olden days a ceremonial send off was given by the family members of the travellers praying for their security and safe return home from yoyage.

From time immemorial, Orissa, having a coastline of 600 km and situated between the two great deltaic regions, of Ganges on the north and of Godavari and Krishna on the south has played an important role in India's maritime trade. Being fertile and strategically important, the Orissan coastline, from river Subarnarekha in the north to river Rishikulya in the south, was dotted with big and small ports.

Ptolemy, the 2nd century Greek geographer, gives a list of ports on Orissan coastline, e.g., 1. Kambyson, mouth of Ganges (possibly mouth of river Hugli), 2. Manada, Manda or Mandu river mouth (possibly the mouth of river Mahanadi), 3. Kannagara (Konark), 4. Katikardama or Katikardamma (possibly Cuttack or Khurda), 5. Palin or Palura (possibly present Paloor village on Ganjam river. and 6. *Aphetarion* possibly Gopalpur- on-Sea. Aphetarion is mentioned as the place from where ships departed for Khryse, i.e., Suvarnabhumi. Hathigumpha inscription refers to the renovation of Pithunda, now in Andhra Pradesh, by king Kharvela. Kalidasa in *Raghuvaṁśa* refers to the king of Kaliṅga as the lord of the sea *Mahodadhipati.*

Hieun-Tsang describes three regions which are identifiable with the present coastal Orissa. These are 1. U-cha, (Oḍra) 2. Kong-U-to (Kongoda), and 3. Kieling-Kia (Kaliṅga). Hieun Tsang also refers to a port town Che-Li-To-La (Charitra) "from where merchants depart for distant countries and strangers come and go and stop on their way."

Besides the ports mentioned by Ptolmey and Hieun-Tsang, other ports, big or small, on the Orissan coast on the basis of literary descriptions or explorations or excavations, are Olandas (Balasore), Chandraval, Paradweep, Astrange, Dosarne (Dhauli), Nanaigam (Puri), Kaina para, Khalkattapatna, Manikapattna and Kaliṅgapattna. Some of these ports are in land and situated on river banks. The *Brahamananda Purana* (10th century AD) informs us that Chilka lake was a big harbour sheltering sea-going vessels. From this harbour vessels sailing for Java, Malaya, Sumatra, Bali, Burma, China, Thailand, Ceylon and other places could carry thousands of passengers.

Explorations at Potgarh in Ganjam district by the Excavation Branch-IV of Archaeological Survey of India, located on the left bank of Rishikulya river, a platform made of brick jelly and laterite kankar soil, running up to a length of about 30 m has been observed in the section cut by the river Rishikulya. The platform, possibly, was meant for loading and unloading of cargo brought by boats. There is a strong possibility that Potgarh was an inland port.

Excavations at Manikpatna by the Orissan Institute of Maritime and South-east Asian Studies, have revealed Ceylonese coins, Arabian egg-white and chocolate glazed wares, Chinese porcelain and celadon wares and Roman rouletted wares.

Khalkattapatna (lat. 86° 02' N and long. 19° 51' 13" E) in Puri district of Orissa has been excavated by the Excavation Branch-IV of the Archaeological Survey of India. Khalkattapatna is situated 11 km east of Konark in Puri district and is located on the left bank of river Kushibhadra which falls into the Bay of Bengal 3 km to the north-east. The right bank of the river Kushibhadra forms a narrow barrier of sand between the site and the Bay and serving as a groyne wall must have provided the site with ideal landing facilities and protection from over flooding due to storms.

Excavations at Khalkattapatna (1984) revealed a brick jelly floor which might have served as loading–unloading platform. Pottery recovered from the excavations consisted of Chinese celadon ware, Chinese porcelain with blue floral designs on white background, egg-white glazed ware and glazed chocolate ware, all of the Arabian origin. The associated indigenous pottery consisted of dark grey and red slipped wares. The shapes met with were bowls, basins, handis, vases, miniature pots, all wheel-turned. Pottery with stamped geometrical designs confined to neck and waist, was also met with.

A total of 143 antiquities were recovered and these consisted of arecanut-shaped beads of terracotta, fragments of bangles of glass and copper, fragmentry animal head of terracotta (horse), a miniature copper bowl and copper coins. Besides pottery of Chinese origin i.e., celadon ware and Chinese porcelain and the egg-white and chocolate glazed wares of Arabian origin, the most important find from excavations were one complete and one fragmentry Chinese circular copper coins datable to circa 14th century AD. The circular copper coin had a square perforation in the centre with a legend in Chinese characters. The occupation at the single phase site can be dated between 12th and 14th centuries AD.

Most of the ports on the Orissan coastline including Khalkattapatna, were inland ports located on river banks. Coastal Orissa, being a deltaic region, is full of rivers from north to south and these rivers in the past were navigable. Bulk of Orissan trade moved through these rivers to the main ports, which were few in number. In two sculptural depictions, i.e., (i) in the Bhogmandapa of Jagannath temple at Puri and (ii) a small medallion in Lingarāja temple, only small boats have been shown, depiction of big boats/ships are few and this factor indicates the popularity of the small boats which were used for riverine trade etc.

It is also likely that these small boats besides being used for riverine trade etc., were shuttling between ports situated on the coastline.

The direct crossing of Bay of Bengal was full of hazards. We know that the Chinese traveller Fa-Hian, who sailed in a big ship on his return journey from Tamralipti, reached Java after an adventurous voyage marked by several hair breadth escapes and hence the crossing of the Bay of Bengal and Arabian Sea must have been undertaken by the big ships and avoided by the small ones. It is therefore possible that the route taken up by the small ships emerging from the ports situated inland, on rivers, was along the coastline to big ports hopping on small ports en route.

The *Periplus of Erythrean Sea* gives an interesting account of the goods which were imported into India and exported from India. In this list some items from eastern India are masalia, muslins, malabathrum, Gangetic spikenard, bdellium, ivory, agate, carnelian, lycium, cotton cloth of all kinds, silk cloth, pearls, long pepper and diamonds. Dosarene is mentioned as a port from where ivory was loaded. Diamonds came from the Mahanadi valley and district of Sambalpur.

A panel in Orissa State Museum depicts the transportation of elephants by ships. It may be gathered that Orissa, where elephants were in abundance, also exported baby elephants which were easy to be carried on boats.

The seaports of Orissa, backed up by fertile lands rich in flora and fauna, were connected by a strong riverine navigation system. Orissan coast being a deltaic region, is criss-crossed by small and big rivers at short intervals, and hence movement of merchandise by river was much easier, convenient and cheaper.

There is a strong possibility that during earlier times, majority of the rivers of Orissa were easily navigable and played important part in the communications network. It can be seen that the hinterlands being full of forests and rivers, road communications and net-works between distant places would have been extremely difficult and expensive if not impossible.

Till the rise of big kingdoms in the later historical period, we are not aware of many land routes from north to south and hence the main route to south was the sea route. This may account for the fact that most of the Hindu and Buddhist centres on the eastern coast are situated at an easily approachable distance from the coast.

The journey from the popular port in the north, Tamralipti, to Anuradhapur (Ceylon) was an important coastal journey and in this journey all the ports on the coast of Orissa played very important roles. The big boats which crossed the Bay of Bengal, en route to Arabian countries passed through the Orissan ports for exchanging cargoes, passengers, and picking up essential supplies, i.e., food etc.

The shuttle service plying between inland ports and seaports, maintained the much needed supply line and kept the sea ports well provided. It must be emphasized that the role played by the inland ports in the maritime activities of Kaliṅgas was an extremely important one. But alas! the large scale deforestation resulting in the erosion of land and silting up of rivers have rendered many of the rivers of Orissa unsuitable for navigation and thus a deadly blow to riverine navigation in Orissa has been delivered.

Khalkatapattna being the only port town on the coast of Orissa excavated so far, the evidence obtained is very important in the maritime activities of the Kaliṅgas. Pottery recovered from Khalkattapatna, egg-white glazed and chocolate glazed wares and celadon ware and Chinese porcelain, clearly point to the maritime relations with Arabian countries (egg-white glazed and chocolate glazed wares) and China (celadon ware and Chinese porcelain). The find of Chinese coins from Khalkattapatna is a definite evidence of foreign seamen and ships visiting Khalkattapatna port.

The inland port of Khalkattapatna situated on river Kushbhadra, thus was not only an important link in the riverine navigation of Orissa, but also occupied an important place in international trade between Arabian countries on the West and Indonesia and China on the East.

REFERENCES

Agrawal, D.P., "Marine Archaeology in Harappan Context", in S.R. Rao (Ed.), *Marine Archaeology of Indian Ocean Countries.*

Bag, A.K., "Ships and shipbuilding Technology in Ancient and Medieval India", in S.R. Rao (Ed.), *Marine Archaeology of Indian Ocean Countries.*

Beals, S., *Buddhist Records of Western World,* Vol. II, pp. 204.

Das, A.C., 1975, *Orissa Historical Research Journal,* Vol. XVI, No. 4 to Vol. XXII, No. 1, Bhubaneswar.

During, Caspers, E.C.L., 1973, "Harappan trade in Arabian Gulf in the 3rd millennium BC" *Proceedings of VIth Seminar for Arabian Studies*, London.

——, 1983, "Triangular stamp seals from the Arabian Gulf and their Indus connections," *Annali*, Institute Universitario Orientale, Vol. 43.

——, 1985, "A Possible Harappan contact with the Aegean World", *Proceedings of VIII International Conference Asso-South Asian Archaeology*, West Europe, Brussels, (Eds.) Janin, S. and Maurizo, T., Institute Universitario Orientale, Naples.

Gerini, G.E., *Researches on Ptolemy's Geography of Eastern Asia.*

Joshi, J.P., "Archaeological Perspective of Marine Activities in Ancient India", in S.R. Rao, (Ed.), *Marine Archaeology of Indian Ocean Countries.*

Mahatab, H.K., 1959, *History of Orissa,* Cuttack.

Majumdar, R.C., 1973, *Hindu Colonies in Far East,* Calcutta.

Mookerji, R.K., 1962, *Indian Shipping,* Allahabad.

Nagaraju, S., 1971, "Chalukya Vinayaditya's intervention in Cambodian Politics", in *Indian History and Culture, Dr. P.B. Desai Felicitation Volume,* Dharwad.

——, 1984, "Palaeography of the Earliest Inscriptions of Burma, Thailand, Combodia and Vietnam", *Svastiśri Dr. B.R. Chabra Felicitation Volume,* Delhi.

Ritti, Śrinivas, Shipping in Ancient India—Keynote address, in S.R. Rao (Ed.), *Marine Archaeology of Indian Ocean Countries.*

Rao, S.R., 1970, *Shipping in Ancient India, India's Contribution to World Thought and Culture*, Madras.

Schoff, Wilfred, H., *The Periplus of Erythraean Sea.*

Sharma Sastry, R., *Kautilya's Arthasastra,* p. 142.

Tripati, Sila, "Ancient ports of Kaliṅga", in S.R. Rao, (Ed.), *Recent Advances in Marine Archaeology.*

15

Kaliṅga-Śri Lankā Relations

V. VITHARANA

Kaliṅga, the ancient Indian kingdom that occupied a part of the sprawling coastal plain and the adjacent low, parallel ridges of the Deccan's Eastern Ghats from the left (i.e., the northern) bank of the Gōdāvarī to the Mahānadī and beyond, has been known to the people of Śri Lankā for the last two-and-half millennia, i.e., from the earliest days of the island's recorded history. According to the brief and sketchy account given in the fourth century Pali historical poem, *Dīpavaṁsa* ('Island Chronicle', Ch. 9) and the more coherent and detailed narrative found in the fifth century *Mahāvaṁsa* ('Great Dynasty', Chs. VI & VII), complemented by the exegeses supplied by the *Vamsatthappakāsinī,* the Commentary to the latter, it was Vijaya, a prince from Siṁhapura of Kaliṅga (which name is not mentioned in the *Dpv.*), evicted from the kingdom owing to his rebellious character along with 700 followers, that founded the '*Sīhala'* (Skt. *Siṁhala)* race in Śri Lankā. They welded themselves with still other immigrants from the region and, of course, the indigenous people (who-ever they were), as it appears, to build up a new civilization in the island with a sense of unprecedented dynamism.

The story as given in the *Mhv.* starts with a Kaliṅga princess being espoused to the king of Vaṅga, and their daughter Suppādevī (called Susīmā in the *Dpv.),* 'very fair and very amorous' *(atīvā rūpinī...atīvā kāmagiddhinī)*, leaving home alone (as destined) and joining a caravan travelling to Magadha. It was attacked by a 'lion' *sīha* or *siṁha* (or, a person called Sīha : *Dpv.*) who took her to a cave where they continued to live, she bearing him son and daughter twins. When they were sixteen, the son, Sīhabāhu, pushed open the heavy stone door of the cave and, taking his mother and sister on his broad shoulders, escaped. They reached the Vaṅga border where the commander, the son of Suppādevi's uncle, married her at the capital city.

The 'lion' in rage began to devastate the country, and the king offered a thousand pieces (increased to three thousand, later) of money as reward for the killer; and Sīhabāhu with a fourth arrow killed his father and took the head to the king to find him dead a week after. The ministers made him king, but he made room for his mother's husband—the Vaṅga commander, and returned to Kaliṅga with the sister. There he built a new capital, Sīhapura (Skt. Siṁha-), and founded new villages over the vast forest tracts of the surrounding Lāla region. He made his sister Sīhavalli, his queen and came to be called 'Sīhala' because he 'took' or 'grasped' the lion (*Sīhamadinnavā*: *Mhv.* VII, 42); and so called were 'all those who had ties with him' (*tena sambandhā ete. sabhepi).*[1]

Sīhavalli gave birth to twin sons sixteen times, of whom the eldest was Vijaya. He, though consecrated prince-regent, had to be banished on account of his evil conduct, as referred to above.

He and his companions first landed at Suppāraka and, on being ejected once again, reached Lankā on the day of the passing away of the Buddha.

There (to make a long story short) he met Kuvaṇṇā or Kuveṇī—a *yakkhiṇī,* with whose help he killed the *yakkha* chieftain and his people on the occasion of a marriage ceremony, and became ruler of the land. He founded the city of Tambapaṇṇi and lived there with the *yakkhiṇī;* and the ministers founded villages even in relatively distant regions. Thus in the island of Lankā (which also came to be called Tambapaṇṇi) a new civilization began to burgeon.

Vijaya and his 700 companions (some of whom were the ministers referred to) together with their progeny, being 'those who had ties' with Sīhabāhu, continued to be called 'Sīhala'—and so even the island, 'after the lion' (*Lankādīpo ayaṁ ahū sīhena Sīhalā iti : Dpv.* 9, 1).

The story of Vijaya does not end at this point, nor are all its details even up to that mentioned here. It has been subject to much criticism and a great deal of interpretation, cynical at times, and certain events that contribute to its coherence have been interpreted in various ways. In the midst of them all, nevertheless, it is not unreasonable to aver that:

(i) the Sinhalas as a people inherit a legend concerning their origin as related (in a fuller manner) in the chronicle, *Mahāvaṁsa;*

(ii) in accordance with it, their eponymous hero, Vijaya, hailed from Kaliṅga of India;

(iii) Vijaya's great-grand mother belonged to the Kaliṅga royal lineage;

(iv) his father and mother were the king and queen of Kaliṅga;

(v) the very name Sīhala (Skt. Siṁhala) appears to have been a title bestowed on Vijaya's father (in Kaliṅga) and inherited by him and his followers, and then by the new race that they founded in the island kingdom of Lankā or Tambapaṇṇi; and

(vi) the island itself came to be called Sīhala (in addition to other names).

Vijaya, it has to be mentioned, did not produce an heir, and was succeeded by the son of the eldest of his 31 brothers (Sumitta) after an interegnum of one year when the ministers ruled the island. The successor, Prince Paṇḍuvāsudeva, arrived from Kaliṅga with thirty-two sons of ministers (*Mhv.* VIII, 1-12). Bhaddakaccānā or Subaddhakaccānā of the royal house of the Śākyas who arrived subsequently was consecrated his queen, and her thirty-two companions became the wives of youths who accompanied the new king.

Vijaya is said to have ruled for 38 years (*ibid.* VII, 74), and the arrival of his nephew marks the fortieth year of his arrival in Śri Lankā. Taking into account the possible progeny of his 700 followers (and the relatively large families that appear to have been a feature of the times), it is possible that by this time there were a minimum of 2,500 families with Kaliṅga blood running in their veins living scattered over the north-central plain of Śri Lankā.

Kaliṅga, which is thus one of the earliest names of an Indian region (along with Vaṅga and Magadha) with which Śri Lankāns became familiar, is also mentioned in the Pali

Buddhist literature that came into the island as a consequence of the introduction of Buddhism by the Ven. Mahinda during the 3rd century BC. The *Majjhima Nikāya* (1, 378) refers to the forests of Kaliṅga, and the *Dīgha Nikāya* (19, 36) to the coastal settlements and the capital city, Dantapura, which however is different from the Siṁhapura mentioned in the legend.

Among the *Jātakas* (the birth stories of the aspirant to Buddhahood) is one entitled *Kaliṅga Bodhi Jātaka* (No. 471), and the story is as follows:

> The king of Kaliṅga reigning at Dantapura had two sons. The royal astrologers predicted that the elder would succeed him and the younger would lead the life of a hermit and a son of the latter would be *cakravarti* of Kaliṅga. On being consecrated king, the elder (Mahā Kaliṅga) felt jealous of his brother (whose son, he thought, would prevent his own son from being king). On hearing of a conspiracy, Culla Kaliṅga handed over his signet ring, sword and scarf to a faithful minister, and retired to a hermitage on a river-bank.

In the meanwhile, the daughter of the Madu king of Sāgala was prophesied also to be a recluse nun, but a son born to her, the sooth sayers said, would be *cakravarti.* Hearing of it, all monarchs of Jambadīpa surrounded the capital in order to possess her; and the king escaped with his queen and daughter in order to be recluses themselves, and set up their abode on a site up stream of the same river as Culla Kaliṅga. The Madu princess was in the habit of floating down streamers of flowers that she wove and one of them happened to rest on the head of the prince as he bathed down stream. 'This should be the delicate work of a young maiden, and none other', he thought and, walking up stream, met her as she kept singing on the bough of a riverside tree. He identified himself as a *kṣatriya,* and was accepted into the family of the royal trio. A son was born to the princess, and they named him Kaliṅga. He learnt the *śilpas* at the feet of the grand father and the father, and when he reached the proper age, the latter handed over to him the ring, scarf and sword with the instructions to meet the minister concerned. Everything went well, and, on being *cakravarti,* he started on a journey through the air attended with great pageantry. But the royal elephant would not go over a certain point in the sky although he was coaxed on. The minister, Kaliṅga Bhāradvāja, came down to the ground to investigate the cause, and he espied a Tree of Enlightenment (of the Buddhas) immediately below. On hearing the words of the learned minister, the king began to coax the elephant once more, but he expired unknown by the king. Another appeared miraclously, and the king descended and began to praise the minister as though the latter were a Buddha. But he explained to the king the unparalleled virtues of a Buddha which led to the monarch to hold a week-long festival of offering to the (Bodhi) Tree. He returned to Dantapura with his parents and spent his days in meritorious activity.

A part of this story (up to the point at which the young prince became king : *danta purē rājā hutvā)* is related in the *Dharmapradīpikāva* (pp.296-302) in such manner that the bravity, resonance and easy-flow of the (by far) pure Sinhala (*Heḷa*) idiom, the creative imagery inclusive of the use of symbols and the realistic portrayal of incidents are held as exemplary of the highest level to which the Sinhala prose idiom may attain.

Time was when the author, Guruḷugomi or Garuḍa Ācārya, himself was regarded as a native of Kaliṅga, and this very fluent poetic prose idiom was referred to as *Kaliṅgu*

Heḷuva, 'the *Heḷa* of (the) Kaliṅga (genre)'[3]—a generous tribute, indeed, to the region that provided the backdrop to an excellent story of romance and devotion.

The reference to elephants in this story reminds one of the record made by Megasthenes, the Greek ambassador to the Mauryan court of Candragupta (3rd century BC), indicating that Śri Lankā exported elephants to Kaliṅga.[4] Says he, 'These elephants are more powerful than those of the mainland and in appearance larger, and may be pronounced to be in every way more intelligent. The islanders export them to the mainland opposite in boats which they construct for this traffic from wood supplied by the thickets of the island, and they dispose of their cargoes to the king of Kalinga'.

It is likely that a corroboration of these statements is hardly possible, and the best that may be gleaned is that trade relations were maintained between the two regions, whatever the commodities were.

The next great Śri Lankā–Kaliṅga link is as lasting as the one before—the arrival of the Buddha's Tooth Relic at Arurādhapura in AD 310. The story is related very briefly in the *Mahāvaṁsa* (37, 92-97) and in almost epic proportions in the twelfth century Pali poem, *Dāṭhavaṁsa*, by the Ven. Dhammakitti, evidently based on a Sinhala poem, *Daḷadāvaṁsa* by name, composed at the request of King Meghavaṇṇa (Kīrti Śri Meghavarṇa or Kit Siri Mevan) during whose reign (301-27 AD) the Relic arrived. The story unfolds, like the first, in the Kaliṅga-Magadha region and extends up to the environs of Śri Lankā.

Guhaśīva, king of Kaliṅga, commenced to pay homage to the Tooth Relic of the Buddha on converting himself to Buddhism, thus incurring the wrath of the priests *(nighaṇṭas)* who complained to Pandu, the suzerain, at Pātalīputra in Magadha. The latter had it brought down to his capital, and the miracles that it performed there led to the conversion of this monarch too. The king of Sāvatthi waged war on him claiming the Relic and the latter, on being defeated, had it despatched back to Dantapura. The Sāvatthi army next appeared at the gate of the city; and Guhaśīva directed his daughter, Hemamālā, and her husband, the Ujjaini prince Danta Kumāra, to disguise themselves and escape from the city with the Relic concealed, and have it delivered to his friend, Mahāsena, the ruler of the Buddhist kingdom of Lankā.

They reached Anurādhapura—the Meghagiri Vihāra located in the Mahā Megha Vana to be exact, during the ninth year of king Meghavaṇṇa (310 AD)—the son of Mahāsena. He enshrined it in a steatite (*phalika*) casket, housed it in the Dhammacakkaghara, held a festival on the expenditure of nine lakhs, and proclaimed that it should be conveyed to the Abhayagiri Vihāra in a procession every year.

The historicity of the arrival of the Relic at Anurādhapura is undoubted, and Fa-Hsien—the Chinese traveller-monk who was in Anurādhapura a century later—describes the Tooth Relic Festival as it was held then, in his memoirs.[5] But the same may not be said of the events that appear to have preceded it in the Kaliṅga region. Contemporary or other records, or even an oral tradition pertaining to these events have likely not surfaced yet in the region, and doubts have been expressed as to the authenticity of the names of the royalty mentioned: king Brahmadatta of Kaliṅga (Buddha's contemporary), his son Kāsirāja and his son Sunanda (*Daṭhāvaṁśa*, 114-133), Guhaśīva's vassal Citrayāna (*ibid.*, 152-158) and Guhaśīva himself. The *Bhagavat Purāṇa* (VIII, 10, 28, X, 63, 7) incidentally mentions a Guha, but not a Guhaśīva. One may only conjecture that the author of the contemporary Sinhala chronicle, *Daḷadāvaṁsa*, of the early fourth century (now non-extant) on which was based the Pali *Dāṭhāvaṁsa*, relied on what he heard personally from Danta Kumāra and Hemamālā the veracity of whose words he neither wanted to check nor had the resources to do so. Anyway, it is a well coordinated story with the general requisites of an epic—royalty (inclusive of a princess), miracle, devotion, conspiracy, secrecy, war, adventure, women, sports, travel, surprise, realization, festivity etc. etc., and (to parody what is said in certain canonical Pali works about the Doctrine of the Buddha) excellent in the beginning, excellent in the middle, and, to the Sinhala-Buddhists of Śri Lankā, very excellent in the end.

And to crown them all, it has brought Kaliṅga into a lasting bond of friendship with Śri Lankā.

The arrival of the Tooth Relic in the island did not merely mark the addition of a *cavaṭṭi* ('bone of the dead,' as referred to it by the *nighaṇṭas* in their complaint to the king of Pāṭalīputr: *Dāṭhāvaṁsa*, 152-158) to the relics of the Buddha that were already enshrined or exhibited locally, nor was it merely the most important event of Meghavaṇṇa's fairly long reign. It marked the initiation of an institution that began to play a paramount role not only in the religious affairs, but also in social and political affairs of the island, specially during the second millennium of the Christian era,[6] and continues to be venerated at the highest level. It has also gathered around it a corpus of elaborate and picturesque ritual and pageantry now known to many parts of the external world.

It became the palladium of the kings of Śri Lankā, and temples were built to house it with the change of their capital cities—Anurādhapura, Polonnaruva, Daṁbadeṇiya, Kuruṇāgala, Kōṭṭē and Seṅkaḍagala or Maha Nuvara (mod. Kandy); and inscriptions dealing with donations (persons, land, villages etc.), protection, regulation, ritual etc. date from the tenth century AD. Special festivals in its honour have been held as from the times of Niśśaṅka Malla of the Kaliṅga lineage (1187-96), and the present-day pageant during the *Āsaḷa (Āsāḷha)* season (August) in Kandy dates from the reign of king Kīrti Śri Rājasiṅha (1747-82) who reigned from the same city.

Subsequent to the arrival of the Tooth Relic in 310 AD, *Kaliṅga* is not mentioned in Śri Lankān annals for another few centuries. This silence should not be interpreted to mean a hiatus in mutual relations as it would have only meant that an occurrence of importance as the above (or even less) did not take place. During the centuries that followed, Śri Lankā maintained religious intercourse with Amarāvatī, Dhānyakaṭaka and Nāgarjunukoṇḍā on the banks of the Kistna on Kaliṅga's southern border, and nothing prevented the Sinhalas of the times from venturing a few miles north-east-wards to reach the latter. Further, the post-sixth century Kaliṅga was a centre of Mahāyāna Buddhism where abodes such as Udayagiri and Ratnagiri were flourishing. There is no doubt that the Śri Lankān Buddhists, some of whom at least professed this 'vehicle' (*yāna*) of Buddhism, referring to it as the *Vaitulya Vāda* (or *Vetulla V.*) and appear to have practised the associated cults to some degree, did maintain contacts with the region as was found necessary. *Vajiriya Vāda* and *Nīlapaṭa Darśana* were Mahāyāna 'schools' that were known in Śri Lankā, and eminent Mahāyāna teachers, Gunavarman and Vajrabodhi, visited the island. Sanskrit *dhāraṇīs* (written also in Sinhala characters) have been found in many places in the environments of Anurādhapura and Mihintalē (9 miles to the east, and the rocky site at which the Ven. Mahinda - the Buddhist missionary—met the King Devānampiya Tissa: 3rd c. BC; and the Nālandā Gedigē, Vijayārāma, Puliyankulama Vihāra and Iṅdikaṭusāya supply sufficient evidence to have once been centres of these 'schools' (see N. Mudiyanse, *Mahayana Monuments in Ceylon*, Colombo, 1967).

A positive sign of the continuing Kaliṅga-Śri Lankā relations is the arrival, during the reign of Aggabodhi II (604-14), of the king of Kaliṅga, his queen and minister who were compelled to leave their kingdom, perhaps owing to an attack by the Cālukya king, Pulakeśin I. They entered the Order (of Monks) under the Ven. Jotipāla. Aggabodhi housed the royal monk at the Mattapabbata vihāra, and the minister monk at the Vettavāsa vihāra, but the latter handed it back to the Community of Monks. The queen, on hearing of the royal nun, built for her the Ratana vihāra. It happened that the royal *thera* (monk) passed away, and Aggabodhi mourned grievously and performed meritorious acts to transfer merit on him (*Mhv.* 42, 44-50).

King Mahinda IV (956-72) fetched a princess from Kaliṅga to be his first *mahesi (ibid.* 54, 9).

Gold *fanams* of the eastern Gaṅga king Anantavarma Coḍagaṅga of Kaliṅga (1075-1146) found in the Kandyan region are suggestive of commercial relations carried on during this period between the two countries.

Such continued contacts made it possible for Vijaya Bāhu I (1055-1110), one of Śri Lankā's greatest monarchs, to obtain his queen, Tiloka Sundarī ('Beauty of the Three Worlds') from Kaliṅga. What doubt can there be about her being as 'fair' as her ancestor, Susīmā alias Suppādevī, who contributed immensely to the origin and the naming of the Śri Lankān race?

Foreign kings, Candrabhānu from Tāmbraliṅga (mod. Ligor in north Malaysia), Ārya Cakravarti from S. India (*Mhv.* 88, 65-66, 90, 43-47) and the Chinese seafarer, Cheng Ho (*University History of Ceylon*, p. 651) have invaded the island or otherwise interfered with its affairs in order to take away the Relic during the late 13th and early 15th centuries.

Further, a very considerable literature, both local and foreign, unequalled by those compiled on any other Śri Lankān sacred site or object, and in more than one language has burgeoned on the subject of the Tooth Relic for the last eight hundred years and many are the references to it in other literary sources.[7]

Numerous also are the foreign delegations and dignitaries that have paid homage to it specially during the recent past, and more so are the local leaders that have paid it obeisance before inaugurating their functions of office. It is also held with a sanctity of a yet higher order by the Buddhists of the Kandyan Hills region who visit the Daḷadā Māligāva—the Temple of the Tooth, at least once a year, specially on periodical exhibition days, and view the *Asaḷa Perahära,* the pageantry in August. They make vows to the Relic to rid themselves of worldly afflictions and to obtain mundane welfare. It is also their custom to wish each other 'the blessing of the Lord of the Tooth', *daḷadā hāmuduruvan gē pihiṭa.*

The story of the arrival of the Tooth is one of the most popular of the Śri Lankān Buddhist stories. The scene of the husband-wife pair journeying on foot to Anurādhaura with the faint halo of the Relic shining over Hemamālā's tresses (within which she had concealed it) has been represented in local temple paintings, and the one at the Käḷaṇiya (Kelani) vihāra (near Colombo) by the modern painter, Soliyas Dias, and its replica in bas-relief adorning one of the halls of the President's House (Janādhipati Mandiraya) in Colombo are widely known. Charles Dias, a dramatist of the early decades of this (20th) century composed a drama on the saga of the Tooth Relic, and he named it 'Hemamālī'. It is also customary for a drama depicting the arrival of the Relic at Anurādhapura and its subsequent history (inclusive of the travails that it underwent during the post-15th century era of imperialist incursions) to be staged in the open air on the occasion of the *Vesak* (*Vaiśāka*) festival marking the full-moon of May. The Māligāva itself (with the octagonal *pattirippuva* fronting it) is likely the island's most distinguished and far-famed edifice; and, given a gilt roof of late, is one of the three most sacred sanctums of Śri Lankā,[8] and one of the most honoured in the Buddhist world.

No reference to the Tooth Relic is complete without a mention of the popular belief in its efficacy to bring rain. The *Dāthāvaṁsa* refers to a torrential downpour that occurred on the occasion of its arrival at the Meghagiri vihāra referred to above:

> *sansibbitam rajatarajjusatānukāri – dhārāsatehi vasadambaramambudena*
> *sabbādisā jaladakūṭa mahagghiyosu – dittacirajjutipadīpasatāvabhāsā* : 371

> (It appeared as though both the sky and the earth were enveloped in a hundred-fold flow resembling hundreds of silver threads. The directions were lit by hundreds of lamps of lightning that shone from the gem-set eaves of the rain-clouds).

This miraclous occurrence would have made a deep impression in the minds of the faithful, which would have been further reinforced by the conception of the teeth of the Buddha obtaining the 'touch' (Skt. *sparṣa*, Sin. *pahasa*) *of the* 'rain' (*varṣā, vahare, vässa, väsi* or *vāhi*) of the 'eighty-four-thousand-fold mass of the Buddha's Doctrine' (*asūhāra dahasak dharmaskandha*), as variantly expressed in the Sinhala classical texts, *Amāvatura* (7), *Dharmapradīpikāva* (196), *Butsaraṇa* (45) etc. *Dharma varṣā, sadhharma varṣā, daham väsi* etc., are expressions that may be heard in a Buddhist sermon even today. This association of the Tooth with 'rain' possibly led to the accretion of ritualistic forms performed in honour of the Relic in anticipation of rain. And it was rain that supplied the vast water resources on which life and prosperity in Śri Lankā lay.

One cannot be certain about the period when the associated ritual activities were initially held, but by the beginning of the 14th century, as evidenced by the prose work, the *Daḷadā Sirita*,[9] the festival of offering to the Tooth Relic, held also as a rain-magic performance, appears to have been well formalized. Composed during the reign of king Parākrama Bāhu IV (1303-33), this work traces the history of the Relic, describes the festival activities and appends 38 regulations (*vyavasthā*) that should govern them. The main text is in the sonorous and alliterative *vṛttagandhi* or *utkalikāprāya* style, but the regulations are couched in one that may well pertain to the 11th or the 12th century. And of them, the 30th is important in the present context. It says:

> *väsi novasnā kala mema lesin daḷadā pūjā karanuva isā*

> ('And to perform in this manner the offering to the Tooth Relic at times when there is no rain').

This makes it possible to conclude that the ritual to the Tooth Relic as a rain-rite was being performed even by the close of the Anurādhapura period (11th century).

An occasion when this efficacy (as supposed) apparently became manifest came by subsequent to the British occupation of the Kandyan kingdom in 1815. The new rulers, in their fanatic endeavour to destroy the local traditional cultural institutions, prohibited the annual *Asaḷa* festival to the Tooth Relic at Kandy from being held. Rain, it is said, gradually ceased to fall in the hill country, and from 1821 it failed to arrive altogether. The chieftains, understanding the cause as they knew, informed of them to John D'Oyly, the British

Resident, who made the Governor, Sir Edward Barnes, aware of the situation. Permission was granted to hold an exhibition of the Relic and to hold the *Perahära* for seven days with the 'water-cutting' ceremony[10] to follow on the eighth. All ritualistic activities were held as planned, and on the final day—which happened to be the 28th May 1828—a torrential downpour inundated the city and the environs, washing away the bridges over the Mahaväli river on the eastern and northern city limits. The flood came to be known as the *daḷadā vatura* ('the inundation of the Tooth Relic') or *guruganvatura* ('the brown inundation'); and Barnes decreed that the festival should be held for 14 days (not seven) annually in the future. Two short poetical works available at the library of the Colombo Museum—the *Dalada Varnanava* and the *Dathadhatu Vamsaya*—describe the phenomenon.

The contribution made by Kaliṅga to the culture of Śri Lankā, first, to the historic scenario of the founding of the Sinhala race (though contested to a degree by historians of the modern era: *University History of Ceylon*, 90-91 etc.) and second, to the corpus of dynamic activities that formed the religious life and environment of these people onwards for nine centuries later is thus clearly manifest. These relations seemed to reach yet another peak when the marriage between Vijaya Bāhu I and Tilaka Sundarī (referred to above) began to make way for a series of events of the highest political importance in the subsequent history of Śri Lankā.

NOTES

1. The Skt. rendering of this term is *Siṁhala* which has been used up to the present day in writing in the Sinhala language too, and it continues to be current in ordinary usage.
   The relevant verse of the *Mhv.* (VII, 42) is also quoted in the 13th century exegetical work, *Dharmapradīpikāva* (p. 55) to explain the etymology of *Siṁhala: siṁhayāge lānaya ādānaya kele no yi siṁhala nam viya*, 'He came to be called "Siṁhala" because, did he not perform the grasping of the lion?'
   Lānaya here is, at times, rendered as *lāyanaya*, 'mowing down' (i.e. to kill), which is semantically more appropriate than a mere 'taking' or 'grasping'.
2. Even the language came to be so called, *Sīhalaṭṭhakathā* ('Commentary in the Sīhala language') being a well-known example in Pali.
   The island is referred to as *Sīhaladīpa* in *Sumaṅgala Vilāsinī* and *Paramatthajotikā*. The Greek *Salai* and *Salike* (for Śri Lankā) appears to be a derivative of *Sīhala*. *Siṁhala* in *Kāvyamīmāṁsa (Ādhyāya 17) & Bhāgavata Purāṇa (19),* and *Siṁhala Dvīpa* in *Kathāsaritasāgara* (dvādaśalambaka) and *Avadāna Kalpalatā (Muktalat vadāna)* are a few of the several examples found in Skt. literature.
3. *Heḷa* and *Heḷuva* are the local terms for pre-modern Sinhala. The commentaries compiled in Sinhala of the times around 2,000 years ago to Pali Buddhist literary works are called *Heḷaṭuvā (Heḷa + aṭuvā)*—the equivalent of *Sihalaṭṭhakathā* (above).
4. J.W. McCrindle, *Ancient India as Described by Megasthenes and Arrian* (Calcutta, 1887), pp.173-75.
5. H.A. Giles, *Travels of Fa-Hsien (399-415 AD)* or *Record of the Buddhistic Kingdoms* (Cambridge, 1923), pp. 69-70.
6. See Dharmaratna Herath, *The Tooth Relic and the Crown* (Colombo, 1994).
7. Literary works on the Relic: *Daḷadāvaṁsa* (4th c., Sinhala, non-extant), *Dāṭhāvaṁsa* (12th c., Pali), *Daḷadā Sirita* (14th c., Sinhala), *Daḷadā Pūjavaliya, Dāṭhāvaṁsa Kavi, Daḷadā Itihāsa Kāvyaya, Daḷadā Haṭane Kavi, Daḷadā Varṇanāva, Daḷadā Perahära Lakara & Dāṭhādhātu Vaṁsaya* (later works up to the first half of the 19th c., all Sinhala).
   The *Mahāvaṁsa* (5th c. Pali) and several historical, epistolary and panegyrical works in Sinhala (13th-18th c.) make reference to the Relic.

Foreign works that make reference to the Relic: *Hmannan* (11th c. Burmese), *Jinakālamāli* (16th c., Pali) of Thailand, and the records of the Chinese traveller monks, Fa-Hsien and Hiuen-Tsiang, and the Chinese works *Sung-Shu* and *Pien-i-tien*.

8. The others are the Śri Mahā Bodhi (Tree) at Anurādhapura and the Holy Mountain, Samantakūta or Samanola (popularly referred to as Adam's Peak).
9. *Sirita* (< *cāritra*, 'behaviour'). The title would mean 'behaviour towards the Tooth Relic.'
10. Lit. 'the cutting of the water.' The rite is performed at a river-ferry well before sunrise. The water is 'cut' with a sword by a *kapu* (lay priest) and a vessel-ful is collected therefrom, to be preserved until the following occasion.

REFERENCES

Sinhala

Daḷadā Sirita, ed. Sorata, Colombo, 1950.
Daḷadā Varṇanāva (author etc. not mentioned).
Dāṭhadhātu Vaṅsaya, ed.(?) D.M.A. Talavatura, Kandy, 1934.
Dharmapradīpikāva, ed. Dharmarama, Colombo, 1951.

Pali

Dāṭhāvaṅsa, tr. Mutu Coomaraswamy, London, 1874.
Dīgha Nikāya, ed. Rhys-Davids & Carpenter (PTS), London, 1890-1911.
Dīpavaṁsa, tr. B.C. Law (*Ceylon Historical Journal* VII, 1-4), Dehiwala, 1959.
Jātaka, tr. V. Fausboll, Trubner, London, 1877-97.
Mahāvaṁśa, tr. W. Geiger, Colombo, 1950, 1953.
Majjhima Nikāya, eds. Trunker & Chalmers (PTS), London, 1948-51.
Vansatthappakāsinī, (ed.) G.P. Malalasekera (PTS), London, 1935.

Sanskrit

Bhāgavata Purāṇa, ed. Krishnacharya, Kumbakonam, 1916.

Modern Works

Giles, H.A., *Travels of Fa-Hsien*, Cambridge, 1923.
Herath, D., *The Tooth Relic and the Crown*, Colombo, 1994.
McCrindle, J.W., *Ancient India as described by Megasthenes and Arrian*, Calcutta, 1887.
Mudiyanse, N., *Mahayana Monuments in Ceylon*, Colombo, 1967.
University History of Ceylon, University Press Board, Colombo, 1959.

16

The Sewn Boats of Orissa

ERIC KENTLEY

Orissa is the northernmost area on India's east coast where a particular type of beach seining boat is found. The most distinguishing feature of this type of boat is that its planks are not nailed to one another but are sewn together with coir rope. It is also built without framing. Although there are important regional variations, this frameless sewn boat is found as far south as Karaikal in Tamil Nadu.

During 1983-84 I undertook a survey of these boats along the east coast, and this paper summarises the findings, focusing on the boats of Orissa.

In published descriptions, these boats are generally referred to as 'masulas' (see, for example, Hill 1958). However, this is not a term employed by, or even known to, the builders and users of the craft.[1] In Orissa the boat is called *padua;* in Andhra Pradesh it is pronounced more like *padava* and amongst Tamil speakers it is *padagu.* However, some metal fastened boats are also called by these names. Therefore as 'masula' is used specifically to mean a sewn boat of this region (albeit not by their operators) and has a widespread currency amongst those interested in ethnographic craft, I will continue to use it here.

Although historically masulas were used as ship to shore transport between beaches and ships anchored in the open roadsteads (see, for example, Hill 1958: 208), this function has now disappeared entirely. With the exception of a very few used as ferries to cross river mouths and backwaters (for example at Navalarevu and Gopalpur), masulas are now all fishing boats, and the vast majority of them are used exclusively for beach seining.

Beach seining masulas are found as far north as Puri and all masulas from here southwards to the river Vamsadhara in Andhra Pradesh are very similar and can be regarded as a single type. The 'typical' example is five-strake boat, although strictly the second strake is not a strake but a large stealer. It has six or seven crossbeams, holding the sides together, and a decked area at the stern. Most boats of this sector are between 7.5 and 8 m in length, although the smallest I measured was 6.75 m (with the exception of one ferry which is described below) and the largest 8.40 m. Length-to-beam ratios are around 3.5 and beam to depth ratios about 2.

The central longitudinal member is normally of *sal (Shorea robusta)*, but Indian laurel or even, allegedly teak may be used. The stem and stern posts are of *Syzigium cuminii.* All planks are mango, including those that make up the stern deck (which are often made from old strakes). The crossbeams are of *casuarina (Cashuarina equisetifolia).* The boats are sewn together with two-ply coir rope with a dried marsh grass, *rella gaddi,* as the wadding material on most seams.

The central longitudinal member on boats of this type is a keel plank: that is, its width is greater than its depth, a handspan (about 16 cm) wide and a hand's width (8-12 cm) in depth, rectangular in cross-section. It should be eight cubits in length (a cubit being the length from the elbow to the fingertips). The ends are slightly tapered and are fastened to the stem and stern posts by horizontal half-lap joints, the projecting lap of the keel plank being below that of the post. The length of the lap is calculated as the width of six fingers and is secured by sewing over a wadding of coir fibre (*not* dried grass) inboard.

The stem and stern posts are adzed into shape from logs, normally tapering from the same width as the keel plank to about 8 cm at the sheerline. Rarely is either a single piece: both posts are usually made of two parts, again scarfed by a horizontal half-lap joint. The lap on the lower section is inboard. The two parts are sometimes nailed together but are more commonly held in position by the sewing that binds the strake ends to the posts. There is a consensus that the stem post should be seven cubits in length, measured on the curve, but five and six cubits are the values given by different builders to the stern post.

Flat on its inner aspect, the surface which takes the ends of the strakes is at 90 degrees to this. The outer surface is usually gently rounded, except around the Andhra Pradesh border area, where it is more wedge-like. The stem post head retains the shape but the stern post head is commonly adzed almost to a point, so that the rope against which the steering oar works can be slipped over easily and made firm. Alternatively the starboard side, or both sides, may be indented.

All planks are of the same thickness, 2.2 cm — seven threads (a thread being an eighth of an inch). Strakes are not necessarily one-piece, but rarely more than two. To make up a strake, the planks are often simply butted together, although they are sometimes plain scarfed and sewn together.[2] Coir is frequently used as the wadding material on such joints, inboard and outboard, whereas dried grass is used on the strake-to-strake seams. I was unable to get an explanation for this. Certainly, coir does not rot as rapidly as grass and is regarded as a superior wadding material. However, it is much more expensive than grass. But the use of grass as the primary wadding material means that the boats must be dismantled after every fishing season and the grass replaced, although this has the advantage that the boats are not left on the beaches during the cyclone season.

The garboard strake, twelve cubits long, butts against the side of the keel plank and posts and is held in position by sewing over a wad of dried grass both inboard and outboard. It is positioned so that it extends beyond the keel plank and onto the stem post a distance of 2.5 cubits and onto the stern post 1.5 cubits, thus forming the basis of the greater sheer forward than aft. For most of its length the garboard strake is parallel sided, but curves at the ends. This curve is roughly cut to shape and then trimmed *in situ* when the third strake is matched up, as the curve is determined by the third strake as it bends towards the posts.

Similarly the second strake, a stealer eight cubits in length, has its gently curved upper side finally trimmed when the third strake is matched up. It ends where the curve of the garboard begins. Amidships, the second strake gives a total width from the edge of the keel plank to its upper side of 1.5 cubits. However, in Edumanipelam, near Baruva, I found one boat which had on its starboard side the garboard and second strake combined in a single wide strake.

In Gopalpur, there was a ferry that had only one strake between the second strake and the cross beams. This measured only 6.20 m in length with a maximum beam of 1.77 m and a depth of 0.42 m. It had five cross beams and three old planks serving as thwarts for passengers. Otherwise it was structurally identical to the beach seiners. It was said to have been built entirely from old parts of a beach seiner and cost Rs. 1,000, whereas the larger boats cost Rs. 8,000.

Again in Gopalpur, there was one beach seining masula with a single board strake on both sides between the second strake and the cross beams. Two other boats here had the same arrangement forward, but two planks aft. Normally there are two full strakes between the second strake and the cross beams, approximately 16 and 18 cubits in length.

Halfway between Bhavanapada and Sonapily, a fishing village to the south, I found a masula with a frame for carrying the net. The top of the third strake had been indented to take three cross beams. These were clamped into position by the fourth strake and onto them were lashed, longitudinally, thirteen thin casuariana poles each about two metres long. I have seen this arrangement nowhere else on the entire east coast. The boat was also unique in having a drainage hole drilled through the keel plank (some 15 cm aft of the start of the keel plank, in the bow).

From the top of the fourth strake to the bottom of the third should be a distance of one metre. If it falls short, a series of planks, a handspan or more in width, will be sewn onto the inner surface of the fourth strake, rising above it to achieve the required height. Even if the fourth strake does give the required height, some builders will still fit this series of planks (which is not strictly an inwale, as it is not fitted to the top strake—it is convenient to call it an inner rail), but so that its top edge is flush with the strake's top edge. This is said to give additional strength. Other builders say that it is unnecessary and merely adds weight. On some boats, particularly in Puri, this rail is fitted so that it rises above the fourth strake at the stern, thus raising the level of the stern deck, but flush with the top edge of the fourth strake along the rest of the boat. The technique for sewing on this inner rail will be described below.

The shape of the boat is held by the insertion of the crossbeams. As noted, most boats have six of these, but some have seven. They are roughly circular in cross-section and the fourth strake and inner rail (if present) are indented to take them. Rarely however do they lie flush with the top edge of the plank: normally they are slightly higher. They are lashed down with coir rope, holes being drilled in the fourth strake and sometimes through the beams themselves to take the rope. There is no standard method.

The fifth beam from the bow on a six-beam boat and the sixth beam on a seven-beam boat are not lashed down. They are removable, to aid loading the net. The first three cross-beams may protrude some distance outboard so that their ends can be used to lift the boat, but this is not common. Most beams are cut off roughly flush with the outer surface of the hull.

Measured along the curve of the fourth strake, the deck at the stern should extend four cubits. The planks that make it up are laid either on the top edge of the fourth strake or on the inner rail. Holes are drilled through them about 2 cm from the edge and they are secured by the sewing which connects the top strake to the fourth strake or inner rail.

The top strake is about twenty cubits in length and relatively narrow, between 8 and 11 cm. It is indented on its upper edge to take two thole pins on either side, staggered. Its lower edge will rest on the tops of the crossbeams, and if these have not been fitted flush

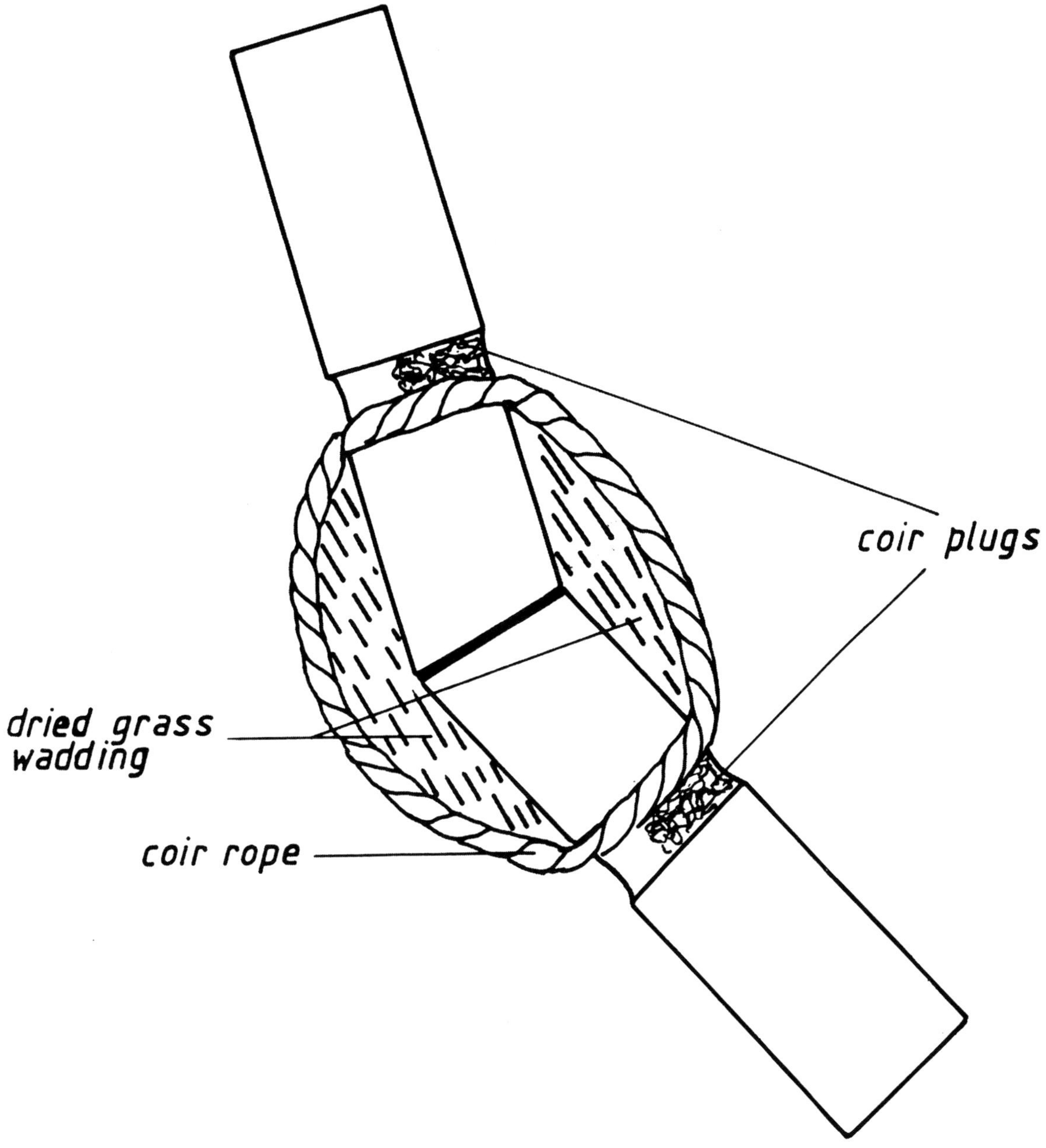

Fig. 1. Cross-section of sewing on Orissa masulas

with the fourth strake or the inner rail there will be a small gap. The planks which make up the top strake are not joined over a wadding of coir. They may in fact not be sewn together at all, save by the sewing that connects them to the fourth strake or the inner rail.

Sewing throughout the boat is with a doubled coir rope and on all strake-to-strake seams, except the top strake seam, it is done over a wadding of dried grass, both inboard and outboard. Builders are able to make a line of holes three fingers apart and two fingers width from the plank edge by eye. The holes are bored with a bow drill, with a 1 cm bit. The lower plank is drilled first, then the upper strake is matched up and marks made so that each hole on this will be vertically above one on the lower strake. No material or treenail is fitted between the strakes. At certain points, particularly where the garboards join the posts, it is common to find that the dried grass has been covered inboard by a waterproof material, such as bits of plastic bags or bicycle tyre inner tubes. The holes are plugged with balls of coir pushed in with a metal punch from inboard. However, on most boats the seam of the third and fourth strakes and the holes on the posts above this line are not plugged. It is thought unnecessary as it is above the waterline.

The top strake seam is never plugged. The pairs of holes on this seam are a handspan apart, and instead of dried grass the sewing holds a 3 cm diameter rope (usually of hemp) inboard and outboard numerous strands of coir rope. The pattern of sewing on this seam is different in appearance to that on the lower seams: it is in fact 'half sewn'. I have not seen boats actually being sewn in Orissa, but verbal descriptions indicate that it is identical to the practice found further south, which I have witnessed. Briefly, the full operation consists of taking a coir rope from a point roughly amidships through the sewing holes to the stem or stern post and then returning it to the starting point. The pattern produced is the same on both sides of the hull—a vertical bar between each vertical pair of holes with a cross between this and the adjacent horizontal pair. For convenience, this can be termed the criss-cross pattern. On the top strake seam, the rope is taken in one direction only. This produces the criss-cross pattern on one side of the hull and a pattern of vertical bars connected by diagonals all running the same direction on the other.

The inner rail, when present, is usually sewn on using a different technique. As on the top strake seam, the pairs of holes are about a handspan apart. Where the rail is fitted flush with the fourth strake, the pairs of holes are bored through both planks; where the rail is fitted above, the lower holes go through both planks but the upper holes are bored through the rail above the level of the strake. The coir rope is passed through a lower hole from inboard, then taken to the hole immediately above, passed through this and back down to the lower hole. It then travels outboard back up to and through the hole above and is taken (now inboard) diagonally to the lower hole of the adjacent pair. This sequence is then repeated until the post is reached where the sewing is finished off, as is all sewing, by knocking in a small wooden plug. Thus the pattern produced inboard is identical *in appearance* to that on the top strake seam, but outboard the pattern is of unconnected vertical bars.

South of the river Vamsadhara, the masulas are larger and slightly different in design. The beach seining masulas are six strake boats, ranging from over 8.5 metres in length with a beam to length ratio of over 4 to over 10 metres in length with a beam to length ratio of over 5.[3] Here, it is the third strake that is a stealer. The second is a tapering strake narrowing to meet the posts as a point.

Beach seiners of this style could be found in the mid-1980s between Kaliṅgapatnam and Dainapeta, about 100 km south of Visakhapatnam. They have disappeared from Uppada where James Hornell sketched them in the mid-1920s (Hornell 1920, 175). Beach seining requires a steep underwater slope, so masulas are not found around the Krishna-Godavari river mouths, and are not seen again until the coastal villages in the vicinity of Kavali. This

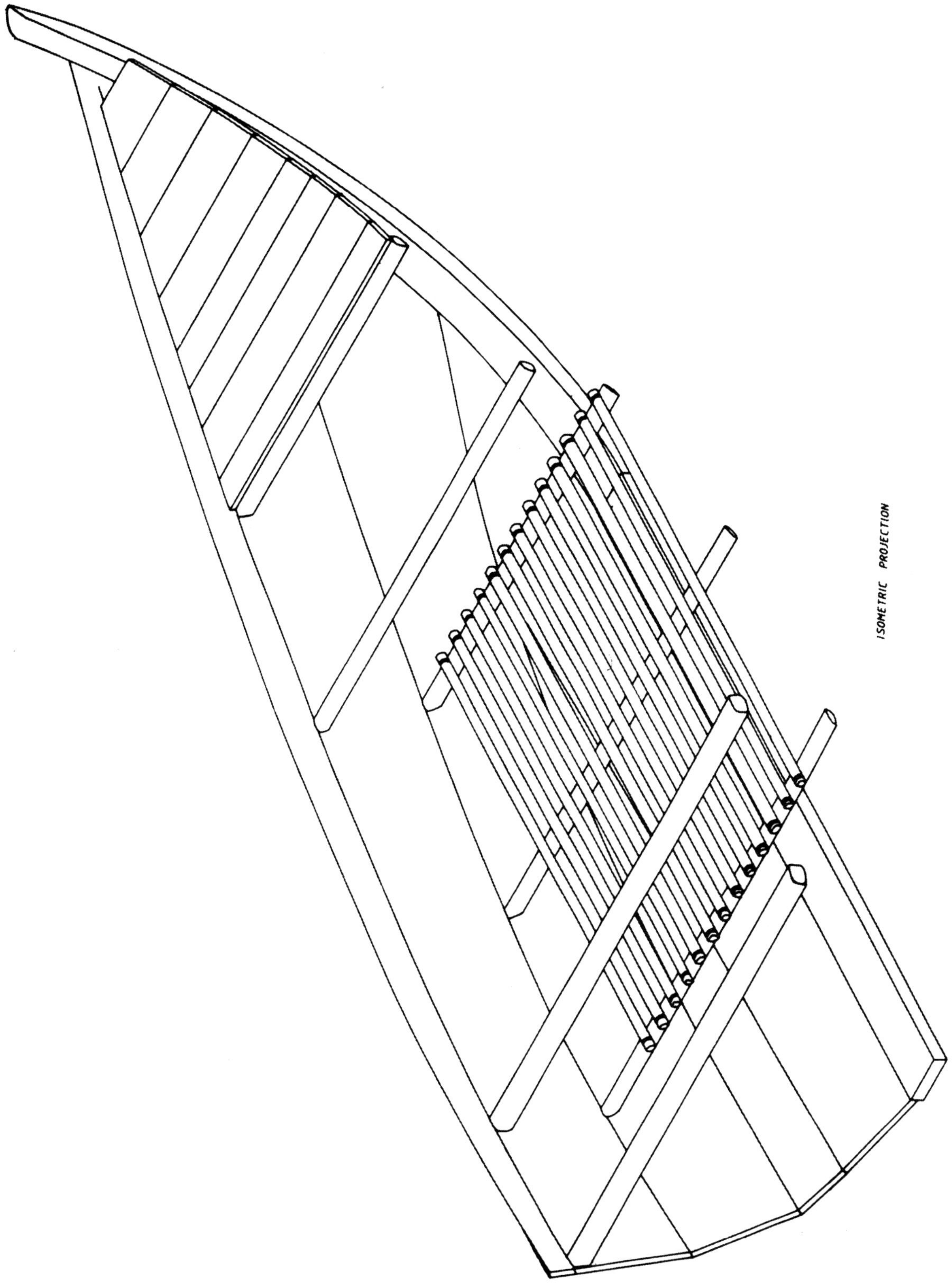

Fig. 2. A net-carrying frame on an Orissa masula

is an isolated group of boats about seven metres in length. It is not until Madras that they are found in numbers. Between Madras and Karaikal, most, but not all, fishing villages have masulas. These masulas are generally over 10 metres in length. From Kavali to Karaikal, the masulas are six strake boats, with the second strake as a stealer like the boats of Orissa.

A further distinguishing feature is the pattern of sewing. The criss-cross pattern on both sides of the hull is only found where the hood ends of the planks are attached to the stem and stern posts. On the strake-to-strake seams, the criss-cross pattern is on one side of the hull only-inboard. Outboard there are simply vertical bars of coir. This is in fact the same pattern described above for sewing on an inner rail on the boats of Orissa.

There are many other differences between the Tamil Nadu masulas and those found further north. For example, the former tend to use *aini (Artocarpus hirsuta)* or *paduk (Pterocorpus indicus P. Macrocarpus)* for the lower strakes and use coir as the wadding material throughout the boat, not dried grass. The central longitudinal member of a Tamil Nadu masula is more plank-like, and the 'heels' of the stem and stern post extend below it and are used as pivot points for 'walking' the masula up the beach. In Orissa and Andhra Pradesh masulas are taken in and out of the water with a straight lift. Again, each of the six or eight oars on a southern masula has a single rower, whereas in Orissa and Andhra Pradesh up to four oarsmen may pull on one of the oars near the boat's centre.

Yet, despite the differences between the Tamil Nadu masulas on the one hand and the Orissa and Andhra Pradesh masulas on the other, in general *appearance* the masulas of Orissa look more like those of Tamil Nadu than those of Andhra Pradesh. The latter are without doubt the best in terms of sophistication and quality of construction. Indeed, disregarding the variations, the highest quality boats are those around Visakhapatnam, and workmanship becomes cruder the further one travels from here.

Undoubtedly this is due in a large measure to the fact that the Andhra Pradesh masulas are built in boat-building communities (although these seem to produce no other boat types), whereas in both Tamil Nadu and Andhra Pradesh they are built in the fishing villages by boat-builders who are also fishermen themselves using the village's fishermen as labour.

Yet the ingenuity of the builders of even the crudest craft should not be overlooked—as I described above someone was inspired to develop at carrying frame for the net and a drainage plug. The masula may have a history stretching back centuries, it may use a plank fastening technique that it found from Puri to East Africa, but innovations like the frame and the plug show that the boats are not fossils of a bygone era but tools under constant adaptation and development.

NOTES

1. Although Hill (1958: 208) dismisses the theory, it may be derived from the town Masulipatnam (which was translated for me as "Muslim town"), now renamed Machilipatnam ("Fish town"): a theory widely accepted amongst fisheries department officials throughout the east coast.
2. However, at Bhavanapada I found one boat which had its forth strake on the port side composed of two planks which were connected by a wooden piece nailed on the inside.
3. A 7-metre masula-the only masula equipped with a sail-used for setting gillnets is also produced in this area, a relatively recent development possibly as a substitute for the *teppa*, the raft of the Andhra (and Orissa) coast, the wood for which (*Albizzia stipulata* or *Eythryna indica*) has become

increasingly scarce and, consequently, expensive. It was not built in Orissa during the time of this study. However I saw a few in use at Paradeep which had been imported from Bimlipatnam in Andhra Pradesh. They were seen nowhere else in Orissa. There is an even smaller masula, less than 5 metres in length, used for backwaters fishing, which I have seen nowhere but at Bimlipatnam.

REFERENCES

Hill, A.H., 1958, 'Some early accounts of the Oriental boat'. *Mariner's Mirror,* xliv: 201-17.

Hornell, James, 1920. 'The origins and ethnological significance of Indian boat designs'. *Memoirs of the Asiatic Society of Bengal* (Calcutta), vii no. 3:139-246.

17

History of Shipping in Bengal

N.C. GHOSH

Bengal is gifted with a number of navigable rivers and a coastline. It is, therefore, natural that maritime activity in Bengal should have developed from very ancient times. This is amply borne by archaeological as well as literary sources. East Indian navigators had defied religious sanctions which prohibited them to sail overseas. The attitude of the ship-wrights of this region had set the sailing over high seas from very early times.

Numismatic finds from Harinarayanpur, 24-Parganas, West Bengal attest earlier sea-faring activities in India from excavation at the site[1] (Roychoudhuri, 1962, pp. XVII & III), Copper coins were recovered from *circa* 4th century BC level. At least two of them bear symbol of rigged ship. Recently two identical copper coins with ship motifs were unearthed from excavation at Kotasur, district Birbhum, West Bengal[2] (Ghosh 1992, 57). Stratigraphically coins were found in a debris deposit which overlies early centuries level and sealed by early medieval occupation. The earliest habitation at the site goes back to *circa* 4th century BC. The cultural milieu of the earliest phase at Kotasur and Harinarayanpur are comparable. The coins from Kotasur are most likely displaced from the earlier level. Beside mast and rolled sail there is a mid-cabin. The former site is quite close to sea while the latter is an inland site situated on a navigable river. Both of them had served vast hinterland.

A number of terracotta seals were discovered from deltaic Bengal. Few of them contain ship motif and legends in Kharoṣṭi-Brāhmi. The finds are dated "from about the second half of 1st century AD to about 5th century AD" (Mukherjee, 1990, 40).[3] Rouletted ware from Tamralipti, an ancient port town now lost and rouletted ware and Roman wine jar pans from Chandraketugarh further attest maritime activity of Bengal in early centuries of Christian era. Rouletted ware and Kharoṣṭi-Brāhmi seals and rouletted ware sherd are now reported from coastal Java, Bali and Thailand[4] (Sharma, 1991, 4). A miniature model of a boat in copper from Deulpota near Diamond Harbour, West Bengal which is assignable to Gupta period, is a notable find (Chattopadhyay, 1994, 64).[5] At Tilda near Tamralipti, a Greek inscription in terracotta seems to record the thanks giving of an unknown Greek sailor to the last "East wind that come with the down" (Euron) (Chattopadhyay, 1994, 63).[6]

Carved and moulded clay-panels adorn brickwork temples of late medieval Bengal. In these terracotta reliefs, which represent processions of warriors, lines of elephants and horses, or local zamindars riding in palanquins, mythological scenes, a particular topic is boating and shipping. The vessels represented may be divided into two categories: river boats and sailing ships. The first group are represented in an accurate and realistic manner while the second group vessels do not bear careful observation by artists. Nevertheless boats and ships merit a close examination from the vantage point of nautical technology (Deloche, 1991, 2).[7] Archaeology is admirably supplemented by literary sources.

Earliest literary composition of Bengal is Carya-pada. It is dated to early medieval times. It contains significant navigational data. The MSS came to possession of Mahamahopadhya Harprasad Sastri in his third visit to Nepal in 1907. Sastri edited and published his collection in 1917, under general caption *Boudha-Gan-O-Dohā*.[8] It contains compositions of different Siddhacharya(s) (i.e., preceptors who attained perfection) of the Sahajiya sect, an offshoot of Buddhism. It was composed in *Sandhya Bhasa* and prepared with equivocal works. The main purpose of the songs was to initiate their disciples into esoteric practices. The parallels in the songs were derived from common avocations viz., brewing, rope-making, basketery, weaving, spinning, shipping, etc. Carya-pada reflects social and economic condition of Bengal (early 8th to 13th century AD), as it was composed in Bengal. The doubt is set to rest when it is found that Carya-pada was written in Bengali script. Songs nos. 8, 10, 13, 14 and 38 particularly bear significant navigational data. Song no. 8 is as under:

Sone Bhaitī karuṇā nābī I
Rupā thoai nāhika thābī II *dru* II
Bāhatu kāmali ganna ubesi
Gelī jāma bāhudai kāise II *dru* II
Khunti upaḍī melili kācchi I
Bāhatu kāmali sadguru Puchi II *dru* II
Maṅgata caṛ hile cau clis cāhaa I
Keḍuāla nāhi kė ki bahabake Pāraa II
Baṁa Dāhiṇa Cāpī mili mili mangā II *dru* II
Baṭata milila mahasuhasāṅga II *dru* II

(I have) filled (my) boat (nābi) of compassion with gold and have left silver with the world. Kamāli (poet) says further that (he is) rowing (Bāhatu), on towards (void), if one birth is totally annihilated how it can recur again (ocean is often used as similie to represent void). Kāmali says, he has pulled Khunti (Bollard) and untitled rope (kacchi), from the (boat), Kamali is rowing (Bāhatu). Seeking in every step instruction of wise preceptor Maṅgata (companion) on board, should (go up and) look around oars-man (keduala) rows (and takes us) across (while rowing he) looks to left and right. He (rows) on towards perfect bliss.

Nābi (boat) is also used in songs nos. 13 and 38. Again *nābaḍi* and *naukā* (boat) both are used (*ibid*. 24). *Nābi, nabāḍi* and *Naukā* are used in context of river as well as sea. *Diṇgā* and *naya* are more commonly used in late medieval Bengali text for boat/ship. Later river and seacrafts were distinguished in waiting and former is known as *pālbihin Naukā* (boat without sail). Boats with *goloi* are often referred to as naukā proper in Bengali language (Janson, 1989, 74).[9]

(ii) *Bahutu*, rowing is available in late medieval Bengali texts in sense of rowing. In slightly modified form *Bāya, Kheyā* are also used for rowing.

(iii) *Sadguru*, preceptor in the verse seems to be an equivocal word here. Another meaning would be an experienced *Kannahār* (*ibid*., 13, 24) or Karnadhar i.e. captain or chief navigator. It is also frequently mentioned as captain of fleet in *Mangalkavya(s)*.

(iv) *Khunti.* It is evident from the context that it represents, here, post (bollard) on quay for securing ropes to it for mooring. In late medieval text *alan* also served the same purpose. In late medieval texts *naṇgar* (anchor) and its synonym *goja* (anchor) were referred to as mooring device.

Anchor has a very fascinating history. Earliest representation of anchor in India is found on an Indus seal. It is triangular in shape and obviously is made of stone. From excavations at Lothal, Gujarat, S.R. Rao reported stone anchors from Harappan level. Vedic literature is replete with word anchor (X - 4.1). Later *Milindipañha* and *Tilakmañjari* ( ) among other literary sources refer to anchor. All of them are of stone. It appears *noṇgar* and *goja* were multipronged and were made of iron. Arab seafarers were very active in Bay of Bengal from 9th century AD onwards and were conversant with multipronged iron made anchor. *Laṇgar* (anchor) is a Persian word. In Arabic it is Misrât (I owe this information to Dr. Niaz, Lecturer, Dept. of Persian, Arabic and Urdu, Visva-Bharati).

(v) *Kacchi*, rope needs no elaboration. Kambalambarpadanam provides some details of rope making. Poets of Carya-pada also referred to basketry (song no.10), spinning (song no. 26), brewing (song no. 3), rope (making) (song no. 8). These professions were in the hands of lower caste women. In an ethnographic survey in early twentieth century in some traditional boat building centres in coastal region, Harnell (1918)[10] recorded stitching of planks for building hull. Yuktikalpataru, a medieval Sanskrit text (Sastri, 1917),[11] Iban Batuta (Needham, 1978, 465 FN.II)[12] also mentioned stitching at planks for building hull. In our field survey in 1991 from Bhiminipatnam to Kankinada, Andhra Pradesh seacoast we came across a traditional boat building centre of Bhiminipatnam. Here carpenters were busy in building various parts of vessel including drilling holes on planks. For stitching, women of their community were busy in rope-making.

(vi) *Mangata car hib Cau dis chahha* : "Climb up and look around' may be read in context of ship/boat (*nāvi*) and ocean (void), in the verse. This is an age old navigational practice which is borne out by archaeological evidences. In one of the terracotta seals from lower Bengal (Mukherjee, *op. cit.*, 61),[13] there is a representation of a masted ship and a rope ladder. The ladder is shown as suspended from the top of the mast. In one of the sculptural panels from Borobodur, a ship with full blown saul is depicted. A ladder is leaning against the mast. A crew is climbing up the ladder (Krom - i-v vols).[14] There is a representation of a masted ship in a panel from Ajanta (Yazdani, 1930-1955).[15] On a high platform against the mast a crew is standing with pole in his hands.

In Middle Ages the Arabs as well as Indian shipwrights had graded their navigator 3rd and highest grade—the muallim—had to be able to navigate his ship at all times out of sight of land, from any port to any part, using only stars and his fund of experience, and never losing his way even if buffeted by storms or current or winds (Bahal, 1988, 44).[16]

The following verse from *Chaṇḍīmangal Kāvya* (Sen, Sukumar, 1986, 230),[17] adds more information:

Gade Dinga Madhukar
Madhey jar Rae Ghar
Pase, Guda Basile Gobar
Disaru basite pat upare Malumkat

Ship (Diṇgā) Madhukar is being built with a mid-cabin seat provided for rowers. A lookout post (mālum-kōt) for Diśāru (direction finder) is raised above the deck. *Malumkat* and *Diśāru* are also referred to by other poets of Mangalkavya(s). He was accompanied by Tārābid (sky-brazer) and Pabanbettā (Aminohydrographer), in voyages. Specialised technical hands ensure skilful handling of ship in dark.

(vii) *Keduol* or helsman steers his craft and keeps watch on left and right—*Baṁ-Dahīna chāpi*. He thus avoids deep sea near coast and coastal reef. He rows along middle path. *Chandimangal Kavya, Padma Purāṇ, Manasamangal* and *Krishnacharitamrita*, late medieval texts are noteworthy as far as selection of mode of construction of vessels. Chulking timber was ideal material for building boats and ships prior to steam-navigation. Teak and a few other species were most sought after wood. The traditional wood-cutters from Kerala know the species, kind, variety and size of timber required for building seaworthy crafts. Our ancient texts are, however, silent on the subject except for an indirect reference to seasoning of wood and a list of unsuitable and suitable timber for construction (*Bṛhat Saṁhitā*).[18] In general timber species barring a few are not durable unless properly treated before use.

Kabikankan Mukundaram in his *Chaṇḍīmangal* narrates:

Hanumanta mahābirā
nakhe kare dui cir
Kå̄thāl Piyāl tāla sālȧ
Gå̄ṁbhāri tamālā dahu
nahlka Ciryā rahe bȧhu
Darubrahma jagay gajāla
Śilāy Sānāyā bāsi
Pāti cāche rāsi rāsi
nānā phule bichtra kalaś
Pitā Putre dohe atigajā le gå̄thiā pāti
Gore diṅgā dehite rupas.
(Sen [ed.] 1986, 230).[19]

* * * *

Kå̄thāla (Skt. Pansa) *artocarpur integrifoliu*
Sarala, pine, Pinus longifolia
Tāl, Palmyra, Patmyra palm
Sāl *Strorca rocusta gaertn*
Piyasal, Indian kino tree, *Petracarpus Morsupium*
Gå̄ṁbhari *Gmetina arboreal*
Tamāl, blackwood, *Cliospyres tomentosa*
Piyāl *Buchanania latifolia*

Ketakadas Khemananda composed *Mansamangal* in 1938-39 AD. He writes:

Asār kȧther Naya
Yadi je sesher jāya
Kastha jayraya khay
Nonā Jale
(Kayal and Dev, 222)[20]

Carpenters were aware of the effect of salt-laden wind on timber. Crafts prior to sailing were painted with begable emulsion. It is prepared from juice of Gab *Dispyros embryopetris.* Sri Krishnacharita (14th century AD) mentions that *Khalapādī* (thin pieces of wood) and *Sarubuthi* (emulsion of Gab, *Dispyros embrypetris* with jute and hemp), were used for repairing leakages and caulking respectively.

Planks for building hull were joined by iron nails. Contemporary Sanskrit text datable to late medieval period[21] which was composed in Bengal (Hazra, 1990)[22] however, mentions stitching of planks as mode of building hull. Time and amount for construction of boat are vaguely hinted in more than one text but hardly these have any historical significance.

Various categories of naval personnel: Keduāl, Karnadhar, Gaṇak, Disāru, Tārābid, Pabanbetta, etc. are noteworthy information. Combined testimony of archaeological and literary sources from earliest time to late medieval times brings out many unknown facts of maritime history of Bengal before steam navigation.

NOTES AND REFERENCES

1. Roychowdhury, Chittaranjan, 1962, *A Catalogue of Early Indian Coins*, Part I, Calcutta, XVII, p.111.
2. Ghosh, N.C., 1992, "Boat/Ship motif on two coins from Excavation at Kotasur, West Bengal." *Science, History, Culture and Archaeology on Land and Water*, (Eds.) B.P. Nayak and N.C. Ghosh, 57, New Delhi.
3. Mukherjee, B.N., 1990, "Kharosti and Kharoshti-Brahmi Inscriptions in West Bengal (India)." *Indian Museum Bulletin,* Calcutta, 40.
4. Sharma, I.K., 1990, Ceramics and Maritime Trade Routes of India, New Discoveries, Paper read at *International Seminar* held at Madras, December 20-21, 1990.
5. Chattopadhyay, Bhaskar, 1994, *An Introduction of the Maritime History of India,* 59, Calcutta.
6. *Ibid.,* 59-60.
7. Deloche Jean, 1991, "Boats and Ships in Bengal Terracotta Art". *Bulletin,* De I'E' Cole Francaise D'extreme-Orient Tome LXVIII, 1-23.
8. Sastri, Harprasad, 1917, *Boudha Gan-O-Doha,* Calcutta, 1-202.
9. Janson, Eric G. *et al.,* 1989, *The Country Boats of Bangladesh,* 74.
10. Hoanell, James, 1918-23. The Origin and Ethnological Significance of Indian Boat Designs, *Memoir of the Asiatic Society of Bengal,* Vol.VII, No. 1.
11. *Yuktikalpataruh Maharaja Śri Bhoraja Rachitah.* Ed. Isvana Chandra Sastri, Calcutta Series, Calcutta, 1917.
12. Needham, Joseph *et al.,* 1978, *Science and Civilization in China,* Cambridge (Nautical Technology), Vol.V, 4, 465 (f.n.1).
13. B.N. Mukherjee, 1990, *op. cit.,* p. 61.
14. Krom, N.J. *Barabudur: Archaeological Description,* I-V Vols.
15. Yazdani, G., 1930-55, *Ajanta,* 4 Vols. London.
16. Bahal, K.N. 1988. "Pilot Ibn Majid who showed Vasco da Gama the Route to India in 1598." *History of Traditional Naviqation,* Rajmanibani G. and Victor Subbaroyalu (Eds.), 141-48.
17. Sen, Sukumar, 1986, Kabikikan Virachita, *Chandimangal,* New Delhi.
18. *Brahatsamhita,* Ed. Pandit Shri Achutyanand Jha Sharma, Varanasi, 239.
19. Sen, *op. cit.,* p. 230.
20. Kyal, Akshay Kumar and Chitro Dev, *Mansamangal Velabdas Khemanand Rachita,* 222.
21. Sastri (Ed.) 1917.
22. Hazra, R.C., 1990, *Isyuktikalpataru: A Work of Bhuja, Professor P.K. Gode Commemoration Volume,* Poona.

18

The Maritime Contacts Between Eastern India and South-east Asia: New Epigraphic Data

B.N. MUKHERJEE

The recently noticed and deciphered inscriptions from West Bengal written in Kharoshṭī and in many cases in a mixed script, consisting Kharoshṭī and Brāhmī letters, indicate that trading communities hailing from the north-western part of the Indian subcontinent migrated to the territory now in lower West Bengal (in eastern India) and became very active as traders from about the last quarter of the 1st century AD to about the beginning of the 5th century AD. Their main settlements were in the region of Chandraketugarh in the district of 24, Parganas (North) and perhaps in the area of Tamluk in the Midnapore district. These were then within the limits of Vaṅga. These trading communities had maritime commerce with South-east Asia. They used to supply *inter alia* Central Asian horses. They were known as Yueh-chih, since they had originally come from the domain of the Yueh-chih or the Kuṣāṇas. Among them there could have been people hailing from the North-West with or without any ethnic connection with the Kuṣāṇas. However, all of them used in the territory of lower West Bengal the North-Western Prākṛit as their language. It was written either in Kharoshṭī (imported from the North-West) or in a mixed script consisting of Kharoshṭī and Brāhmī letters (evolved by the immigrants in their new habitats in ancient Vaṅga).[1]

In the light of the above data, a seal-matrix made of tin assumes significance. It was unearthed at Oc-eo. The rectangular shaped matrix measures 0.018 × 0.114 m. Its thickness is 0.008 m. The letters engraved on it in reverse were considered by G. Coedes as belonging to the Brāhmī script. He thought that the inscription consisted of one line and read it as *apramāda* (*apramādam*).[2]

Coedes did not notice the second line of the legend. Since the characters belong to a matrix, these are engraved in reverse and from right to left to ensure their correct forms in the stamped impression. Keeping this feature in mind the first letter can be read as Brāhmī *a*. Coedes read the second letter as *pra* of the Brāhmī script. But there is really no distinguishing stroke for indicating subscript *r*. The straight line attached to the lower portion of the left vertical line of the character, which may be taken as *pa*, can be considered as a stroke for medial *u*. In that case the character is *pu*. However, it can also be read as the letter *ḍa* of the Kharoshṭī script. The third letter is Brāhmī *ma* with a sign for medial *i*. The fourth one appears more like a Kharoshṭī *ha* than a Brāhmī *da*. The first two letters of the second line are easily decipherable as Brāhmī *ra* and *na*. But no letter in the Brāhmī script looking like the third character (from the right) of the second line is known. On the other hand, it can be easily read as the letter called shin in Aramaic and Iranian alphabets (like Parthian). The letter is now known to have been employed also by the Kharoshṭī using immigrants in ancient Vaṅga (though it does not occur in the Kharoshṭī documents discovered so far in the North-Western section of the subcontinent).[3]

The last character of the seal inscription thus proves that it is in a mixed script consisting of Kharoshṭī and Brāhmī letters. The feasibility of the use of such a script has already been proved by the discovery of a large number of short inscriptions in Kharoshṭī-Brāhmī in lower West Bengal.[4]

The inscription can now be read as *Apumidaranaś* (taking *inter alia* the second and the fourth letters of the first line as Brāhmī) or, more meaningfully, as *Aḍamiharan (a) š ( ).* The latter can be accepted as the Prākṛit rendering of the Iranian expression *Artamihrnś,* meaning the "King (or lord) (š<) (*Xśayathiya*) of the Artamihr (family)." While the Iranian word *arta* literally means "law" or "justice," the term *mihr* (< mithra) can signify "a deity (sun)," or "a friend."[5]

Thus the reading *Aḍamiharan(a) š ( )* is meaningful. Again, as it is not unexpected in a seal inscription, the reading may allude to a personal name. Such proper names as Vakamihira, Yolamira, Miraboyana, etc. are known from epigraphic records.[6]

No doubt, one may argue that the alternative reading *Apumidaranas* may be taken as a personal name. Even in that case, the last letter is to be taken as a non-Brāhmī character. On the basis of the collective evidence of the palaeographic features of the Brāhmī letters, *a, ma* and *na,* the inscription may be dated to *c.* 3rd century AD.

Thus there is no doubt that the seal inscription is in the mixed script, consisting of Kharoshṭī and Brāhmī letters. Since the Kharoshṭī-Brāhmī script was used by the trading communities from the North-West settled in Vaṅga in the early centuries of the Christian era, the discovery of a Kharoshṭī-Brāhmī inscriptions at Oc-eo should indicate their connection with that locality. As the inscription concerned is on tin, which should have been available in the area of Oc-eo,[7] the seal-matrix was probably done locally. This suggests the presence of Kharoshṭī-Brāhmī using people (traders) at that market town. This inference is supported by the discovery of the representation of a male head in tin at Oc-eo, bearing affinity to the head of the Kuṣāṇa ruler Miaos on his coins.[8] Figures with Iranian head-dresses are noticeable on some engraved gems found at Oc-eo.[9] The Kharoshṭī-Brāhmī using communities, hailing originally from the North-West, came from an area which had been included in the Yüeh-chih or Kuṣāṇa domain. So they could have been generally known as Yüeh-chih. Among them there could have been Yüeh-chih and Iranian ethnic elements.

The evidence from Oc-eo alludes to the presence of members of such communities. It is interesting to note that Ptolemy noted in about the middle of the 2nd century AD a place called Thagora on the Great Gulf, identifiable with the Gulf of Thailand, and somewhere above a promontory on the Gulf (present Mui Bai-Bung).[10] So Thagora should have been at or not far from the site of Oc-eo. As we have suggested elsewhere, the name Thagora, i.e. Tukhāra, indicates a settlement of the Tukharas in a locality included in ancient Fu-nan (basically comprising the territories of Cambodia and south Vietnam). The Tukhāras were identical with or closely related to the Yüeh-chih.[11] So the communities hailing from North-Western India and settled in Vaṅga could have been known as Tukhāra as well as Yüeh-chih. It is significant that in about the middle of the 3rd century AD, K'ang T'ai was heard at the court of Fu-nan about the Yüeh-chih traders selling horses.[12]

Thus the Kharoshṭī using trading communities in Vaṅga not only had trade relations with South-east Asia, but they also reached Fu-nan and had established a settlement there by about the middle of 2nd century AD. With them the habit of using the mixed Kharoshṭī-Brāhmī script and Prākṛit reached Fu-nan.

The presence of the Kharoshṭī-Brāhmī using people on the coast of the Malay Peninsula (now controlled by Thailand) is indicated by an inscribed seal of carnelian stone. These and several other inscribed seals and seal-matrices have been unearthed at Khuan Lukpad (Khlong Thom) in Karabi province.[13] The engraved seal in question bears a circular inscription in the mixed script. As we have shown elsewhere,[14] it can be deciphered as (VII) *Atarañа* (taking the third and fourth characters respectively as Kharoshṭī *ra* and *ña*) or *Atarajha* (considering only the third letter *ra-* as written in Kharoshṭī). It is palaeographically datable to *c.* 2nd or 3rd century AD.

The legend *Artarajha*, (i.e. *Artarāja,* Sanskrit *Ṛitarāja*) may literally mean "the law(ful) king". However, it may have been used as a personal name.

According to the *Liang-shu*, during the epoch of the Wu dynasty in China (AD 220-80) an envoy of Fu-nan came to Chü-li (or Tou-chu-li) and then through a maritime route reached the mouth of the river of T'ien-chu,[15] i.e. the Ganges.[16] It appears from K'ang T'ai's statement that the mouth of the Ganges was in the area of Tāmralipti.[17] The envoy returned with horses.[18] T'ou-chü-li (Tokola emporium mentioned by Ptolemy) was on the western coast of the Malay peninsula (now in South Thailand).[19] In the same peninsula was perhaps the area of Ko-ying or China-ying, where the Yüeh-chih traders (from Vaṅga) used to import horses in *c.* 3rd century AD.[20] The last noted inscription indicates the presence of the Kharoshṭī-Brāhmī using people (perhaps the same as the Yüeh-chih from Vaṅga) in the zone concerned in *c.* 3rd century AD.

The use of Kharoshṭī-Brāhmī in other parts of Thailand in about the same period is suggested by two Kharoshṭī-Brāhmī inscriptions. A rectangular carnelian bead (0.9 x 0.45cm), found at Khao Sam Kaeo (Chumphon province), bears a legend in the mixed script.[21] It can be read as *Akhisati*, taking the last two letters (*sa* and *ta* with the sign of medial *i*) as written in Kharoshṭī.[22] It may be taken as a personal name.

A Kharoshṭī-Brāhmī inscription appears in a small seal impression unearthed at U Thong in central Thailand. It is now in the Lopburi Museum, Thailand.[23]

The oval shaped sealing displays a male(?) figure sitting on a backless chair or stool. He sits with his body facing one-fourth to front and the rest to right (i.e. to his left). The head is turned to right (i.e. to his left). The right hand hangs down, while the left hand is stretched out. The latter is perhaps holding an indistinct object.[24]

There is an inscription on the edge of the sealing which can be meaningfully read only from inside. The first letter from the right is Kharoshṭī *ḍha*, and the first character from the left is Kharoshṭī *va*. Hence the legend should be read, as it is usual with Kharoshṭī writings, from right to left. In that case the first letter is Kharoshṭī *ḍha*. The second and third characters are Brāhmī *ta* and *a* respectively. The last letter is, as noted above, Kharoshṭī *va*. Its form is similar to that of the same letter in the Palatu Dheri inscription (no. C).[25]

The legend can now be read as *Ḍhata'ava*. Palaeographically the inscription may be dated to the 4th-5th century AD (as indicated especially by the form of Brāhmī *ta*).[26]

The legend *Ḍhata'ava (Dhṛitayavah)* may literally mean "the holder of (or adherent to) speed". It may also be translated as "the holder of a barley-corn", taking the uncertain object held in one of the hands of the male figure as a grain of barley.[27] Otherwise the legend may be taken as referring to a personal name.[28]

It appears that during the period of Fu-nanese domination of Thailand,[29] the use of Kharoshṭī-Brāhmī was introduced there by the traders using that script. Both Fu-nan and the area of Thailand under it received the script by *c.* 2nd or 3rd century AD.

There is an indication about the continuity of the use of this mixed script, at least sporadically, in the Mon kingdom of Dvārāvatī in the period after the end of the domination by Fu-nan in about the middle of the 6th century AD.[30] On one variety of the inscribed silver coins of Dvārāvatī, the usual Brāhmī legend *Śrī-Dvārāvatīsvara puṇya*[31] has been written in the mixed script as *Śrī-Dārāvatisvaro-puṇya.*[32] Here the fourth (*va*), fifth (*ti*), sixth (*śva*) and seventh (*ra*) letters are in Kharoshṭī and the rest are in Brāhmī (Fig. 5). Palaeographically the coin-legend is datable to the late 6th or 7th century AD.[33]

This evidence shows that even in the 6th or 7th century AD, the mixed script was considered in Thailand as important enough to be employed, even if sporadically, on such official products as coins. We do not know whether the script was used even in later centuries.

It was only natural that Kharoshṭī and not only Kharoshṭī-Brāhmī was made known to S.E. Asia by the traders from Vaṅga, hailing ultimately from the Kharoshṭī-using zone in the North-Western section of the subcontinent. We can refer at least to one instance.

A fragmentary graffito is noticeable on a potsherd unearthed during an excavation at Sembiran in the Tejakula district of Bali (Indonesia).[34] The surviving letters are in Kharoshṭī and may be read from the right to left as *Tośavi...* Palaeographically the fragmentary graffito can be dated to *c.* 2nd century AD.[35] I.W. Ardika and P. Bellwood, the excavators, believe that the potsherd was originally a part of an open dish-like vessel imported from outside (India).[36] Even if it was an imported item, its evidence indicates contact of Bali with some Kharoshṭī using people.[37]

The language of the above noted inscriptions is Prākṛit.[38] The influence of the North-Western Prākṛit is discernible at least in two inscriptions[39] (nos. 1 and 4).

The above data suggest that the Kharoshṭī and Kharoshṭī-Brāhmī scripts and the Prākṛit language were used among certain communities in some localities of South-east Asia in the early centuries of the Christian era. South communities might have hailed from India, especially Vaṅga. They were probably connected with international trade. Thus the scripts and Prākṛit reached South-east Asia in the wake of the activities of the traders.[40]

NOTES AND REFERENCES

1. B.N. Mukherjee, *Economic Factors in Kuṣāṇa History* (cited below as *EFKH*), Calcutta, 1970, pp. 37-38; Kharoshṭī and Kharoshṭī-Brāhmī Inscriptions in West Bengal (India) (published in the *Indian Museum Bulletin,* Vol. XXV), Calcutta, 1990 (cited below as *KKBIWB),* pp. 9f, 33-35 and 65-67.
2. L. Malleret, *L'Archaeologie du Delta du Mekong*, Vol. II, Paris, 1960, p. 383; III, Paris, 1962, Pl.LXI, no. 652.
3. *KKBIWB*, p. 63, Pl. IV.
4. *Ibid.,* pp. 44f.

5. R.G. Kent, *Old Persian Grammar, Texts, Lexicon,* 2nd edition, Connecticut, 1953, pp. 170, 181, 203; G.D. Davary, *Baktrisch, Ein Wörterbuch,* Heidelberg, 1982, pp. 230, 274.
6. G.D. Davary, *op. cit.,* p. 231.
7. A Malleret, *op. cit.,* Vol. II, pp. 265-71.
8. *Ibid.,* Vol. III, Pl. XCVIII-C; B.N. Mukherjee, *Kuṣāṇa Silver Coinage,* Calcutta, 1982, Pl. I, no. 6.
9. A Malleret, *op. cit.,* Vol. III, Pl. LXVI, no. 1274; Pl. LXXIII, 1315.
10. Ptolemy, *Geographike Huphegesis,* VII, 2, 7.
11. *Journal of the Asiatic Society,* 1974, p. 143.
12. *EFKH,* p. 37.
13. *Encyclopaedia of Southern Culture,* Songkhla (in the Thai Language), Vol. III, 2529 B.E. or 1986 AD, p. 1201 f; K. Veeraprajak, "Inscriptions from South Thailand", *SPAFA Consultative Workshop on Archaeological and Economical Study on Śrīvijaya,* Jakarta, 1985, pp. 131-43; H.P. Ray, "Early Trade in the Bay of Bengal," *The Indian Historical Review,* Vol. XIV, nos. 1-2, pp. 87f.
14. See our article in the *N.C. Majumdar Commemoration Volume* (edited by D.Mitra), to be published shortly. See also the *Encyclopaedia of Southern Culture,* Vol.III, p. 1202.
15. *Liang-shu,* Ch. 54, f. 22f; S. Lévi, "Deux peuples mśeconnus," *Melanges Charlez de Harvez,* pp. 22-23.
16. *KKBIWB,* p. 17.
17. L. Petech, *Northern India According to the Shui-Ching-Chu,* Rome, 1950, p. 53; *KKBIWB,* p. 17.
18. Supra, no. 15.
19. *KKBIWB,* pp. 17, 21, no. 34. Tokola may have been at or near Tokua Pa.
20. K'ang T'ai's *Wu shih wai Kuo Chuan* quoted in the *Tai-p'ing Yu-Lan,* ch. 359; *Etudes Asitatiques,* Vol.II, p. 250. According to another theory, it was on the east coast of Sumatra.
21. *Encyclopaedia of Southern Culture,* Songkhla, Vol. VIII, 2529 BE or 1986 AD, p. 3227.
22. *Ibid.,* p. 3228. Here the inscription has been taken as written only in Brāhmī and read as *Akhidaro.* But the third letter is definitely Kharoshṭī *sa* and not Brāhmī *da.* The character is probably Kharoshṭī *ta* with the sign of medial *i.*
23. *Muang Boran Journal,* April-June, 1986, Vol. 12, no. 2, pp. 9f; *Journal of the Asiatic Society,* 1991, pp. 85-86.
24. *Ibid.*
25. S. Konow, *Corpus Inscriptionum Indicarum,* Vol. II, Pl. I, *Kharoshṭī Inscriptions with the Exception of those of Aśoka,* Calcutta, 1929, Pl. XXIII.
26. A.H. Dani, *Indian Palaeography,* Oxford, 1963, Pl. X A.
27. This suggestion was kindly communicated to me by Dr. S.C. Banerji.
28. *The Asiatic Society Monthly Bulletin,* December 1990, p. 2.
29. J.A. Cady, *South-east Asia, Its Historical Development,* pp. 52f.
30. *Ibid.,* pp. 54f.
31. M. Mitchiner, *Oriental Coins and Their Values—The Ancient and Classical World, 600 BC-AD 650,* London, 1978, p. 650. For different varieties of inscribed silver specie of Dvārāvatī see *ibid., The Śilpakorn Journal,* Vol. 34, no.2, 1991, pp. 68-69; *Inscriptions in Thailand, Pallava and Later Pallava Script* (in the Thai language), Vol. I, 2529 BE or 1986 AD, pp. 113, 127.
32. *The Śilpakorn Journal,* Vol. 34, no. 2, 1991, pp. 51f. Here the inscription has been wrongly described as written only in the Kharoshṭī script.
33. See our article in the *N.G. Majumdar Commemoration Volume* (edited by D. Mitra) (to be published shortly).
34. I.W. Ardika and P. Bellwood, "Sembiran: The Beginnings of India's Contact with Bali," *Antiquity,* Vol. 65, no. 247, p. 225.
35. *KKBIWB,* p. 73 and Fig. 79.
36. *Antiquity,* Vol. 65, no. 247, p. 229.
37. *KKBIWB,* p. 38.
38. *Ibid.,* pp. 14-15.
39. S. Konow, *op. cit.,* pp. xcv f.
40. *KKBIWB,* pp. 34-35.

19

Marathas and the Sea

A.R. KULKARNI

Maratha country is fortunate in having a long coastline, with natural harbours for anchoring small and big ships, and rocky islands to serve as sentinels of these harbours on the west coast. Nature has showered all its gifts on the Maratha country but the Maratha man has failed to exploit these natural resources either for commercial purposes or for political ambitions. Marathas could alone claim, in the 17th century, among other Indian powers as the only major power which could think of organizing navy for political purposes. The reason was obvious. They had to deal with the European powers who had occupied parts of the Maratha country on the west coast for establishing their factories, and also for striking their roots in the Indian soil. In order to protect their infant kingdom from the devilish motives of the European powers, the Marathas had to devise ways and means to check the growing ambitions of these traders-cum-rulers. Shivaji, the founder of the Maratha power, who had made Konkan region on the west coast as the base of his state, had to deal with these European powers on the west coast, which he could do only by organizing naval power. The Mughals and the Adilshahi rulers of Bijapur, were certainly aware of the menace of these European powers on the west coast, but as they did not come directly in conflict with them for their very political existence, they did not pay much attention to the establishment of a naval organization. On the contrary they utilized the services of the Siddis of Danda Rajapuri to check the growing activities of the Marathas in the Konkan. The Siddis and the Portuguese, who had come to stay as political powers on the west coast in the Maratha country, and who were supported by the Mughals, the Bijapurians and the English, as occasion demanded, were thus the only enemies of the Marathas with whom they had to fight on land as well as on sea of which they were the masters.

Marathas dominated the political scene of Indian history nearly for two centuries, namely the 17th and 18th but it was only during the brief period of Shivaji's short regime, in the 17th century some attempts were made to build navy, which included the construction of marine forts and also warships of various sizes. The foreigners therefore could refer to the Maratha fleet as 'Shivaji's Armada'[1] in their official correspondence. We also find a few references to the commercial activities of the Marathas during this period. The pioneering work of Shivaji could not be continued in the subsequent period and this splendid edifice was destroyed due to the infighting between the Peshwas and the Maratha Admirals of the House of Angres with the help of the English a little before the tragedy of Panipat of 1761.

In this brief resume of the maritime history of the Marathas, it is proposed to consider the beginning of Maratha naval activities under Shivaji, his naval policy emerging out of experience, the construction of marine forts and the development of dockyards, the encounters with the Siddis and the Portuguese, the commercial activities, and lastly in brief the extinction of the Marathas as a naval power.

Shivaji's successful encounter with the Bijapurians in 1659 opened him the gates to the Konkan and brought under him Kalyan, Bhivandi and Panvel which were adjacent to the north province of the Portuguese. He realized shortly that without navy he would not be able to control the creeks on which these places of trade and commerce were situated. He also realized that the timber which was available in plenty in Kalyan-Bhivandi area could be fruitfully utilized for constructing ships and developing a dockyard. A Portuguese source of 1659 mentions that Shivaji built a navy at Kalyan, Bhivandi and Panvel.[2] As Kalyan creek was joined to Vasai, the Marathas required the Portuguese *cartazes* for plying their ships on the Arabian Sea. The sea from Thana to Chaul was under the control of the Portuguese. However within a period of two years, it seems, Shivaji made good progress in developing his navy, and even the Portuguese were worried about him, as the Viceroy of Goa gave orders to stop the issue of *cartazes* to Shivaji. By plundering the ports of Rajapur, Dabhol and also later on capturing them by 1661, Shivaji brought under his control the major part of Ratnagiri district, and thereby gave a threat to the Siddis as well as to the Portuguese.

A Dutch record of 1664 says that Shivaji built the marine fort on the rock island near Harney port (Ratnagiri district) and he had forty *galbats* well equipped and he built sixty anew taking advantage of the fighting between the Adilshahi rulers and the Mughals, and that he was quite friendly with the Dutch. The marine fort mentioned here is Suvarna Durga.[3] His first naval expedition, which he personally led in 1664 was against Basrur, the chief port of Shivappa Naik of Bidnur (Karnatak), and the foreign powers indirectly involved in this were the Portuguese and the Dutch, and also the English to some extent. Shivaji acted very diplomatically. He simultaneously invaded Bardesh, not to create confusion in the minds of the Portuguese, and captured Kudal, Sawantiwadi and plundered Vengurla to check the Dutch. The English were anxiously waiting for the Portuguese to get the possession of Bombay island from them, and Shivaji was waiting for the Portuguese navy to move towards the north to give effect to this order of transfer of Bombay issued by the Portuguese king. Shivaji with his armada of 85 *Shibads* and three big *galbats* assaulted Basrur and plundered it on 8th February 1665, the day on which Bombay was transferred to the English by the Portuguese. The booty thus resulting out of the sack of Surat in 1664, and Basrur in 1665 was utilized for strengthening the base of the infant Maratha kingdom in the Konkan by building a strong navy and a few marine forts.

This successful encounter against Basrur had far-reaching consequences as far as the maritime history of the Marathas was concerned. As the contemporary chronicler Sabhasad records, 'He brought his own ships, well-equipped, and led them personally'. This is the unique example in medieval history, where a king was personally leading the armada. This personal experience taught Shivaji not only the importance of navy as a limb of the state, but also the technique of naval warfare, importance of the coastal ports and marine forts guarding them, the geography of the west coast up to Bhatkal, as he had to cross many port-towns from Malwan to Basrur (a distance of about 300 kilometres by land-route), like

Vengurla, Goa, Karwar, Gokurna, Kumtha, Honavar, Ganguli, Bhatkal, etc.[4] The main objective of Shivaji's navy was to constrain the activities of the Siddis rather than to pick up quarrels with the strong naval powers like the Portuguese or the English. The Marathas had no ambition to extend their power beyond the seas, hence the question of naval conflict with any foreign power did not arise. Secondly, as the Marathas were not born traders, and the country itself was not producing any exportable commodities, the development of a mercantile flotila was not given any serious consideration by them.

Shivaji had major encounters with the Siddis from 1661 till his death in 1680. But it must be admitted here that with all his tactics, and land-victories, Shivaji could not defeat the Siddis on sea and capture their strong hold Murud-Janjira. To check the Siddis, he planned to conquer the Khanderi island, about 18 km south of Bombay, which he thought would serve as a good naval base. In October 1679, he landed on that small rocky island with men and material and fortified it.[5] This involved the English in a conflict with the Marathas. However, in spite of their superior artillery and maritime supremacy, the agility of the Marathas, and their small boats in big numbers, forced the English to withdraw, and allow them to take possession of the island of Khanderi. But the occupation of Underi island, lying close to Khanderi, by the Siddis, defeated the purpose of Shivaji, and the Siddi menace continued to threaten the Marathas through the subsequent course of their history.[6] The Portuguese who were a decadent power during the period of Shivaji, avoided major conflict with the Marathas, except some minor skirmishes arising out of some local issues.

Nothing spectacular happened from the point of view of maritime history of the Marathas during the period of Sambhaji, the successor of Shivaji, in spite of his daring and adventurous spirit. The age-long enmity with the Siddis and the Portuguese continued, but no tangible results were achieved by the Marathas during the period of Sambhaji or Rajaram against their coastal enemies. Sambhaji's effort to capture Underi from the Siddis failed miserably. The Maratha assault on Janjira fort in 1682 met with similar fate. As Sambhaji was involved in conflict with the Mughals, he could not deal with the Portuguese effectively. The Portuguese, however, wanted to remain neutral, and therefore concluded a treaty with Sambhaji in 1684, by which mutual non-aggression at sea was conceded by both the parties.[7] Shivaji was fully aware that for the development of coastal trade as well as foreign trade escorting fleets were necessary. Jadhunath Sarkar has aptly remarked, "A merchant fleet is also the nursery of a national fighting navy."[8] It is quite clear from the references in the East India Company's records that Shivaji had established commercial relations with Mocha (Western Arabia), Persia, Bussera, Aden, Muscat etc."[9] Chaul, Dabhol, Kalyan, Bhivandi, Vengurla, Pen Rajapur, etc. were the main port-towns engaged in coastal trade, during this period.[10] A factory record of 1662 mentions that Shivaji was fitting out two vessels of considerable burden which he intended for Mocha.[11] Another report of the year 1664-65 says that Shivaji had possessed himself of the most considerable "ports belonging to Deccan, to the number of eight or nine, from whence he sets out two or three more trading vessels yearly from every port to Persia, Bussera, Mocha, etc."[12] Elsewhere it is stated that 'a junk of Sevagee arrived from Aden the pasy-day with little or nought in her.'[13] A letter of 1674 mentions that he had at Rajapur four or five three-masted vessels which used to be employed in trade to Muscat and other places.[14]

As regards the articles of trade, we have not enough information, but it seems that rice and salt were the two major trading commodities. It is recorded that in the storm of 1669, several of Shivaji's ships and rice-boats were lost, "one ship whereof was very richly laden."[15] About salt, it is mentioned that 'a salt fleet having for convoy a ship of 250 tunns and some frigates' had gone to Trombay from Bombay to purchase salt.[16]

Since Shivaji's escape from Agra, and his recovery of the ceded territories, the English were trying to be friendly with him, and were hopeful of a treaty of friendship with him. The record says, "He (Shivaji) is much a friend to our nation, if to any, and exceedingly desires our trade again in his ports, and in truth his ports of Rajapur, Dabhol, Keley, etc. are of exceeding and indispensable necessity for the trade of Bombay, they yielded great quantities of goods of all sorts proper for Europe, and were cheaper than that of Surat and other places, where they were dearer by 25% than that of Rajapur". Similarly, the Company believed that the trade in Shivaji's country would consume more quantities of European commodities particularly copper and tin useful for mints. Shivaji had also promised to settle a warehouse of his merchants in Bombay, "for putting of great quantities of goods which he hath lying by him."[17]

Thana, Kalyan, Bhivandi, Alibag, Vijaydurg, Vasai and Malvan were the chief ship-building centres of the Marathas, with their dockyards at Alibag and Vijaydurg. Teak wood of fine quality required for shipbuilding was available in plenty in these areas.[18] According to Sabhasad, the chronicler of Shivaji, "He had built six types of ships like Gurabs, Galbats, Sibars, Tarandes, Tarus and Pagars... in this manner seven hundred ships were equipped in the sea."[19] It is difficult to get the numerical strength of Shivaji's navy, though we find some stray references to his 'armada' in the English records. Sabhasad says that the Maratha navy was formed into two squadrons of 200 vessels each and commanded by two admirals Darya Sarang and Mai Nahak.[20]

In 1670, as per one English report some 60 or 70 vessels of Shivaji were at the mouth of Bombay port.[21] Again, it is reported in the same year that he was with a considerable fleet at Nagaon, near Bombay.[22] "There is a report that Sevagee's armada is coming out, consisting of 6 ships and 40 gorabs" says one document of 1673.[23] In a record of 1675, it is mentioned that he had 57 small frigates, well manned to deal with the Siddis.[24] References are also found to Shivaji's great preparations at sea, equipment with men, provisions and all manner of materials.[25] It seems that the English people did not always apprehend any danger from Shivaji's fleet. According to them "his fleet consisting only of small grabbs and slight and inconsiderable boats, very ill fitted, and his men totally inexperienced to the sea."[26] However they were scared of "the deeper designs for his Armada. But his designs are so well laid and secretly carried on that no judgement can be made of them till they are executed."[27]

Shivaji was known as a great fort builder. He was born in a fort and died in a fort. To him fort was the essence of the kingdom. He, not doubt, utilized land and hills in his territory for constructing forts, but did not spare sea also when he understood the importance of navy. A modern author, James Douglas, writes, 'It was a great mercy that Shivaji was not a seaman, otherwise he might have swept the sea as he did the land.... He liked the sea, but the sea did not like him.'[28]

The *janjiras* or marine forts of Shivaji were of two types—those which were built on rocky island, surrounded by sea on all sides, but the second one were coastal forts or the head-land forts, constructed on the seashore with their entrances from the land side and rears facing the sea. Sindhudurg, Anjanwel, Yeshwantgad or Reddi, Vijayadurg or Gheria, Jayagad, Ratnagiri, Kolaba, Khanderi, were some of the major marine forts of Shivaji, either constructed or renovated and fortified by him during his period to fight mainly with the Siddis, and protect the Marathas from the European powers on the west coast.[29]

Shivaji poured a lot of money in these forts of Konkan.[30] He used latest technology by borrowing the services of skilled artisans, particularly the Portuguese, yet it must be admitted that none of his forts could surpass the Danda Rajapuri marine fort of the Siddis in any respect.[31] The main function of these forts was to serve as storehouses, and guard the sea against the activities of the enemy. This purpose must have been fairly achieved by these forts during the period of Shivaji.

Shivaji's naval policy has been epitomized by his contemporary Ramachandrapant Amatya in one of the sections in his treatise on Maratha polity entitled 'Ajnyapatra' or Royal Edict' written before 1717.[32] Jadhunath Sarkar says, 'Nothing proves Shivaji's genius as a born statesman more clearly than his creation of a navy and naval bases.'[33] While pointing out the importance of navy, Amatya, the author of *Ajnyapatra* says, "Navy is an independent limb of the state. Just as a king's fame for success on land is in proportion to the strength of his cavalry, so the mastery of the sea is in the hands of him who possesses the sea. Therefore a navy should necessarily be built". The salient features of Shivaji's naval policy as pointed out by Amatya are:

> Fast *gurabs*, neither very great nor very small should be built and should be of middle size. Large *galbats* as they are not useful without the help of wind should not be built. All naval force should be fully and well-equipped with brave and efficient fighters, guns, short guns, matchlocks, ammunition, grenades and other material of naval use (Fig. 1).
>
> Every unit of the navy comprising five *gurabs* and fifteen *galbats,* should be separately arranged under one admiral called *Sarsubha.* For the expenses of the navy the revenue of a particular territory should be apportioned to control the behaviour of the naval servants.
>
> Trade should be encouraged, as it will cause the growth of income of the state through customs. In the sea *tarandi,* (ships of the *kolis*) and merchants should be protected and allowed to move freely. If the ships of the foreign merchants, besides those of the enemy, not possessing permits, are coming and going, then they should not be allowed to move without inspection. They should be treated with sympathy and all necessary help be given to them after charging a little custom duty. If there is a big merchant, he should be treated a little more hospitably according to his importance on behalf of the government. An effort should be made to see that the foreign merchant feels assured in every way and attracted and enters into commercial intercourse with the kingdom.
>
> If the navy and the hostile ships meet each other and begin fighting, all should strive to join in the fighting. If the wind is not favourable whatever may be our strength, without coming into contact with the enemy and gradually cutting off our contact from the enemy, our fleet should be brought under the protection of a sea-fort. The safety of ships and sailors should never be risked. A treacherous enemy

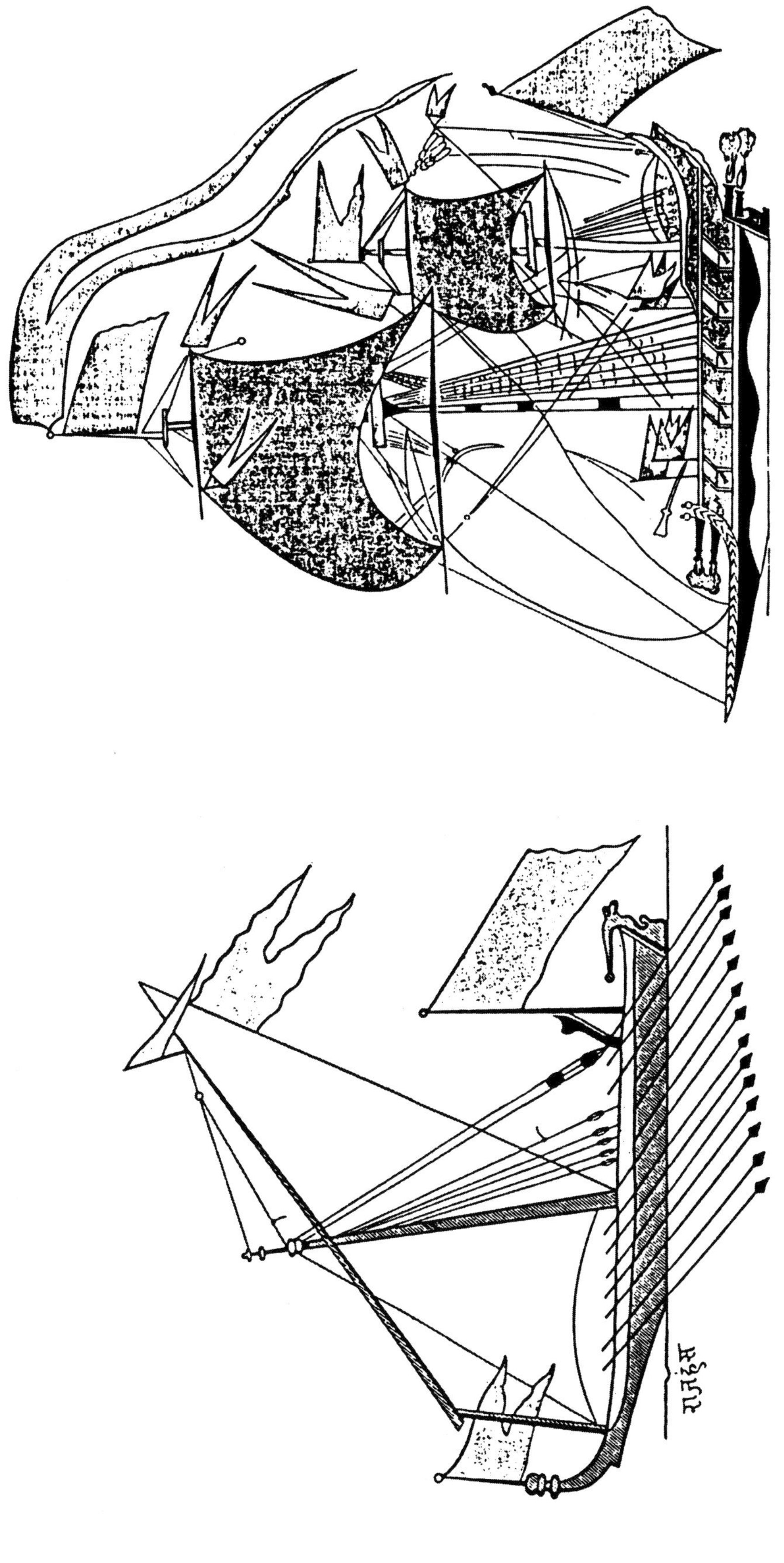

a b

Fig. 1. a, Marāṭhā *glabat Rajahams*; b, Marāṭhā gurāb (18th century AD), Apte B.K., *A History of the Marāṭhā Navy and Merchantship*, Bombay, 1973

> should not be called near, and never be trusted ever if he seeks a promise of safety.
>
> It should be done a week or two before the rising of storms, and that should not be done in the same port or under the protection of any sea-fort or in the open sea. If sheltering is done every year at one and the same port, the men of the fleet, however often warned, are sure to give a great deal of trouble to the same port of the country.... The sheltering should be done only in fortified ports.... Disorder should not at all be allowed to take place in the territory where the ships are sheltered. Trees should not be cut without royal permission.

Thus, it can be seen from the above features of the naval policy, how minutely Shivaji had worked out the details of the naval policy and how much he was interested in developing navy for political as well as economic purposes.

The subsequent history of the Marathas shows gradual departure from the policies laid down by Shivaji, in every aspect, which caused the ultimate ruin of the Maratha power. This is true of naval policy as well. Shivaji tried to institutionalize administration, but the later administrators worked for making their offices hereditary. This is how the Peshwaship became the prerogative of the Bhat family and the house of the Angres of Kolaba and to some extent of the Dhulaps as the perpetual holders of the Admirality. It is really an irony of history that the Peshwas who were the sons of the sea, not only neglected the development of navy so essential for the prosperity of their own *watan* land, the Konkan, but also became instrumental in destroying the house of Angres, with the help of the British.[34] Kanhoji Angre (1669-1729) the terror of all the powers of the west coast, was the last great Maratha seaman, who excelled in every aspect of naval leadership like personal courage, organization of navy, technique of naval warfare, etc. He was just emerging as a strong sea-fighter during the period of Sambhaji (1680-89) and was made *Sarkhel* or the Chief Admiral by Rajaram, in recognition of his successful skirmishes against the Siddis, the major enemy of the Marathas.

Division was a curse to Maratha power, and the House of *Chhatrapati* was no exception to it. After the release of Sahu from the Mughal camp, he should have legally occupied the Maratha throne, but due to the obstinancy of Tarabai, the widow of Rajaram (1689-1700) the Maratha *gadi* was divided into Satara and Kolhapur, which led to the division of loyalties among the Maratha *Sardars.* Balaji Vishwanath, the first Peshwa, succeeded in winning Kanhoji Angre to Sahu's camp, and by a treaty, Kanhoji obtained ten sea-forts and sixteen land forts, *Sarkhelship*, and a territory of 34 lakhs revenue with Kolaba as his capital.[35] This is the departure from the principle or policy of Shivaji, who was against military *saranjams,* or permanent land assignment.

Though the foreign powers denigrated Kanhoji as a pirate, he was a competent man on sea, who could subdue the Siddis, the Portuguese, the English and the Dutch. He died in 1729 at the age of 60 after firmly establishing the authority of his House in the Konkan. But later on, the dispute between his two sons Sambhaji and Manaji over property led to the destruction of the house of the Angres. Manaji was supported by the Peshwa Balaji Bajirao and also the English. After the death of the first three sons of Kanhoji namely Sekhoji, Sambhaji and Manaji, the last son Tulaji became the *Sarkhel.* He was quite successful in maintaining the integrity of the Konkan against the foreigners. But he could not fight against his own people, particularly the Peshwa. He was defeated twice by the combined forces of the Peshwa and the English first at Suvarnadurg (1755) and then at Vijaydurg (1756).[36] This practically put an end to the Maratha naval power, and the Marathas were reduced simply to a maritime community, leading their lives as fishermen rather than as naval fighters.

NOTES AND REFERENCES

1. B.G. Paranjape (Ed.), *English Records on Shivaji* (henceforth ERS), Pune, 1931, Part I: 416, p. 307.
2. P.S. Pissurlencar, *Portugez-Marathe Sambandha,* PISSU, Pune, 1967, p. 41.
3. *Shivakalin Patrasar Samgraha:* SPS (Marathi), Shri Shiva Charitra Karyalaya, Pune, 1930, Vol. I: 1023, p. 272-73.
4. For a detailed description of this expedition, please refer to T.S. Shejwalkar, *Shri Shiva Chhatrapati* (Marathi), Bombay, 1964, pp. 110-22.
5. *ERS* II : 389, p. 215.
6. Jadunath Sarkar, *Shivaji and His Times,* 5th (Ed.), Calcutta, 1952, pp. 268-75.
7. PISSU, pp. 112-15.
8. Sarkar, *op. cit.,* p. 246.
9. *ERSI,* 106, p. 97.
10. A.R. Kulkarni, *Maharashtra in the Age of Shivaji,* Pune, 1969, pp. 219-22.
11. *ERS,* I: pp. 44, 48.
12. *ERS,* I: 106, p. 97.
13. *ERS,* I: 170, p. 134.
14. *ERS,* I: p. 7.
15. *ERS,* I: 164, p. 132.
16. *ERS,* I: 189, p. 146.
17. *ERS,* I: 429, p. 315.
18. *ERS,* I: 333, p. 232.
19. S.N. Joshi (Ed.), *Sabhasad Bakhar,* Pune, 1960, p. 65.
20. *Ibid.,* p. 65; Sarkar, *op. cit.,* pp. 252-54.
21. *ERS,* I: 230, p. 167.
22. *ERS,* I: 235, p. 171.
23. *ERS,* I: 416, p. 307.
24. *ERS,* II: 131.
25. *ERS,* I-275, II: 384, 385, 472.
26. *ERS,* II, p. 6.
27. *ERS,* II: 119, p. 68.
28. James Douglas, *Bombay and Western India,* London, 1893.
29. Sabhasad, *op. cit.,* p. 68; G.S. Sardesai (Ed), *Shivaji Souvenir* (Marathi), Bombay, 1927, p. 119.
30. V.K. Rajwade (Ed.), *Marathyanchya Itihasachi Sadhane,* Vol VIII, Kolhapur, 1903, letter No. 22.
31. Shivaji had utilized the services of Portuguese artisans for building his warships, and the marine fort of Sindhudurga. See Pissurlencar, *op. cit.,* pp. 42 and 54.
32. S.V. Puntambekar (Ed.), *A Royal Edict,* translation of Amatya's *Ajnyapatra,* Madras, 1929. Please see the Chapter IX on Navy, pp. 48-52.
33. Sarkar, *op. cit.,* p. 245.
34. G.S. Sardesai, *New History of the Marathas,* 2nd Ed., Vol II, Bombay, 1958, pp. 355-66.
35. Sardesai, *op. cit.,* pp. 32-33.
36. Sardesai, *op. cit.,* pp. 355-66. For a detailed discussion about the Angres, see D.G. Dhabu—*Kulabkar Angre,* Alibag, 1939; Manohar Malgaonkar, *Kanhoji Angre : Maratha Admiral,* Bombay, 1959; B.K. Apte, *History of the Maratha Navy and Merchantships,* Bombay, 1973.

20

Trade and Politics in Eleventh Century Bay of Bengal*

HERMANN KULKE

In the year 1025 the South Indian king Rajendra Cōḷa is praised in of one of his inscriptions for "having despatched many ships in the midst of the roling sea and having caught Sangrama-vijayottunga-varman, the king of Kaḍāram [Śrivijaya], together with the elephants in his glorious army, (and) the large heap of treasures, which (that king) had rightfully accumulated."[1] The inscription moreover enumerates thirteen other port cities on the Malay peninsula, Sumatra and the Nicobar islands which were raided by the South Indian navy.

Rajendra's mighty overseas expedition against Śrivijaya was a unique event in India's history and its otherwise peaceful relations with the states of South-east Asia which had come under India's strong cultural influence since about a millennium. The reasons of this naval expedition are still a moot point as the sources are silent about its exact causes. Nilakanta Sastri concluded in his monumental work on the Cōḷas that "we have to assume either some attempt on the part of Śrivijaya to throw obstacles in the way of the Cōḷa trade with the East, or more probably, a simple desire on the part of Rajendra to extend his digvijaya to the countries across the sea."[2] The American historian G.W. Spencer interprets the naval expedition of the Cōḷas as the culmination of their politics of plunder and expansionism which the Cōḷas had been employing already since decades in wars in South India and Śri Lankā.[3] Most likely all of these explanations have a certain truth-value. But there are reasons to assume that South India's war against Śrivijaya primarily has to be seen in the much wider context of contemporary political and economic developments in the Indian Ocean.

The late 10th century witnessed the synchronous rise of three new and powerful dynasties, the Fatimids in Egypt (AD 967), the Songs in China (960 AD and the Cōḷas (AD 985), which soon began to interfere in the Indian Ocean trade system. The decline of the Abbasides of Baghdad and the rise of the Fatimids in Egypt as the dominating power of the Muslim World not only caused the shift of Muslim trading activities from the Persian Gulf

---

* This paper is based on a lecture delivered at the Department of History, Utkal University, on February 9, 1993. I am grateful to Prof. K.S. Behera for inviting me to his Seminar. An enlarged version of this paper will be published by Prof. Om Prakash in the proceedings of the International Seminar: The Bay of Bengal in the Asian Trade and Cultural Network, 1500-1800 (New Delhi, December, 1994).

to the Red Sea. It also increased considerably the importance of the Malabar coast in the hinterland of the emerging Cōḷa power. Whereas the Persian Gulf trade with India followed mainly the coastal line to the great harbours of Gujarat, ships from the Red Sea and Aden, particularly during summer monsoon, easily crossed the Arabian Sea directly to the Malabar coast of South India. In the Far East the Song dynasty from the outset began to promote and control maritime trade more successfully than any other Chinese dynasty. But India and South-east Asia, too, emerged during these decades as active participants in the international power struggle and maritime trade between the Near East and China, the terminals of Indian Ocean trade. The spectacular attack of the Cōḷas on Śrivijaya has to be seen in this broader context of the rise of new powers, the shift of trade routes and, as a consequence of these processes, a struggle for market shares.

The rise of the Cōḷas from 985 to 1025 took place in a breathtaking swiftness. From their dynastic core region in the Kaveri delta king Rajaraja subdued all kingdoms of South India with their coastal regions, penetrated into central India and conquered the off-shore islands Śri Lankā and the Maldives. In the twenties of the eleventh century his son Rajendra undertook, as a culmination of this Cōḷa expansionism, his two unique expeditions to Bengal and to South-east Asia. The Cōḷas appear to have followed a systematic plan, even though it might have evolved only stepwise. After the conquest of the whole of South India and its flourishing ports at the Coromandal and Malabar coasts, they occupied Śri Lankā and the Maldives as important maritime trading centres in the Indian Ocean, and then subdued all possible Indian opponents on the eastern coast up to Bengal (e.g. the Somavamsa of Orissa) and finally attacked Śrivijaya, which dominated South-east Asia's trade routes through the Straits of Malacca and the Sunda Straits.

During the last centuries of the first millennium AD India and South-east Asia went through similar processes of state formation which elsewhere have been subsumed under the term "from early to imperial kingdom."[4] The result of this development was an increased capacity of the state to extract socially produced surplus and to mobilize men and means. Suffice it to mention here the rise of the Rasthrakutas in Central India in 752 and of the Angkor state in AD 802. More or less simultaneously with the aggressive expansionism of the Cōḷas under Rajaraja and Rajendra, the kingdom of Angkor for the first time extended its frontiers far beyond its dynastic homelands and subjugated parts of Laos, central Thailand and the northern part of the Malay Peninsula. It soon became the dominating power in the Gulf of Siam and Mainland South-east Asia and was therefore bound to get into conflict with Dai-Viet and Champa who were competing for the control of the important maritime trade routes at the eastern coast of Mainland South-east Asia.[5] And, most important in our context, Angkor penetrated very directly into the sphere of interest of Śrivijaya on the northern Malay Peninsula. Since centuries Śrivijaya had controlled the southern part of the Malay Peninsula up to Ligor and Chaya and temporarily even the Isthmus of Kra.

Since the middle of the 11th century another "imperial kingdom" and important competitor arose in the northeastern Bay of Bengal. The kingdom of Pagan united central and coastal Burma with parts of the northwestern coast of the Malay Peninsula. Pagan was thus, perhaps for the first time in the history of South-east Asia, able to link maritime trade in the northern Bay of Bengal directly with China through its access to the land route to Yunnan. During this period Burma's relations with countries on the opposite side of the Bay of Bengal and with Śri Lankā appear to have been very strong as can be seen e.g. from the influence of Orissan architecture in early Pagan.

The Malay World of present Malaysia and Indonesia was divided between Śrivijaya in the west and the kingdom of Mataram in Java. In the early 10th century Mataram had shifted its capital from near Yogyakarta in southern central Java to northeastern Java near Surabaya. The causes of the abandonment of one of Asia's most impressive sacred spaces around the Borobudur and Prambanam are still unknown. But there are good reasons to assume that this shift aimed at the control of the fertile rice growing plains southwest of Surabaya and at a more direct access to, and perhaps even control over, the spice trade route to the Molukkas which passed along the northern coast of Java. The west of the Insulinde and its important trade routes were, since the late 7th century, under the control of Śrivijaya. Sometimes termed as a thalassocracy or "Ocean State," Śrivijaya appears to have been a confederation of habours and their respective hinterlands rather than a centrally administered agrarian state,[6] but its richness was proverbial. In the year 956, on the eve of the above mentioned rise of the new great powers of the Indian Ocean, the Arab geographer Ma'sudi reported that even the fastest ship wouldn't be able to visit in two years all the islands of this kingdom whose Maharaja extracts more profit from his own country than any other ruler of the world.[7]

The relations of the South-east Asian states with their great neighbours, India and China, were intensive but of very different nature. India was for South-east Asian countries the holy land of Buddhism and Hinduism and certainly an important trading place. But politically and increasingly economically, too, China was the undisputed "Middle Kingdom." All kingdoms of South-east Asia and particularly those which were small and harassed by their neighbours sent tributary missions to the imperial court of China.[8] For South-east Asian historiography and, of course, for the historiography of the Indian Ocean trade system it is of greatest importance that Chinese officials reported meticulously about these missions, their gifts, requests etc. Chinas own interest in the "southern barbarians" of *K'un-lun,* the countries of South-east Asia, increased considerably unter the T'ang dynasty (618-907).[9] Their rule coincided with the heydays of trans-oceanic of Arab and Near Eastern merchants in China.

The reunification of China under the Song dynasty and the rise of the Fatimides and of the Cōḷas in the second half of the tenth century initiated a new era in the maritime history of Asia. Shortly after his accession to the throne the first Song emperor issued orders for the regulation of maritime trade and revenues. About two decades later, a "Bureau of Licenced Trade" was established for buying up foreign goods which were then sold as a government monopoly. In 987 the Chinese government gave an instruction which appears to have been one of the major causes of the struggle and changes which occurred in the Bay of Bengal during the eleventh century. In this year China dispatched four missions vested with imperial authority and gifts to foreign countries to induce "foreign traders of the South Sea and those who went to foreign lands beyond the sea" to come more frequently to the Chinese ports on the promise of special facilities and import licences.[10]

Śrivijaya was the first country to react to the Chinese offer and sent a tribute mission already in the next year. But during its stay in China the mission was informed that its country has been attacked by the east Javanese kingdom of Mataram. During a stop-over in Champa the mission received the news that Mataram was still continuing its war against Śrivijaya. The mission therefore returned to China and placed Śrivijaya under imperial protection. But a Javanese embassy to China in 992 confirmed that the war was still going on.[11] The reasons of this conflict are unknown. But in this case, too, we may assume that it was caused by a competition between these two states which were most directly involved in the spice trade with China.

During these years of increasing tensions we are informed about a number of peculiar "rituo-political" donations of South-east Asian rulers to China and India. The annals of the Song dynasty report that in 1003 the king of Śrivijaya "sent two envoys to bring tribute. They told that in their country a Buddhist temple had been erected in order to pray for the long life of the emperor and that they wanted a name and bells for it by which the emperor would show that he appreciated their good intentions. An edict was issued by which the temple got the name of *Ch'êng-t'en-wan-shou* ("ten thousand years of receiving [blessings] from heaven [i.e. China]") and bells were cast to be given to them."[12] Already in the next year Śrivijaya sent again envoys to China who were followed by four embassies till 1018. Śrivijaya was obviously most eager to win China's favour.

Exactly during these years when Śrivijaya's king had a temple constructed for the welfare of the Chinese emperor, Śrivijaya entered into the same type of diplomatic relations with the Cōḷa state in South India. In the year 1005 the Cōḷa king Rajaraja donated the revenue of a whole village for the maintenance of a Buddhist shrine which the king of Śrivijaya had constructed in Nagapattinam, the major port of the Cōḷa state. The foundation stone of this shrine in the South Indian harbour might have been laid already about two years earlier in 1003, in the year when the king of Śrivijaya informed the Chinese emperor about the construction of a Buddhist shrine for his welfare. It is tempting to assume a direct connection between these two unusual and more or less synchronous deeds of Śrivijaya's king whose name Chulamanivarmadeva is clearly mentioned in both the Chinese and Indian sources. Śrivijaya obviously tried to establish friendly relations with the two big powers of East and South Asia in order to maintain and strengthen its privileged position in the maritime trade in eastern Asia. Previously China might have been more important for Śrivijaya than South India. But after the conquest of South India's ports, the Maldives and Śri Lankā, the Cōḷas controlled the central section of the Indian Ocean trade route in a very similar way as Śrivijaya dominated its southeastern section. During this period of incipient trade rivalry in the bay of Bengal both states obviously still tried to maintain their friendly relations. After his accession to the Cōḷa throne in 1014, Rajendra continued this policy. In 1015 he confirmed by a new inscription his father's donation to Śrivijaya's temple at Nagapatinam. In the same year and in 1018, he received precious gifts from Śrivijaya for a Hindu temple and its Brahmins in the Cōḷa port.[13]

During these years Angkor, mainland South-east Asia's major power, also entered into a kind of rituo-political relations with the Cōḷas. In 1012 king Sūryavarman under whom, as already mentioned, Angkor became the dominating power in the Gulf of Siam, chose a very unusual gift for the Cōḷa king. For the protection of his own royalty (*atmalakṣmī*) he presented to Rajaraja a war chariot with which he had defeated his own enemies. In this case, too, it is left to us to speculate about the reasons of the truly princely gift by the king of Angkor to his colleague on the Cōḷa throne. It is likely that Angkor has entered troubled waters with his penetration into Śrivijaya's sphere of influence on the Malay peninsula. The isthmus of Kra has always offered an alternative to the long and often dangerous maritime trade route to the Gulf of Siam through the Straits of Malacca, particularly for those merchants who wished to avoid the rather restrictive staple rights of Śrivijaya. It is quite possible that in the early eleventh century Angkor tried to reactivate the route via the Isthmus of Kra which would have diverted a part of the maritime Bay of Bengal-China trade directly through the Gulf of Siam which now had come under Angkor's control.

Our sources are silent about a direct conflict between Śrivijaya and Angkor in the eleventh century. But in the eighth century several inscriptions in Champa reported that people from Java and other islands, "men living on food more horrible than cadavers, frightful, came in ships" and desecrated temples and idols.[14] In the mid-eleventh century Sadasiva, Sūryavarman's *purohit* and brother-in-law, claims in his famous Sdok Kak Thom inscription that his forefather Sivakaivalya had consecrated Angkor's "state cult", the Devarāja cult, in AD 802 in order "to prevent his land of Kambuja from ever being [again] dependent (*āyatta*) on Java."[15] This reference in a inscription of the year 1052 shows that in eleventh-century Angkor there existed still an awareness of a possible threat from Java, which in the eleventh century context certainly also referred to Śrivijaya. It might have been this wish never to become again "dependent on Java" which induced the king of Angkor to present to the ruler of South India his own war chariot for the sake of his *atmalakṣmī*. Obviously the Cōḷas, too, meanwhile had become rivals of Śrivijaya and thus potential allies of Angkor.[16]

It is not surprising that in this period of hectic diplomatic activities of various states of the Bay of Bengal, the Cōḷas sent their first embassy to the Chinese court. It had a stop-over in Śrivijaya for several months and reached China in 1015. As this happened only ten years before the swift attack of the Cōḷa navy on the ports of Śrivijaya, one may assume that the South Indian envoys had done excellent intelligence work in view of a possible future conflict with Śrivijaya. The mission to China was a great success. The Cōḷas were recognized as a "Tributary State of the First Class," the highest possible distinction of a non-Chinese state by the imperial court. The Cōḷas had thus gained the same status as the Fatimids, Śrivijaya and Java. Together with China, these states represent the four major powers of the Indian Ocean.[17]

As already mentioned, Rajendra Cōḷa initially seems to have continued his father's policy of friendly relations with Śrivijaya as he reconfirmed his father's grant to Śrivijaya's Buddhist temple at Nagapattinam and received valuable presents from the king of Śrivijaya. But there are reasons to assume that during these years the competition between the major powers of the Bay of Bengal had increased considerably. In 1016 the east Javanese kingdom of Mataram was attacked and its capital ransacked by west Javanese troops with obvious approval or even support of Śrivijaya. For more than a decade Mataram ceased to be Śrivijaya's rival in the spice trade of the eastern islands. As if Śrivijaya was aware of its precarious position after having become the sole big power of maritime South-east Asia, it sent regularly envoys to China in 1016, 1017 and 1018.

The Cōḷas did not remain mere spectators of Śrivijaya's rise to an unchallenged regional power with control over the vital maritime trade routes in South-east Asia. They, too, started a new round of eliminating possible rivals in the off-shore islands of South Asia. In 1017 the last remnants of the ancient kingdom of Śri Lankā were destroyed. Polunnaruva with its easy access to the eastern coast and its ports became the new Cōḷa capital of Śri Lankā. In the next year Kerala with its important Malabar ports was finally subjugated and the "many ancient islands", the Maldives, were again attacked. In 1020, only five years after their first embassy had reached China, the Cōḷas sent again envoys to the Imperial Courts.[18] Few years later, in 1022/23 the Cōḷas accomplished their grand design by their victorious march through Kaliṅga up to the Ganges, eliminating all possible rivals on the eastern coast of the subcontinent.

It appears as if the Cōḷa state had been trying to copy the Śrivijayan model, i.e. to gain the undisputed control over ports and those maritime routes which passed through its sphere of influence. The exact reasons why these two major regional maritime powers of South and South-east Asia discontinued their successful rituo-political diplomaitic relations and why the Cōḷas attacked Śrivijaya in 1025 are still unknown. But apparently their competition had reached a level where their traditional means of settling conflicts were no longer valid. In the year 1023, the Chinese emperor had even urged Arab envoys to shift their trade from the Central Asian Silk Road to the Silk Road of the Sea.[19] In this situation, the immensity of stake in maritime trade might have induced the famous South India merchant guildes of the Ayyavole and Manigraman to play a more active role in this maritime big power game. They may have tried to influence the Cōḷa court in a similar way as the (British) Rangoon Chamber of Commerce exerted pressure on the British Government on the eve of the annexation of Upper Burma in 1885. But, of course, this is a mere conjecture as our sources are totally silent on this point.

The Cōḷa raid of fourteen flourishing port cities on the Malay peninsula and Sumatra appears to have shocked the counties of South-east Asia as none of them sent envoys to China for three years. In 1028 the Song emperor therefore complained that "in recent years foreign shipping rarely came to Canton". He sent instructions to the fiscal superintendent of Canton to invite the merchants to return to Canton. Already few weeks later a mission from Śrivijaya arrived and was treated with great honours. O.W. Wolters therefore rightly remarks that "Śrivijaya was still in business."[20] Although hampered by internal struggles between several port cities - most likely a result of the Cōḷa raid - Śrivijaya regained its dominant position in the western Malay world with its important Straits. It returned to its traditional means of diplomacy in order to improve its position at the Chinese court. In 1079 it donated the sheer unbelievable amount of 6,00,000 gold pieces for the repair and maintenance of a Taoist shrine in Canton.[21] From a Chinese report of the 12th century we learn that Śrivijaya "is the most important port-of-call on the sea-routes of the foreigners, from the country of Sho-po (Java) on the east and from the countries of the Ta-shi (Arabs) and Ku-lin (Quilon) on the West; they all pass through it on their way to China."

The Cōḷas appear to have been rather reluctant to convert their military success into a more permanent political dominion, for instance by the establishment of a fortified settlement of Tamil merchants in the Straits of Malacca. In fact, such a settlement of the Manigraman merchant guilde had already existed at Takuapa at the Isthmus of Kra during Pallava rule in the late 8th century.[22] After their raid of Śrivijaya the Cōḷas seem to have confined themselves to another mission to China in the year 1033. But towards the end of the eleventh century, particularly under the reign of Kulottunga I (1070-1118), the Cōḷas renewed their activities in the Bay of Bengal.[23] In 1068 they interfered again in Śrivijaya by a naval expedition on behalf of a pretender to the throne of Kaḍāram, Śrivijaya's second capital on the Malay peninsula. At the Chinese court, however, this assistance to prince of Śrivijaya did not enhance the reputation of the Cōḷas as they were now termed in official Chinese annals as a tributary or "vassal" state of Śrivijaya. This obviously false estimation might have been deliberately caused by Śrivijaya's envoys at the Chinese court. The "misunderstanding" was corrected only by a new mission of the Cōḷas to China under Kulottunga in 1077. It consisted of 72 persons most of whom being traders. They were accorded two exceptionally high privileges of protocol. Śrivijaya had to send two missions in 1079 and 1088 in order to receive the same honours.[24] The involvement of the Cōḷas and in particular of Kulottunga in the Śrivijayan affairs during these years is a controversial matter. It is likely that Kulottunga's name occurs as the name of the ruler of Śrivijaya in a Chinese transliteration in the above mentioned Cantonese donative inscription of the year 1079, as the same name occurs in the Song annals as the name of the Cōḷa king who sent the mission in the year 1077.[25] From this evidence, the renewed naval activities of the Cōḷas in 1068 and other scattered evidence one may infer that the Cōḷas supported one faction of the Śrivijayan court or one port-city of its confederating. Another faction therefore might have spread the news that the Cōḷa kingdom has become a "vassal state" of Śrivijaya. After all, this time was a period of intensive power struggles in Śrivijaya. Only few decades later Palembang lost its dominating position among the port-cities of Śrivijaya in favour of Jambi. But Indian merchants continued their trade with Śrivijaya as we know an inscription of the Ayyavole guild of the year 1088 which was found near Barus in Sumatra.[26]

Kulottunga maintained friendly relations also with the great kingdoms of Mainland South-east Asia. In the year 1114 soon after his enthronement king Sūryavarman II, the famous builder of Angkor Wat, sent a mission to the Cōḷa court which presented a precious stone to Kulottunga. And in an inscription at Pagan the Burmese king Kyanzittha (1077-1112) even claims to have converted the "Choli prince" to the teachings of the Buddha by a personal letter written on gold leaves in which he praised greatness of the Buddhist triratnas.[27] All these rituo-political missions and donations appear to have been connected with the promotion of trade as Kulottunga is the only Cōḷa king whose name is associated with a harbour. The remaining of Visakhapattanam in Andhra Pradesh as *Kulottuṅgacōḷapattanam* seems to indicate Kulottunga's interest in trade with countries on the opposite side of the Bay of Bengal, i.e. with Burma and with Cambodia via the Isthmus of Kra.[28]

The decline of the Cōḷa power since the late twelfth century by no means caused a decrease of South Indian trade in the Bay of Bengal and China. The twelfth and thirteenth centuries were a period of greatest activities of the two South Indian guilds of the Ayyavole and Manigraman merchants, mainly, of course, in South Indian itself and in Śri Lankā.[29] But Burma, too, remained a region where South Indian merchant guilds were active during this period. An inscription of the 13th century at the only Hindu temple at Pagan, which was most likely built for Indian merchants, reports a donation by a member of the South Indian *nānādeśi* merchants.[30] The weakening of the Cōḷa state since the mid-13th century allowed other kingdoms at the Bay of Bengal and their harbours to participate more actively in the

Indian Ocean trade. This can be inferred from the famous Motupalli inscription of king Ganapati of the Kakatiya kingdom in northern Andhra Pradesh who promised in the year 1244 "safety to traders by sea starting for and arriving from all continents, islands, foreign countries and cities."[31] Recent excavations at Manikapatnam, an ancient maritime habour at the Chilka Lake in Orissa, appear to corroborate the increase of Chinse trade in this region of the Bay of Bengal during this period.[32]

Particularly impressive is the thirteenth century evidence for the presence of a large South Indian merchant community in China and for Chinese traders in South India. More recent discoveries at Quanzhou (which under the Southern Song dynasty had gradually surpassed Canton as China's main port and place of large colonies of foreign merchants) have brought to light a well preserved lower portion of a Hindu temple and about 200 sculptures, all in purely late but localized Cōḷa style.[33] This temple and the large number of Hindu sculptures is the earliest known infallible evidence for the existence of a large South Indian colony in China. A bilingual Tamil-Chinese inscription of the year AD 1281 reports the dedication of a Saiva statue in yet another Hindu temple at Quanzhou. Its author might have been the son of the last Cōḷa king Rajaraja III who would have sought the help from the Chinese emperor two years after the eclipse of his dynastic fortune.[34] Two months before this dediction a Mongol envoy, Yang Ting-pi, had already been despatched to India-most likely to South India, "underscoring the reciprocal nature of this relationship."[35]

The evidence for the presence of a Chinese merchant community in South India during these years is equally impressive. Till 1867 the ruins of a three-storeyed Chinese pagoda existed in Nagapattinam. From Chinese sources we know that it was constructed in AD 1267. China thus seems to have followed the example of Śrivijaya and its Buddhist monastery at Nagapattinam. Moreover altogether 1838 Chinese coins have been discovered in the neighbourhood of Nagapattinam, most probably belonging to a coin-hoard. They are dated from the 2nd to the 13th century. The latest of them belong to a time bracket of 1265 to 1275 which corresponds exactly with the date of the construction of the Chinese pagoda. If we add to this evidence the findings of Chinese ceramics at South India, the greatest amount of which belongs to the thirteenth and fourteenth centuries,[36] it becomes clear that these centuries were a period of intensive and mostly direct trade relations between South India and China.[37]

The establishment of the Delhi Sultanate in 1206, its temporary extension to the Central and South India in the early fourteenth century, the subsequent establishment of the Deccan and Madurai Sultanates and the spread of Islam in India's ports and along the maritime trading routes in South-east Asia further increased India's importance in the Indian Ocean trade system. Through its Indian and foreign Muslim trading community India's ports became more directly linked with the "international" Muslim trade in the Indian Ocean. South Indian Muslim merchants like the Telugu Klings and Tamil Chulias were particularly active in the Malay world.[38] And moreover the conquest of Bengal by Muslim armies seem to have considerably enhanced the maritime activities of Bengal as it drew the harbours of Bengal into the orbit of the Delhi Sultanate and transoceanic trade of Muslim merchants which connected the Near East, South India with South-east Asia and China. An indication of these increased activities of Bengal trade with China are the envoys which the Sultanate of Bengal sent regularly to China during the early 15th century.[39]

In the early 15th century two events were of greatest importance and significance for the last century of the Indian Ocean trade system before the coming of the Europeans: the foundation of Malacca and the maritime expeditions of the Ming dynasty under the imperial eunch Zheng He. His six expeditions between 1405 and 1433 firmly established China's temporal hegemony over in the "Southern Sea," viz. South-east Asia, and extended temporarily China's dominant maritime position stepwise up to Śri Lankā, South India, the Persian Gulf, the Red Sea and to East Africa. Whereas Malacca during these years and initially under direct influence of Zheng He's expedition rose to the major trade centre of the Indian Ocean,[40] the Mings broke off their systematic and successful maritime expansionism as suddenly as it had begun. Both events, the foundation of Malacca and Zheng He's expeditions, were the climax of a bundle of interrelated all-Asian processes which has been exemplied in this paper by a more detailed depiction of the eleventh century struggles for political and economic domination in the Bay of Bengal. The result of these processes and their dynamics was the emergence of a close-matched network of intensive political, economic and cultural relations covering the whole world of the Indian Ocean. The very basis of this Asian maritime network were interlinked regional networks with their own distinct history in the Near East, South, South-east and East Asia. The existence of this system of distinct yet interlinked networks facilitated the swift and successful entry of the early European powers and merchants into the Indian Ocean trading system.

NOTES AND REFERENCES

1. *South Indian Inscriptions,* II, p. 109.
2. K.A.N. Sastri, *The Cōḷas,* Madras 1955, p. 220.
3. G.W. Spencer, "The Politics of Plunder: The Cōḷas in Eleventh Century Ceylon," in: *Journal of Asian Studies,* 35 (1976), pp. 405-20; idem, *The Politics of Expansion. The Cōḷa Conquest of Śri Lankā and Śrivijaya,* Madras 1983.
4. H. Kulke, "The Early and the Imperial Kingdom. A Processural Model of Integrative State Formation in Early Medieval India," in: *The State in India 1000-1700,* ed. by H. Kulke, New Delhi 1995, pp. 233-77; idem, "The Early and the Imperial Kingdom in South-east Asian History," in: *Southeast Asia in the 9th to 14th Centuries,* ed. by D.G. Marr and A.C. Milner, Singapore 1986, pp. 1-22.
5. K.R. Hall, "Eleventh-Century Commercial Developments in Angkor and Champa," in : *Journal of Southeast Asian Studies,* 10 (1979) 420-434.
6. H. Kulke, "Kadātuan Śrīvijaya'-Empire or Kraton of Śrivijaya. A Reassessment of the Epigraphical Evidence, in: *Bulletin de l'École Française d'Extrême Orient*, 80 (1993), pp. 159-80.
7. G.R. Tibbetts, *A Study of the Arabic Texts Containing Material on South-East Asia,* Leiden 1979, p. 38.
8. The report of a rather early mission from Holatan on Java in the year AD 430 is very informative for this type of East Asian diplomacy. "My country once had a large population and was prosperous and never bullied by other countries. But now the situation is different and we have become weak. My neighbours vie with each other in attacking me. I beg Your Majesty to extend Your protection from far. I also hope that there will be no trading restrictions which will affect the coming and going of our merchants. If you pity me I hope that you will send missions ordering these countries not to maltread us so that Your Majesty's reputation as the protector of the weak will be known everywhere. I hope that you will instruct the Canton officials to send back my ship and not permit

them to rob and hurt my traders. I wish hereafter to send missions every year." Liu Sung shu, 5, 33b, quoted by O.W. Wolters, *Early Commerce. A Study of the Origins of Śrivijaya,* Ithaca 1967, p. 151.

9. Wang Gungwu, "The Nanhai Trade. A Study of the Early History of Chinese Trade in the South China Sea," in: *Journal of the Malay Branch of the Royal Asiatic Society,* 31, 2(1958), pp. 1-135. See also P. Wheatley, "Geographical Notes on Some Commodities Involved in Sung Maritime Trade," in: *Journal of the Malay Branch of the Royal Asiatic Society,* 32, 2(1959), pp. 5-140 (21); Jung-Pang Lo, "Maritime Commerce and its Relation to the Sung Navy," in: *Journal of the Economic and Social History of the Orient,* 12 (1969), pp. 57-101.
10. See particularly P. Wheatley, *op. cit.,* p. 24ff.
11. G. Coedés, *The Indianized States of Southeast Asia,* Honolulu, 1968, p. 132.
12. W.P. Groeneveldt, *Historical Notes on Indonesia and Malaya Compiled from Chinese Sources,* Jakarta 1960, p. 65.
13. For the policy of the Cōḷas during the eleventh century see K.A.N. Sastri, *The Cōḷas,* Madras 1955, p. 220; G.W. Spencer, *The Politics of Expansion. The Cōḷa conquest of Śri Lankā and Śrivijaya,* Madras 1983 and K.R. Hall, *Trade and Statecraft in the Age of the Cōḷas,* New Delhi 1980.
14. G. Coedes, *op. cit.,* p. 91.
15. H. Kulke, "The Devarāja Cult," in: *Kings and Cults. State Formation and Legitimation in India and Southeast Asia,* New Delhi 1993, p. 344.
16. K.R. Hall, "Khmer Commercial Development and Foreign Contacts under Sūryavarman I," in: *Journal of the Economic and Social History of the Orient,* 18(1975), pp. 318-36.
17. K.R. Hall, *op. cit.*
18. N. Karashima, "Relations between South India and China in Cōḷa Times," in: *Professor K.A. Nilakanta Sastri Felicitation Volume,* Madras 1971, p. 69 f.
19. K.N. Chaudhuri, *Trade and Civilization in the Indian Ocean. An Economic History from the Rise of Islam to 1750,* Cambridge 1985, p. 56.
20. O.W. Wolters, *op. cit.,* p. 251.
21. Tan Yoek Soeng, "The Sri Vijayan Inscription of Canton (AD 1079)," in: *Journal of Southeast Asian History,* 5(1964), pp. 17-26.
22. K.A.N. Sastri, "Takuapa and its Tamil Inscription", in: *Journal of the Malay Branch of the Royal Asiatic Society,* 22(1949), pp. 25-30.
23. See particularly K.R. Hall, "International Trade and Foreign Diplomacy in Early Medieval South India," in: *Journal of the Economic and Social History of the Orient,* 21(1978) 75-98 and K.A.N. Sastri, *The Cōḷas,* p. 316f.
24. O.W. Wolters, *The Fall of Śrivijaya in Malay History,* London 1970, p. 93.
25. For details see Tan Yoek Seong, *op. cit.*; I am grateful to Tansen Sen, who kindly sent me a copy of his unpublished paper "Relations between China and the Cōḷa Kingdom of South India: AD 850-1279."
26. K.A.N. Sastri, "A Tamil Merchant Guild in Sumatra," in: *Tijdschrift voor Indische Taal-, Land- en Volkenkunde,* 72(1932), pp. 314-27.
27. J. Stargardt, "Burma's Economic and Diplomatic Relations with India and China from Early Medieval Sources," in: *Journal of the Economic and Social History of the Orient,* 14(1971), pp. 38-62.
28. Ranabir Chakravarti, "Kulottunga and the Port of Visakhapattanam," in: *Indian History Congress Proceedings,* 42(1981), pp. 142-45.
29. Meera Abraham, *Two Medieval Merchant Guilds of South India,* New Delhi 1988, pp. 127-181; Burton Stein, "Coromandel Trade in Medieval India," in: *Merchants and Scholars. Essay in the History of Exploration and Trade,* ed. by J. Parkar, Minneapolis 1965, pp. 47-62.
30. *Epigraphia Indica,* VII, pp. 197-198.
31. *Epigraphia Indica,* XII, p. 196.
32. For a first report see K.S. Behera ???? It is to be hoped that these promising excavations will be continued as they may reveal for the first time the great maritime importance of the Orissan coast in the Late Middle Ages.

33. John Guy, "The Lost Temples of Nagapattinam and Quanzhou: A Study of Sino-Indian Relations," in: *Silk Road Art & Archaeology,* 3(1993/94), pp. 291-310.
34. T.N. Subrahmaniam, "A Tamil Colony in Medieval China," in: *South Indian Studies,* 1978 (quoted by J. Guy, p. 298).
35. J. Guy, p. 300.
36. The same picture emerges from the few findings of Chinese ceramics which so far have become known from Manikapatnam. For South India see Y. Subbarayalu, "Chinese Ceramics of Tamil Nadu and Kerala Coasts" paper presented at the International Seminar: Techno-Archaeological Perspectives of Seafaring in the Indian Ocean (with focus on 4th *c.* BC-15th *c.* AD), New Delhi 1994.
37. Haraprasad Ray, "commodities Involved in the Trade between South India and China during Ming Dynasty (AD 1368-1644)," paper read at the International Seminar: The Bay of Bengal in the Asian Trade and Cultural Network, 1500-1800, New Delhi 1994; proceedings to be published by Om Prakash.
38. S. Arasaratnam, "The Chulia Muslim Merchants in South-east Asia 1650-1800," paper presented at the 10th Conference of the International Association of Historians of Asia, Singapore 1986.
39. T. Yamamoto, "International Relations between China and the Countries along the Ganges in the Early Ming Period," in: *Indian Historical Review,* 4 (1977/78), pp 13-19.
40. Wang Gungwu, "The Opening of Relations Between China and Malacca, 1403-5," in: *Malayan and Indonesian Studies. Essays presented to Sir Richard Winstedt,* Ed. by J. Bastin and R. Rollvink, Oxford 1964, pp. 87-104.

21

Orissa in Chinese Historical Records

HARAPRASAD RAY

Aśoka's invasion of Kaliṅga in the third century BC was a turning point in India's relation with the outside world. Aśoka was adamant to occupy Kaliṅga because of its prosperity and importance as a trade centre, controlling overseas communication. This is evident because Aśoka started sending holy unissaries throughout South-east Asia afterwards. It is possible that it was the tales of these areas brought to Pataliputra by the traders and holy people who might have used Tamralipti and the Kaliṅgan ports (may be Puri or Manikpatna on the Chilka lake) that fired the imagination of Aśoka, the great. Traders, monks or priests and the crews comprised the passengers of the boats, sailing beyond the Jambudvipa.

As a matter of fact being a Buddhist has never prevented a king from invading his neighbours and expanding the territorial borders. We have ample examples from Chinese history. The Wei Dynasty (AD 220-265), Eastern Wei (AD 534-550), Western Wei (535-556), Qi, Liang and others who were great champions of Buddhism never ceased fighting with each other till their enemies were annihilated. We have a story current about the Tang King Gao Zu (AD 618-626) who was helped in regaining his kingdom by the armed monks (*Bhikshus*) of the Shaolin monastery at Luoyang, the ancient kingdom of China.

The Earliest Phase

I would like to presume that one of the early large scale Indian exoduses was the result of Aśoka's invasion of Kaliṅga, the Brahmanic cult, under pressure from the patrons of Buddhism took refuge in the Suvarnadvipa, Javadvipa and Śri Lankā (Sinhala) with its followers.

These waves of migration were normally neither preceded nor followed by royal invasion. Early colonisation was generally a peaceful venture. The principalities in the early port towns as well as the local chiefs inland welcomed for their own reason artisans, masons, traders and also the holy men, the intellectuals of India, for exchange of goods, or royal taste, and also to arm themselves with legitimacy and recognition. The Indian scholars had very early given the country an elaborate and definitive social laws and customs through their *Srauta* and *Grihya Sutras* which were later amalgamated into the *Smritis* and other *Dharmasastras.*

The early development of Asian trade was taking place through the India-Middle east route expanding farther than Rome around 1st Cent AD with diffusion of the knowledge of the use of the monsoon winds for navigation during the 1st millennium BC. This is confirmed by archaeological and linguistic evidence.[1] At the same time the South-east Asian sailors and traders were in contact with eastern India. Archaeological evidences supporting this view during the last several years strongly suggest that there was widespread communication, including trade, all around the shores of South China by 1000 BC. This is indicated by the rapid spread of very distinctive jade ornaments, many elements of pottery decoration and manufacture, and carnelian, and then a variety of glass beads, along the coast, of northern and southern Vietnam, southern Taiwan, most of the Philippines, and except for the jade ornaments, much of eastern Indonesia, while it has not yet been convincingly proved, the only known and likely source for the carnelian, and then later, the various early glass beads, is the east coast of India around Madras. The carnelian beads start showing up in the Philippine site around 1000 BC.[2]

The acceleration of archaeological survey and excavation in South-east Asia, particularly in Thailand over the past twenty years has produced quite a number of : beads, bronzes, seals, coins, an ivory comb, ceramic vessels and so on, of western origin, which can help us to extend back to at least the middle of the first millennium BC, the physical evidence for regular exchange systems spanning the Bay of Bengal. Since the scale of Indianization in the first millennium AD was so vast that scholars like Van Leur have long believed that it must have been preceded by an extended period of regular, but less intense, and archaeologically less visible, contacts.[3]

The earliest Chinese evidence on India-China trade through South-east Asia comes from Chinese records. This was a sea-land-sea voyage. The famous passage referring to Hungzhi in one of the earlier historical works entitled *Han Shu* (History of former Han Dynasty) written by Ban Gu (AD 32-92) give definite information about trade between China and India via South-east Asia since the time of Emperor Wudi (140-87 BC) of the Former Han Dynasty, till the early part of 1st Century AD. Rhinoceros horns, elephant tusks, tortoise shells, pearls and jades, silver, copper, fruits, and cloths were the items exchanged.[4]

The Chinese traders sailed into the South China Sea in merchant ships of the foreigners known to China as the Yues (The Austronesians) who took them to the southeastern coasts of Thailand (i-lu-mo) and then to *Shenli* at the neck of the Malay peninsular for a ten-day-long overland trip to *Fugan dulu* to the west of the peninsula near Tavoy. Starting in October-November, the voyages would reach the west coast of Malayan peninsula in about ten months around June-July, and another two months sailing would take them to Huangzhi (Vaṅga, i.e. Gange). In early Christian era, another route through the Singapore strait (*Long-ya-men*) passed through Pizong on the east coast of the peninsula. This was faster as it took ten months to reach the then border of China at Xianglin (Ri-nan). From the description it appears that this route was preferred during the return voyage taking advantage of the favourable monsoon winds. Interpreters the chief among whom acted as the envoy accompanied the crew some of whom must have included private traders also.[5]

This is the first reference to South-east Asia acting as the springboard for voyagers to the eastern part of the Indian Ocean. The area visited by the Chinese is adjacent to the Kaliṅga territory, and Kharavela's expeditions into the eastern India were likely to have drawn Kaliṅga into the wide trade network of the 2nd BC to 1st Cent. AD.

Next we find the Funanese (Indo-Chinese peninsula) embassy in Tanmai (Tamralipti) looking for horses. Horses had great attraction for the emperors and kings, it was a necessity for survival against the enemies. We do not know if the Funanese king supplied to China some of the horses brought from India or the Chinese envoy from the Wu Kingdom (3rd Cent. AD) was successful in acquiring horses from India via Tamralipti. The Southern Bengal port of Tamralipti (enjoyed the prestige of an international port as vouched by the *Periplus* and Ptolemy. Terracotta objects and a large number of seals, in Kharosthi and Brahmi—Kharosthi scripts discovered in southern Bengal prove that the merchants of Kushana or Yuezhi origin exported horses and perhaps also rice to South-east Asia. The evidence of Kang Tai (3rd Cent. AD) of Wu Dynasty indicate contact between India and China through the South-east Asian kingdoms of Funan. Geying, *Ye-po-ti* (java—Sumatra). Takkola and Linyi where substantial number of Indian colonies existed as proved by discovery of Brahmi-Kharoshti inscriptions and other historical data.[6]

Whosoever were the carriers of these scripts the South-east Asians, the Kalingans and their neighbours were surely among them.

In the *Milindapanha (Questins of King Menander*) we have proofs of a network of traders existing between India and China through Takkola in the South-east Asia.[7]

Fa Xian's (Fa Hien) account (*Faxian Foquo Ji,* Record of the Buddhist Kingdom) leaves us in no doubt that Indian colonists in Java kept up the intercourse with their mother country and carried on trade with China. We learn that they were in considerable numbers already; otherwise Faxian would hardly have said that their religion was flourishing there. It is also apparent that till 5th Century AD no Chinese lived or traded there.[8]

If we link up Faxian's testimony with the records of Tang dynasty (AD 618-906) we may not be wrong in considering these Indians in Java as overwhelmingly Kaliṅgans.

From the account of the History of the Former Han Dynasty, it appears that the mutual trade between India and China brought the Indians to the China coast a little before the commencement of the Christian era followed later by the persians, on the coast of Leizhou peninsula near modern Guangzhou (Canton). This was the time when the Chinese began to trade towards the south, but arrived in the Malaya archipelago certainly not before the fifth century AD, as Fa Xian's testimony proves; probably they moved into the area much later, for their first notices of these countries look as if they had been obtained from hearsay, foreign travellers and traders, rather than from personal knowledge.[9]

The Tang-Song Upsurge

Both the (Old) History of the Tang dynasty (j 197) and the *New History of the Tang Dynasty* (j 222) mention Java as Ga-ling, the Chinese name for Kaliṅga, the Hindu settlers at the time of Tang dynasty (AD 618-906) were clearly from Orissa in overwhelming number, and as was the case with Banka (Vaṅga), Dvaravati, Ayuthia, Lavapuri (Lopburi) etc. in the South-east Asia and such places as Pandu, Vasishthasrama in Assam, and many other myriad places, the Kaliṅga settlers in Java gave the name of Kaling or Kaliṅga to Java and when asked as to their original moorings they informed the Chinese that they were Kaliṅgans. The Chinese on the otherhand, thought that the place inhabited by these Kaliṅgan was named Kaliṅga, and thus bestowed this appellation on their adopted country Java, but when they began to visit Java themselves which by all indications was not before the seventh century, they learnt its correct name and called it Java.[10]

According to the *New history of Tang Dynasty* (j 222 : 2) during AD 627-649 several envoys were sent to China, between 766-779 three envoys went to China, in 813 they presented four *Senaqi* slaves (probably Zanj) i.e. present day Zanzibar, known to India during those days as Kaliyadvipa (the Island of the Blacks, the same meaning conveyed by the Arabic name Zanzibar). Other presents included parrots of different colours, pinka-birds. The present of female musicians in 873 is significant dancer; were they the predecessors of present day *Bayijis* (musician-dancer)?

The *New Tang history* also mentions about the poisonous girls in Java known as early as *Arthasastra* in 4th century BC as *Visakanya* in India. It mentions that when one had intercourse with them, he gets painful ulcers and dies, but his body does not decay. The *History* also tells us that the ancestor of the Galing dynasty was named Jiyan, in 674 the ruler, a woman, was named *Simo* (Ximo) who was virtuous and completely devoid of any greed. *Jiyan* may stand for *Gyana* or Jina while *Simo* may be *Sima* or some similar name which can be discovered from ancient record; written archaeological or from local tradition.[11]

It is in the account of Xuanzang who visited Orissa about AD 639 that we get a clear picture of the Orissa which was divided into four regions: *Ucha* (Odra), Gong-wu-to (Kongoda), Jie-Jing-jia (Kaliṅga) and *Jiaosolo* (Kosala, i.e. South Kosala).

Xuanzang was believed to have gone to the Odra country from Raktamrittikavihara near present day Bahrampur in West Bengal. In fact Xuanzang went to Odra from Tamralipti from where it was nearly 700 lis, and not from Karnasuvarna, the venue of the Raktamrittika Vihara. There is a doubt about the identification of the capital of Odra of that time. According to some, it was at present-day; Dhauli, 7 miles (11.2 km) south of Bhubaneswar, identified with Dosara of Ptolemy, its ancient name being Tosali. From here Puspagiri *Sangharama* was on the South-west on a big mountain, i.e. Khandagiri, 4 miles (6.4 kms) west of Bhubaneswar near Khudra, known even today.[12] Identification of Khandagiri with Puspagiri is uncertain, we have to leave it to later historians and archaeologists. It is possible that, that part of the Khandagiri which contains Kharavela inscription, was the seat of the government.

Zhelidalo (Chelitala) a port of Odra formed the south-west frontier of the country. It abouted on the sea and was *Zoli* in area (6-7 kms). The note in Chinese says "in Chinese it means the city of departure". The merchant sailed out into the sea from here. The travellers came, stopped and went their way. All sorts of rare and precious articles were collected here: in its outskirt were storeyed *Sangharams,* five in number. People sailed for Sinhala from here. *Zhelidala* is identified by some with present-day Puri which might have been called Charitrapura. Waddle places it at Charitatola on the old Mahānadī delta bed 15 miles 924 kms) down the lower course of the river from Cuttack. Here on the highest point of the river opposite the Kandrapura canal remains of ancient port has been found at a village called Nendra.[13]

But both the above identifications are tenuous. They neither conform to sound nor to the historiocity of the place. Following its sound it represents *Zhelidalo.* I think *dalo is tala* which means 'lake' in India. In that case *Zheli* may perhaps represents *Chili* of *Chilika*, in which case the word will be Chilika—*tala* the lake Chilika. In Chinese transliteration it is quite normal to miss one or more sound; as for example, Lakhnauti is *Cha-na-ji*, Nasiruddin is Nading, while *Ai-ya-si-ding* represents Ghiyasuddin, and so on.[14] Although Xuanzang has been mostly correct in transcribing the names with Sanskritic origin, in this case it is possible that he missed a sound or two of the local name of the place, specially in view of the pilgrim's remark that "their spoken words, and expressions differ from Central India."[15]

If this interpretation is accepted then we can look for this port somewhere between the southern end of Chilika Lake and the sea.

From Balugaon, a simple sail boat takes one into Chilika Lake with its catamarans bearing decorative designs as well as sampans which have a distinct South-east Asian look. Separated from the Bay of Bengal by a narrow sandbar, the Chilika must have been a natural harbour for Kaliṅgan ships. Indeed, recent excavations at Manikpatna on this lake have unearthed copper coins from Śri Lankā with "Śrimad Sahasamalla" engraved on them.

Chinese celadon pieces and Roman roulette wares have also been excavated from this area. In this connection the engraving of the purely African animal giraffe on the walls of the Konark temple is very significant because in China this exotic animal was as much an object of curiosity as a good omen for bringing prosperity. The first present of giraffe to the Chinese emperor was from the independent sultans of Bengal around 1415 AD.[16] Whether this premise is correct or not will depend on digging up the ancient history of this area.

Dr. N.K. Sahu has tried to restore the world as Sritra indicating Srikshitra, the ancient name for Puri.[17] But, if the name was Srikshetra during 7th century AD Xuanzang would have transcribed it as *Shi-li-cha-da-lo* as he did in case of Srikshetra while describing it as situated northeast of Samatala.[18] Describing it as situated northeast of Samatala, i.e. Srihatta in Bangladesh for Myanmar. *Kangodamanadala* where Xuanzang went from Odra is north of Ganjam, near Chilika, the country being 2000 *li* southwest of Zhe-li-dalo, forests intervening in between.[19] Southwest of Kangoda, is *Kaliṅga* known as Dantapura. It also included a part of modern Andhra Pradesh including Mahendra Parvata where Rajendra Cōḷa's inscription has been found.[20] From Kaliṅga, 800 *li* to its northwest, was *Kosala* which had Chanda (on the north of Wardha river) or a place somewhere in Chatisgarh as capital (Wairagarh, Kanker or Raipur).[21]

The basis for China's interest in Kaliṅga could be its rich maritime trade which comprised muslins of different varieties procured from Bengal and other neighbouring countries and also locally produced, pearls, diamonds, topazes, caned chests and intricate wood carvings. The foreigners demand for jewellery was satisfied by the delicate, filigree ornaments in gold and silver made by Kaliṅgan artists. Elephants were also among the inventory of export.

The dawn of seventh century saw the rise of Islam, and at the same time the Buddhist upsurge had created almost complete Indianisation of China. It was then primarily the Central Asian route from India to China that was more in use. The northeastern route from India was also used as vouched by Vijing (late seventh century AD). The Chinese did not normally venture beyond the South-east Asian region at that time. The Indians and the Arabs were dominating the sea trade. The Kaliṅgans were settled in Java. The South Indians had also joined the trade and were spreading their network through their guilds like the Nanadesin, etc.

The Chinese shipbuilding technology had developed and they were venturing out upto the South Indian coasts; we hear about the Chinese using compass in a work called *Pingzhou Ketan (Pingzhou Chats*) of 1119 by Zhu Yu. These were the days of big ships. The Kaliṅgans, called Ho-ling or Jia-ling, were the principal traders in Java, Sumatra and China even during the early 12th century as confirmed by Zhu Yu who says that "On large *Jailing* (Kaliṅga) sea-going ships every several hundred men, and on small ones a hundred and more men, choose one of the more important traders as head-man, who with an assistant headman manages various matters".[22] These ships were not Chinese either in build or crew.[23] They traded between Quanzhou in China and the Arab countries in the West.[24]

Before probing further into Orissa's place in Chinese records. I would like to give details of the commodities involved in trade between India and China with South-west Asia forming the nexus. Although these details are for the period AD 960-1279 when the Song dynasty was in power and even upto the end of the Mongol dynasty (from 1279-1368), the power that shook the world for a time and whose successors after being converted to Islam ruled over India as the Mughals for more than three centuries. The same Mongols were overthrown by the Chinese national power merely within 90 years. The inventory of trade does not differ much in the following centuries of 14th to 16th century and after. Some of these items may even have been exported from Utkal.

The primary focus of trade until 11th century was the Chinese market, and the commodities involved reveal their source and the different producing centres. West Asian origin included higher quality aromatic essences, exotic animals and glasswares. Śri Lankā, the island of gems (*Ratnadvipa*) was there, South-east Asia provided forests products like benzoin, pine resin, dragon's blood (from *Daemonorhops*, Blume, or climbing rattan),[25] camphor, nutmeg, (*jatikosa*, Malayan *pala,* Chinese: *roudou kou*) and clove. Bronze-casting was in advanced stage in India, and judging from its scale, it will be natural to conclude that the tin of India must have entered into the sinews of commerce.[26] Later accounts, specially the 15th century travelogues repeatedly report that many of these forest products were being manufactured and processed in the forest areas of India, especially in Kerala.

Cinnamon was obtained from various species of laurel growing in China, Tibet, Burma, Śri Lankā and India, the Himalayan and the Malabar area being the best source. Zhao Rugua (13th Century) the Chinese author ascribed the home of cardamom to a variety of centres, such as, Cambodia (Kampuchea), the northern part of the Malay Peninsula, Java, Sumatra, Śri Lankā and the Coromandel (Cholamandalam).

Among dye-stuff, lac a red dye with a greater affinity for silk than cotton, was native to Pegu, Siam and Assam, the Pegu product being the best quality having demand in India and China. Indian rhinoceros and its horns formed one of earliest prized exports, and we hear from the poets of China that they adorned the imperial gardens of Han China. Tortoise shell, ivory and pearls were exported by the Indian merchants, but they surely had variety of sources extending from Somali and Berbera coasts to India. The parrots, specially the Indian ring-necked parakeet was a prized item because of its skill in imitating human speech. The Indian traders surely did good business in myrth (*quggula*). The Timor and Samban white sandalwood famous for its fragrance did get exported to China along with the Indian red variety used for colouring, construction and medicinal purposes.[27] Steel swords were dispersed through India in a large quantity. The black pepper (*piper nigrum*) the most important commodity exported to China was a native of Kerala from where it appears to have been introduced into Java also.[28]

Cotton textiles produced in Bengal, parts of Bihar and Orissa, the coastlines of Andhra Pradesh and Tamilnadu and Gujarat, played an important role in India-China trade. Those produced in South-east Asia did not count for much and the region had to depend mainly on India for this trade with China.

The items which clearly had an exclusively Indian provenance in India-South-east Asia—China trade were diamonds, carnelian, madder of the kind obtained from *Rubra cordifolia*, Linn, indigo and putchuk. Foodgrains, sugar and timber which earlier moved from the west coast of India to the West, started flowing into the China market but in this venture the increased supply from South-east Asia of forest products was naturally possible.[29]

The above inventory may possibly give some indication as to why some areas slid gradually into secondary place. The South Indians who included a part of the then Kaliṅga region were there with the Arabs. It is possible that the long distance trade (*Longue duree* of Braudel) involving the trade ports from the Mediterranean upto China's south and south-east coast was dominated by the rich adventurous and large ship owners like the Karamis, the Jews, the Ehettys and others. Orissa's share has yet to be worked out.

Particulars in the trade of China comprised Arabs, (including the Persians), Jews, the *Kunlun* merchants of the South-east Asia and the Indians. Indian literary references indicate Indian participation in trade in the South-east Asian and China sectors since very early times. On the basis of iron objects found at Taungthaman, Myanmar (Burma), and onyx and carnelian found in the Tabon caves, Palawan, Myanmar, it has been concluded that commercial links between India and this part of South-east Asia existed in the fifth century BC.[30]

The nature of Indian participation in this trade needs to be delinked from the historiography of Indianization of South-west Asia; the Indians participated in trade. Indic modes, materials and spiritual, followed in an extensive and diverse fields. The comings and goings of traders in transit increased Indian participation in South-east Asian life. Many scholars have expressed their opinions on Indianization of South-east Asia. Lately scholars have started focussing on the fact that it was the exigency of state formation which encouraged Indonesian potentates to adopt policies aimed at engendering forces leading to increased Indianisation.[31] A lot has been said and theorised on Indianisation of South-east Asia and the exercise is still continuing.

The *History of Song Dynasty* (AD 960-1279)[32] call Bali as the country of the Brahmanas, although Brahmanism has been supplanted by Buddhism to a great extent. Their Kings used to send Embassies to the Chinese court between 992 and 1132 with presents like ivory, pearls, silk embroidered with flowers and gold, silk of different colours and designs, tortoise shells, betel trays, short swords with hilts of rhinoceros-horn or gold, rattan mats plaited with figures, white parrots and small pavilions made of sandalwood, adorned with all kinds of precious materials.[33] How many of these Brahmin population comprised the Kaliṅgans and Odras is difficult to assert, but some of the articles like ivory, pearls, cotton goods, betel trays, mats and parrots were surely from these areas. This is because the products mentioned as coming from Bali or other countries must not be taken too literally. The Chinese as a rule did not ascertain whether the articles which they found or which were brought to them, were really produced by the country itself. However mention has been made of silkworms being reared by the Javanese and this deserves our attention. It also shows that substantial part of Indian export of cotton fabrics of different varieties went to China through these insular areas. It is also very likely that textile products were being manufactured in these Kingdoms also. The Indians particularly those belonging to South Indian guilds possibly controlled these centres.

It is an interesting thing to note how these Indians who were Kaliṅgans in the earlier periods were by and by supplanted by their neighbours, the Andhras and the Tamils. I think the political situation in these areas was behind such vicissitudes. I draw the attention of the scholars to the necessity of probing these human migrations in depth.

The Yuan Continuation and Ming Recession

After early 12th century, the next appearance of the name of Orissa is to be found in Wang Dayuan's *Daoyi Zhilue* (Records of the Foreign Lands) compiled in 1350 after the author had visited the countries of the South-east and South Asia, as well as some of the Central Asian countries. The country has by then acquired its present name from Udra or Odra. It is now called *Wu die* in Chinese.[34] The first sentence in the notice is translated as, "it is the old name of *Yinjiali*.[35] It seems that this is due to a wrong reading by omitting the first character *guo* (the doubt having arisen because of its meaning being "country"). We think the four characters *quo-yin-jia-li* stand for the country's name. The second character which should be *ling* has been wrongly written as *yin* due to the copyist's error or the author's negligence. Thus it should read as *quo-ling-jia,* the fourth character *li* having been interpolated. *Guo-ling-jia* is the ancient Kaliṅga which was written in the earlier dynasties as *Ho-ling* or *Jialing*. The sentence should then mean, "it is the old name of Kaliṅga." This is also a mistake which is very natural for a foreigner who is not likely to know that they were two countries for a long time before Odra, present-day Utkal—Orissa, replaced the other names.

The country is described by Wang as bare and swampy, its hills and woods, are rare. The people depend on agriculture, the soil being fertile gives three bumper harvest in a year. The people are honest and more prosperous than their neighbours. The taxes are one-tenth. The natural products include kingfishers feathers, wax, cotton and fine textiles.[36] The Chinese paid for these items with gold, silver, coloured satins, white silks, cloves, nutmeg, white and blue chinaware, drums, lutes, etc.[37]

The author also gives the weight of Orissa silver coins as 2.8 *gian* i.e. about 14 grams (present standard), 10 such coins being equivalent of 10 *liang* worth of Chinese paper money (i.e. equal to half kilograms of today). Each silver coin fetched 11,520 cowries. Each unit of 250 cowries. Each unit of 250 cowries could buy one "pointed basket" of cooked rice. On an average 73 *dou* (bushels), 6 *sheng* (pint) (1 *sheng*=1 litre, 10 *sheng*=one *dou* (bushel), i.e. 736 litres of rice could feed two men for a year comfortably. The prosperity of the country drew the Chinese to its ports, and 90% of those coming did not return, so easy it was to gain a livelihood there.[38] This is the testimony of the Chinese who visited the place personally.

Orissa's prosperity in 14th century depended on its rice trade; both the Northern Maldive Islands,[39] and Kozhikotte[40] depended on Orissa for their supply of foodgrains which was carried to their ports by the Orissa traders; in exchange, the traders used to carry a shipload of cowries to Orissa and Bengal where they could get more than a shipload of rice. This is how cowries became the ordinary folks currency in Orissa and Bengal till the end of 19th century.

By the turn of the fifteenth century, Orissa's rice trade was still very extensive, some of the rice eating states like Pandaraina on the Malabar coast (named *Da Ge-tan* in Chinese) depended entirely on the Malabar coast (named Da Ge tan in Chinese) Orissa for their yearly supply of rice.[41] We also find the modern name Orissa being included in the sailing charts of the Chinese sailors as given in the *Mao Kun Map* which is a part of *Wubeizhi* (Weapons Manual. Folio 10) at about 20° 25 N, 85° 57' E. Manikapatna is also given in the *Mao Kun Map* as *qu-ba-dan* at 19° 43 N, 85° 28' E while Puri is shown there as Orissa Pagoda (*Wu-li-she ta*).

After these official records and travelogues we come to the age of the European when not only inter-state relation between the Asian countries is jeopardised, the trade system based on the free market operation is thoroughly sabotaged and the countries are separated from each other, the soldiers from India are taken to fight against the Chinese during the wars of 1840 (Opium), 1856-60 (the period of the Heavenly Kingdom) and 1901 (Boxer), which created distrust against the Indians among the Chinese. The dawn of Independence in 1947 and the birth of National Governments in both the countries brought both India and China closer to each other inch by inch a process which is still continuing.

The recent discoveries of Chinese celadon, porcelains and coins confirm the written records bequeathed to us from China. The excavations of Khalkatapatna (86° 4' 4" E, 19° 51' 13" N) on the left bank of the Kushabhadra river in Puri district and at Manikapatna on the left bank of the water channel connecting the Chilka lake with the Bay of Bengal, have yielded Chinese celadon and blue and white porcelain wares belonging to the period between 12th and 14th centuries. Two Chinese copper coins, one complete and the other damaged with square perforation in the middle and inscription in damaged Chinese characters will throw' further light on overseas maritime activities of Orissa and its relation with China. The celadon sherds from the Barabati Fort, Cuttack, assure Cuttack a place in the maritime map. Some of the examples may be from 16th cent. and even later period. They are to be carefully studied with the help of Chinese scholars.

I have seen hundreds of sherds which represent the rough to finest examples of Chinese celadon and procelains ranging from 14th to 16th centuries and later. The proper study of these procelains will establish the historiocity of Orissa ports like Manikapatna which I would like to identify with Chilkatala i.e. Zhelidalo of Xuanzang, and other ports like Kaliṅgapattanam, Palour (of Ptolemy), Gopalpur, etc.

Echo of the Maritime Past

Most Orissa rivers have a Goddess of navigation installed at the mouth of a river. Chitresvari is worshiped at Kauda on the Budhabalong river in Balasore. Kakat Mangala is another deity connected with sailing. Villagers at Jharpipal and Sarupipal claim that many families from the areas went to Java and Sumatra. At Palur in Ganjam, locals talk of the lighthouse which was on the top of one of the hills. Buoys have been found on the river Baitarini and the remains of a Port Office at Chandbali point to maritime activity in the area.[43]

During the full moon day of November (month of Kartika in India) the plump white moon casts its glow on the crowds which move to the water's edge holding gaily coloured paper boats. A ritual dip is made and then the boats are set afloat. And as these paper boats bob on the Mahānadī waters (which flow in to the Bay) each with obligatory oil lamp, an annual pageant is re-enacted in memory of Orissa's spirit of seafaring. The sister keeps fast, draws rice powder ships with waves around, recounts her pining for her brothers who are fare away across the seas, and pray to the goddess Mangala who protects the sea farers for the safe return to the brothers, many of whom perished in rough seas. This celebration commemorates a distinguished period in Kaliṅgan history when merchants set sail for distant lands in South-east Asia. This is known as the festival of *Bali Jatra,* the voyage to Bali.[44] What more poignant memory can there be than this traditional festival of South-east Asian nexus in Sino-Indian Trade.

NOTES AND REFERENCES

1. Charles Verliden, "The Indian Ocean. The ancient period and the middle ages" in Satish Chandra, ed., *The Indian Ocean: Explorations in History, Commerce and Politics,* Delhi, 1987, pp. 27-35.
2. Wilhelm G. Solheim II, "Remarks on the 'Indianization' of Funan: An economic history of South-east Asia's first State," *Journal of South East Asian Studies,* 14, 1983, pp. 169-70.
3. Ian C. Glover, "Recent archaeological evidence for early maritime contacts between India and South-east Asia," Paper presented at the *Techno-archaeological Perspectives in sea faring in the Indian Ocean,* NISTADS, New Delhi, 28th Feb.—3rd March, 1994, p. 1.
4. Hanshu, J. 28B, *Zhonghua Shuju* edn. Vol. 6, pp. 669-71.
5. Haraprasad Ray, "The Identity of Hauangchiki : An ancient Indian Kingdom in intimate contact with Han China," *Indian Historical Review,* 17, 1-3, 1993, pp. 1-34.
6. B.N. Mukherji, *Kharoshti and Kharoshti-brahmi Inscription in West Bengal (India).* Indian Museum Bulletin No. 25, Calcutta, 1990, p. 34.
7. *Ibid.:* also, Xu Yunqiao, Ed. *Kangtai Wushi Waiquo Zhuan Jizhu (Collection of Kangtai's Notices on Foreign Countries during Wu dynasty with Annotations),* Singapore, 1971, pp. 17-24.
8. W.P. Groeneveltd, *Historical Notes on Indonesia and Malaya Complied from Chinese Sources,* 1887, reprinted, Jakrata, 1960, p. 8.
9. *Ibid.,* p. 2.
10. *Ibid.,* p. 15.
11. *Ibid.,* pp. 13-4.
12. Ji Xianline, *et al.* Eds. *Da Tang Xiyu Ji Jiaozhu, Tang Xuanzang Bianji Yuanzhu (Xuanzang and Bianji's journey to Western Region during the Tang dynasty Annotated),* Beijing, 1985, pp. 812-13, 815.
13. *Ibid.,* p. 816.
14. Haraprasad Ray, *Trade and Diplomacy in India-China Relations: A study of Bengal during the Fifteenth century,* New Delhi, 1993, pp. 60-61.
15. Ji Xianlin *et al. op. cit.,* p. 812: Samual Beal, *Si-yu-ki, Buddhist Records of the Western World,* reprinted, Delhi, 1969, II, p. 204.
16. Ray, *op. cit.,* p. 72.
17. K.S. Behera, "Xuan Zang and Cultural Communication between China and Orissa in Eastern India," Paper read at the *International Symposium On Xuanzang Studies,* at Yanshi and Xian, China, 16-20, April 1994, p. 6.
18. Ji, *et al., op. cit.,* p. 803.
19. *Ibid.,* p. 817-18.
20. *Ibid.,* pp. 819-25.
21. *Ibid.,* pp. 823-24.
22. Zhu Yu, *Pingzhou Ketan* (Pingzhou Chats) (AD 1119). Congshu Jicheng Chubian edn., bk. 2754, p. 2.
23. F. Hirth and W.W. Rockhill, *Chau Ju-kua: His work on the Chinese and Arab Trade in the Twelfth and Thirteenth Centuries,* entitled *Chu-fan-chih,* 1911, reprint, New York, 1966, p. 31, n. 4.
24. *Ibid.,* pp. 78-79.
25. O.W. Wolters, "The *Po-ssu* Pine trees," *Bulletin of the School of Oriental and African Studies,* 23.2. 1960, pp. 327, 333-34.

26. Lotika Varadarajan, "Indian Participation in the trade of the Southern Seas," in Satish Chandra, ed., *op. cit.,* pp. 51-52.
27. P. Wheatley, "Geographical notes on some commodities involved sung maritime trade," *Journal of the Malayan Branch of the Royal Asiatic Society",* 32, 1959, pp. 65-67.
28. Wolters, *Early Indonesian Commerce,* New York, 1967, pp. 136-37; Wheatley, *op. cit.,* p. 107; S.M.H. Naimar, *Arab Geographer's Knowledge of South India,* Madras, 1942, pp. 34-35, 46, 103, : J. Innes Miller, *The Spice Trade of the Roman Empire,* Oxford, 1969, pp. 80-81, 83.
29. A Lewis, "Maritime Skills in the Indian Ocean," *Journal of the Economic and Social History of Orient, (JESHD*), 16, 1973, pp. 256-57.
30. J. Stragardt, "Burma's economic and diplomatic relations with India and China from early medieval sources," *JESHD,* 14, 1971, pp. 43-48; also see Vardarajan, *op. cit.,* p. 95, n. 28.
31. Wolters, *op. cit.,* 1967, pp. 240-47; K.S. Sandhu and P. Whealtly, eds. *Melaka,* Kuala Lumpur, 1983, pp. 4-7; also Varadarajan, *op. cit.,* p. 96, n. 30.
32. Tou Tou and Ouyang Xuan, *Sonqshi* (History of the Song dynasty), Tongwen Shuju edn, j. 489.
33. Groeneveldt, *op. cit.,* p. 17.
34. Su Jiqing ed., *Daoyi Zhilue Jiaoshi [Records of Islands (By Wang Dayuan) Annotated]* (1350), reprinted, Beijing, 1981, 377-78.
35. W.W. Rockhill, "Notes on the Relation and Trade of China with the Eastern Archipelago and the coast of the Indian Ocean during the Fourteenth Century," *T'Oung Pao,* 16, 1915, p. 444.
36. Su Jiqing, *op. cit.,* pp. 375-76.
37. *Ibid.,* p. 376.
38. *Ibid.*
39. *Ibid.,* p. 264.
40. *Ibid.,* p. 325.
41. Feng Chengjun, ed., *Xingcha Shenglan Jiaozhu (Overall Survey of the Ocean Shores (by Fei Xin) Annotated),* (1436), repreinted Taipai, 1970, *Houji,* p. 16).
42. J.V.G. Mills, *Ma Huan: Yingyai Shenglan. The Survey of the Ocean's Shores)* (1433) Hakluyt Society, London, 1970, p. 289.
43. For boats, etc. of Orissa see, Sila Tripati, "Traditional boat building and navigational techniques of Southern Orissa," *Journal of Indian Ocean Studies,* 3, 1, 1995, pp. 66-79; see also, Sunil Kumar Patnaik, "Trade routes and communication pattern of ancient Orissa," *Indica,* 30, 1 & 2, 1993, pp. 47-55.
44. See, *Ibid,* p. 50.

22

Traditional Navigational Landmarks on the East Coast of India

B. ARUNACHALAM

Much before the compilation of coastal marine surveys and mapping of the Admiralty naval charts on the Indian Coast, Indian sea-farers have been using conspicuous landmarks for identification of different sections of the coast and recognition of specific port locations during coasting voyages as well as overseas voyages. While sailing along the coast off-shore at a visible distance from land or while approaching the shore it is necessary to constantly identify specific landmarks such as the mouth of a river, the vegetation character, the hills in the horizon, the skyline profile or any built up feature that stands out strikingly, for knowing the whereabouts of the vessel and its location fix, for purpose of safe and sure course of navigation. Even offshore reefs and rocks, bars and banks, islands, and even the nature of bottom sediments like sand and mud on the sea floor, apart from the visible signs of nature of sea-life are all practically useful indicators.

On the east coast of India stretching between Kanyakumari in the south and the Ganges mouth, seafarers native to this coast as well as those from west coast of India frequenting the Bay have used such landmarks for identification in the mediaeval past. Compared to the west coast of India, the east coast has relatively fewer port locations and also fewer identifiable landmarks. This is due to the fact that the coasts in the Bay of Bengal are low and shelving over long distances with intervening stretches of large river deltas. The shore is mostly associated with plantations of coconut palms, alternating with belts of sand dunes and hills where it is low and shelving; tidal mangroves and salt marshes adjoin river mouths extensively. Because of this low character of the coast, and the retreat of the hill line inland, away from the sea any cultural feature, isolated hills and topographical features stand out as useful landmarks. The low gradient of the sea-floor in the inshore waters makes it a marked surf zone and shoals and banks occur at frequent intervals at depths less than 10 fathoms. The river mouths are mostly bar-ridden and the bars and spits are all of a shifting character. As a result, the entire coast is relatively more dangerous to approach except in known waters, and it is in this context landmarks gain significance. In coasting voyages, the vessels have to keep at a distance in fairly deep water and approach the shore only through rehearsed channels.

The accompanying map depicts all the significant and conspicuous landmarks that have been traditionally used by the seamen on the East coast over the centuries, prior to the completion of systematic charting of the coast in the 19th century. The information compiled in this map is drawn from literary references, sailors' manuals, especially of the seamen of Gujarat and Kutch who have visited the different sections of he coast in the 16th to 18th centuries and travel accounts. On account of the general low sky profile of the coast, wherever the coast is relatively bold in relief or is backed by even a low plateau, such an area stands out prominently in relief as for example the high coast between Bhimlipatnam and Visakhapatnam and to a distance further south, as well as between Kaliṅgapatnam and Barava; sea-cliffs and headlands thus become useful for local identification. The SW-NE orientation of this coast, while proceeding in a northerly/southerly voyage brings in sharp focus this bold relief of the coastline. Visakhapatnam itself is identified by the Dolphin Nose, the cliff headland along the shore front. The *Nagari Nose* to the south end of the nagari hill-ridge is a conspicuous landmark used for fixing the location of Pazhaverkadu (Pulicut) while sailing from the south. The ridge running parallel to the coast also aids in locating Kistnapatnam in south Andhra coast. The hill at Thirukazhukunram (with a temple on its top at present) known to the Europeans as the Finger Peak or the Sadras Hills was a striking landmark for approach to Chaturangapatnam (Sadras) from the south, in line; it is also sighted behind as well for Mahabalipuram (Seven Pagodas) for a considerable distance offshore. Similarly, the St. Thomas Mount with its church spire on top together with the cathedral spire of San Thome and the twin temple gopurams of Mylapore and Tiruvallikeni hail the approach of Madras from the south, till the Fort St. George was seen. The Simhachalam Hills in the back-drop of Visakhapatnam, and the Nilguri Hill in the backing hinterland of Baleshwar (Balasore) are prominent hill features readily recognisable, giving identity to the ports in their foreground. The Sugar Loaf Hill behind Pentakonta is again a striking landmark. The isolated Santapilli peak behind the coast in a northwesterly rhumb, when viewed from south of the coast is not only the identity indicator of Santapilly port, but also an indicator of caution for approach to the port in that rhumb, on account of the Santapilli rocks in the foreground.

Cultural features have provided traditional navigational landmarks over a long period of time in the navigational history of the east coast especially in the low plains and delta zones. The shore temple and the Olakanneswar temple (Old Light House) behind have been a useful combination used to identify the port of Mahabalipuram during the Pallava period. The Shore Temple was further a pointer to the dangerous rocks to its south. Three circular temple domes appearing in line, with the tallest as the western most while approaching from the south in a NNW rhumb is a location pointer to Jaganath Puri (called the Jagat of the East Coast) by the west coast seamen. These temple spires appears to segregate on approaching the shore closer in a NW rhumb until they become three individual features quite close to the shore. The singular Black Pakoda to the north of Jaganath Puri is the famous Sun Temple of Konarak. The port of Paringpettai (Porto Novo) is always identified by the four temple gopurams of the temple of Chidambaram appearing to the SW of it and in line with the woods on the mouth of the Kollidan river. The two temple spires of Tirunagari and Tiruvenkadu help in identifying the old port location of Tirumullaivasal. Similarly, the church spire is an identification landmark for the ports of manapadu as well as Tuttukudi (Tuticorin). While the mediaeval part of Nagapattinam is recognised by a temple, the five minarets of the mosque painted white are used to identify the port location

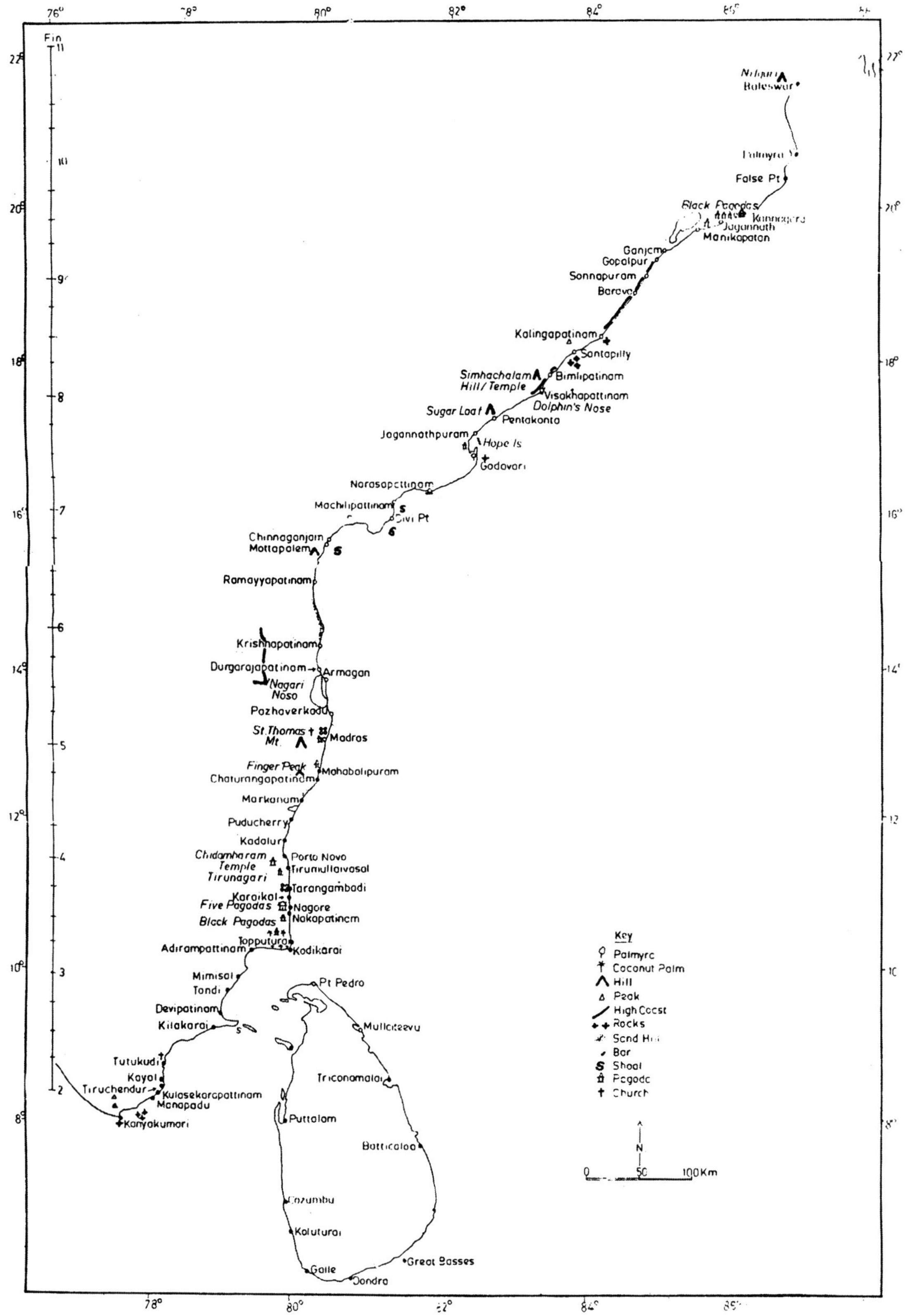

Fig. 1. Map showing significant landmarks on the East Coast

of Nagore. Tarangambadi (Tranquebar) and Cuddalore are identified by their forts on the sea-side, while the skyline of built-up promenade is used to identify Puducheri (Pondicherry). A few locations are identified by vegetation character, in the absence of other conspicuous features. An isolated thicket of Palmyras was used to identify Point Palmyra on the Orissa coast, as distinct from the False Point. Godavari (Coringa) and Hope Island are identified by the appearance of dense mangroves. So too, Kodikarai is recognised by the abrupt turn of the coast, and the mangroves giving place to coconut plantations. Offshore shoals and banks indicate the proximity of ports of Ganjam, Machhilipatnam, Motapalli, Durgarajapatnam, Kilakkarai and Pamban. Rocky reefs characterise the neighbourhood of Manapadu, Santapalli and Kaliṅgapatnam. The shiny reddish low laterite plateau backing the coast provides a distinction to the coast between Guddalore and Markanam.

Limited as these traditional navigational landmarks are, they have served the useful purpose of directing navigation in the historical past of the East coast. These traditional landmarks still continue to serve the interests of country-crafts, inspite of the coming in of light houses and beacons in the 19th and 20th centuries.

List of Contributors

I. Wayan Ardika
Post Graduate Department of Anthropology, Faculty of Letters, Udayana University, Denpasar, Bali, Indonesia.

B. Arunachalam
Department of Geography University of Bombay, Mumbai.

Kishor K. Basa
Post Graduate Department of Anthropology, Utkal University, Bhubaneswar.

K.S. Behera
Professor and Head Department of Ancient Indian History, Culture and Archaeology Utkal University, Bhabaneswar.

U.N. Dhal
Former Head, Post Graduate Department of Sanskrit, Utkal University, Bhubaneswar.

M.K. Dhavalikar
Retired Director, Post Graduate and Research Institute, Pune.

N.C. Ghosh
Retired Professor and Head of Department of Ancient Indian History, Culture and Archaeology, Visva-Bharati, Santiniketan.

Lallanji Gopal
Former Head, Department of Ancient Indian History, Culture & Archaeology, Banaras Hindu University, Varanasi.

Eric Kentley
National Maritime Museum, Greenwich, U.K.

A.R. Kulkarni
Professor Emeritus Vice-Chancellor Tilak Meharashtra Vidyapeeth (Deemed University) Gultekadi, Pune.

Hermann Kulke
Chair of Asian History, Kiel University, Germany.

B.N. Mukherjee
Carmichael Professor of Ancient Indian History, Culture, University of Calcutta, Calcutta.

A.N. Parida
Reader, Post Graduate Department of Ancient Indian History, Culture and Archaeology Utkal University, Bhabaneswar.

G. Victor Rajamanickam
Principal Investigator, CSIR Project Head, Department of Industries and Earth Science, Tamil University, Thanjavur.

K.V. Raman
Professor and Head Department of Ancient History and Archaeology,University of Madras, Chennai.

Haraprasad Ray
School of Languages, Jawaharlal Nehru University, New Delhi.

I.K. Sarma
Former Director, Salarjung Museum, Hyderabad.

B.K. Sinha
Superintending Archaeologist (Retd.) Excavation Branch, A.S.I., Bhubaneswar.

R. Sivakumar
Research Fellow, CSIR Research Project on *Indigenous Traditions of Navigation in Indian Ocean,* Tamil University, Thanjavur.

Haryati Soebadio
Former Minister, Social Welfare, Government of Indonesia, Indonesia.

L.N. Swamy
Research Fellow, CSIR Research Project on *Maritime History on South India*, Tamil University, Thanjavur.

V. Vitharana
Retired Professor in Sinhala, Ruhuna University, Sri Lanka.

PLATES
(PHOTOGRAPHIC DOCUMENTATION)

A. Deities Associated with the Ocean and Navigation

Pl. 1. Varuṇa, Bhubaneswar, Orissa State Museum

Pl. 2. Lakṣhmī, "daughter of the milky ocean", Pitalkhora, c. 2nd century BC, Prince of Wales Museum

Pl. 3. Avalokiteśvara as a saviour from perils, including of ship wreck, Kanheri

Pl. 4. Aṣṭamahābhaya Tārā, as a saviour, among others, from ship wreck, from Ratnagiri, Orissa

Pl. 5. Viṣṇu Anantaśāyīn, Dasavatar temple, Deogarh

Pl. 6. Viṣṇu Anantaśāyīn, on the bank of the Brchmani river at Sarang, Orissa

B. The Indus Civilization Period

Pl. 7. Ship on a stone seal, Mohenjo-daro (after Mackay)

Pl. 8. Ship on a terracotta amulet, Mohenjo-daro

Pl. 9. A Dockyard, Lothal

Pl. 10. Persian gulf seals, Lothal

Pl. 11. Model of a terracotta boat, Lothal

C. Indo-Roman Period

Pl. 12. Roman amphora, National Museum, Rome

Pl. 13. Fragments of Roman amphoras, Arikamedu

Pl. 14. Fragments of Arretine dishes, Arikamedu

Pl. 15. Yavan Couple, Pitalkhora, c. 2nd century BC

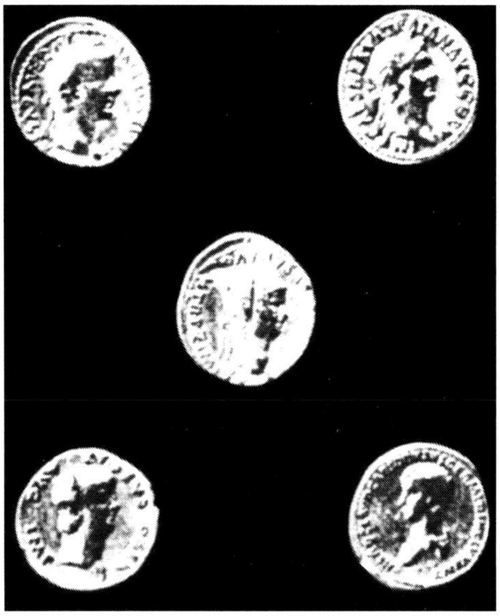

Pl. 16. Roman coins found in India

Pl. 17. Rouletted ware, from Sisupalgarh, Orissa

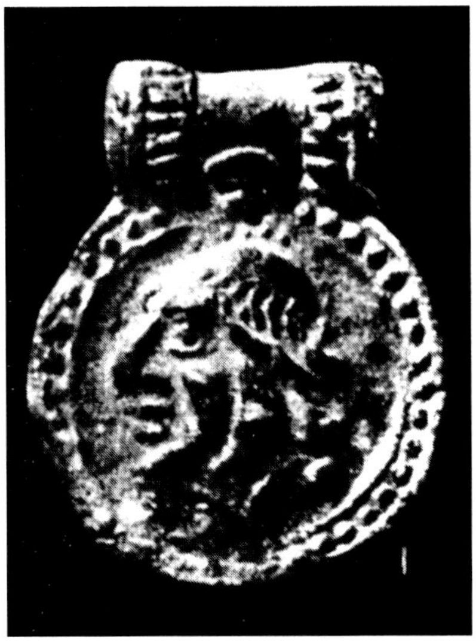

Pl. 18. Terracotta bullae, Sisupalgarh, Orissa

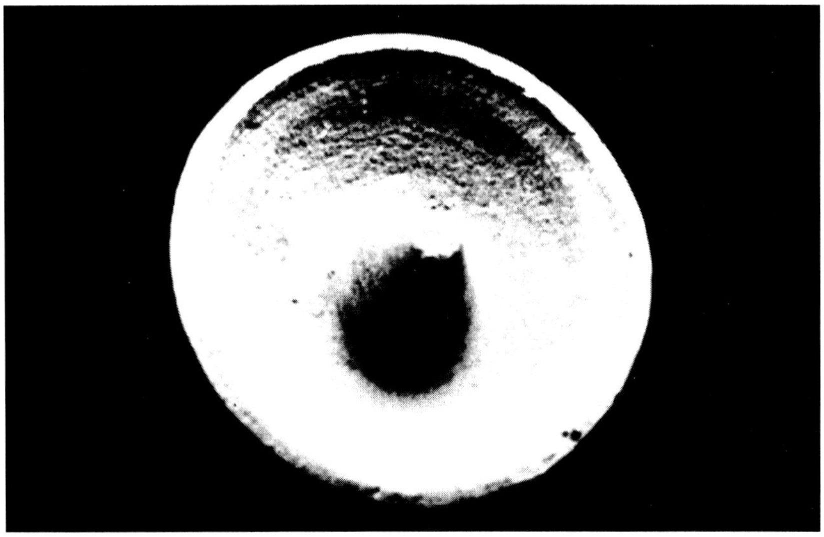

Pl. 19. Small pot with protrusion in the centre from Manikpatna, Orissa

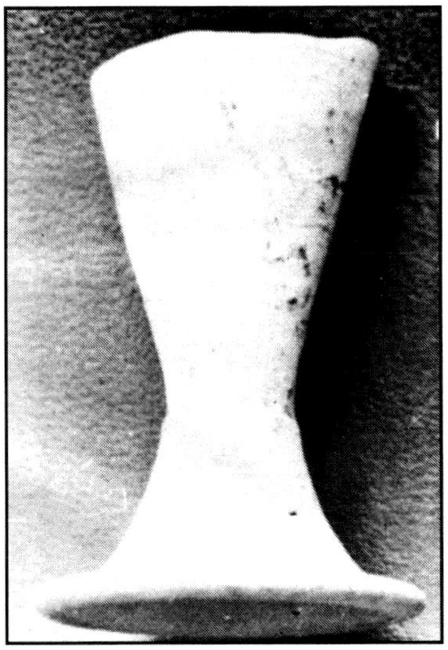

Pl. 20. Pedestal goblet, from Palur, Orissa

Pl. 21. Black and red ware sherds, from Palur, Orissa

Pl. 22. Terracotta pots, Ter, c. 2nd century AD

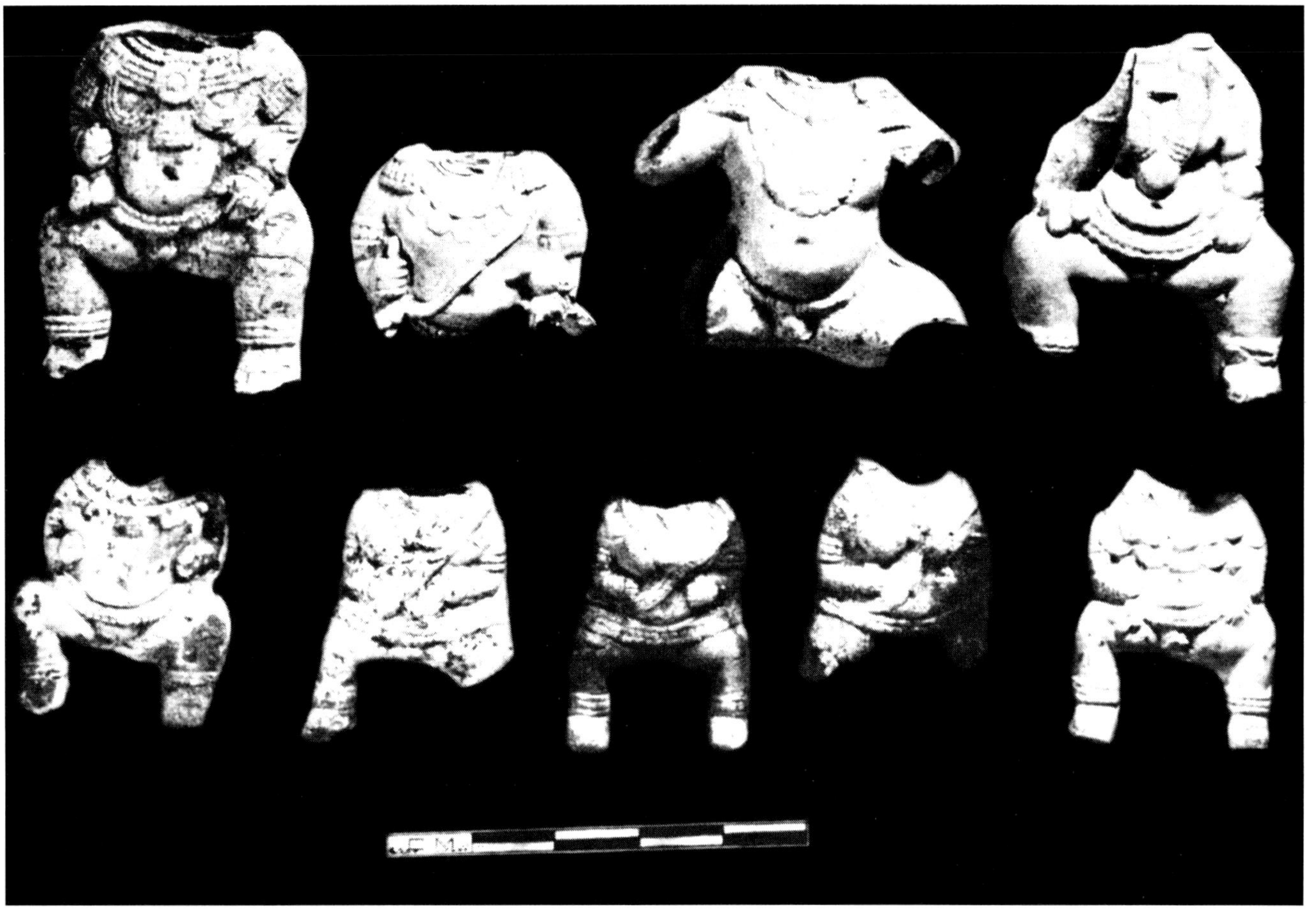

Pl. 23. Kaolin figurines, Ter, c. 2nd century AD

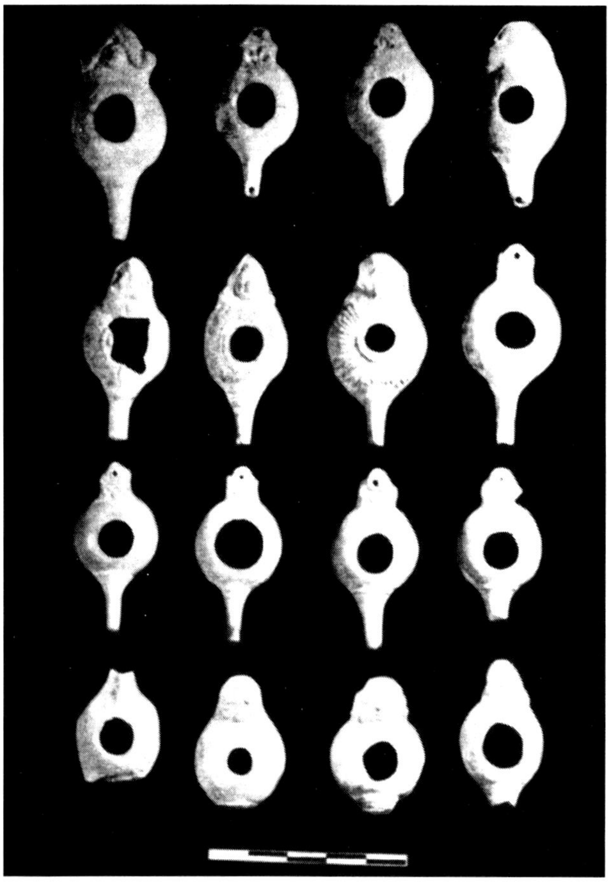

Pl. 24. Roman terracotta lamps, Ter, c. 2nd century AD

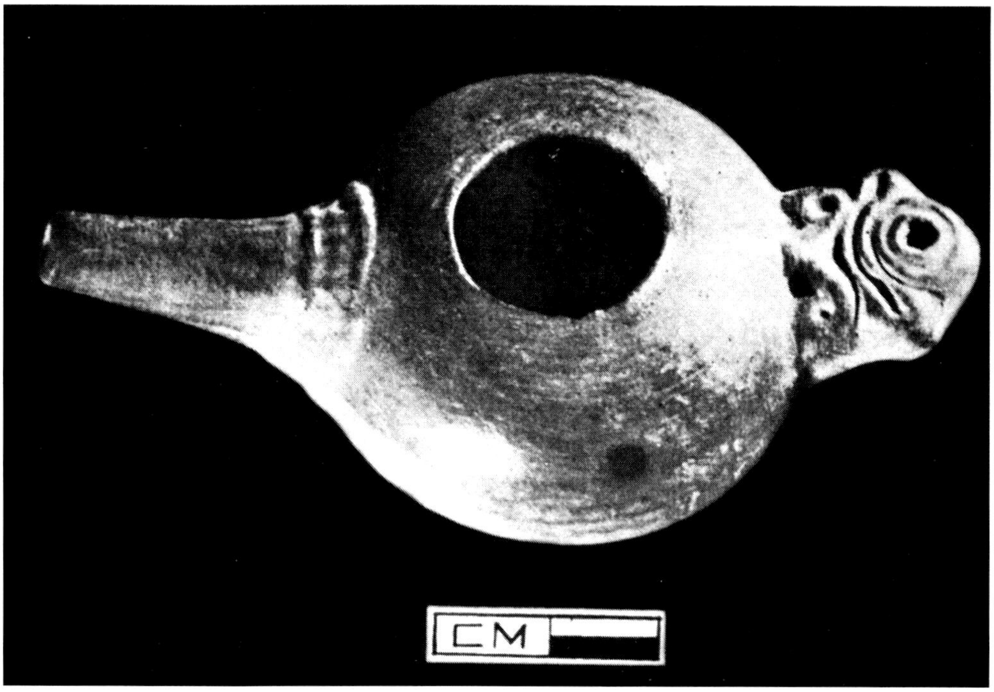

Pl. 25. Roman terracotta lamp, Ter, c. 2nd century AD

Pl. 26. Bronze mirror, Brahmapuri

Pl. 27. Repousse emblem depicting the legend of Perseus and Andromeda, c. 2nd century AD, from Brahmapuri

Pl. 29. Ships engraved on Roman coins

Pl. 28. Bronze handle of a jug, c. 2nd century AD, from Brahmapuri.

Pl. 30. Ship with two masts on Sātavāhana coin

D. Cultural Links with Sri Lanka, Indonesia and China

Pl. 31. Dhyani Buddha, Polonnaruwa, Sri Lanka

Pl. 32. Coin of Sahasamalla, King of Sri Lanka from Manikpatna, Orissa

Pl. 33. Borobudur, the perforated stupas, c. 800 AD, Indonesia

Pl. 34. Representation of a ship, c. 800 AD, Borobudur, (Indonesia)

Pl. 35. Dhyani Buddha from Borobudur

Pl. 36. Śiva liṅga, Bali

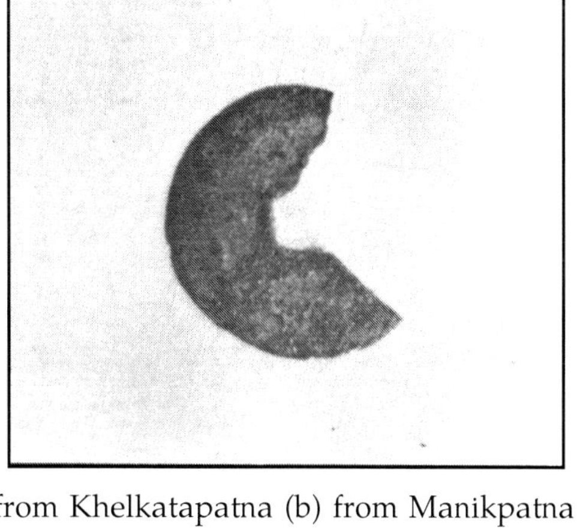

Pl. 37. Chinese coins in coastal Orissa (a) from Khelkatapatna (b) from Manikpatna

Pl. 38. Gaṇeśa, Indonesia

E. Representations of Boats and Ships in Indian Art

Pl. 39. Representation of a boat, c. 2nd century BC, Bharhut

Pl. 40. A barge with prow in the form of a griffin, c. 1st century BC, Sanchi

Pl. 41. A canoe with planks joined together, c. 1st century BC, Sanchi

Pl. 42. Impression of a seal showing a sea-going vessel, c. 2nd century AD, Chandraketugarh (West Bengal),

Pl. 43. Seal impression showing a boat c. 2nd century AD, Chandraketugarh

Pl. 44. Seal with a masted ship flying a banner, c. 3rd century AD, Chandraketugarh (West Bengal)

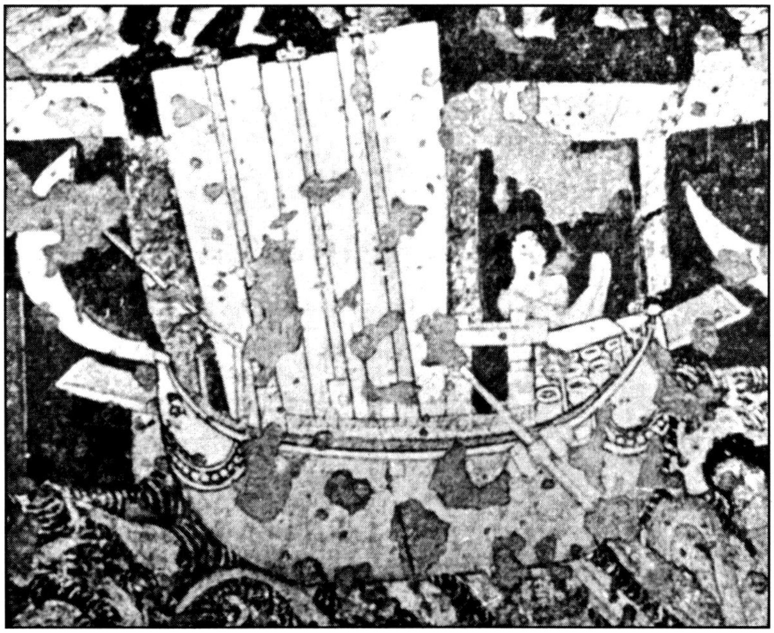

Pl. 45. Representation of a ship, Ajanta painting, c. 6th century AD

Pl. 46. Boats carrying elephants, c. 9th century AD, Bhubaneswar

Pl. 47. Mahmud of Ghazni's fleet of boats, c. 1026 AD

Pl. 48. Vīragal showing naval battle with armed soldiers on boats, c. 11th-13th century AD, Eksar

Pl. 49. Vīragal showing a long canoe-shaped ship, c. 12th century AD, Goa Museum

Pl. 50. Vīragal showing a naval battle in a shipyard, c. 12th century AD, Goa Museum

Pl. 51. The clinker style boat, c. 13th century AD, Koṇārak

Pl. 52. Marttanda Bhairava dancing on a boat, c. 13th century AD, Koṇārak

Pl. 53. Representation of a clinker style boat on the Bhoga Mandapa, c. 15th century AD, Śrī Jagannātha Temple, Puri

Pl. 54. Representation of ship in Bustan manuscript, c. 16th century AD

Pl. 55. Job Charnock founding Calcutta, c. 1690 AD, (after Sir Richard Temple)

Pl. 56. Representation of boat in a palm leaf manuscript, c. 18th century AD, Orissa

Pl. 57. An Orissan *Patia* boat, partly of reversed clinker style. North Coast (Orissa)

Pl. 58. Details of the boat (of No. 57)

Pl. 59. Backside of the boat (of No. 57)

Pl. 60. Bow of an Orissan *Masula* (after Eric Kentley)

Pl. 61. Taking an Orissan *Masula* to the water (after Eric Kentley)